PRAISE FOR
PRACTICAL JULIA

"As a career computational physicist and early participant in the Julia community, Lee has had a front row seat to the development of the Julia ecosystem. He has written numerous technical articles on Julia, and has a great skill in explaining complex topics in a simple way. This book is a great starting point for the reader's journey into Julia—with the first part covering the fundamentals of the language and second part diving into a variety of different scientific disciplines."

—VIRAL SHAH, CO-CREATOR OF THE JULIA
PROGRAMMING LANGUAGE AND CEO OF
JULIAHUB

"This is a nice deep dive which covers a lot of ground, from the basics on how to define arrays and use the type system all the way to biochemical modeling and scientific machine learning. Lee gives a very nice in-depth treatment, showing not only the most standard ways to do things, but also some different library options along with a good explanation of the pros and cons to the choices. I think this is a great book for any Julia user's shelf."

—CHRISTOPHER RACKAUCKAS, RESEARCH
AFFILIATE AND CO-PI OF THE JULIA LAB,
DIRECTOR OF MODELING AND SIMULATION
AT JULIA COMPUTING, AND APPLIED
MATHEMATICS INSTRUCTOR AT MIT

PRACTICAL JULIA

A Hands-On Introduction for Scientific Minds

by Lee Phillips

no starch press®

San Francisco

Printed in the United States of America

First printing

27 26 25 24 23   1 2 3 4 5

ISBN-13: 978-1-7185-0276-5 (print)
ISBN-13: 978-1-7185-0277-2 (ebook)

Publisher: William Pollock
Managing Editor: Jill Franklin
Production Manager: Sabrina Plomitallo-González
Production Editor: Miles Bond
Developmental Editor: Jill Franklin
Cover Illustrator: Gina Redman
Interior Design: Octopod Studios
Technical Reviewer: James Foster
Copyeditor: George Hale
Proofreader: Audrey Doyle

For information on distribution, bulk sales, corporate sales, or translations, please contact No Starch Press® directly at info@nostarch.com or:

No Starch Press, Inc.
245 8th Street, San Francisco, CA 94103
phone: 1.415.863.9900
www.nostarch.com

Library of Congress Control Number: 2023016515

To Gianna and Maxwell

About the Author

Lee Phillips was a theoretical and computational physicist at the Naval Research Laboratory for 21 years. He has presented his research in numerous scientific papers and at international conferences. He has also written many popular articles on science and its history, and on the use of computers in research. He's involved with science education and outreach, including serving on the Board of Directors of the Friends of Arlington's Planetarium and maintaining their website.

About the Technical Reviewer

James Foster is an applied mathematician with a doctorate in mathematical optimization, specializing in the modeling and optimal planning of energy systems. He has worked across industry and government, and taught both pure and applied mathematics courses at the university level. An enthusiastic contributor to the open source community, he is particularly involved in the development of the JuMP modeling language for optimization in Julia. He also serves as a Carpentries instructor and lesson maintainer, teaching foundational computational skills to researchers.

BRIEF CONTENTS

CONTENTS IN DETAIL

PART I
LEARNING JULIA

7
DIAGRAMS AND ANIMATIONS   189

8
THE TYPE SYSTEM   213

PART II
APPLICATIONS

9
PHYSICS   269

10
STATISTICS   305

ACKNOWLEDGMENTS

This book obviously could not exist without Julia, and for Julia, I'm grateful to its creators, Jeff Bezanson, Stefan Karpinski, Viral B. Shah, and Alan Edelman. Their vision for a new language for scientific computing must have seemed wildly ambitious at the time, but a decade later it has more than delivered on all its promises.

Thanks to the hundreds of developers and maintainers of Julia's packages for science, mathematics, and graphics. The word *ecosystem* is certainly overused, but Julia's composability eases the formation of symbiotic combinations that place unprecedented, expressive power at the numericist's fingertips.

Thanks to my children, Gianna and Maxwell, to whom this volume is dedicated, for suffusing my long nights of research and writing with a sustaining glow of pride.

To my fellow physicist, author, and man-about-town Kevin Jensen, your willingness to share a three-hour cup of coffee whenever our coordinates happen to intersect, your constant friendship, lively interest in my projects, and bottomless well of tolerance added more leavening to my toils than you suspect. And to Janet, for graciously suffering the combined effect of both of us in her house at the same time.

Karina Mejía, I've never known anyone both so kind and so unwilling to take a single molecule of crap from anyone. You never stop challenging me nor infecting me with your certitude that the success of my endeavors is as inevitable as the next astonishing Tegucigalpa sunset. I am sincerely grateful to both you and Kevin for getting my jokes.

My teacher and friend Monica Toro helped me punctuate the completion of writing with a magical vacation in Medellín. I'll never forget her hospitality and companionship. She also forced me to describe this book in Spanish during our lessons.

My editor at No Starch Press, Jill Franklin, is responsible for putting the publisher and me together. Although we don't always agree on the minutiae of punctuation, her devotion to detail and clarity made this a better book. And that's not always an easy thing for an author, by nature a member of a species with an overdeveloped ego, to admit.

Dr. James Foster contributed the benefit of his experience and expertise to provide a superb technical review, improving both the code and the exposition in countless instances. I was lucky to have him looking over my shoulder.

Despite the vigilant attention of the two aforementioned guardians of quality, we all know that errors are inevitable. Any dropped balls that remain on the ground are entirely my responsibility, although the sun was in my eyes.

Thanks to Bill Pollock for creating and maintaining a commodious home for such an excellent library of books, and for inviting me in. I'm proud to be part of the family.

For their comradeship, hospitality, and occasional reminders to get back to work by innocently asking, "How's that book going?" during the gestation period, I am grateful to my sisters, Melicia and Meredith, and their families, and my friends Patricia Munguía, Mileisha Zelaya, and Juán Calderon.

Thanks to David Harutunian for the tour, from which I used one photograph herein, and Wayne Large for permission to use his photomicrograph.

I am indebted to the editors of various publications, especially Jake Edge of *LWN* and Nathan Mattise at *Ars Technica*, for working with me over the past several years to help refine my approaches to writing about Julia.

I depend entirely on open source software for all my research, computing, and document preparation. Aside from Julia itself, the tools in my workshop that I use throughout each day are Linux and the GNU userspace, Vim (and Neovim), ImageMagick, TeX and LaTeX and the associated ecosystem, Pandoc, Mutt, Git, Rsync, Zsh, and OpenSSH.

And to all those for having forgotten to mention I am smacking my head about now, I'll make it up to you.

INTRODUCTION

I often feel that the American programmer would profit more from learning, say,
Latin than from learning yet another programming language.
—Edsger Dijkstra

Julia is a fairly new programming language. It emerged into the public sphere in 2012 after two and a half years of research by four computer scientists at MIT. Julia's creators explained why they needed to create a new language: they were "greedy."

There were already languages that were fast, such as C and Fortran. They were well suited to writing programs that ran on giant supercomputers to simulate the weather or design airplanes. But their syntax was not the friendliest; programs in these languages demanded a certain amount of ceremony. And they didn't provide an interactive experience; one could not improvise and explore at the terminal, but had to submit to an edit-compile-run discipline.

Other languages existed that dispensed with ceremony and that one could use as interactive calculators, such as Python and MATLAB. However, programs written in these languages were slow. Also, such languages often were not well suited to keeping large programs organized.

Julia's creators were greedy because they wanted it all: a language that was as easy to use as Python but was also as fast as Fortran. The solutions that people bolted on to Python (for example) to make it faster often involved rewriting the time-consuming parts of their programs in a faster language, such as C. The resulting chimera meant maintaining code in two languages, with the resulting organizational, personnel, and mental overhead issues. This is called the "two language problem," and one of the motivations behind Julia was to eliminate it.

Julia is now widely acclaimed as a real solution to the two-language problem. In fact, it's one of only three languages that belong to the "petaflop club," reaching the very top rank of performance on giant number-crunching problems (the other two are Fortran and C++). Uniquely, Julia combines this high level of performance with the ability to serve as an interactive calculator, whether with its highly polished read-eval-print loop (REPL), in development environments of various kinds, or in browser-based notebooks.

For those who have worked with Python, Octave, MATLAB, JavaScript using Node, or other REPL-based language systems, the Julia experience will be familiar. You can simply type julia in a terminal, and you'll see a brief startup message and a welcoming interactive prompt. Now you can type expressions and get immediate results printed back out on the terminal. You can define variables and functions, operate on arrays, import libraries of functions, read data from the disk or the network, and generally use the language as a sophisticated calculator. You never have to declare the types of variables nor spin any other boilerplate that comes between you and your work.

Those are the similarities to other interpreted languages. You'll also encounter some differences. You might notice occasional delays of a few seconds that usually don't occur with languages like Python. This happens because Julia isn't really an interpreted language, but it is doing both precompilation of code and just-in-time (JIT) compilation behind the scenes.

As you'll discover, this trade-off is worthwhile when your calculations get big. Your experience with other interactive languages may cause you to expect things to grind to a halt, but you will find, instead, that your code will execute with the speed of a compiled language like Fortran.

As you explore further, you'll discover that Julia is not like other languages you may be familiar with. At first, it seems superficially the same. You can type 1 + 1 and get 2 back. But you'll learn that Julia is neither object oriented like Python, nor traditionally functional like Haskell, nor is it like whatever JavaScript is. The language is organized around a different principle, and that's the source of much of its power.

Why Is Julia Popular with Scientists?

Julia is organized around something called multiple dispatch, which is enabled by a powerful and flexible type system. Later, you'll learn more about what these things mean and how to take advantage of them in your programs. For now, file this idea away for future reference: the multiple dispatch system is as important a reason as Julia's famous interactivity and speed for its success in the scientific world. While Julia is not the first language to incorporate this feature, it's the first one to combine it with the other virtues that make it genuinely useful for the research community.

It is this design feature that enables an unprecedented level and ease of code reuse and recombination. This, as much as any benchmark, is what delights the researchers who have adopted Julia as their computational tool. Julia is taking off with scientists largely because it allows them to use each other's code and recombine libraries to create new functionalities in ways not envisioned by the library's authors. You'll see many examples of this in later chapters, especially in Part II. You'll also see how the type system and Julia's metaprogramming abilities allow you to bend the language to fit your problem perfectly, with no compromise in performance.

What Will This Book Do for You?

After reading Part I, and whatever interests you in Part II, you'll be able to take full advantage of Julia to solve any computational problem that confronts you. You will know how to explore and visualize data, solve equations, write simulations, and use and create libraries. The emphasis here is on applying Julia to research problems. The approach is direct and practical, with a minimum of theoretical computer science. I'll teach you how to write efficient code that runs on a laptop or on large distributed systems. Whether your interest is in scientific research, mathematics, statistics, or just fun, you'll learn how to make intelligent use of this tool and how to enjoy doing so.

This book starts at the beginning, assuming that you have never touched Julia. I don't assume any particular knowledge of numerical methods or computational techniques, explaining everything of this sort as needed. I assume only that you've had some contact with basic programming concepts. In other words, when I describe how to write an if statement in Julia, I'll expect that you're familiar, in a general sense, with the concept of using conditions.

How to Use This Book

The material in Part I builds sequentially, so, ideally, you'll read those chapters in order. The chapters in Part II, by contrast, depend only on the material in Part I, not on each other. You can successfully read the biology chapter without looking at the physics chapter. Of course, I encourage everyone to read every chapter! Here's why: some particular techniques are developed in application chapters in which they are most likely to be relevant. However, due to the nature of scientific research, any bit of computational knowledge can potentially find application in any discipline. For example, a biologist may find the material in the physics chapter about differential equation solvers to be useful in modeling population dynamics. Since the chapters in Part II are not in any particular order, however, it will probably be most natural to read the chapter of immediate interest to you first, and return to the others at your leisure.

The book has an extensive index, which should make it easy to root out any subject, no matter where it is hiding.

In order to get the most out of a book such as this, read it with a Julia prompt open, so you can try things out as you encounter them in the text. The hands-on approach cements ideas far more effectively than simply reading. As you follow along, you'll find that you want to try out variations of my sample code and learn how the language behaves through trial and error. You won't break anything. If you get into a weird state that you don't know how to fix, you can simply exit the REPL and start it up again. In addition, the Julia REPL has a well-implemented documentation mode, where you can access all the gruesome details about any particular function to supplement what's in the text.

This book has a companion website at *https://julia.lee-phillips.org* where you can find runnable versions of all the major code listings in the text, datafiles used by the programs, color versions of the illustrations, example animations, and videos of simulations.

Book Overview

In Part I, after the preliminaries dealing with installation and the coding environment, we focus on learning Julia: the syntax, data types, concepts, and best practices. This part also contains chapters about the module and package system and visualization.

Chapter 1: Getting Started Introduces the hardware and experience needed for running Julia and benefiting from this book, and provides a guide to installation on various operating systems. We also review the most common coding environments and end with some recommendations.

Chapter 2: Language Basics Provides an introduction to the concepts, syntax, and data types of Julia that will equip you with a solid, basic understanding of the language.

Chapter 3: Modules and Packages Describes how to organize your Julia programs, how to incorporate code from others into your work, and how you can be a part of the Julia community.

Chapter 4: The Plotting System Concentrates on Julia's powerful Plots package. You'll learn how to make and customize every common type of 2D and 3D plot and how to create interactive graphics and finished illustrations for publication.

Chapter 5: Collections Introduces data types such as sets, strings, arrays, dictionaries, structs, and tuples. This chapter covers comprehensions and generators, operators over collections, array initialization and manipulation, and Julia's various types of strings.

Chapter 6: Functions, Metaprogramming, and Errors   Delves further into functions, treating different ways to define and supply arguments, and higher-order functions. It includes an introduction to metaprogramming, involving the use of symbols, expression objects, and macros to write code that manipulates code.

Chapter 7: Diagrams and Animations   Shows how to use a flexible and powerful package for mathematical and other diagrams, and a more specialized tool for drawing node-and-edge graphs. We'll explore two packages providing different approaches for creating animations, and we'll use several of these packages in later chapters to create illustrations and videos.

Chapter 8: The Type System   Covers more details about Julia's different kinds of numbers and other objects, the type hierarchy, type assertions and declarations, and how to create our own types. It explains how to use the type system in concert with multiple dispatch to organize our programs and the connection between types and performance. In addition, a section on plotting recipes reveals the unique power of Julia's plotting system.

Part II contains chapters devoted to particular fields of research, plus a final chapter on parallel processing. Each chapter uses one or more specialized packages widely used in an area of application, and tackles at least one interesting problem in its specialty.

Chapter 9: Physics   Shows how to enrich numbers with units and uncertainties, a subject of potential interest to scientists in many fields. A detailed example of thermal convection demonstrates how to use a powerful fluid dynamics package. The chapter ends with an introduction to a state-of-the-art package for solving differential equations.

Chapter 10: Statistics   Discusses concepts in statistics and probability theory, such as distributions, and relates them to functions and types provided by relevant Julia packages. It applies these ideas to the simulation of the spread of an infection, and it introduces dataframes by slicing and dicing real data about COVID cases.

Chapter 11: Biology   Explores agent-based modeling and shows how to use Julia's Agents package to simulate the evolution of creatures who learn how to avoid being captured by predators. It builds on some ideas from the statistics chapter to analyze the results.

Chapter 12: Mathematics   Focuses on symbolic mathematics (computer algebra) and linear algebra. It describes two main approaches to the first topic, including hybrid numerical-symbolic techniques. It covers the basic use of linear algebra packages to solve equations and efficiently perform matrix operations by taking advantage of the type system.

Chapter 13: Scientific Machine Learning   Explores concepts and techniques in a relatively new area that exploits ideas from machine learning to infer properties of models. It shows how to use automatic differentiation in several contexts, and introduces probabilistic programming through Julia's Turing package.

Chapter 14: Signal and Image Processing   Focuses on signals and images. The signal section covers Fourier analysis, filtering, and related topics, using a bird call as the working example. The image section uses feature recognition in the problem of counting blood cells and examines several techniques for image resizing, smoothing, and other manipulations. In this context it delves further into advanced array concepts.

Chapter 15: Parallel Processing   Explains how to run our programs on more than one CPU core or computer. The chapter discusses the different concurrency paradigms and how to take advantage of multithreading and multiprocessing. We'll see how to run our programs on a network with machines all over the world, with no change to the code.

FURTHER READING

- For details on the inspiration for the Julia language, see "Why We Created Julia": *https://julialang.org/blog/2012/02/why-we-created -julia/*.

- My article in *Ars Technica*, "The Unreasonable Effectiveness of the Julia Programming Language," explains the underlying reasons for Julia's wide adoption among scientists: *https://arstechnica.com/science/ 2020/10/the-unreasonable-effectiveness-of-the-julia-programming -language/*.

- If you're a Python programmer and want a very brief rundown of the differences in syntax, see "Julia for Python Programmers" by Dr. John D. Cook, at *http://www.johndcook.com/blog/2015/09/15/julia-for -python-programmers/*.

- If, instead, you come from Lisp, take a look at "A Lisper's First Impression of Julia" by Pascal Costanza at *https://p-cos.blogspot.com/ search?q=first+impression+of+Julia*. It's from 2014, but still of interest.

- For the original theoretical justification explaining the need of a new language and how Julia's design decisions meet that need, see "Julia: A Fresh Approach to Numerical Computing," authored by Julia creators Jeff Bezanson, Alan Edelman, Stefan Karpinski, and Viral B. Shah (*http://arxiv.org/abs/1411.1607*).

- For another version of Julia's creation story, see Klint Finley's "Out in the Open: Man Creates One Programming Language to Rule Them All" (*https://www.wired.com/2014/02/julia/*).

- "Julia Joins Petaflop Club" from Julia Computing is an astronomical (in both senses) application of Julia (*https://cacm.acm.org/news/ 221003-julia-joins-petaflop-club/fulltext*).

- "Julia Update: Adoption Keeps Climbing; Is It a Python Challenger?" by John Russell (*https://www.hpcwire.com/2021/01/13/julia -update-adoption-keeps-climbing-is-it-a-python-challenger/*) provides some interesting historical perspective.
- "Why I Switched to Julia" by Bradley Setzler is a case study of Julia used in econometrics that shows a 100-fold speed increase over Python with NumPy: *https://juliaeconomics.com/2014/06/15/why-i -started-a-blog-about-programming-julia-for-economics/*.

PART I

LEARNING JULIA

1

GETTING STARTED

You don't have to see the whole staircase, just take the first step.
–Dr. Martin Luther King Jr.

 As mentioned in the introduction, to learn a programming language, it's not enough to read a book—not even one as good as this. Experimenting and writing programs yourself is essential. After absorbing a key concept in the book or running a code sample, try to construct variations of the code and run them. Writing your own variations will help you achieve fluency in the language.

This chapter first covers how to install Julia on all the major operating systems, and then discusses the various types of coding environments. We'll see how to install each one, and explore their unique features, advantages, and disadvantages.

Installation Guide

Of course, to be able to do any of this you will need access to a Julia system. If you're already set up to run Julia code, you can safely skip this whole section. If not, you can skip the subsections covering installation on operating systems that you don't use, but you should probably read everything else.

Hardware Requirements

For learning Julia, almost any computer will be sufficient. It should have at least 2GB of RAM, but twice that amount will be more comfortable. You'll need about 0.5GB of free disk space to install Julia, but you should have at least 3GB of additional space for the packages that you'll install for plotting and other purposes.

These modest requirements are fine for learning the language and even for doing many real calculations, although you may require beefier hardware for larger-scale projects. Julia is used for calculations at every scale, and it can make efficient use of all types of hardware from laptops to GPU array processors to the world's largest supercomputers (see "Further Reading" on page 23 for an example). I have run every example calculation in this book on a very modestly powered laptop, so all of the code here should run with no problems on any machine that you're likely to be using.

Julia runs on Linux, FreeBSD, macOS, and Windows. At the time of writing, Julia is fully supported on these systems:

- Linux 2.6.18+: x86-64 (64-bit), i686 (32-bit), and ARMv8 (64-bit)
- FreeBSD 11.0+: x86-64 (64-bit)
- macOS 10.9+: x86-64 (64-bit)
- Windows 7+: x86-64 (32- and 64-bit)

These installation requirements may change, so check *https://julialang .org/downloads/* for up-to-date information.

Julia also runs on some system versions and architectures not listed here, but with reduced support, weaker guarantees, or possibly hampered functionality. It can also take advantage of more specialized hardware—for example, graphical processing unit array processors, which we'll discuss in later chapters.

Prerequisites

To use Julia effectively, you need to know a few things about how to operate your computer. You need a basic knowledge of the terminal and the command line: how to create and change directories (folders), view a list of files, find out how much storage space is available on your hard drive, and delete files.

Every operating system has various graphical utilities for accomplishing those tasks, both built-in and as third-party software, but it is a good idea for the computational scientist to become familiar with the command line and use it routinely. There's a good chance you'll find yourself in a remote computing situation some day, where the command line may be the only way to communicate with the remote machine.

It's also a good idea, even if your personal computer uses some other operating system, to learn how to perform these rudimentary tasks on Linux, as that is by far the most common frontend OS on compute servers for scientific work. If your daily driver comes from Apple, that won't be a problem, as the basic commands in the macOS BSD-derived terminal are nearly the same as on Linux. If you're accustomed to Windows, you may need to learn some translations; however, that is beyond the scope of this book, and you won't need to know the Linux dialect to use Julia on your personal computer.

You'll also need to be familiar with an editor on your system that can save files in a plaintext format. Most programmers use Vim, Emacs, or a more elaborate integrated development environment (IDE)—options that we will discuss further in the next section. You can use any editor you're familiar with, but graphical editors such as Word are not the best choice. However, if you really want to use such programs, they'll work. Just be sure to save your creations as plaintext files, and use a monospaced font, which will work better for writing code.

Julia Versions

Most people, no matter their platform, will download Julia from the official Julia website at *https://julialang.org/downloads/*. Whether you get it there or somewhere else, keep in mind that Julia, although it's been stable for several years, is still undergoing rapid development. *Stable* in this context means that you can expect no breaking changes: programs that you write now, or have written using any version of Julia from v1.0 onward, will continue to work as you upgrade your Julia installation in the future, with few exceptions. However, *rapid development* means that the particular version you have installed can make a substantial difference.

Regarding the language implementation itself, the Julia team has made continuous progress in speed and responsiveness since the first public release, and that's likely to continue, which is reason enough to recommend using the most recent stable language version. Regarding the ecosystem generally, many important packages, which are libraries of Julia code that you can use in your own programs, are also progressing rapidly, and new ones are emerging every month. Older Julia versions may not be compatible with new, or newer versions of, important packages.

In the download section of the Julia website, you will find downloads corresponding to various "releases," or recent versions, of Julia. Most people will be best served by the one identified as "Current stable release." "Upcoming release" is a beta version of the next stable release. It will have more recently added features, but it will also have slightly more compatibility problems with various packages and may be afflicted with some minor bugs. Depending on when you are reading this, the "Long-term support" release may or may not have all of the features this book uses. In general, to avoid any confusion arising from possibly different behavior from the code samples here, ensure that you install Julia v1.6.0 or greater and avoid beta releases.

Installation

This section contains instructions for various options to install Julia on every OS for which it is available. You only need to pay attention to the sections that apply to you.

As an alternative to these instructions, which leave you with a Julia binary ready to run, you can download the Julia source code at the same location as the other download links. As Julia is completely free and open source software, the source is always available for experts to inspect and compile themselves. If you want to run Julia on an unusual system for which a binary is not supplied, this is your only option.

On Linux and FreeBSD

Almost every Linux distribution has its own package management system: an official mechanism for installing programs and keeping them updated. Using the official package manager has two advantages. First, it is integrated, meaning that dependencies among all the installed programs should be automatically resolved and everything will work together. The second benefit is security: packages in the official repositories are generally vetted and unlikely to contain malicious code.

Unfortunately, it takes considerable time for software to be packaged and included in the official repositories of most Linux distributions. Projects such as Julia that are undergoing rapid development should generally not be installed using the package manager. The distribution's version will lag too far behind the current versions that you can get directly from the Julia project. This is less of a problem for certain Linux distributions that employ a rolling release schedule and keep their packages up to date, but it makes the use of the package manager in, for example, Debian-based distributions a poor choice for Julia.

For these reasons, if you are on Linux, the best strategy is to go to the Julia download page at *https://julialang.org/downloads/*. Look for the heading "Current stable release" and, under that, find the entry for your machine's architecture. Most people will want the 64-bit download for "Generic Linux on x86." Clicking the download link copies a file to your computer with the extension *.tar.gz*. It will be a little more than 100MB.

The default location for browser downloads for most people is the *Downloads* directory inside their home directory, but your browser may be configured differently. After you have found the download location, you should see the file you just acquired, named something like *julia-1.X.0-linux-x86_64 .tar.gz*, which indicates v1.X.0 of Julia, built for Linux systems with the x86, 64-bit architecture. The double extension indicates that this is a compressed tarfile. You can uncompress and un-archive the file with a single command (substituting the actual downloaded filename):

```
tar zxvf julia-1.X.0-linux-x86_64.tar.gz
```

The tar command should already be installed on any normal Linux system. After entering this command, you should see the names of a bit more than 2,000 files scroll by in your terminal, indicating the creation of subdirectories and the un-archiving of the files needed for an initial installation of Julia to work. You won't need to do anything directly with any of these files except one. After the process is complete, which should take under a minute, you'll have a new directory with a name taken from the beginning of the archive's name. For the example *julia-1.X.0-linux-x86_64.tar.gz* download file, that directory is *julia-1.X.0*. The installation will take up about four times the space of the tarfile, which you can delete after the tar command completes successfully.

The next step is to set up your system so that entering julia in the terminal starts the Julia program that you just installed.

To make the final installation step, first check your path by entering **echo $PATH**. If */usr/local/bin* is listed, navigate there. If it's not, but there's another directory in your path where you like to keep local commands, go there. Otherwise, it's a good idea to establish such a directory, which can be */usr/local/bin* or something else. The method for doing that varies a bit depending on your shell. For the most common case of bash and bash-compatible shells, add this line to your *.bash_profile* startup file (which you can find in your home directory):

```
PATH=/usr/local/bin:$PATH; export PATH
```

After you have navigated to */usr/local/bin* or to your local command directory of choice, make a symbolic link to the file */bin/julia* within your new Julia installation directory, and call it *julia*. For our example, the command is:

```
ln -s $HOME/Downloads/julia/julia-1.X.0/bin/julia julia
```

To create the link you need to be root, or use sudo.

You can keep your downloaded Julia installation anywhere, but you'll need to update the link set in the command if you move it.

To check that your new Julia installation is working, open a fresh shell and enter **julia**. An interactive prompt should appear, waiting for you to type your first line of Julia code.

On macOS

You can install Julia on your Apple computer the same way you install any other application. Navigate to the Julia download page, find the section for your desired version, and click the 64-bit link in the table. A normal macOS *.dmg* file will be downloaded to your system, which should open itself. You should see the Julia icon of red, green, and purple circles arranged in a pyramid. Drag this to your *Applications* folder as usual.

When you double-click this icon, a terminal should open with the Julia interactive prompt ready for your first command.

The next step is to make arrangements so you can start Julia from the terminal command line and not need to click the icon, which will be convenient later on. These preparations also will allow you to run saved Julia programs without using the REPL.

Enabling this behavior requires two steps. If the Julia interactive prompt is still waiting for you, press CTRL-D to quit the REPL or enter **exit()**. Next, at the shell command line, enter the following command to delete any existing julia command that might be left over from a previous installation:

```
rm -f /usr/local/bin/julia
```

Then enter the following (change *Julia-1.X.app* to match the version that you have installed):

```
ln -s /Applications/Julia-1.X.app/Contents/Resources/julia/bin/julia /usr/local/bin/julia
```

You may also want to check for the presence of julia commands elsewhere in your path, such as in /usr/bin, and delete them or move them out of the command path, so that you don't inadvertently invoke an older executable from a previous installation.

This command creates what's known as a *symbolic link* to the actual Julia binary program stored deep within your *Applications* folder. Now you can type **julia** in any terminal to start the interactive Julia shell or to run Julia programs.

On Windows

Some installations of Windows do not have a modern terminal set up. You will need such a program to run Julia effectively and to follow the examples in this book. If you don't already have a good terminal installed, a reasonable option is the Windows Terminal, a free program available from the Microsoft Store. Before doing anything else, install this terminal or something equally capable and make sure that you know how to start and use it.

Navigate to the Julia download page and find the section for your desired version (see "Julia Versions" on page 5).

If you know you're on a 64-bit version of Windows, click the 64-bit download link. If you're on 32-bit or are not sure of the architecture, click the 32-bit link. This will get you a Julia install that will work on both architectures, but using the 64-bit build has some advantages if you know you can use it.

This will download a *.exe* installer, which you should run next. It will inform you of the installation directory; be sure to make a note of it.

The following instructions to set up Julia to run from a terminal will work for recent versions of Windows. If you're running Windows 8 or earlier, you'll find specific installation instructions linked from the Julia download page.

Recent versions of the installer offer a checkbox for setting the Julia path. If yours doesn't, or you prefer to choose the path yourself, follow this procedure:

1. Open Run by pressing **Windows key-R** and enter the following command to open the System Variables window so you can edit the path:

`rundll32 sysdm.cpl,EditEnvironmentVariables`

---

2. Click **New** and enter (or paste) the path the installer told you about (you copied that information, right?). If you've lost the path, look for a program with "julia" in the name in *C:\Users\<your_username>\ AppData\Local\Programs*.

3. Click **OK**, open a terminal, and enter `julia` to test your setup. You should see a terminal-flavored rendering of the Julia logo, a brief message, and an interactive prompt, waiting for your first line of Julia code.

Another option on Windows is provided by package managers. The open source edition of the popular Chocolately package manager, for example, installs a reasonably up-to-date Julia version.

Using Docker

Read this section if you know what Docker is and you are sure that you want to install Julia by using a Docker image.

If that's you, you are fortunate that a Docker community exists for Julia. Go to *https://hub.docker.com/_/julia*, which contains a description of the image for using Julia. I won't list the details of what systems and versions are supported, because those are likely to change frequently. The page has up-to-date information for installing and using the Julia container on your machine. Aside from that, everything else in this book applies identically to Julia run from within a Docker container and Julia installed in the conventional way.

Privacy Note

The Julia team is scrupulous in pointing out a privacy issue that, although of no concern to most people, and something that most would take for granted in any case, deserves to be mentioned. Julia's package management system (something we'll discuss in later chapters) is designed with the expectation that you are connected to the internet, and it will download software as needed for you to complete your tasks. This means that, of necessity, your IP address, what you downloaded, and when, are stored on a server somewhere, at least for a while.

The Julia Coding Environment

With the basic Julia system installed, let's turn to the various options for interacting with it. Different methods of talking to Julia are best suited for different situations. Also, if you have a favorite editor or IDE, this section will explain how you can program in Julia without changing your workflow.

Table 1-1 is a brief table of the coding environments discussed next and their salient advantages and disadvantages:

Table 1-1: Coding Environment Comparison

Environment	Advantages	Disadvantages
REPL	Nothing to install, quick, useful modes	Graphics in separate windows, repetitive entry
Text editors	File organization, editing convenience, REPL integration	No graphics, limited interactivity
Jupyter	Huge community, inline graphics, interactivity, multiple languages, good for sharing	Poor organization, no version control, hidden state, browser text entry
Pluto	Inline graphics, sophisticated interactive controls, reactive and consistent, full REPL integration, backed by normal Julia file	Julia only, browser text entry
VS Code	Integrated editor, REPL, graphics, good language support	Less powerful as an editor than Vim or Emacs

Let's take a more detailed look at each of these options.

The Julia REPL

When you enter julia in the terminal, you enter the *REPL*, or *read-eval-print loop*. You'll see a welcome message and the prompt will change from your system's shell prompt to Julia's.

REPL Modes

The REPL has several modes. The initial mode, with the julia> prompt, is the normal mode in which you will spend most of your REPL time. Here you can enter any Julia expression, press ENTER, and Julia will print the result of the expression. Even if you don't know any Julia yet, try it out to make sure everything is working correctly. Enter an arithmetic expression such as 1 + 1, and you should see the result immediately after pressing ENTER.

This mode of operation will be familiar to you if you've used Python, Node, APL, or any other REPL-based language. Unlike Python, Julia is compiled rather than interpreted. This difference will have implications in how you use the REPL in later chapters, but for now, you can use the Julia interactive interface just like any other REPL you may have used before.

The Julia REPL's normal mode is a sophisticated environment with a few tricks up its sleeve to make your work easier. It has a "paste mode" that lets you paste in code samples you may have copied, for instance, from a web page, and that may be littered with the julia> prompt and have code interleaved with explanatory text. The REPL will know to just execute the actual code on any line starting with julia>, provided the first line pasted starts with it. (At the time of writing, paste mode does not work on Windows.)

The REPL is fully readline capable. This means you can use the up arrow and down arrow to recall earlier commands and edit them before repeating them. This feature even works well for multiline code blocks such as function definitions. To search for a previous command, you can press CTRL-R and type some text contained within that command. Your command and code history is saved between REPL sessions, so you can quit the REPL, come back the next day, and still recall your commands with the arrow keys. The history is stored in the *.julia/logs/repl_history.jl* file within your home directory. This file contains all the code you enter, and it even timestamps each entry, but it does not record the results Julia returns.

Another useful REPL mode is the help mode. Press **?**, and the prompt will change to help?>. Enter any Julia function, data type, operator, or library, and you will see a nicely formatted description of the item you entered, often with a useful collection of examples.

```
help?> Base
search: Base basename AbstractSet AbstractSlices Broadcast broadcast broadcast! AbstractString
AbstractDisplay

  Base

  The base library of Julia. Base is a module that contains basic functionality
  (the contents of base/). All modules implicitly contain using Base, since this is needed
  in the vast majority of cases.
```

Later on you'll learn how to document your own functions in a way that hooks into the REPL help system.

The REPL also has a shell mode, activated by pressing **;**, that allows you to enter system shell commands from within the REPL session:

```
julia> ilj = "I love Julia"
"I love Julia"

# Enter ";" here to switch to shell mode.

shell> echo $ilj
I love Julia
```

We can use shell mode for simple commands. As the listing shows, we can interpolate Julia variables, but piping and redirection won't work.

Another REPL mode you will use often is the package mode, activated by pressing **]**, which we'll cover in Chapter 3 when we explore how to use packages and modules. For now, just be aware that the package system in Julia is an integral part of the language and environment, so much so that it's built into the REPL. Julia developers don't need to wrestle with several competing third-party package systems, nor with the inevitable "dependency hell" that afflicts some other languages.

To exit out of any of these modes back into the normal (sometimes called "Julian") REPL mode, press BACKSPACE while the cursor is at the starting position.

TAB works in any REPL mode to generate context-aware completions. If there is a unique completion, it is entered for you at the cursor; otherwise, the REPL presents you with a list of options.

REPL Colors

To help you to know which mode you're in, the REPL colors each of its prompts differently. The colors help visually separate the prompts from the expressions you enter and their results. The REPL also uses colors in certain types of output, such as help output, to distinguish elements like keywords and variables from normal text. The default colors work well when using a terminal with a black or dark background, which is the most popular choice. However, they are too light to be easily legible on a white or very light background. I use such a background for the illustrations in this book, as it prints better than the black background I usually use on my computer. If you use a light terminal background, or simply prefer a different appearance from the default, you can edit a configuration file to change any of the REPL colors.

In your home directory, you will find a directory called *.julia* (note the dot: in most people's shells, as they are typically configured, this directory will not be listed using the usual commands unless you add a flag to request listing of "invisible files," and graphical file management tools may or may not show the directory by default). Within *.julia*, there may already be a *config* directory; if not, create one. Enter the *config* directory and edit the *startup.jl* file (or create it if it doesn't exist). Add the following to *startup.jl*:

```
function customize_colors(repl)
    repl.prompt_color = Base.text_colors[28]
    repl.help_color = Base.text_colors[178]
end

atreplinit(customize_colors)
```

You have just written your first Julia function. Julia runs the *startup.jl* file every time the REPL starts (the *.jl* extension is used for Julia programs). This function simply defines two variables: one for the color of the prompt in normal mode and the other for help mode. The two numbers in square brackets are ANSI color codes, which are understood by most modern terminal programs. I've chosen two colors that work well on my monitor when using a white terminal background. If you want to pick your own colors, you can find tables of the 256 ANSI colors and their codes by searching the web for "ANSI color codes." I've redefined only these two colors because the other defaults happened to work well. If you want to change some other colors, you can define the `repl.shell_color`, `repl.input_color`, and `repl.answer_color` variables as well.

Julia also understands several color *names*, but too few to allow an ideal selection.

Unicode Characters

Julia allows the use of Unicode characters in variable names and for other identifiers. This means you can make formulas in your Julia programs look more like real math, using, for instance, Greek letters and subscripts. Some people have set up their systems to allow them to type such characters easily. Even if you haven't, you can still use these characters thanks to a Unicode input mode provided by the REPL. If you enter a backslash (\) followed by a string of ASCII characters, then press TAB, one of three things will happen. If the REPL recognizes the string as one of its codes for a Unicode character, the entire entry, beginning with the backslash, will be replaced by that character. If the code you typed is the beginning of a character code or one of several possible codes, the tab completion mechanism will work in the normal way. If the REPL does not recognize what you typed, it will do nothing.

A complete list of the Unicode character codes recognized by the REPL is maintained at *https://docs.julialang.org/en/v1/manual/unicode-input/*. Those familiar with LaTeX syntax will be happy to know that all the Greek letters and some other symbols that have LaTeX commands are on the list unchanged. For example, to input α in the REPL, type **\alpha** and then press TAB. There is much more—even a wide selection of emoji.

If you want to know the LaTeX-style abbreviation for a particular Unicode character, perhaps one that you've copied from the documentation, enter the help mode in the REPL, paste in the character, and press ENTER. If an abbreviation exists, the help system will tell you what it is.

Figure 1-1 shows a simple example of what you can do with an expanded character set.

```
julia> α₁ = 10
10

julia> α₂ = 3
3

julia> 👾 = 13
13

julia> (α₁ + α₂) / 👾
1.0
```

Figure 1-1: Using Unicode in the REPL

This is more than just fun and games. The ability to employ a wider collection of characters, including Greek letters and subscripts, allows us to make our code more concise and expressive.

Text Editors

Julia programmers use text editors routinely, either in addition to or in coordination with the REPL. I'll go over some of the relevant features of the most-used programmer's editors here. If you use something else, be sure to search for any enhancements, either built-in or in the form of third-party plug-ins, specific to Julia. These enhancements typically include syntax highlighting, which helps immensely in avoiding typos in your code, and can include more sophisticated features, such as code formatting and execution.

Vim

Vim is an excellent editor for programming in any language, and it has valuable Julia support. I recommend installing the `julia-vim` plug-in, available at *https://github.com/JuliaEditorSupport/julia-vim*, where you will also find its documentation. The plug-in requires Vim version 7.4 or greater. To take the best advantage of `julia-vim`, ensure that the built-in `matchit` plug-in is enabled by executing the `:runtime macros/matchit.vim` Vim command, which should be in your Vim startup file. This plug-in adds a Julia file type with syntax coloring and awareness of the block structure of Julia syntax. It extends the `matchit` operation by allowing you to jump to the end or beginning of function definitions and other blocks by entering `%`. You can also select or delete blocks, or the bodies of blocks, in the same way that Vim allows you to operate on other text objects.

The plug-in also emulates the REPL's LaTeX-style entry of Unicode characters. For this it provides two options: you can have it wait for you to press TAB, as the REPL does, or it can expand the entry on the fly as soon as it sees a character (usually a space) that seems to indicate the end of the entry (the on-the-fly mode does not support emoji, however).

Another option for recent versions of NeoVim or Vim is to install language support for tree-sitter, which adds syntax-aware highlighting and other features to the editor. If you have Vim version 8.0 or greater, which I highly recommend, or the NeoVim fork, you can interact with *any* REPL directly, including the Julia REPL. By "interact," I mean that you can remain in an editing buffer containing your Julia program and send selected lines, expressions, or blocks directly to the REPL for execution. The execution is asynchronous, so you can continue editing while Julia is churning through a time-consuming command. Communication with the REPL is two-way, so you can also send results printed in the REPL back into the editing buffer. The following instructions apply to Vim, but NeoVim users should be able to adapt them to that program.

First, install the `vim-sendtowindow` plug-in, which lives at *https://github .com/karoliskoncevicius/vim-sendtowindow*. After opening the editing buffer of choice, execute the `:term julia` Vim command. If you have the julia command set up properly (see "Installation" on page 6), a new Vim buffer should open with the Julia REPL running within it, below the editing window.

Now you can select any text in the editing window and press the spacebar followed by j to send it to the REPL. If you'd prefer some other shortcut for this operation, the vim-sendtowindow web page explains how to set it up. You can also define shortcuts for sending text to the right, left, and up, which is handy for sending text *from* the REPL and in case you prefer to split your windows vertically. The :term command, with its asynchronous execution of commands, is built into Vim. The plug-in provides a convenient way to send text back and forth between the editing and terminal buffers. The author of vim-sendtowindow maintains a list of plug-ins with similar functionality on its website.

Similar REPL interactions are possible with earlier versions of Vim, using plug-ins such as ScreenSend, but the term command in version 8 makes REPL interaction smoother and less error prone.

Emacs

Emacs is a powerful programmer's editor with sophisticated Julia support available. The official Julia major mode for Emacs, called julia-emacs, is developed on GitHub at *https://github.com/JuliaEditorSupport/julia-emacs*. The creators of the Julia language are contributors to the project, which is probably one of the reasons that a deep and detailed knowledge of the language's structure and syntax is built into the mode. Once installed, Emacs will display Julia code using a variety of colors and font styles to clarify its syntax. It also provides movement among and manipulation of code structures such as blocks.

To install julia-emacs, first enable the MELPA repository (*https://melpa .org*) and add **(require 'julia-mode)** to your Emacs initialization file. For most people, this will be *.emacs* in their home directory. For a smooth experience, you should be running a version of Emacs that is at least 24.1. If your version is earlier, an upgrade would be advisable for using Emacs and Julia together.

Emacs shines at interacting with REPL-based languages, and Julia is no exception. Several minor modes are available specifically for Julia interaction. One of the most popular is julia-repl, also developed on GitHub and available at *https://github.com/tpapp/julia-repl*. It's designed to work with the aforementioned julia-emacs, and you must have at least version 25 of Emacs installed.

To install julia-repl, edit your *.emacs* initialization file, adding the following lines:

```
(add-to-list 'load-path path-to-julia-repl)
(require 'julia-repl)
(add-hook 'julia-mode-hook 'julia-repl-mode)
```

Now you can start a Julia REPL right from within Emacs. It will run in an ANSI terminal, with the full complement of text colors and formatting. A table of keyboard shortcuts is available on the mode's GitHub page. You can perform the usual sending of fragments, whole blocks, or the entire buffer to the REPL for execution. In addition, the built-in knowledge of Julia allows the mode to do such things as listing all the methods of a function, which will make more sense after you read Chapter 8.

Jupyter Notebooks

You can use Julia from within a web browser, in two main ways, in what is referred to as a *notebook* interface. The older way is the Jupyter Notebook. Jupyter popularized the notebook concept in the free software arena, and it's widely used in the Julia, Python, and R communities. In fact, the word *Jupyter* is a mashup of the names of those three programming languages.

If you want to use or explore a notebook interface and do not have a particular reason to use Jupyter, proceed directly to the next section and learn about Pluto. Pluto offers the same style of notebook interactivity as Jupyter while improving on the concept. For those who need to use Jupyter to collaborate with others using the system, who want to use other languages (besides Julia) with the same notebook interface, or who desire to explore existing Jupyter Notebooks, this section is designed to get you started.

If you already have Jupyter set up and working on your computer, you merely need to install the Julia backend. In the Julia REPL, press] to enter the package mode (see page 11). Make sure you're connected to the internet, and enter the `add IJulia` command to download and install the Julia backend for the notebook and the packages that it depends on. This is a fairly big install and will take some time, but the REPL will keep you informed with an animated display showing the progress of the downloads and the precompilation of modules. When the process is complete, enter `jupyter notebook` either at a separate system shell prompt or using the REPL shell mode to launch the notebook.

If you don't already have Jupyter installed, after the installation described earlier is complete, enter the following lines in the Julia REPL:

```
using IJulia
notebook()
```

Julia will ask if you want to install Jupyter using the `Conda` package. Answer in the affirmative. This next phase of installation should be quicker than the `IJulia` install, but may still take some time. When the software is ready, Julia will open a window or tab in your default browser with the starting Jupyter page. To start up Jupyter in future sessions, repeat these commands in a Julia REPL.

When the Jupyter Notebook page opens, you'll have a drop-down list of installed kernels, or language backends. Choose the Julia kernel, and a new tab or window will open. On that page, you can enter Julia expressions in "cells." When you press CTRL-ENTER while the cursor is in a cell, Julia will evaluate the expression and print the result in an output cell underneath it.

Because we are in a web browser, the system can take advantage of the ability to format text and display graphics. Figure 1-2 shows a Jupyter Notebook after I've executed a few cells.

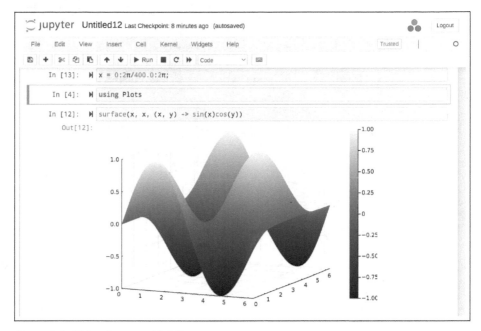

Figure 1-2: Using Jupyter with Julia

The last cell is a command to create a surface plot, which directly embeds the plot in the page.

You don't need to worry about saving your work with Jupyter, as it makes frequent autosaves, as indicated with the notice near the top of the page in Figure 1-2.

Sharing your work is as simple as sending the on-disk form of the notebook to your colleagues. Everything is in one file, including the graphs and other images, which by default are encoded as SVG. Jupyter Notebook files have the *.ipynb* extension, and are stored in the directory where you started the REPL.

If you are going to use Jupyter extensively, consult the detailed documentation at *https://jupyter.org* to learn more about all of its features.

Pluto: A Better Notebook

Pluto is a notebook interface to Julia that uses a web browser, similarly to Jupyter. Although it's a young project, it's already used routinely by a large community and has significant advantages over Jupyter. Its only shortcoming is that it is Julia-only, but this specialization allows Pluto to take better advantage of what Julia has to offer than frontends that support multiple kernels.

Pluto does not depend on anything aside from a modern web browser and Julia. To install it, press] to enter the package mode in the Julia REPL and execute the **add Pluto** command. After everything downloads and installs, press BACKSPACE to exit the package mode, and execute this code in the REPL:

```
using Pluto
Pluto.run()
```

A new window or tab will open in your default web browser with the Pluto welcome page, which looks like Figure 1-3.

welcome to **Pluto**.jl

New session:

Open a <u>sample notebook</u>

Create a <u>new notebook</u>

Open from file:

Enter path or URL... `Open`

Recent sessions:

⊙ <u>Plutotest</u>

Figure 1-3: The Pluto welcome page

Here you'll see links for opening a fresh notebook, continuing work on an existing one, or examining sample notebooks. The sample notebooks cover a variety of subjects and are well done and instructive.

A Pluto notebook is a web page where you can enter Julia expressions in "cells." Pressing CTRL-ENTER while the cursor is in a cell will cause Julia to execute the code in that cell as well as all the cells that depend on it. If, for example, you define, or redefine, a variable in a cell and execute it, and you have a second cell that uses that variable, Pluto will execute that second cell after the first one is done. If a third cell depends on the result from the second cell, Pluto will execute that one next, and so on. After each cell is run, its result is displayed *above* the input cell. You can watch the progress of execution passing from cell to cell by observing the animated progress bars on their left borders.

Pluto determines the order of execution by calculating a *dependency graph* for all the cells on the page. Using the dependency graph means that the results shown on the page are independent of the visual order in which they are arranged, and of the order in which you decide to execute cells.

What you see is completely determined by the code in the cells, so you can share your notebooks with collaborators and everyone will see the same, consistent notebook. This is the major advance over other notebooks, such as Jupyter, where the results displayed on the page are the consequence of the order in which the cells were run and may even depend on cells that have been deleted.

Pluto's behavior is, in some ways, similar to a spreadsheet, and offers the same live, reactive experience. Even die-hard terminal users such as myself enjoy using Pluto for certain kinds of exploratory computation. Its ability to embed graphics and, as we'll see in later chapters, incorporate graphical controls such as sliders and color pickers creates a rich environment for experimenting with code and data.

Figure 1-4 shows a Pluto page with a simple matrix calculation. I created it by clicking the link to start a new notebook in the welcome page. Pluto opened a new tab and the browser switched to it, and I entered expressions in three cells and pressed CTRL-ENTER to evaluate them.

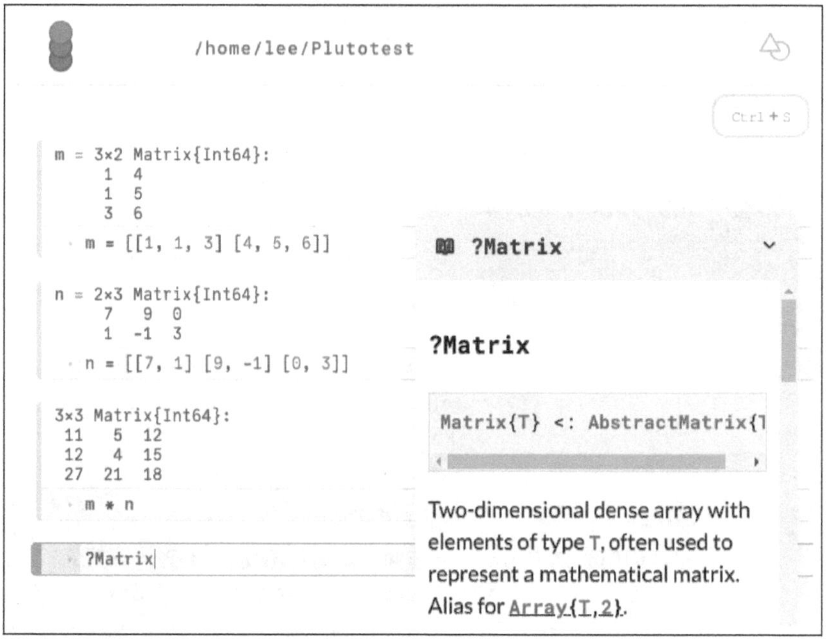

Figure 1-4: Matrix calculations in the Pluto notebook

Figure 1-4 shows the main elements of the Pluto interface. At the top is the path of the notebook file. Until you type this in, a message in that space will invite you to do so. To the right of that is a save button, but you only need to use it if you change the location of the file and want to save immediately. Every time you execute a cell, Pluto saves your work automatically.

In the first two code cells I've defined two small matrices, m and n, and in the third cell, I asked for their matrix product. (This is a preview of the array operations that we'll explore in Chapter 2.) Keep in mind that in Pluto, the results are printed above the input cells.

So far, we could have done this the same way in the REPL. The difference here is that if we change any of the numbers in m or n and run the cell with its new definition, the matrix product is instantly recalculated and the revised result replaces the old one without any further action by the user. In the REPL, we would have to type m * n again, and the new result would be printed below that, possibly scrolling other information off the screen.

In Pluto, because the results displayed are independent of the order in which they appear on the page, we can rearrange the cells to provide a good exposition, without worrying about affecting the calculations. We can combine Julia expressions with text formatted using Markdown or HTML, and turn our notebook into an article or a live explanatory text.

In the final cell, I've entered a question mark (?) followed by the name of a data type, Matrix. As soon as you enter the question mark and begin typing, a live help window opens, displaying documentation about what you've typed so far. As you add letters, the documentation changes to reflect what you've typed, and you can stop when you see what you want.

The help window stays there, displaying documentation about whatever you type into any cell, whether or not you ask for help. If it becomes distracting, click the little down arrow to tuck the window away. Because of Pluto's close integration with Julia, it has other conveniences, such as tab completion, that work the same way as in the REPL.

The text file that backs the notebook page, stored at the location you entered at the top, is a normal Julia module file. You can import it into other Julia programs, edit it directly, and put it into version control. You are not locked into the Pluto notebook, but can use the code you develop there in other Julia projects.

Pluto is a new and innovative way to develop programs and carry out exploratory computation that is fun to use. Even if you turn to it only now and then, you should install it and become familiar with the interface. Follow Pluto developments and find more documentation at *https://github.com/fonsp/Pluto.jl*.

Integrated Development Environments

Both Vim and Emacs can serve as capable IDEs for Julia by installing the plug-ins described in their respective sections earlier. Traditional IDEs don't afford as much of a critical advantage for languages like Julia as they might for more verbose and ceremony-laden languages such as Java or C++, where many developers consider them essential. A text editor is all you need for writing Julia programs.

However, some users prefer a "real" IDE or may already be accustomed to one. The Julia IDE situation is in flux at the moment of writing. An IDE called Juno, consisting of a plug-in for the Atom editor, was essentially the official IDE for Julia, but work on it has ceased. As the language moves forward, Juno will not keep up. IDE development for Julia has shifted to a plug-in for VS Code, a popular IDE from Microsoft.

You can download VS Code from its GitHub repository at *https://github .com/microsoft/vscode* and compile for your system. A quicker route for Linux, macOS, or Windows is to download the appropriate package file from *https://code.visualstudio.com/Download* and follow your system's normal install procedure. Microsoft also offers branded versions as binary downloads. These may contain small enhancements, and are released under a Microsoft product license.

After installing the base VS Code program, you will install the Julia plug-in, which you can do from within the IDE. Figure 1-5 illustrates how to do this.

Figure 1-5: Installing the Julia plug-in within VS Code

The screenshot shows the left-hand area of the VS Code window, with the extension icon selected. I've entered "Julia" into the extension search box at the top, and the program is displaying a list of publicly available extensions that match. When you perform this search, the list will likely look different, but you want the extension titled simply "Julia," which, in this case, is at the top of the list. Click the blue **Install** button to download and install the plug-in.

Quit VS Code and restart it after installing the plug-in. If you have set your path properly, as described in "Installation" on 6, press CTRL-SHIFT-P (CMD-SHIFT-P on macOS) to open a command window and execute the `Julia: Start REPL` command. A Julia REPL should open in a pane at the bottom of the window. It behaves just like the normal REPL described on page 10, with all REPL modes available, and using your color and other customizations.

In addition to typing directly in the REPL, you can open an existing or new file for editing. Julia code is syntax colored, and there are syntax-aware commands for moving through the code and manipulating its structures. The documentation at *https://www.julia-vscode.org/docs/stable/* consists largely of blank pages at the time of writing, but I expect this situation to be improved soon. Open the command window and type **Julia:** to discover Julia-specific commands and then scroll through the list. If you see a command you'll be using often, this list contains buttons next to each command that allow you to define keyboard shortcuts.

I recommend defining a shortcut for the "Send Current Line or Selection to REPL" command. This allows you to send any expression or statement directly from the editor to the REPL for execution.

If you execute a plot command in the REPL, the plot appears in its own dedicated pane within the VS Code window. Figure 1-6 shows the main part of the window as it appears on my laptop, with the light background selected from among VS Code's three appearance options.

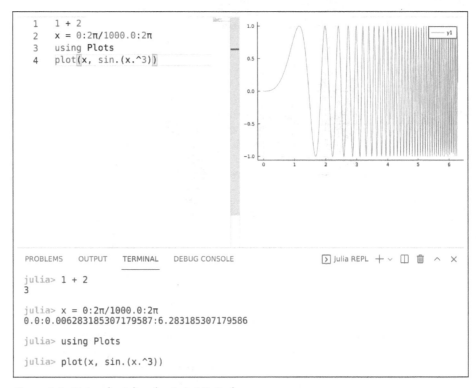

Figure 1-6: Using the Julia plug-in in VS Code

In the top pane, I'm editing a file with a few lines of Julia code, which I've sent directly to the REPL in the bottom pane. Although you may not understand all the language syntax yet, you may be able to form an idea of what the expressions are intended to return. After trying some arithmetic to see if the setup is working, I define a range of numbers, assigned to the x variable, and then plot a function applied to each value in the list. At the top right, the plot window has appeared.

Recommendations

As the choice of tools is a matter of personal preference, I've tried to provide enough information about all the main ways of interacting with Julia and editing Julia programs to allow you to choose the methods that most appeal to you. If you are already in the habit of using Vim, Emacs, or any other tool for programming, you don't need to learn anything new or change your workflows to use Julia. Use what you are familiar with, as Julia can easily adapt to it.

If, however, you're not yet committed to any specific tooling, I have a recommendation. I suggest that you install Vim, along with the Julia-specific plug-ins described in "Text Editors" on page 14. Vim takes some getting used to, but the long-term rewards are worthwhile, as it is an efficient and flexible editor, and it makes working alongside the REPL easy.

If Vim is new to you, to ease the burden of learning both a new language and an unfamiliar editor simultaneously, consider working through Pluto, as well as in the REPL directly, while you take your time to become comfortable with a new editor.

Be aware that this reflects my personal preferences, and you may prefer a different environment. For example, if you find working in a browser-based notebook appealing, there is no reason you can't do all of your Julia work within Pluto. My only negative recommendation is not to stick with a primitive editor that has no REPL or language support, as doing so will hold you back in the long run.

FURTHER READING

- My article "The Scientist's Linux Toolbox" in *Linux Pro Magazine* (*https://www.linuxpromagazine.com/Issues/2020/241/Scientist-s -Toolbox*) provides more information about Julia and other software useful to scientists computing on Linux.

- In "An Introduction to Pluto" (*https://lwn.net/Articles/835930/*), I describe the development of the Pluto notebook, give some examples of its use, and contrast it with the popular Jupyter Notebook interface.

- A useful ANSI color code table is available at *https://misc.flogisoft .com/_media/bash/colors_format/256_colors_bg.png*.

- Go to *https://gitforwindows.org* for a Windows solution that provides Git, a terminal program, and some more conveniences.

2

LANGUAGE BASICS

Learning another language is not only learning different words for the same things, but learning another way to think about things.
–Flora Lewis

 Sometimes people new to programming ask why there are so many computer languages. They all have different syntaxes. Some use braces and semicolons, like C and JavaScript; some use whitespace, like Python; some are notorious for a proliferation of parentheses, like the Lisp family; and some use keywords, like Julia.

However, differences in syntax are not the real reason. With experience, variations in language punctuation become trivialities. It's also true that some languages are faster than others, or have different demands on memory, although these are often properties of implementations rather than the languages themselves, but performance is not the real reason either.

The fundamental reason for the persistence of different languages and language families is that they are based on different ideas. Each language represents a unique conceptual framework in which to express computations. When we write a program, we are not simply telling a machine what to do. If that were the case, we would all write in the machine code into which our programs are ultimately translated. Instead, we are telling *people*, including ourselves, about a computation. Computer languages are human languages.

As you begin your journey through Julia, it's important to keep this in mind. You are not learning merely a collection of incantations for getting the computer to do what you want. You are learning a way of thinking: a set of concepts that you can use to organize computational ideas. If you master these ideas, your programs will do what you expect, will perform well, and will be clear to others and even to your future self.

That being said, most of these overarching ideas will come out in the application chapters in Part II. In this chapter, we cover the nitty-gritty: the bricks and stones out of which you will build your cathedrals.

These elements are the blocks with which you structure your Julia programs—functions, loops, and decisions—and the data types they interact with, such as strings, various kinds of numbers, and collections. After you finish this chapter, you will know enough about Julia to write your first programs.

The Syntax: Data Types, Expressions, and Blocks

In this section we'll learn about the fundamentals of Julia syntax for creating the basic structures used in almost every Julia program. We'll also be introduced to our first Julia data types.

Throughout this chapter I'll refer to the REPL, but these references apply equally well to any interactive environment for Julia, such as Pluto or VS Code.

Types of Numbers

All values in Julia have a *type*, just as in almost all programming languages. One of the basic types is that of a number, but, just as in mathematics, there are different types of numbers. In math we have positive and negative numbers, integers and real numbers, and more exotic varieties such as complex numbers and quaternions. Positive integers, or counting numbers, have been with us since before recorded history, but somebody had to invent all the other kinds of numbers. In "User-Defined Types" on page 234, you'll learn how you can invent your own kinds of Julia numbers if you want to, but for now, let's look at some of the built-in types.

NOTE *Perhaps more than any other chapter in this book, it is important to read this one with the Julia REPL open and try things out as you read about them. Experiment with variations of the examples in the chapter until you feel comfortable with the syntax. You will use everything in this chapter repeatedly in all your programs, so making these details second nature now will be helpful.*

If you type a number without a decimal point into the REPL and press RETURN or ENTER, Julia will give you the same number back. A number by itself is an *expression*, which means something that returns a result. Since the result of evaluating a plain number is the number itself, that's what you get. These whole numbers, by default, are given the type of Int64, which just means an integer that takes up 64 bits of storage. (I'm assuming a 64-bit system, which is a pretty safe assumption these days. If you are using a 32-bit system, replace Int64 with Int32 throughout this chapter.)

A number with a decimal point has the type Float64. The numbers 1 and 1.0 may have the same values, but they are different to the computer. The first is an Int64, and the second is a Float64. This difference has various repercussions that will appear in our later work.

Since Julia is intended, among other things, for scientific calculation, naturally it can deal with complex numbers as well. The syntax for entering complex numbers uses im for the imaginary unit (the square root of −1). So to enter the number $3 + 4i$, you write 3 + 4im. The type of that number is called Complex{Int64}, because the numerical parts happen to be integers. The type of 3.4 + 1.1im is called Complex{Float64}. This notation means that it's a Complex type that has Float64 parts.

You can write very big or small numbers using the usual computer version of scientific notation: 6.02e23 means 6.02×10^{23}. Numbers written in this way are Float64s, even if you write the mantissa as an integer. The exponent must be an integer, and if you prefer, you can use an uppercase E.

Julia will rewrite your entry in "proper" scientific notation. For example, if you enter 1234e19 in the REPL, it will repeat the value as 1.234e22. And apparently, it prefers the lowercase e.

There are a few other numerical types, such as the unsigned integer UInt64, but this is enough for now. We'll go deeper into the type system in Chapter 8.

Operations and Expressions

Addition, subtraction, and multiplication work as you would expect on all these types of numbers. The order of operations is the same as in mathematics and is similarly overridden using parentheses.

Julia performs obvious *type promotion* when needed. The expression 1 + 1 involves only integers, and the result will be the integer 2; there is no reason to return any other type. But the expression 1.0 + 1 involves a floating-point number, so it will return the Float64 result 2.0.

Try some arithmetic in the REPL involving operands of various types, including complex numbers, to make sure you understand how promotion works. Integers are promoted to floats, and both of those are promoted to complex numbers, as needed.

Division and Rational Numbers

Julia has *three* kinds of division. Every language has to decide what to do about expressions such as 1/2. The problem is that both operands are integers, but the result is not. Some languages, such as Fortran and Python 2, evaluate that expression to be zero, because that is the result of taking the integer part before the decimal point in the answer. Other languages will promote the result into a float and return 0.5; that's what Julia does.

If you want a form of division that behaves like Fortran, you can use the division symbol (÷): 1 ÷ 2 gives 0 and 4 ÷ 3 gives 1. To enter this operator in the REPL, enter \div followed by TAB (see "Unicode Characters" on page 13).

The third form of division uses the // operator to define `Rational` numbers, which are ratios of two integers. Using this data type, you can perform exact arithmetic on rationals without converting the results into floats. For example, the expression 1//2 + 1//3 evaluates to 5//6. Julia reduces rational numbers to their simplest form, so if you enter 4//6 in the REPL, it will return the result 2//3.

What do you think you get if you enter 1//2 + 1//2 in the REPL? If you tried it, you may have been surprised to find the result printed as 1//1 rather than simply 1. The result of expressions involving only `Rational` numbers is a `Rational` number. If instead you evaluate 1//2 + 0.5, you get the `Float64` number 1.0.

Exponentiation and Infinities

To raise a number to a power, use the ^ operator. Here are the results of exponentiation of various types of numbers:

```
julia> 2^3
8

julia> 2^0.5
1.4142135623730951

julia> 2^-1
0.5

julia> (1 + im)^2
0 + 2im

julia> (1 + im)^(1 + im)
0.2739572538301211 + 0.5837007587586147im

julia> 0^-1
Inf

julia> (0//1)^-1
1//0
```

All of those results should be as expected, but the last two infinite results merit some discussion. Division by zero, as in the next-to-last expression shown or the equivalent 1/0, evaluates to `Inf`, which has the `Float64` data type. The `Rational` number 1//0 is also infinite, but it has the `Rational` data type. It behaves as an infinity should: since adding a finite number to infinity doesn't change it, we have 1//0 + 1 yielding 1//0. The type promotion rules still apply, so if, instead, we evaluate `1//0 + 1.0` we get `Inf`: still infinity, but the `Float64` infinity.

Dividing by infinity gets us zero, as it should. However, we get a `Rational` zero or a `Float64` zero, depending on the operands:

```
julia> 1/(1//0)
0//1

julia> 1.0/(1//0)
0.0
```

There are other sizes of floating-point numbers, just as there are integers. If we contrived to divide a/b where a had the value 1.0 of type `Float32` and b had the value 0.0 of the same data type, Julia would return yet another kind of infinity: `Inf32`. You'll learn how to make variables contain types of your choosing in "User-Defined Types" on page 234.

Modular Arithmetic

Another useful operator, `%`, returns the remainder when dividing its first operand by its second. For example, `5 % 2` returns `1`. As with the other arithmetic operators, integers yield an integer and floats yield a floating-point result.

Chains of Expressions

We've briefly seen the use of the semicolon to separate expressions and, in the REPL, to suppress the printing of a result (see page 11). If we have a list of expressions on a line, separated by semicolons, the result of the chain of expressions is the result of the last expression:

```
julia> 1; 2; 5+3
8
```

We assign values to variables in Julia using the `=` operator. Since the value of a chain of expressions is the last one, the assignment

```
r = (1; 2; 5+3)
```

results in r having the value 8. If we had omitted the parentheses, r would have been assigned the value 1, because then the assignment `r = 1` would have been a separate expression.

Coefficient Syntax

In cases where it is not ambiguous, we can juxtapose a literal number with a variable (or function, as we'll see later) to signify multiplication. If the juxtaposition creates an ambiguity, Julia will complain, and we must revert to using the `*` operator.

Multiplication written this way has one important difference from the use of `*`. It has a higher operation precedence than the other arithmetic operations, so it is an exception to the usual order of operations. A few examples should make this clear:

```
julia> w = 2
2

julia> 2w
4

julia> 2^2w
16

julia> 2^2*w
8

julia> 1/2w
0.25

julia> 1/2*w
1.0
```

In an expression such as 1/2*w, the 1/2 is calculated first and the result is multiplied by 2. But since juxtaposition binds more tightly than explicit arithmetic operators, in the expression 1/2w, the 2w is calculated first.

This unusual syntax feature, along with the ability to use Greek letters and other Unicode symbols, helps to make math in code look more like math.

Expression Blocks

Another way to group expressions together is with a begin...end block. This unit of code starts with the keyword begin and, as do all blocks in Julia, ends with the keyword end. You can enter blocks directly in the REPL. Julia sees that you are defining a block and will not print the prompt until the structure is complete:

```
julia> begin
            1
            2
            5 + 3
        end
8

julia>
```

As with chains of expressions separated by semicolons, the result of this group of expressions is the final one. You can even assign the result of the block to a variable:

```
julia> eight = begin
          1
          2
          5 + 3
       end
8

julia> eight
8
```

The value of an expression is printed by default in the REPL and in
other interactive environments such as Pluto. However, if you are running
a program stored in a file, you need to use `print(expression)` to see the value
on the terminal.

Logic

Logical values are represented by `true` and `false`, which are of type `Bool`. The
important logical operators are logical AND, which is represented by `&&`, and
logical OR, which uses `||`. These operators are *short-circuiting*, which means
that, going from left to right in an expression, once the final value of an expression can be determined to be `true` or `false`, Julia will stop and not evaluate the remainder. For example, in the expression `false && more stuff`, as
soon as Julia hits the `&&` operator, it will stop and return `false`, and never try
to evaluate the `more stuff`. It can do this because the result of this expression must be `false`, regardless of whether the `more stuff` is true or false. The
programmer must be aware of this and not depend on all parts of a logical expression being evaluated. In an expression such as `false && (cc = 17)`,
the part after the `&&` is never even looked at, and, therefore, the assignment
never happens.

If you need to ensure that all parts of a logical expression are evaluated,
use the operators `&` and `|` instead. These are the bitwise AND and OR opera-
tors. They transform numbers, as we'll see in later chapters, but act as logical
operators when applied to `Bool`s.

`Bool` values usually arise from the evaluation of comparisons, which use
the operators `>`, `<`, `<=`, `>=`, `==`, and `===`. The negations of the equality tests are
`!=` and `!==`. The `<=` operator can also be spelled using the nicer-looking Unicode symbol $\leq$, and `>=` is synonymous with $\geq$. The expression `1 < 5` evaluates
to `true`, `5 ≥ 5` is also true, and so on.

You may have noticed that there are two equality comparisons. The first,
`==`, compares two values, regardless of type. So `5 == 5.0` will give us `true`, even
though one number is an integer and the other is a float. The other equality comparison tests whether two values are identical in all respects. It only
returns true if no program could be written where it could possibly make a
difference which value was used. Therefore, the expression `5 === 5.0` returns

false because it is certainly possible for a program to distinguish between integers and floats.

Comparisons such as > don't usually need associated negations, because the negation of > is <=. In fact, mathematicians sometimes pronounce that comparison as "not larger than." If you need to express this as an explicit negation, you'll have to negate a whole expression using the syntax !(a > b), at least at the time of writing. Including negated comparisons in the language, which would be written as !<, for example, is under consideration.

Looping: while Blocks

So far we've learned about one kind of block: the expression block using begin. A common way to write a *loop*, or piece of code that is to be repeated until some condition no longer holds, is with another kind of block: the while block. As with all blocks, it is terminated with the end keyword. The condition that terminates the block uses the comparisons that we learned about in the previous section. Listing 2-1 is a simple example of a while block in action in the REPL.

```
julia> j = 0;

julia> while j < 5
           println(j^2)
           j = j + 1
       end
0
1
4
9
16
```

Listing 2-1: Looping in the REPL

The println() function prints its value on a separate line. But why did we have to use this at all, when expressions in the REPL are supposed to be printed automatically?

The begin blocks return a result, which is the last expression evaluated in the block. But while blocks do not return a result, so there is nothing to print. Whatever we want to see, we have to print explicitly. This is probably a good thing, as loops can evaluate many expressions and are likely to produce a mass of output that we don't want.

Notice also the initialization of the j variable before the start of the loop. In the REPL, this creates a *global* variable that is accessible and modifiable anywhere. After the while loop is finished, the value of j equals 5. This is another behavior that differs between the REPL (and other interactive contexts such as Pluto) and programs in files. (I'll explain this in more detail in "Scope" on page 52.)

if Blocks

Julia has conventional conditional evaluation control flow using the logical comparison operators (see "Logic" on page 31) and the keywords if, elseif, and else. You may nest your if blocks at will; each one is terminated with the end keyword.

Here is a little program that we can run in the REPL to tell us if a number is even or odd:

```
if n % 2 === 0
    "That number is even."
elseif n % 2 === 1
    "That number is odd."
else
    "I only deal with integers."
end
```

If, before entering this block, you define n to be a number, it will give you the answer. If n is undefined or something besides a number, you'll get an error message.

The === comparison between two integers makes the code refuse to handle any kinds of numbers other than integers. Try the code with, say, n = 6 and then with n = 6.0 to see what happens.

Unlike while blocks, if blocks return a result, so an explicit print() statement isn't needed.

NOTE *I've used indentation to clarify the structure of the code blocks in the examples throughout this book. Indentation has no syntactic meaning in Julia, but using it is a good habit that makes programs easier to read. You can indent code lines any way you please, or not at all, and it will not affect their execution. Spaces are needed to separate tokens, and newlines are equivalent to semicolons in their role as statement and expression separators. Otherwise, Julia doesn't care about whitespace in general.*

Arrays

The various numbers that we've seen so far are all types that hold single values. Arrays are a class of Julia data types that hold *collections* of values. Scientific calculation typically involves operations over vectors, matrices, or higher-dimensional arrays, and Julia offers a convenient, concise syntax for manipulating these data structures, as well as excellent array performance.

Try typing [1, 2, 3] in the REPL. This is the syntax for creating a one-dimensional array, also called a *vector*, of three elements. Its data type is called Vector. As before, the REPL will print the expression back, but this time in a different form:

```
julia> [1, 2, 3]
3-element Vector{Int64}:
 1
```

2

3

It also prints, before the value, a bit of information about the kind of value that it's about to display. Julia routinely does this in the REPL when printing anything more complicated than a simple data type. The information is provided to help you interpret the display. This is useful because, when constructing arrays, Julia may change the types of some of the elements that you included under some circumstances, and it's good to know about that. Also, the feedback about the shape of the array tells you whether your array operations did what you expected.

Here is a case where Julia changes some numerical types:

```
julia> a = [4, 5.0, 6]
3-element Vector{Float64}:
 4.0
 5.0
 6.0
```

We give a a value entered as a literal array with three elements: an integer, a float, and another integer. The message from the REPL confirms that this is a 3-element Vector, but the notation Vector{Float64} means that the elements of the Vector are all of type Float64. Julia has *promoted* the integers to floats. We can confirm this by looking at the numbers it prints, which are now all adorned with decimal points. When you initialize an array with a literal expression like the one just shown, Julia will always try to make the types of its elements uniform by promoting values as needed. This helps performance for later calculations using the array. The vertical arrangement of numbers is the way Julia prints vectors when possible. As we'll see shortly, it has conventions for printing arrays of various shapes.

Sometimes it's impossible to promote elements so that they all have the same type. The elements of an array can be anything, including other arrays, as shown in Listing 2-2.

```
julia> a = [4, [5.0, 6], 7]
3-element Vector{Any}:
 4
  [5.0, 6.0]
 7
```

Listing 2-2: A heterogeneous array

Julia is still following the printing convention of arranging the elements in a column. The first and third elements are integers, and the second element is a vector. But notice how Julia promoted the integer 6 in that vector to a float so that all of *its* elements would have the same type. The message from the REPL tells us that the type of the complete vector is Vector{Any}, which means it's a Vector that can hold a mixture of any types. This particular array has two elements of type Int64 and one element of type Vector{Float64}.

We can get the value of, or assign a value to, an element of an array by *indexing* using square brackets. Array indices in Julia, as in Fortran and many other languages designed with scientific and mathematical work in mind, start at 1.

In the following example, I've entered a few array indexing expressions into the REPL after performing the assignment in Listing 2-2:

```
julia> a[1]
4

julia> a[end]
7

julia> a[2]
2-element Vector{Float64}:
 5.0
 6.0

julia> a[2][2]
6.0
```

Notice the use of the keyword end to point to the last element of an array; this is convenient when you don't know its length. The second element of the array is another array; we can index into that array in one expression using a double index, as in the last expression. If you do need to find the length of an array, use the length() function.

Ranges

Julia can construct ranges of numbers with a special notation. The syntax 1:5 represents a range of integers from 1 to 5 inclusive, counting by 1. You can count by numbers other than 1 by using a version of the syntax with three numbers. For example, 1:3:12 represents a range with the numbers 1, 4, 7, 10. The range can count down as well, using a negative step, as in 5:-1:2. Finally, any of the numbers in the range specifier can be a float rather than an integer, in which case all the numbers in the range will be floats.

Ranges are not arrays. They live in a kind of dimension of potentiality, ready to be brought to life by being used. In the meantime, they take up almost no space. One way to bring them to life is with the collect() function that turns them into a bona fide Vector:

```
julia> collect(1:5)
5-element Vector{Int64}:
 1
 2
 3
 4
 5
```

```
julia> [collect(1:2:10), collect(2.5:-0.5:0)]
2-element Vector{Vector{Float64}}:
 [1.0, 3.0, 5.0, 7.0, 9.0]
 [2.5, 2.0, 1.5, 1.0, 0.5, 0.0]
```

The first example turns a range into a vector, while the second uses two collect() operations inside a literal vector, resulting in a vector of two vectors.

The most common use of ranges is in for loops, which is covered in "More Looping: for Blocks" on page 46.

Ranges are also useful in indexing expressions to extract more than one element from an array:

```
julia> v = collect(0:5:20)
5-element Vector{Int64}:
  0
  5
 10
 15
 20

julia> v[2:4]
3-element Vector{Int64}:
  5
 10
 15

julia> v[end:-2:1]
3-element Vector{Int64}:
 20
 10
  0
```

These examples show how we can extract subsets of arrays and conveniently reverse the order of elements by using a decreasing range. We can extract noncontiguous elements by supplying the range with a step. For instance, v[1:2:5] yields [0, 10, 20].

Arrays: Beyond the First Dimension

The Vectors we've seen up to now are Arrays of one dimension. Even though the elements of a Vector may contain other collections, the Vector itself is still one-dimensional. Julia has arrays with any number of dimensions. Those with one dimension have their own type because they are a common special case, and optimizations can be applied to routines that calculate on them.

Matrices

Arrays with two dimensions also have a particular type, called a `Matrix`. Matrices arise in many contexts in mathematics and physics, and in all kinds of calculations. They represent linear transformations that rotate vectors, encode the coefficients of systems of linear equations, are used as simple data tables, and much more.

Think of a matrix as a rectangular table of values. You can enter such tables directly to define them:

```
julia> m = [5 6
            7 8]
2×2 Matrix{Int64}:
 5  6
 7  8
```

When entering the definition of the matrix m into the REPL, I press ENTER after the number 6 to insert a line break. Julia's REPL knows that the input is not complete because of the unclosed square bracket, so it doesn't try to evaluate anything, but instead waits for more input. After I close the bracket and press ENTER, the REPL sees a complete expression, makes the assignment to the variable m, and returns the expression, preceded by a description of its shape (2×2), type (Matrix), and the type of the collection's elements (Int64).

You can take advantage of this behavior to break an expression between lines, as in the following example:

```
julia> (1 + 1
         + 1
       )
3
```

Without the opening parenthesis, the addition on the first line would have been performed immediately because it's a complete expression.

Matrices vs. Vectors of Vectors

Make sure that you understand the difference between the 2×2 `Matrix` m and this vector:

```
julia> v = [[5, 6], [7, 8]]
2-element Vector{Vector{Int64}}:
 [5, 6]
 [7, 8]
```

The latter is a one-dimensional array, whereas the former has two dimensions.

Some indexing should make this clear:

```
julia> v[1]
2-element Vector{Int64}:
 5
 6
```

Here, the first element of the Vector v is itself a vector.

A double index selects the second element of this first element:

```
julia> v[1][2]
6
```

In this case, we get the number 6.

A colon standing alone means to select everything—in this case, the entire second element, which is a Vector:

```
julia> v[2][:]
2-element Vector{Int64}:
 7
 8
```

In this example the stand-alone colon is unnecessary, as just v[2] would yield the same result.

Since m is a Matrix, or a two-dimensional array, we select its elements using two indices:

```
julia> m[1, 1]
5
```

In this expression, the index [1, 1] means row 1, column 1, where the number 5 resides.

In a Matrix, the colon index is useful:

```
julia> m[2, :]
2-element Vector{Int64}:
 7
 8
```

Here it's selecting the entire second row.

Scalar Indexing

The usual way to index an n-dimensional array is with n indices: one for a vector, two for a matrix, and so on, as in the examples just shown. If you use the wrong number of indices, you'll get an error:

```
julia> m[1, 2, 3]
ERROR: BoundsError: attempt to access 2×2 Matrix{Int64} at index [1, 2, 3]
```

Julia is complaining that we tried to index a two-dimensional array as if it had three dimensions.

What do you think we would get if we used just one index on m, as if it were a vector? Oddly enough, we don't get an error, but it may not be obvious at first why we are getting these particular results:

```
julia> m[1]
5

julia> m[2]
7

julia> m[3]
6

julia> m[4]
8
```

Apparently we can access the four elements of this matrix as if they were arranged as a one-dimensional array, and they seem to be arranged by column. This is indeed the case, and it reflects how the numbers in the matrix are arranged in memory. The numbers 5, 7, 6, and 8 are the contents of the matrix reading down by column, starting with the first column and then the second. This is called *column-major order*, and is the way the elements are stored in memory.

Concepts like "two-dimensional arrays" are abstractions that make it easier to think about calculations and write programs. In the machine, the elements of the array are stored in one long row. The numbers in a Julia Vector, Matrix, or other Array type are guaranteed to be stored contiguously. Using a single integer as an index is called *scalar indexing*.

The scalar index can go from 1 to the total size of the matrix. If we try m[5], we get an error message because the matrix contains only four elements.

The Julia programmer doesn't have to be overly concerned with the machine representation of data structures or think much about how they are arranged in memory, but this detail is important. A calculation that loops over the elements of a matrix should proceed in column-major order rather than row-major order because the former method accesses contiguous values in memory and will be more efficient.

Indexing Arrays with Arrays

In addition to numbers and ranges, elements of an index expression can themselves be vectors. Listing 2-3 sets up a slightly larger matrix so we have more room to play.

```
julia> m = [11 12 13 14
            15 16 17 18
            19 20 21 22];
```

```
❶ julia> m[2, [2, 3]]
2-element Vector{Int64}:
 16
 17

julia> m[[1, 2], [3, 4]]
2×2 Matrix{Int64}:
 13  14
 17  18
```

Listing 2-3: Indexing with vectors

After defining a 3×4 Matrix, I extract the elements from the second and third columns of the second row by using a vector for the column part of the indexing expression ❶. Since the result is one-dimensional, Julia puts the elements into a Vector.

Then I pull out the elements in the first two rows and the third and fourth columns. Since the result is two-dimensional, it becomes a (smaller) Matrix.

We've seen that when we access elements of a multidimensional array using a single index, Julia interprets that as an index into the one-dimensional array made by taking the elements in column-major order.

When indexing an array, you can refer to all of its dimensions:

Array[rows, columns, third_dimension, fourth_dimension]

With this style, each of the expressions separated by commas must be a Vector or a number. (A number is treated as a Vector with one element, as evaluating 5[1] shows.) The Vectors can be in the form of range expressions or simple colons, which are interpreted as the Vectors they represent.

Alternatively, you can index it as if it were a Vector:

Array[Array]

When using this second style, the Array in the index expression can have any shape. The result will have the shape of that Array. It can be larger than the original Array because you can repeat elements. The only limitation is that, if the original Array has n elements, you can use indices only in the range $[1, n]$. The same limitation applies to the first style, but to each individual indexing vector, where n means the length of the array along that dimension. In other words, you can't index elements that don't exist.

Let's take another look at the second indexing style with a couple of examples, using the Array m defined earlier:

```
julia> m[[2 3
          4 5]]
2×2 Matrix{Int64}:
 15  19
 12  16
```

```
julia> m[[end 1 9
          9  1 end]]
2×3 Matrix{Int64}:
 22  11  21
 21  11  22
```

In both of these cases, the result has the same shape as the array used as an index. The end keyword picks out the last element in the source array. In the first style of indexing, it picks out the last element along the relevant dimension.

Concatenation Operators

It's not always convenient to use line breaks to signify the end of a row when defining matrices, so in Julia, you can use a semicolon instead:

```
julia> m1 = [6 7
             8 9];

julia> m2 = [6 7; 8 9];

julia> m1 == m2
true
```

The line break and the semicolon are both ways to spell the *vertical concatenation operator*. This has another name, vcat, so another way to construct the m1 or m2 matrix is with vcat([6 7], [8 9]). In this expression, [6 7] and [8 9] are two *arguments* to the vcat() function.

The space used to separate the numbers 6 and 7 in the definitions of m1 and m2 just shown is an operator, too, called the *horizontal concatenation operator*. It has its own explicit function as well, called hcat(). It's important to understand the difference between [6, 7], which is a Vector containing two elements, and [6 7], which is a 1×2 Matrix formed by horizontal concatenation invoked by a space. (Tabs can be used as well as spaces for this purpose.)

The following are a few final examples to clarify the results of the two different directions of concatenation. Here's one way to construct a matrix:

```
julia> [[6 7]; [8 9]]
2×2 Matrix{Int64}:
 6  7
 8  9
```

This construction combines vertical and horizontal concatenation in one expression. The spaces between the numbers concatenate them horizontally into arrays with a single row each. The semicolon vertically concatenates each of those matrices into a larger matrix with the first row on top of the second.

Replacing the semicolon with a space produces a different shape, horizontally joining the two one-row matrices into a longer one-row matrix:

```
julia> [[6 7] [8 9]]
1x4 Matrix{Int64}:
 6  7  8  9
```

In the third example, we'll ask for two *vectors* to be horizontally concatenated:

```
julia> [[6, 7] [8, 9]]
2x2 Matrix{Int64}:
 6  8
 7  9
```

The result in this example surprises some people new to the language. You may not immediately understand why we don't get the same result as in the previous example. Horizontal concatenation really means, for a Matrix, joining along the second dimension. Since a Vector doesn't have a second dimension, Julia first has to change each Vector into a 2x1 Matrix, and then join them along the column dimension.

But there is no such issue when we ask Julia to *vertically* concatenate the vectors because that means to join them along their first dimensions:

```
julia> [[6, 7]; [8, 9]]
4-element Vector{Int64}:
 6
 7
 8
 9
```

The result of this is a longer Vector.

Tuples

A Tuple is similar to a Vector, with the important difference being that you cannot change it once it is created. Initialize a Tuple the same way you create a Vector, but use parentheses instead of square brackets or omit them entirely if that does not create an ambiguity, as shown in Listing 2-4.

```
julia> tup1 = (5, 6)
(5, 6)

julia> tup2 = 5, 6
(5, 6)

julia> tup1 === tup2
true

❶ julia> tup1[1]
 5
```

❷ julia> **tup1[1] = 9**
ERROR: MethodError: no method matching [...]

Listing 2-4: Some properties of tuples

This example shows that the parentheses are optional, and that two tuples containing the same values (in the same order) are indistinguishable because they pass the === comparison.

NOTE *When a tuple contains only one element, it must be written with parentheses and a comma after the element–for example, (3,).*

We can index tuples ❶ as if they were vectors, but we can neither *assign* values to element locations ❷ nor change the tuple in any way.

What is the use of a vector-like collection that can't be changed? Tuples can be used to store lists of values that we want to ensure can't be altered accidentally. Their main use is supplying arguments to functions and collecting results, as we'll see shortly.

Membership

Julia provides another logical operator that tests for membership in a collection. It's the in operator, which can also take the form ∈, entered in the REPL with \in followed by pressing TAB. In this case, the Unicode version is preferred because it comes with a negated form, meaning "not in," that looks like ∉ and is entered in the REPL with \notin followed by TAB.

Here are some examples:

```
julia> 2 ∈ [1, 2, 3]
true

julia> 2 ∉ [1, 2, 3]
false
```

❶
```
julia> 2 ∈ [1, 2.0, 3]
true
```

❷
```
julia> [2, 3] ∈ [2, 3, 4]
false
```

❸
```
julia> [2, 3] ∈ [[2, 3], 4]
true
```

Membership uses comparisons of values ❶, not object identity, which may not be what you were expecting.

In ❷, we get false because the Vector [2, 3] is not one of the members of the Vector [2, 3, 4]. In the following example ❸, we get a true result because the Vector [2, 3] *is* a member of [[2, 3], 4].

Strings and Characters

Julia is a bit unusual in that single and double quotation marks have different meanings: single quotes indicate characters and double quotes are for strings. Char and String are two distinct data types.

Characters

A Char is entered with a pair of single quotes. Julia was created in the age of Unicode, so it was spared the painful transitions of older languages such as Python. Julia is fully Unicode aware. A Char can be any Unicode character, such as '5', 'a', 'ñ', or 'Σ'. Under the hood, it's a 32-bit value representing the character with its UTF-8 encoding. The value has some of the properties of a number, but it is not, in fact, a number.

Characters have an ordering, so you can ask 'a' < 'z' and Julia will tell you true.

NOTE *In many languages, single and double quotes can be used interchangeably, and both signify strings or characters, with characters being strings with only one letter or other symbol. Like Elixir and SQL, Julia distinguishes between string and character data types: "ab" is a string, but 'ab' is a syntax error.*

You can add an integer to a character, as in 'a' + 1, and Julia will give you the next character, 'b'. Subtraction gives similar results. You can even subtract two characters to find the distance between them: 'c' - 'a' yields 2, which means that 'a' + 2 yields 'c'. However, addition of characters is not allowed.

Strings

A String is entered with double quotes, like "François". It is a type of collection, similar in some ways to a Vector, but with some complications. As it is a series of characters, you can make one by joining together single characters. The operator for this, unusually, is *. The designers of Julia decided not to employ the more usual + for several reasons, one of them being that addition is commutative, but the joining of characters certainly is not: 'a' * 'b' yields the string "ab", but 'b' * 'a' yields a different string, "ba". You can also build up a string by joining other strings: "Fran" * "çois" becomes "François".

Since strings are collections, you can use the membership operator with them, but only for testing the occurrence of characters: 'a' in "abc" yields true.

If you want to test for the occurrence of a string, even one consisting of a single character, in another string, use the occursin() function: occursin("a", "abc") will give you a true result.

One of the complications that arises when treating strings like vectors is when trying to index them:

```
julia> n = "François"
"François"
```

```
julia> length(n)
8

julia> n[end]
's': ASCII/Unicode U+0073 (category Ll: Letter, lowercase)

julia> n[1]
'F': ASCII/Unicode U+0046 (category Lu: Letter, uppercase)

julia> n[5]
'ç': Unicode U+00E7 (category Ll: Letter, lowercase)

julia> n[6]
ERROR: StringIndexError: invalid index [6], valid nearby indices [5]=>'ç', [7]=>'o'
```

Everything was going fine until the last expression. Extracting single elements from the String gives us the Char that we expect. Why doesn't n[6] just return the sixth character? Even stranger, if we try n[8], we don't get the last letter, but 'i' instead. If we try n[end], we *do* get the final letter.

The cause of these mysteries is that different Unicode characters take up different amounts of space. The index into a String counts the number of *bytes*, or 8-bit units, from the beginning of the String. Ordinary ASCII letters like "F" and "r" take up one byte each, but "ç" happens to take up two bytes. So it starts at position 5 when counting bytes, but the next character is at position 7, as the error message advises us. And we got the error because we are not allowed to index "inside" a character.

There are complicated ways to avoid this problem by finding out the legal indices for any String. Fortunately, you won't have to learn these techniques, because one rarely needs to index strings directly. If you need to iterate over the elements of a String or any other collection, there is a far easier way to do so, which we'll cover in the next section.

For very long strings, especially those that contain line breaks and may contain quote characters, there is a more convenient syntax. Delimit these strings using three double quotes:

```
julia> ls = """
       Line one.
       Line two "with a quoted section"!
       We're done.
       """
"Line one.\nLine two \"with a quoted section\"!\nWe're done.\n"

julia> print(ls)
Line one.
Line two "with a quoted section"!
We're done.
```

In this example, using print() displays strings somewhat differently from how they are returned as results.

More Looping: for Blocks

So far, we've learned one way to iterate over a section of code, or loop, by using a while block in conjunction with a condition for stopping the iteration. This is appropriate for situations when we want to do something repeatedly until something changes—for example, when reading data from a network socket until the socket is closed or calculating a progressively more accurate solution to an equation until the error is smaller than some tolerance. In other situations, we simply want to iterate a fixed number of times or iterate over the members of a collection. This is where for loops come in.

To loop a fixed number of times, use a range expression. This loop repeats the calculation in Listing 2-1:

```
julia> for j in 0:4
           println(j^2)
       end
0
1
4
9
16
```

This version is simpler because we didn't have to add 1 to j on each iteration. The variable takes on the sequence of values in the range expression, progressing to the next one each time through the loop. As with while loops, for loops do not return results, so we need an explicit println() statement.

We can use any kind of range expression:

```
julia> for q in 8:-2:1
           println(1/q)
       end
0.125
0.16666666666666666
0.25
0.5
```

Here we're counting down by twos from 8 to 1.

NOTE   *You may substitute = for the keyword in in any for block if you prefer. There is also a third, fancier option: you can use the membership symbol ∈, which we first met in "Membership" on page 43.*

You may nest as many for blocks inside each other as required. In cases where you have a contiguous loop body, meaning you don't have to do anything between the updates of any of the loop variables (such as the counters i and j in the following listing), Julia provides a concise syntax that avoids deeply nested structures on the page:

```
julia> for i ∈ 0:3, j ∈ 4:6
           println([i, j, i + j])
       end
[0, 4, 4]
[0, 5, 5]
[0, 6, 6]
[1, 4, 5]
[1, 5, 6]
[1, 6, 7]
[2, 4, 6]
[2, 5, 7]
[2, 6, 8]
[3, 4, 7]
[3, 5, 8]
[3, 6, 9]
```

All the looping instructions are on one line, and we need only one end statement.

The same for block syntax lets us loop over vectors, matrices, or other containers:

```
julia> for x in [-19 23 0]
           println(abs(x))
       end
19
23
0
```

In this example, x takes on the values in the 1×3 Matrix, applying the absolute value function to each one.

The loop can be over Vector and Tuple data types as well, but a Tuple needs to be enclosed in parentheses if used in the for statement.

You can loop over arrays of any dimension:

```
julia> for x in [[-19 23 0]; [-1 22 -17]]
           println(abs(x))
       end
19
1
23
22
0
17
```

The elements are printed in column-major order, reflecting their layout in memory.

Since strings are containers, too, you can loop over them:

```
julia> for c ∈ "François"
           print(c * " • ")
       end
F • r • a • n • ç • o • i • s •
```

Here we don't have to worry about the varying lengths of Unicode characters as the for loop knows how to step from one character to the next.

Functions

Projects in Julia are organized around sets of *functions*. These resemble functions in mathematics, in that they are maps of values to other values. In Julia the input and output values can be of any type.

Here is how to define a function:

```
julia> function double(x)
           2x
       end
double (generic function with 1 method)
```

The double() function takes a number and returns twice the number. For now, don't worry about the message that the REPL returns. You'll find out what it means in "Functions and Methods: Multiple Dispatch" on page 229.

Simple functions like this one have an alternative syntax. You can shorten this function definition block as follows:

```
double(x) = 2x
```

Notice that we don't need a print() statement because a function returns the last expression that it evaluates. Try it by entering expressions like double(-3.1) in the REPL. Anything where 2x makes sense will work, but if you supply an argument where it doesn't, such as a string, Julia will respond with an error message.

In the definition of the function, the (x) part is actually a Tuple with one element, x, which is double()'s single *argument*.

Functions can have any number of arguments. Here is one that gives the length of a vector from the origin if you supply the x-, y-, and z-coordinates of its end:

```
julia> function length3d(x, y, z)
           sqrt(x^2 + y^2 + z^2)
       end
length3d (generic function with 1 method)

julia> length3d(1, 1, 1)
1.7320508075688772
```

Use the return statement if you want the function to stop and return a value. We can use this to modify our `length3d()` function to accept only positive coordinates:

```
julia> function length3d(x, y, z)
           if x < 0 || y < 0 || z < 0
               return "I only work with positive coordinates."
           end
           sqrt(x^2 + y^2 + z^2)
       end
length3d (generic function with 1 method)
```

If we call `length3d()` with all positive arguments, all is well:

```
julia> length3d(1, 1, 1)
1.7320508075688772
```

But a negative argument hits the return statement:

```
julia> length3d(1, 1, -1)
"I only work with positive coordinates."
```

When you invoke the name of a function with parentheses and arguments, you are causing the function to execute using those arguments. This is called *calling* the function. If you supply the wrong number of arguments, such as trying to call `length3d(1, 1)`, you'll get an error. When we want to *refer* to the function without calling it, we simply use its name without parentheses or arguments: for instance, `length3d`. We can assign functions to variables, pass them as arguments to other functions, and generally treat them as any other value.

The function in Listing 2-5 takes a value and another function as arguments and announces the result of applying the supplied function to the argument. It works with any function of one argument, as long as you supply an argument x that f can handle.

```
julia> function tellme(f, x)
           print("The result is ")
           f(x)
       end
tellme (generic function with 1 method)
```

Listing 2-5: A function with a function as an argument

Now if we call `tellme(double, 3)` we will see the string `The result is 6` printed on the terminal. If we call `tellme(abs, -17)`, the function prints `The result is 17`.

These two examples use the `double()` function that we defined and the built-in absolute value function.

I mentioned previously that you don't need to use `print()` statements to see the result a function returns, so you may wonder why there is one here. A function returns the last expression it evaluates or returns immediately if it reaches a return statement. If we had omitted the print() statement and had only the string in its place, the value of the string would be evaluated as itself, but not returned, because it would not be the last expression. Function execution would proceed to the next line and return the value f(x).

The print() statement is not an expression, but a *statement*, meaning that it does not return a result; instead, it has the *side effect* of causing something to be written on the terminal. So the function produces that side effect and continues to the next (last) line, which is an expression, whose value it returns.

A side effect is anything that changes the state of the world, such as creating a file, printing to a terminal, or downloading something from the internet. A *pure function* is a function that has no side effects, but just returns a result. Writing pure functions when possible makes your code easier to debug and reason about, and it helps make your functions *composable*, which is the topic of the next section.

Composing Functions

Just as in math, *composing* functions means to supply the output of one function as the input of the next. Julia supplies three syntaxes for function composition. The first two are the same as common mathematical notations, but the third is a somewhat different idea. Here are all three methods, used for applying our double() function twice:

```
julia> double(double(3))
12

julia> (double ∘ double)(3)
12

julia> 3 |> double |> double
12
```

The first way uses the syntax for applying a function to an argument, where the argument is the function applied to the number 3. The number gets doubled and the result is itself doubled.

The second way uses a symbol that mathematicians sometimes use for composition and has a neater appearance, especially as we can compose as many functions as we want inside the first set of parentheses, something that, using the first method, leads to a proliferation of brackets. The series of functions are combined into a single composite function, applied to the argument list in the second set of parentheses. You can enter the little circle in the REPL using \circ followed by TAB.

The final option goes from left to right, whereas the previous two acted from right to left. It uses the *pipe operator* |> to create a *pipeline*. A value at the beginning, in this case 3, is fed to the first function in the pipeline, and the result of applying that function to the value is passed along to the second function, and so on. This method is a favorite of people who don't like parentheses; it's especially suited to expressing the processing of data through a series of transformations.

The three syntaxes for function composition are exactly equivalent. Which one to use is a matter of preference and convenience in a particular situation.

Creating Anonymous Functions

Sometimes you need to define a function "on the fly," without giving it a name. This happens when you want to supply a function as an argument to another function, but the one you supply needs to live only as long as the computation performed by the outer function. That is, it's disposable.

The syntax for anonymous functions makes their operation as maps explicit, using the operator -> to indicate the mapping. To define an anonymous doubling function, write x -> 2x.

If the function has multiple variables, enclose them in parentheses: (x, y) -> x/(1 + y).

We'll make extensive use of anonymous functions in Chapter 4, where they'll make it easy for us to plot mathematical functions.

Broadcasting

One of the most useful and innovative operators in Julia is the humble dot. With this single character you can turn any function into one that operates element by element on an array, a process called *broadcasting*.

You can transform your own functions into array functions simply by appending a dot to their names:

```
julia> f(x) = 2x
f (generic function with 1 method)

julia> f.([1, 2, 3])
3-element Vector{Int64}:
 2
 4
 6
```

Here we define a doubling function and broadcast it to the elements of a vector. Naturally, broadcasting works with arrays of any shape.

There is much more to say about the central idea of functions in Julia. As with most topics in this chapter, this is just an introduction. You will meet other facets of functions in later chapters as we need them.

Scope

The *scope* of a variable refers to the region of code where it is visible and modifiable. When you define a variable outside any block, with a statement like a = 1, the variable a is *global* because you've defined it in the *global scope*.

The interactive style of computation in the REPL or Pluto leads to the routine use of global variables, as we improvise within an interactive workspace where it's convenient to have everything immediately available. When writing permanent programs in files, however, it's a good practice to limit your use of global variables. They are best confined to constants that need to be available to more than one function in your project.

If you need to use such global constants, declare them with the const keyword; for example, const e = exp(1). This both ensures that you won't accidently change their value later and helps the compiler to generate faster code.

This practice has several benefits. For one, it allows you to move a function from one file to another or reuse your functions without worrying about whether they depend on global quantities defined elsewhere. It keeps functions self-contained.

Loops and functions have somewhat different scoping rules in noninteractive contexts. After we master them, we'll learn about a slight modification to the rules that makes working in the REPL more convenient.

Not all blocks create local scopes. Expression blocks, beginning with the begin keyword (see "Expression Blocks" on page 30), do not establish their own scopes. Their scope is the same as the scope of whatever they're contained within. If the begin block is at the top level, it's in the global scope.

The same holds for if blocks: they're simply part of their immediate environment as far as scope is concerned.

The other blocks introduced in this chapter establish *local scopes*, but there are two different varieties. One type of scope applies to function definition blocks while a different type applies to for and while blocks.

Scoping Rules for Functions

Inside a function definition, all variables are local unless you decorate them with the global keyword. You can use this notation one time, anywhere within the function definition, because variables can be of only one variety in any one block.

If you assign to a variable that doesn't already exist as a local variable, a new one is created. If it *does* already exist, because the function definition is inside another block where it's defined, that preexisting variable is used.

None of this has to do with variables supplied as function arguments. Those are simply local; but see "Mutability" on page 55.

A few examples should help to make this clear:

```
s = 0
function glos()
    s = s + 1
```

```
end

glos()
```

If you save this listing in a file and run it by entering julia *filename*, you'll get an error message complaining that s is undefined. Although s is already defined to be 0 in the global scope, its assignment within the function definition creates a new local variable. However, this variable is undefined on the right-hand side of the statement.

This program file, however, runs without error:

```
s = 0
function glos()
    print(s)
end

glos()
```

It prints out 0. Since there is no *assignment* to s within the function body, no new local variable is created and the function uses the existing global variable.

What if we really had intended, in the first example, to use that global s?

```
s = 0
function glos()
    global s = s + 1
    print(s)
end

glos()
```

This program prints out 1. The declaration of s as global within the function means that the variable inside the function is the same as the one outside.

We've looked at the relationship between variables defined inside a function and global variables. We also need to consider what happens if a variable inside the function block shares a name with a *local* variable outside the function. This can happen if everything is enclosed within another block—say, another function definition:

```
function outer()
❶   s = 0
    function glos()
❷       s = s + 1
    end
    glos()
    print(s)
end

outer()
```

When this program is run, it prints 1. The variable s is a local variable because it's defined inside a function block ❶ . Therefore, according to the scoping rules, when it's assigned to inside the inner function glos() ❷, a new local variable is *not* created; rather, the existing one is used.

Scoping Rules for Loops

Both kinds of loops, for blocks and while blocks, create local scopes, but they have one small change in behavior from function blocks.

If you assign to a variable inside a loop, and a variable with the same name already exists in the global scope, two things happen: the variable is treated as local within the loop, with the value of its global version unaffected by whatever happens inside the loop, and Julia prints a warning about this on the terminal when you run the program from a file (but not from the REPL, as discussed in the next section).

The reason for the warning is that *shadowing* a global variable inside a loop creates an ambiguity: Julia is not sure whether you mean to create a new local variable or use the global one. Rather than refusing to run your program, Julia picks one option, but warns you that you may have intended something different. Remove the ambiguity by using the local or global keyword to decorate the variable inside the loop.

An even better solution for program files is to put the loop and the variables it references inside a function. Then the variables will not be in the global scope and Julia will not issue a warning. In general, while we do many calculations in the REPL outside functions, it's a good practice to place as much as possible inside functions when writing program files.

The behavior, therefore, is exactly the same as in the case of function blocks, aside from the warning. Julia issues this warning in the case of loops, but not function definitions, because while functions generally use only the variables passed in as arguments and their private, local variables, it is common for loops to be initialized by variables set up outside the loops. When everything is local, as when the loop and its initialization are all inside a function, there is little chance that the programmer repeated the variable name inadvertently. However, when the variable external to the loop is global, there is the distinct possibility that this happened by accident. The loop could have been copied from another file that used the same variable names by chance, or the global variables could have been defined somewhere in the file thousands of lines away from the loop. To help keep you safe, Julia follows the scoping rules, but warns you about existing global variables shadowed in the loop.

Modification of Scoping Rules in Interactive Contexts

Inside the REPL, Pluto, or other interactive contexts, different scoping rules for while and for loops apply. Function blocks use the same rules in both interactive and noninteractive contexts.

In the REPL, if a variable is assigned within a loop, and the variable does not exist in the global REPL scope, a new local variable is established. If, however, a global variable with the same name already exists, that global variable is used and no warning is issued.

This modification to the scoping rules makes work in the REPL, with all of its global variables, more convenient. It also simplifies the process of debugging parts of functions inside the REPL. Imagine that a loop, along with its initialization, is copied from within a big function defined in a file and pasted into the REPL. In the file, the initialization variables are local, but when pasted into the REPL, they appear in the global scope. The REPL rule exceptions allow loops and their initializations to behave the same way they do in their natural habitat, nested within function blocks.

Mutability

In several places in this chapter, the === operator appears as a test of strict equality: two values are only equal in the === sense, or identical, if they have the same types as well as the same values.

Now that we know more, we can revisit the === comparison in other contexts. The following example might surprise you:

```
julia> [1] === [1]
false
```

Both sides of the comparison look the same: both are Vectors and both contain the same single value with the same Int64 type. And, as you can check, 1 === 1 is true.

The reason for the result in the listing just shown is that every time you create an array, you are creating a new object with its own location in memory. The two arrays on the two sides of the comparison are not identical because they reside at different memory addresses. It is possible to write a program that distinguishes between them, which is the formal criterion that forces the === comparison to yield false.

A number, in contrast, is just a number, with no particular location in memory. The integer 1 is always identical to itself.

This becomes clearer if we assign these objects to variables. If we make the assignments v1 = [1] and v2 = [1], the comparison v1 === v2 will yield false, while v1 == v2 gives us true. The two variables have the same *values*, but are different objects. They are not identical. Think of the variables as references, or pointers, to the memory addresses where the arrays begin.

Arrays are *mutable*. Here is one consequence of the mutability of arrays:

```
julia> a = [1]
1-element Vector{Int64}:
 1

julia> b = a
1-element Vector{Int64}:
 1
```

❶ `julia> b[1] = 7`
```
7
```

❷ `julia> a`
```
1-element Vector{Int64}:
 7
```

`julia> b === a`
```
true
```

First we define a to be a Vector with one element. Then we set b to be equal to a. We then change ❶ the first (and only) element of b to be 7. After that, when we take a look at a ❷, we find that *it's* changed, too. Its first element is now also 7. The clue to why this happens is in the last line: b and a are not simply equal, they are *identical*. When we make the assignment b = a we make b point to the same memory address as a. The two variables are now pointers to, or names for, the same object. So if we change, or *mutate*, one, we see the same change in the other.

Some objects in Julia are *immutable*:

`julia> a = 1`
```
1
```

`julia> b = a`
```
1
```

`julia> b = 7`
```
7
```

`julia> a`
```
1
```

After making the assignments to a and b, they become alternative names for the numbers 1 and 7. A table keeps track of the names we've given to values, and it lives somewhere in memory, but the variables are names for values, not for memory addresses.

In the second line, we tell Julia to also use b as a name for the number 1. After that, we change our mind and want b to mean 7, but that does not change the assignment of a as a name for 1. You can't mutate the number 1. It will always be 1, and has always been 1. But you can mutate an array by changing what it contains.

Functions That Mutate Their Arguments

We can mutate an array by assigning directly to one of its elements with an indexing expression. We can also mutate an array by adding an element to its end, making it larger. We can always do this with concatenation. For example, if v is a Vector of numbers, v = [v; 7] sticks the number 7 onto the end, increasing its length by one.

However, in calculations where we are going to be doing that many times, this is inefficient. If we get to a point where there is not enough room in memory to keep the elements of v contiguous, Julia will have to relocate it, perhaps repeatedly. A more efficient option is to use a built-in function made for this purpose. If we call push!(v, 7), that mutates v just as in the concatenation version, but more efficiently. When push!() runs out of space, it moves the array and reserves memory for its later expansion. Every time it finds it needs to do this, it reserves a geometrically increasing amount of space. The function is designed to handle the common scenario of a loop in which an array is appended to in a time- and space-efficient manner.

The use of the exclamation point in the name push!() warns and reminds the user that this is a function that mutates its argument(s). It's not part of the actual syntax, but a strongly held convention. Usually functions in Julia use their arguments as inputs to a calculation that returns a result: what we called "pure functions" earlier. Functions with ! in the name change their arguments, and may or may not also return a result. The push!() function does return a result as well: the mutated array.

As the use of the exclamation point is a convention rather than a rule enforced by the language, it's possible for any function to mutate its mutable arguments, but the convention is valuable, and Julia programmers are careful in following it.

The opposite of push!() is pop!(), which mutates its argument by removing its last element and returning that element as a result.

Strings Are Immutable

Although the String type is a collection, like Vector, Matrix, and the other array types, it is immutable.

We can index a string, but we can't assign to its elements, because strings cannot be changed:

```
julia> s = "abc"
"abc"

julia> s[1:2]
"ab"

julia> s[3] = 'Z'
ERROR: MethodError: no method matching setindex!(::String, ::Char, ::Int64)
```

This shows that we can index the string just as we index a vector, but we're not allowed to change any of its elements.

If we want to make a new string, we have to define it literally or build it from parts of existing strings or from characters, using concatenation and indexing. Here is a little function that takes a string and returns a decorative version of it:

```julia
julia> function string_decorator(s)
           decorated = ""
           for char in s
               decorated = decorated * char * " • "
           end
           decorated[1:end-5]
       end
string_decorator (generic function with 1 method)

julia> string_decorator("Julia")
"J • u • l • i • a"
```

The end-5 in the last line of the function is there to omit the final bullet and the space before it—a bullet takes up four bytes.

In general, the technique used here of building up a string by repeatedly redefining it is a good idea only for small strings and limited numbers of redefinitions. Because strings are immutable, each time through the loop creates a new object, which is wasteful of memory.

Here's how to write a function that performs the same task without creating a bunch of strings:

```julia
julia> function better_string_decorator(s)
           a = String[]
           for char in s
               push!(a, char * " • ")
           end
           join(a)[1:end-5]
       end
better_string_decorator (generic function with 1 method)

julia> better_string_decorator("PARTY!")
"P • A • R • T • Y • !"
```

The built-in join() function takes an array of strings and joins them together into one longer string. It will convert other types to strings if there is a sensible way to do so, which means join([5, "6", 'X']) returns "56X".

A sort of opposite to join() is split(). This function takes a string and turns it into an array of shorter strings:

```julia
julia> split("a    b c")
3-element Vector{SubString{String}}:
 "a"
 "b"
 "c"
```

```
julia> split("a||b||c", "||")
3-element Vector{SubString{String}}:
 "a"
 "b"
 "c"
```

It splits on whitespace of any length, unless you supply a second argument in the form of a character or string. In that case, it will use the second argument as a delimiter; the delimiters themselves are discarded.

Comments in Code

An introduction to a language would not be complete without including the syntax for comments.

A single-line comment in Julia begins with a hash mark (#) and can appear on its own line or following a line of code. In other words, Julia ignores everything after a naked # character.

To include a multiline comment, begin it with #= and end it with =#.

Congratulations

If you've mastered everything in this chapter, you are now able to write useful Julia programs to solve many types of problems.

Most of the programs you write will not be completely self-contained, however. Modern programmers build solutions by combining their own code with functions from existing libraries written by others and by themselves. The next chapter will introduce a system built into Julia that helps you manage these libraries and your own programs.

3

MODULES AND PACKAGES

Information about the package is as important as the package itself.
–Frederick W. Smith, founder of FedEx

In the previous chapter, I mentioned that Julia programs are organized around collections of functions. The functions are the verbs of your program, meaning they describe what it does. You could spend your whole Julia programming life working in the REPL or in Pluto while saving programs in files using nothing more than function, variable, and data type definitions.

But when it comes time to develop projects that build on your previous work systematically, or to allow other people to use your code in their projects, you will want to take advantage of the structures Julia provides to organize and share your programs. Even if you never reuse or distribute your own code, you will use code from the Julia standard library, from other official Julia packages, and perhaps from other researchers. In any case, familiarity with Julia's module and package system is essential.

Modules

Julia programmers make liberal use of modules both in the REPL and in program files, and borrowing existing facilities for plotting, solving equations, serving websites, and countless other activities is routine. *Creating* modules, however, is of little use in the REPL. The modules you create will live in files, ready to be used as needed.

Understanding Namespaces

A *namespace* is a grouping for names that distinguishes them from identical names existing in other groups. We need namespaces because functions and variables may be defined in different places but happen to have identical names, and we need a way to make it clear which object we are referring to.

When we define an object in the REPL we can refer to it later with its name. For example, after an assignment such as a = 1, the variable a will return 1. We say that a is defined in the *global namespace*. The terminology varies: sometimes it's *top-level namespace* and sometimes *main namespace*. In any case, the *current namespace* is the one in which we're working.

When we need to refer to objects defined elsewhere, we have two options. We can call them by their unadorned names, as if they had been defined in the current namespace, or we can refer to them with a name such as SomeModule.a. In the latter case, we say that a is in the SomeModule namespace, and we have used a *qualified name* for it.

The two names SomeModule.a and a can refer to different objects—perhaps even to different types of objects. The identifier a might be a variable that we've defined in the REPL, and SomeModule.a might be a function defined in the SomeModule module. In the next section, we'll learn how objects from other modules sometimes wind up in our current namespace and when we need to use qualified names to refer to them.

Using Installed Modules

A Julia installation comes with many modules ready for use. The resources in two particular modules, Base and Core, are always automatically available, which is why we can invoke the functions that we used in the previous chapter, such as abs(), without loading anything explicitly. Most of these essential functions are in the Base module. Base also supplies such basics as the + operator, which is also a function under the hood. The Core module exists at an even deeper level and contains such foundation stones as the Int64 data type. Although you can't do much without Base, you can arrange for it to not be loaded. The small Core module is necessary for Julia to work, however, so it's not optional.

The *standard library* is a collection of modules that's always installed with Julia but that you need to load explicitly to be able to use. The modules in the standard library provide functionality that is commonly needed across a variety of computations, but that is less fundamental than, for example, the arithmetic operators. You will never need everything in the standard library in any particular program, but a typical program will make use of several of its modules.

You can load the resources in a module with either the using or import statements.

NOTE   *Most modules have uppercase initials and use "camel case" for their names, such as LinearAlgebra from the standard library. Although you're free to ignore such naming conventions (including the use of ! explained in "Functions That Mutate Their Arguments" on page 56) in your own projects, following them will make your code easier to read for other Julia programmers.*

The using statement provides access to everything in the module. It brings all the names that the module creator has marked for export into the current namespace. So, for example, after executing using Plots, we can use the plot() function directly, as in plot(x -> x^2).

We can use any name that we know of, however, even if it's not exported. Julia has no secrets. Prefix the unexported name with the name of the module and a dot. For example, Plots.surface(x, y, f) will work regardless of whether surface is exported. In this case, we are invoking surface in the Plots namespace.

The other way to use resources from other modules involves the import statement. The only difference between import and using has to do with how we use names. If we execute import Plots, Plots.surface(x, y, f) will work, but just using surface(x, y, f) will not. The import statement provides access to everything in the module, just as using does, but *not in the current namespace*. You must use the module's namespace.

You can use either statement with a list of modules separated by commas: using Module1, Module2, Module3.

To show the difference between the using and import statements, we'll use two modules from the standard library: the LinearAlgebra module, which contains functions for solving sets of linear equations, inverting matrices, and other linear algebra operations, and Random, which provides random number functions.

Listing 3-1 uses some functions from the standard library.

```
using LinearAlgebra
import Random

❶ function randexp()
      17
  end

  a = [1 1]
  b = [0 1]

❷ dot(a, b) |> println
```

❸ Random.randexp() |> println

❹ randexp() |> println

Listing 3-1: Two ways to import a module

The first two lines make the resources from the two standard library modules available in the rest of the program. The difference between the `using` and `import` statements is in how we refer to those resources.

The `using LinearAlgebra` statement allows us to use all of the *exported names* from this module directly. The exported names are those that appear in an `export` statement in the module. We can use the `dot()` function ❷, which computes the dot product of two vectors, directly, because it's exported by `LinearAlgebra`, and the `using LinearAlgebra` statement pulled it into the current namespace. (The dot product of $[a, b]$ and $[c, d]$ is $ac+bd$.) We can refer to the function using `LinearAlgebra.dot()` as well; the two names refer to the same object.

NOTE   *Sometimes* import *and* using *statements incur significant delays. Julia is precompiling some functions in the module to make their use more efficient.*

The other way to use resources from other modules involves the `import` statement, as we used in the second line: `import Random`. The only difference between `import` and `using` has to do with the use of names. Since we *imported* `Random`, to use its functions we must prefix them with the name of the module ❸.

If we pull in a module with `using` and already have some of its names defined in our program, Julia will print a warning. The next section describes other ways to handle this problem.

We use the `import` statement when we have names that happen to be the same within more than one module or that are identical in an imported module and in our program. The use of module namespaces will remove the ambiguity. For example, our program has our own `randexp()` function, which is different from the one supplied by the `Random` module. It returns 17, which I chose at random when I wrote the function, hence the name.

After the definition of `randexp()` ❶, we define two vectors, a and b. We calculate their dot product using the `dot()` function, which is exported by `LinearAlgebra`, and pipe its output to `println()` so we can see it.

The next line calls the `randexp()` function from `Random` and prints the result. This function returns a number randomly selected from the exponential distribution.

Finally we call `randexp()` ❹ from the program's global namespace and print the result: 17.

Here is the output from one run of the program:

```
1
0.11747991328811039
17
```

When you run it, the second number will be different because it's randomly generated (see "Random Numbers in Julia" on page 307).

Selective Importing and Renaming

So far we've seen two Julia statements, each of which allows a program to refer to objects defined elsewhere. Both statements give access to everything in the target module, but differ in how we refer to the module's objects.

We can supplement either command with specifications that provide more control.

The as keyword lets us pick a name to use for the module within our program. If we change the second line in Listing 3-1 to import Random as Rnd, we need to change the line that uses it to Rnd.randexp() |> println.

We can append a colon to the module name to limit the import to only specified objects. Optionally, we can use the as keyword to rename those objects to names of our choosing. These methods can serve to avoid conflicts with existing names. Here is Listing 3-1 with some modifications:

```
using LinearAlgebra
❶ import Random: randexp as rrexp

function randexp()
    17
end

a = [1 1]
b = [0 1]

dot(a, b) |> println

❷ rrexp() |> println

randexp() |> println
```

This program has the same results as the previous version, but the import statement ❶ imports only the randexp() function from Random and renames it as rrexp(). When we call it ❷, we have to use its alias because its original name, randexp(), is unknown in its current environment.

Creating Modules

In Julia, there is no relationship between modules and files or between filenames and module names. A file can contain any number of modules, and a module may be split among many files.

We define a module in a program file using the module keyword. This begins a structure that resembles a block and is terminated with the end keyword, but is different from the blocks described in Chapter 2. Because it's common for entire files to comprise the contents of a module, the conventional style does not indent module bodies. Such a practice would lead to uselessly indenting most of the file. Another distinction concerns scope: variables defined within a module, but outside any of the blocks that define local scopes, are global to the module. Each module has its own global scope, so a file with more than one module has more than one such scope.

As an example, let's begin with a simple case: Listing 3-2 is a small program containing two modules, with everything contained within a single file.

```
module M1
export plusone
plusone(x) = x + 1
end

module M2
export minusone
minusone(x) = x - 1
end

❶ using .M1, .M2

println(plusone(99))
println(minusone(101))
```

Listing 3-2: A program containing two modules

This program defines two modules, M1 and M2. Each module defines one function, which it lists in an export statement. Usually export lines go near the top of the module, but they can appear anywhere. Running the program prints 100 twice.

The using statement ❶ brings the exported names of the two modules into the global namespace of the file. The dots in front of the module names mean that we are referring to modules defined *within the current module*. But it doesn't appear as if we're in a "current module": the statement is simply at the top level of the file.

We're always in a module in Julia. The top-level module is automatically called Main if we don't name it ourselves, so M1 and M2 are modules within the Main module.

If we had used import rather than using, we would have been obliged to mention the module namespaces when invoking their functions. Although we need to use the dot when importing to indicate *where* the module is, its names are still given in the module statements. For example, the plusone() function is M1.plusone().

Dots in module import statements have a significance similar to their use in directory names in Unix-like operating systems. Single dots refer to the current "directory," or module, and a double dot goes up one level to the enclosing module.

Listing 3-3 shows an example.

```
module M1
export plusone
plusone(x) = x + 1
```

```
❶ module M2
  export minusone
  minusone(x) = x - 1
❷ using ..M1
  println(plusone(200))
  end

  end

❸ using .M1, .M1.M2

  println(plusone(99))
  println(minusone(101))
```

Listing 3-3: Relative module imports

We've moved the definition of module M2 inside M1 ❶. Within M2 we import M1 ❷, which is now a *sibling module*: the double dot tells Julia to go up one level before looking for M1. After this using statement, plusone() is available within M2, so we can call it directly within the println() statement.

Back in the top level, which is the Main module, we again want to import every exported name from M1 and M2 into the global namespace, but now we need to specify that M2 is within M1 ❸.

This program prints 201 followed by the same output as the previous example in Listing 3-2.

If we simply want to insert the contents of a file into the current file, we use the include() statement with a string argument giving the file's pathname. This is equivalent to pasting the file's contents at the location of the include() statement. It doesn't use any of the module namespacing machinery, pulling objects in the included file into the module's namespace. Using file inclusion, we can split large modules among different files, helping to keep our code organized.

Documenting Functions with Docstrings

The previous chapter described how to use the REPL's help system to get information about functions. We can document our own functions so that the help system can provide nicely formatted information about them.

Place a string literal immediately before the beginning of any function definition to document it, creating what's called a *docstring*. The help system, as well as any other Julia documentation system, will associate this string with the function, and format and display it when the user asks for help. Here is a somewhat silly example, where I added some help text to Listing 3-3 to document the plusone() function:

```
module M1
export plusone
"""

    plusone(x)
```

```
Add _one_ to the **number** `x`.

# Example

For example, `plusone(1)` returns 2.
"""
plusone(x) = x + 1

module M2
--snip--
```

In this example I use the triple-quoted string syntax explained on page 45 to conveniently embed newlines and other characters without needing to escape them. Most help strings are written this way.

> ## MARKDOWN IN DOCSTRINGS
>
> The documentation system understands a version of Markdown syntax and will format the output appropriately. Markdown is a simplified system of text markup where you can specify italics, boldface, and code using underscore, double underscore, and backtick delimiters, with asterisks accepted as alternatives to underscores. A blank line starts a new paragraph, and indenting text by four spaces sets it as code. Lines beginning with hash marks are not comments, as in Julia code, but become headings: # Heading, ## Subheading, and so on.

The example demonstrates some of the documentation conventions the Julia community uses. Begin the help text with the function signature, followed by an imperative statement of what the function does. After that can come more explanation and examples.

Figure 3-1 is a screenshot of a REPL session where I included the *modutst.jl* file.

```
julia> include("modutst.jl")
201
100
100

help?> plusone
search: plusone PartialQuickSort

  plusone(x)

  Add one to the number x.

  Example
  =========

  For example, plusone(1) returns 2.
```

Figure 3-1: Using the documentation system

In the REPL, the `println()` statements are run and produce the output shown previously. I pressed ? to enter help mode and typed the name of the function. After showing the results of a fuzzy search on the name, the REPL renders the docstring of the most likely choice. The terminal REPL renders code using a contrasting color and italics with an underline. Other environments may use different typography.

For more details about Markdown formatting, see "Further Reading" on page 81.

We've learned how to reference modules defined in the current file using dots and extend the current file using `include()`. Before that, we were loading external modules with the same `using` and `import` statements, but with no dots in front of the module names. Somehow in those cases, Julia knew where to find the files containing the module definitions, and that is the subject of the next section.

The Package System

The most convenient way to interact with Julia's package system is with the REPL's package mode. Press] to enter and BACKSPACE to exit this mode.

Enter the package mode and have another look at the prompt. It looks something like `(@v1.8) pkg>`, where `v1.8` shows the currently installed Julia version. The part within the parentheses informs us of our current *environment*. We are always in some environment in the REPL. The environment is the project to which the package mode applies its commands.

When we start the REPL we're in the default project. Everything we do in the package manager applies to that environment, unless we change it with the `activate` command.

Enter **activate** **.** to change the environment to the current directory, or **activate** *path* to change it to a specified path. A simple **activate** changes to the default environment for the version of Julia in use.

How to Add and Remove Packages

The most important package command is `add`. To use it, enter **add** *packageName* from within the REPL's package mode.

The `add` command does two things: it downloads and precompiles the latest compatible version of the requested package, if it's not already installed, and it records the package as a dependency of the current environment. The second step ensures that the set of package versions used in the project can always be reproduced, either by its author on a different computer or by a colleague.

We will have to add any packages that are not in the standard library. This includes the vast majority of packages in the Julia ecosystem, such as `Plots`, for making scientific graphics, or `BenchmarkTools`, for timing and profiling programs.

If any package previously installed with `add` is no longer needed, we can remove it with the `rm` *PackageName* command, also from within package mode.

The rm package mode command deletes a package from the list of direct dependencies of your project, but it does not immediately erase any files from the disk. An automatic garbage collection process runs periodically, reclaiming disk space by purging packages that no other installed package depends on and that haven't been used for over 30 days. To reclaim disk space right away, call the garbage collector manually. Detailed instructions are in the package system manual (see "Further Reading" on page 81).

The Load Path

The current environment influences where using and import look for packages and defines the default location for package commands. When executing statements like using Plots or import Random that mention package names without dots, Julia looks for the packages in a series of places derived from a vector of strings named LOAD_PATH.

We can ask the REPL to show us the default initial value of LOAD_PATH:

```
julia> LOAD_PATH
3-element Vector{String}:
 "@"
 "@v#.#"
 "@stdlib"
```

The contents of LOAD_PATH are clearly not filepaths. They're a notation that the package manager translates into the appropriate paths for the system and installation. To see the results of the translation and the current values of the paths, we can call the load_path() function from Base:

```
julia> Base.load_path()
2-element Vector{String}:
 "/home/lee/.julia/environments/v1.8/Project.toml"
 "/home/lee/Downloads/julia/julia-1.8.1/share/julia/stdlib/v1.8"
```

We've already mentioned that Base contains the functions we almost always need, but they're not all exported. Ones that are used infrequently, such as load_path(), need to be accessed in the Base namespace.

My current load path contains two items. The first is a directory that Julia set up when I installed it. It corresponds to my default environment. When I execute a command like add Plots in the REPL, if I haven't switched environments with the activate command, the package manager adds the current version of the Plots package as a *dependency* in the default *project*. It records the fact that this project depends on a particular version of Plots being available, and using Plots will import the functions from that version. This path is the translation of the second element in LOAD_PATH, "@v#.#". The notation simply means "the default environment"; notice how its structure resembles the prompt in package mode.

The package manager records these direct dependencies, the ones specified with add commands, in the *Project.toml* file. This file contains lines such as:

```
Plots = "91a5bcdd-55d7-5caf-9e0b-520d859cae80"
```

This line shows that the particular version of the `Plots` package, made specific with a unique identifier called a *UUID*, is a dependency of the project that contains this file—in this case, the default project associated with my installation of v1.8 of Julia.

The second path returned by `Base.load_path()` comes from the last element of `LOAD_PATH`, which refers to the standard library. As mentioned previously, the standard library consists of modules that are part of the Julia installation, so they don't need to be installed with `add`. I left my installation in the download folder where my web browser put it, so that's where its standard library lives.

The `LOAD_PATH` has three elements, but we see only two in its current translation by `Base.load_path()`. The first element, which is simply @, refers to the *current environment*. Julia searches for packages in the order in which they appear in `LOAD_PATH`, so it searches the current environment first. To change the current environment, execute **activate *path***.

The current environment has two purposes: it comes first in the load path, so imports of packages will load the versions, if any, that have been added as dependencies in the environment, and the package system `add` command inserts a dependency there.

An environment is really nothing more than a place in the filesystem with a *Project.toml* file and a *Manifest.toml* file. The latter is a list of the entire *dependency graph* of the environment: all the packages that need to be loaded to satisfy the dependencies of the ones explicitly `added`, with their UUIDs, the list of dependencies of each of those dependencies, and so on. If we use the `activate` command on a path where there is no existing environment and execute one or more `add` commands, Julia will create these two files there and fill them with the specified package information.

NOTE *If we can't use the filenames* Project.toml *or* Manifest.toml *because they conflict with another tool, we can use* JuliaProject.toml *and* JuliaManifest.toml *instead. If Julia sees either of those files, it will use it and ignore the one without the* Julia *prefix.*

Environments contain no Julia code, only a list of dependencies. They may document a set of consistent modules that work for a particular purpose. For example, after using Pluto, we'll discover that Julia has created an environment alongside the normal default environment whose *Project.toml* and *Manifest.toml* files contain a list of the modules that Pluto needs to work properly.

The Nature of a Package

I've mentioned *package* many times, and have used the term more or less interchangeably with *module*, a tradition well established in the Julia documentation. Now let's make the relationship between these concepts precise and explore how packages are related to environments.

A package is a Julia module associated with a *Project.toml* file containing a few critical pieces of information. The file containing the module and the *Project.toml* file must be laid out in the filesystem as shown in Figure 3-2.

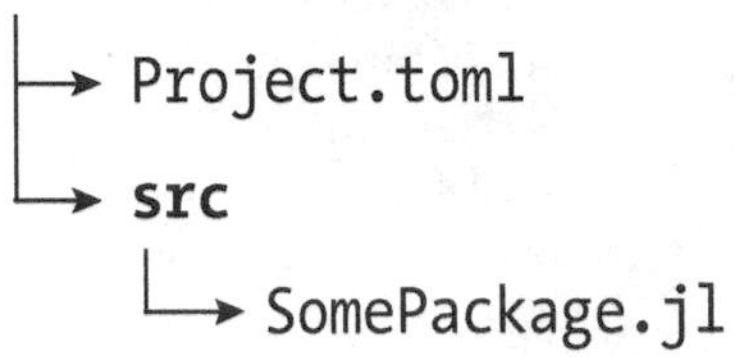

```
├─→ Project.toml
└─→ src
      └─→ SomePackage.jl
```

Figure 3-2: The filesystem layout of
a package

Alongside the *Project.toml* file is a *src* directory, inside which must be the Julia program file, named after the package. Inside this file is the definition of a module also named after the package, which in this case is module SomePackage. The structure shown in Figure 3-2 is usually placed inside a directory also named after the module, *SomePackage* in this case, but that is not strictly required.

For this arrangement to qualify as a package, the *Project.toml* file must provide the name of the package, its UUID, its authors, and its version number, in the format shown in Listing 3-4.

```
name = "SomePackage"
uuid = "842ca1f4-56d0-4d49-a6c9-7b9c77404c7a"
authors = ["Ada Lovelace <ada.l@example.com>"]
version = "0.1.0"
```

Listing 3-4: A package's Project.toml file

The name must match the name of the module defined in *src/Some Package.jl*. If we have these two files, one within a *src* directory, we have a package. We can think of a package as an environment with a module inside and with these four pieces of information in *Project.toml*. In practice, as soon as we add dependencies to our package with the add command executed within the package's environment, we will also have a *Manifest.toml* file alongside the *Project.toml* file that contains the complete dependency graph.

We can do all of our Julia development within *.jl* files, possibly using include() to split the code among several files, and share our work by emailing those files to colleagues. Many Julia programmers do no more than this and don't bother creating packages.

The Benefits of Packages

After the exploratory REPL phase of your program development is over, and it's time to save your code in the filesystem so you can use it later, possibly as a resource in other programs, I would like to encourage you to take advantage of Julia's package system.

It's sophisticated, easy to use, and will save you from dependency conflicts down the road. Most programs use modules from the standard library and other packages, and all are developed with a particular version of Julia itself. As all these components evolve, the possibility of conflict arises and, with time, becomes inevitable in large programs that use many external resources. The package system records the exact versions of all the resources your program uses, so you or anyone else can reproduce that environment in the future, and the program will always work.

In the absence of dependency management, a statement like using `Plots` in your program imports whatever version of `Plots` is used by the environment in which a future user, including yourself, happens to run it. You may have used a feature that is later removed from the package, or a future version may introduce a bug that breaks your program. Without package management, your program is loading unknown code because you're not being specific about what you mean by `Plots`.

Packages often depend on other packages. A future user of your program, encountering a conflict with `Plots`, may try to resolve it by using a different version. But that version will depend on different versions of other packages, and some of those will have their own dependencies. Trying to sort out the dependency graph of packages manually to find a workable set quickly becomes a maddening task. It's such a common headache in languages without good package management that there's a name for it: *dependency hell*. Julia's package system manages the dependency graph automatically. You can have various versions of Julia and of any number of packages installed on your machine at the same time with no issues. If you keep your programs in packages, you can upgrade the versions of modules that it imports without changing your actual code, and if the new versions create problems, you can downgrade as needed.

If you decide to share your programs through the official community channels, you must use packages. The official repository, from which you get resources when you use the add command, is based on packages and the Git version control system, which I'll treat in "Julia and Git" on page 77.

How to Create Packages

It's easy to create packages. First, we navigate to the directory in the filesystem where we want the package to be and start the Julia REPL. We can use any directory, and we can always move it later.

NOTE *We don't have to start a new REPL session just to change locations in the filesystem. To continue in an existing REPL session, we can move around the filesystem while staying in the REPL using two Julia function versions of the familiar Unix commands pwd and cd. The REPL maintains a notion of the current directory, which is where we gave the julia command that started the REPL, and it stays there unless we change it. The pwd() function in the REPL returns a string with the full pathname of the current directory. To change it, enter* **cd(new_directory)**, *substituting the name of the desired destination. (The name is a string, as returned by pwd(), so must be enclosed within quotes.)*

Within the REPL, press] to enter package mode, and execute **generate Floof**. That's all we need to do to create a new package named Floof.

Back in the system shell, or using the REPL's shell mode, we'll find the new directory named *Floof*, and within it, the minimal package files shown in Figure 3-2. Floof's *Project.toml* file will contain lines similar to Listing 3-4, but with the name *Floof* and a new, unique UUID. The authors field is populated from our Git configuration, so it'll be empty if we haven't installed Git (see "Julia and Git" on page 77). The generate statement gives our new package a version number of 0.1.0, which we can change.

Descending into the *src* directory, the *Floof.jl* file has the following contents:

```
module Floof

greet() = print("Hello World!")

end # module
```

This defines a tiny module, called Floof, with one function, greet(), that greets the world. Julia sets up a minimal package with everything in place so we can begin development of our module. We'll make one change to this file for now: add the statement export greet after the first line.

Let's experiment with this new mini-package. First, we'll exercise it without using the package system:

```
julia> include("/tmp/Floof/src/Floof.jl")
❶ Main.Floof

julia> Floof.greet()
Hello World!
julia> using Floof
❷ ERROR: ArgumentError: Package Floof not found in current path

julia> using .Floof

❸ julia> greet()
Hello World!
```

We put the Floof package in the */tmp* directory. The first action in the REPL is to include the program file directly. This is equivalent to pasting it directly into the REPL. The feedback ❶ from the include() statement confirms that Floof is loaded into Main, which is always the name for the top-level module.

Now we can use anything in the Floof module by mentioning its namespace. It has only one ingredient, the greet() function, which does what's expected when we call it.

We would prefer to call this function without having to type the module name, so we need to import its name into the current namespace. We tried to do this with the using statement, but Julia won't let us ❷. After remembering that we need to prefix local modules with a dot, everything works as expected ❸. (I've omitted the stacktrace from the error message to save space, as I will do routinely.)

Importing a name, whether with using or import, without a dot prefix tells Julia to import a package rather than a local module. This wakes up the package system, which consults the LOAD_PATH to search for the package. Although Floof is indeed a package, it's not on the LOAD_PATH, which by default includes the activated environment, the default environment, and the standard library, in that order. Since we haven't activated an environment, and the Floof package is in neither the standard library nor the default environment, Julia can't find it.

If we're determined to import greet() into the global namespace, we can activate the environment that contains the Floof module. But first, we should quit and restart the REPL. Otherwise, this new attempt to import will generate an error complaining about a conflict with an existing name. After starting a fresh REPL, we can do this:

```
(@v1.8) pkg> activate /tmp/Floof
  Activating environment at `/tmp/Floof/Project.toml`

julia> using Floof

julia> greet()
Hello World!
(Floof) pkg> add Random
```

After activating the Floof environment using its pathname, we exit package mode. Back in the REPL's normal mode, after importing Floof's names into the global namespace with using, a simple greet() invokes the function. This works only because we edited *Floof.jl* to export greet. Then we re-enter package mode—observe the prompt, which now indicates the Floof environment. The add Random command adds this package, which contains utilities related to random number generation, to the dependency list for Floof.

We can add paths manually to LOAD_PATH:

```
julia> push!(LOAD_PATH, "/tmp/Floof/")
4-element Vector{String}:
 "@"
 "@v#.#"
 "@stdlib"
 "/tmp/Floof/"

julia> using Floof

julia> greet()
Hello World!
```

We do this, again, in a fresh REPL. The package system found `Floof` in the last entry in `LOAD_PATH`; it will find it regardless of the current environment.

Floof's *Project.toml* file now contains two additional lines. Here are its contents after executing `add Random`:

```
name = "Floof"
uuid = "fdb9266c-3340-4b10-958f-2cb27e4e2988"
authors = ["Lee <lee@example.com>"]
version = "0.1.0"

[deps]
Random = "9a3f8284-a2c9-5f02-9a11-845980a1fd5c"
```

The lines after the `[deps]` label will record every dependency that we manually add with an add statement.

A new *Manifest.toml* file has appeared alongside the *Project.toml* file with these contents:

```
# This file is machine-generated - editing it directly is not advised

[[Random]]
deps = ["Serialization"]
uuid = "9a3f8284-a2c9-5f02-9a11-845980a1fd5c"

[[Serialization]]
uuid = "9e88b42a-f829-5b0c-bbe9-9e923198166b"
```

Manifest files are for recording the dependency graph of a package or environment. For each dependency added manually, the system looks up its dependencies, and the dependencies of all of those dependencies, and so on, until it finds every dependency. Each of these dependencies is another package; all of them together, with all of their dependency relationships, is the dependency graph. As you can imagine, Manifest files can get rather large, but this one is not because `Random` apparently has only one dependency, a package called `Serialization`, and `Serialization` has no dependencies of its own.

Now that we have our very own package, we should be able to add it as a dependency to other packages and environments, just as we did with other packages like `Random` and `Plots`:

```
(Floof) pkg> activate
  Activating environment at `~/.julia/environments/v1.8/Project.toml`

(@v1.8) pkg> add /tmp/Floof
ERROR: Did not find a git repository at `/tmp/Floof`
```

First we use the activate statement with no argument to go back to the default environment. We try to add `Floof` to that environment, but the package manager has a complaint about not finding something called a *git repository*.

Julia and Git

Git is a *version control system*: a program that helps you keep track of your work as it changes over time. Git, in addition, focuses on collaboration, although it's immensely useful to the solo creator as well.

Git is independent of Julia, but since its creation in 2005 by Linus Torvalds, the creator of Linux, its superiority over all other version control systems has led to a near monopoly in the free software community. Julia is part of this community, and Git is an intimate component of the development of the language and its packages.

If you don't already have Git installed and would prefer to continue your study of Julia without pausing to install Git and learning how to use it, skip this section for now. You can always return later. See "Further Reading" on page 81 for a link to an excellent learning resource. There are also many articles and several books about Git.

I recommend installing Git and using it in your projects before your personal library of code becomes substantial. The small investment in time and effort to become familiar with a few basic operations has a huge payback. You'll be able to travel back in time to past states of your programs, keep a log of changes, create alternative versions of your programs where you try out ideas, and merge the ideas into the main line of development when they're ready.

If you're already using one of the older version control systems, you can continue to do so. However, if you reach the stage where you would like to contribute your Julia programs to the community, you will have to use Git. As we're about to see, Git is also required for adding your own packages as dependencies in your own projects and environments on your personal machine, which is something you may want to do even if you don't share your programs.

As shown in "How to Create Packages" on page 73, Julia complained when we tried to add my Floof package. The package system won't let us add a package until we put it in a Git repository. Dependency management, which is the reason for the package system, tracks not simply packages, but versions of packages. Julia's package system works with Git to track these versions. The rest of this section assumes Git is installed.

To allow the package system to deal with Floof, we have to put it in a Git repository and make an initial commit. In the */tmp/Floof* directory, we execute **git init** in the system shell to create the repository, then **git add .** and **git commit -m "Begin repo"** to begin tracking the contents.

Back in the Julia REPL, we try again:

```
(@v1.8) pkg> add /tmp/Floof
    Updating git-repo `/tmp/Floof`
  Resolving package versions...
    Updating `~/.julia/environments/v1.8/Project.toml`
```

```
[fdb9266c] + Floof v0.1.0 `/tmp/Floof#master`
  Updating `~/.julia/environments/v1.8/Manifest.toml`
[fdb9266c] + Floof v0.1.0 `/tmp/Floof#master`

(@v1.8) pkg> status
    Status `~/.julia/environments/v1.8/Project.toml`
  [336ed68f] CSV v0.8.4
  [31c24e10] Distributions v0.24.15
  [fdb9266c] Floof v0.1.0 `/tmp/Floof#master`
  [23fbe1c1] Latexify v0.14.12
  [91a5bcdd] Plots v1.10.6
  [c3e4b0f8] Pluto v0.15.1
```

It works this time: the package manager responds that it's added Floof to the *Project.toml* and *Manifest.toml* files. The string in square brackets is the initial part of the UUID that the package manager has assigned to this version of Floof. The #master string refers to the branch name in Git.

The status package command returns a list of all the dependencies added to the current environment (not the entire dependency graph), and we see that Floof is among them.

If we want to remove a dependency—say, Floof—we enter rm **Floof** in package mode: note that when removing packages, we use just the package name, not the whole path on the filesystem. This does nothing to our files; it simply removes Floof from the *Project.toml* file. However, it may not remove it from *Manifest.toml* because it may be listed there as a dependency of some other package.

If you've made your program into a Julia package and are tracking it with Git, you'll be prepared to request that it be included in the official repository if the day comes when you feel it will be of use to a wider audience. If you complete this step, any Julia user anywhere in the world can simply tell their package REPL to add *YourPackage*, and they'll be able to use and build on your work. Sharing and collaboration are embedded in Julia's DNA. Chapters 9 and 12 demonstrate several interesting examples of how packages can be combined to create new capabilities.

The Relationship Between Package Versions and Git Commits

We've seen how to request status at the package prompt to see a list of dependencies and abbreviations of their UUIDs, and how to see the complete UUID in the *Manifest.toml* file. We may be aware that Git identifies commits with a unique hash, but if we examine the hash of our project with git log, we won't see anything that looks like Julia's UUID.

Here is the relevant section of the default environment's *Manifest.toml*, which is in *.julia/environments/v1.8/Manifest.toml* within the user's home directory:

```
[[Floof]]
deps = ["Random"]
```

```
git-tree-sha1 = "478b184e365f8d114ab757e18c6ab060fc590920"
repo-rev = "master"
repo-url = "/tmp/Floof"
uuid = "fdb9266c-3340-4b10-958f-2cb27e4e2988"
version = "0.1.0"
```

Random is listed as a dependency because we had added it to the project earlier. In the last two lines, we see the full UUID and the initial version assigned by the package system. Before that, we have the path and the branch name from Git. Above that, we see something called the git-tree-sha1, which is a Git hash, but it's not the commit hash that we see by default when we enter **git log**. Within Floof's directory, if we enter this command with an option, we can see more:

bash> **git log --pretty=raw**

```
commit 460ef22bb5c86863d07493e36be791977acd62e7
tree 478b184e365f8d114ab757e18c6ab060fc590920
author Lee <lee@example.com> 1630788711 -0600
committer Lee <lee@example.com> 1630788711 -0600

    make a repo
```

The hash recorded in *Manifest.toml* is the *tree hash*. Most Git users are unaware of this hash because it's rarely needed for anything. The tree hash encodes the actual contents of all the tracked files in the commit. Julia's package manager uses this rather than the commit hash because it's more reliable. Git provides powerful commands, such as rebase, that let users rewrite the commit history. If a conflict arises and something breaks, ideally we would like to identify the actual file contents of the programs involved. In practice, to identify a commit from the information recorded in *Manifest.toml*, we need to ask Git for the raw commit log and search for the tree hash.

Version Updating and Pinning

Another crucial package system command is update *PackageName*. Execute this operation to get the latest version of *PackageName* installed in the environment. Julia will check the registry for a new version, and download and precompile it if there is one. If *PackageName* has any dependencies, Julia will check their versions against the ones already installed, and download and precompile anything that's changed. It will continue through the entire dependency graph, leaving us with a consistent environment, with no further action on our part.

If *PackageName* is our own project that we're developing locally, the update command will cause the package manager to check its Git repository. If the tree hash at the HEAD of the tracked branch, as recorded in Git's log, has changed, Julia will install the new version into the environment and precompile it. The *Manifest.toml* file will contain the new tree hash. If we've edited the source file but not yet made a new Git commit, the package manager won't do anything. Even if we change the version number recorded in *PackageName*'s *Project.toml* file, that will not cause Julia to take any action. The package manager cares only about the tree hash. This means, for example, if we soft-reset to an earlier commit, then `update` in Julia, the package manager will revert to the version that our `HEAD` now points to, pulling the files from the Git repository and *not* from our working tree.

It's possible for an `update` to lead to a conflict, where the current versions of two packages cannot work together. Use the `pin` command in the package manager to force it to hold particular packages at certain versions. Sometimes that's the only way around a conflict until the bugs are fixed.

The three versions of `pin` are `pin PackageName`, which holds *PackageName* at its current version; `pin PackageName@2.4.2`, which, in this example, holds *PackageName* at version 2.4.2; and `pin PackageName=UUID`, which holds the package using its UUID rather than the version number to identify the version.

How to Find Public Packages

How can we discover if there is a Julia package that might help us write our program? The most productive approach is probably a general web search for projects or problems similar to ours, using Julia—this will quickly surface the most popular relevant packages. Of course, talking to people working in the same area is invaluable, if such a community is available. Asking on the Julia Discourse forum will almost certainly yield helpful replies, unless our project is quite niche or esoteric.

Since practically all development of public Julia packages takes place on GitHub, this is the place to search directly for solutions, especially if the previously mentioned approaches did not lead to anything appropriate, or if specific criteria are important to our project, such as recency of development.

There are several sites that seem to offer a way to search through packages, but provide nothing beyond what GitHub offers directly, aside from incorrect and outdated information and an even worse interface. The best strategy for searching on GitHub is to use a language qualifier. For example, in the project search box we would enter `phylogenetics language:Julia` to look for projects that mention phylogenetics in their title or keywords, and that are written in Julia (and possibly other languages). This is effective because Julia packages are written in Julia, and it's necessary because Julia packages often do not have a "Julia" keyword, so using that as a bare search term misses many projects.

Crucially, we can then sort the resulting list based on several criteria, including recency of last update and the number of "stars" the project has. The latter, despite its unpleasant associations with internet popularity and gamification, is actually a useful proxy to uncover packages that are widely used and therefore more likely to be valuable and to have a community around them.

The individual project pages in GitHub will contain a rendering of their README files, which range from a few cryptic phrases to a full introduction and tutorial with screenshots and animations. The README sometimes contains a link to further documentation; if it doesn't, one can click one of the project's documentation badges, but there is no guarantee that will lead to any actual documentation. Lack of documentation is not a good sign, but there may be linguistic or other reasons for the lapse. We can always look at the source code, all of which will be a click away on GitHub. Julia code is unusually easy to read, and obviously is the final source of truth about the operation of any package.

After we discover a package that we want to try, it's time to return to the REPL and `add` it to our project. We can add packages in the official registry, listed in the GitHub project `JuliaRegistries/General`, simply by using its name. In the probably unusual circumstance where we want to add a public project that is not in the general registry, we can add it using its URL. In package mode, we enter

```
add https://github.com/developer/projectname
```

for example, to add the project `projectname` by developer `developer`. This will only work if we are pointing at a proper Julia project with a *Project.toml* or *JuliaProject.toml* file. After adding the project, it will appear in our *Manifest.toml* file with the extra field `repo-url`.

Conclusion

This chapter describes some essential ingredients for using Julia effectively and making it possible for others to incorporate our programs into their work. Programming is rarely done in isolation. There is no need to reinvent the wheel if a solution to a part of your problem is as close as an `import` away. In later chapters, we'll expand on these ideas and look at even more powerful ways to combine the resources of several packages. But first, in the next chapter we'll explore an essential package that nearly all scientific Julia programmers use as we delve into the plotting system.

> **FURTHER READING**
>
> • More details on what you can do with docstrings, mostly of interest to package developers, are available at *https://docs.julialang.org/en/v1/manual/documentation/*.
>
> • When making those docstrings, you may need to know more about Markdown syntax: *https://www.markdownguide.org/basic-syntax*.
>
> • The *.toml* file extension stands for "Tom's Obvious, Minimal Language" designed by Tom Preston-Werner: *https://github.com/toml-lang/toml*.
>
> • A good resource for getting started with Git is *https://git-scm.com*.
>
> *(continued)*

- For detailed information about the package system, including instructions on how to submit your creations to the official repository, or *registry*, go to *https://pkgdocs.julialang.org/*.

- A package system summary, and my first adventure in contributing to a public package, are available at *https://lwn.net/Articles/871490/*.

- For workflow tips, visit *https://docs.julialang.org/en/v1/manual/workflow-tips/*.

4

THE PLOTTING SYSTEM

There is nothing worse than a sharp image of a fuzzy concept.
–Ansel Adams

This chapter introduces the large and rich subject of visualization in Julia. Plots and diagrams play a role in scientific communication equal in importance to words and equations. Julia's plotting ecosystem is diverse and powerful; you'll be able to craft a solution to any type of visualization challenge without leaving the language. The ability to keep both your calculation and its visualization within a single program simplifies the process of exploring and reporting results.

Plotting in Julia is a hotspot of rapid development. This is mostly good, as it means new features and packages arise regularly. The downside, however, is a higher than average incidence of conflicts among packages, incomplete documentation, and bugs, exacerbated by the frequent need for plotting routines to depend on external graphics libraries. With this in mind, I've confined the treatment in this chapter to packages that seem to be stable and mature. The examples here should work over the long term. I've avoided discussing some potentially useful packages that still have too many rough edges.

Plots

The main, and in a sense "official," plotting package for Julia is Plots. Later in the book we'll explore other graphical methods, but this chapter is about the package at the center of Julia's visualization universe.

Plots is not in the standard library, so we need to install it in the package manager with **add Plots**. The initial installation will take some time, as Plots has many dependencies, all of which need to be (automatically) installed as well. Precompilation of this assortment of packages will take a few minutes.

Plots is a unique approach to providing a programming language with plotting abilities. It's often described as a plotting *metapackage*, because Plots doesn't do any actual plotting on its own. Rather, it orchestrates the creation of visualizations by calling on a choice of *backends*.

The Backend System

The backend is the package that actually draws the picture. Each backend has particular strengths and weaknesses, and is suitable for a different type of application. The job of Plots is to provide a unified interface to all of the backends and to apply a degree of intelligence in translating our plotting call into a form that the backend can understand. It tries to figure out what we mean and how to produce the plot we want.

The advantage of using a plotting metapackage is that we can change the backend used in a program without having to change the plotting commands. During research, we may want to have a simulation code produce rough plots directly in the terminal or 3D plots that we can rotate with the mouse. Later, we may want to run the simulation again, but this time save publication-quality plots to disk. With the Plots system, we can accomplish that by simply changing one line of code that selects a different backend.

Some of Plots's backends are automatically installed when we install the package, but we'll need to install others manually, as separate packages (these are subject to change, but we'll be prompted to install a missing backend when we try to use it). When we add the Plots package, one backend that always comes along for the ride is the default backend. Recently this default has been GR, a reasonably fast and featureful plotting engine. To see the list of available backends, execute the **backends()** function in the REPL. To see the currently active backend, execute the **backend()** function.

To activate a backend, we use the appropriate name that backends() returns to form a function and simply call it. If it's installed, the function responds by confirming the name of the package. If not, we'll get an error message explaining that we need to add it.

Here is part of a REPL session showing the process:

```
     julia> using Plots

❶  julia> backends()
     10-element Vector{Symbol}:
      :pyplot
      :unicodeplots
      :plotly
      :plotlyjs
      :gr
      :pgfplo
      :pgfplotsx
      :inspectdr
      :hdf5
      :gaston

❷  julia> backend()
     Plots.GRBackend()

❸  julia> unicodeplots()
     Plots.UnicodePlotsBackend()

     julia> hdf5()
     ERROR: ArgumentError: Package HDF5 not found in current path:
     - Run `import Pkg; Pkg.add("HDF5")` to install the HDF5 package.

❹  (@v1.6) pkg> add HDF5
        Resolving package versions...
         Updating `~/.julia/environments/v1.6/Project.toml`
       [f67ccb44] + HDF5 v0.15.6
       No Changes to `~/.julia/environments/v1.6/Manifest.toml`

     julia> hdf5()
     Plots.HDF5Backend()

     julia> backend()
     Plots.HDF5Backend()
```

Asking for available backends ❶ returns a list in the form of a Vector of Symbols, indicated by the leading colons. "Symbols and Metaprogramming" on page 167 will explain the Symbol data type, but for now, think of it as a string.

Asking for the current backend ❷ returns Plots.GRBackend(). The multiple names for each backend is somewhat confusing, as the capitalized form used to refer to a package differs from the lowercase form used to activate it. The form that backend() returns isn't used for anything.

The next move is to make `UnicodePlots` the current backend ❸; the operation was confirmed. Then we change our mind and decide to plot with HDF5, but our attempt to switch to it gives us an error because it's not in the load path. Apparently we never added it to the environment. After adding HDF5 in package mode ❹, we switch to it and call `backend()` to confirm.

The package system doesn't consider the various backends to be dependencies of `Plots`. This was a deliberate choice to spare users from having to install all of the backends when installing `Plots`, as there are many of them, and most users will need only a modest subset. This creates occasional incompatibilities, however, as `Plots` and its various backends evolve, since the package system cannot automatically keep them in sync. If something doesn't work, try a different backend if possible; otherwise, search the web and the resources in "Further Reading" on page 121 for a resolution.

Modes of Interaction with Plots

If you are following along in Pluto, you can enter each plotting command in a new cell and produce a sequence of figures embedded in the page. If you're using the REPL, each plot should reuse the display window opened by the first, replacing the existing plot. If you want to close that window, use the statement `closeall()`. Closing it using your window manager sometimes leads to errors in the REPL, a known bug.

If you're saving plot commands in a program file, you may have noticed that you don't see any output when you run it. First, you need to include the statement `gui()` at the point in the program where you want to display the current state of the plot. However, the plot window thus created will vanish when the program exits, perhaps so quickly that you may not be able to see the window at all. You need to make the program pause until you're done admiring your plot. One way is to insert the `readline()` statement directly after `gui()`. This statement waits for input at the terminal. When you're ready to dismiss the plot window, simply press RETURN and it will vanish, and the program will continue.

2D Plots

The term *2D plot* refers to a variety of visualizations involving maps between two variables. The basic type, a *line plot*, takes the form of a curve, or set of curves, for functions of a single variable, where typically the independent variable is represented by the horizontal x-axis and the dependent variable by the vertical y-axis in a rectangular coordinate system. The *polar coordinate plot* maps an angle to the distance from some origin, in a polar coordinate system. A third common type is a *parametric plot*, where both variables depend on a third variable, called the parameter. These three basic types, along with other varieties such as bar and pie charts and scatterplots, are all called *two-dimensional plots*, and they are all handled by the `plot()` function provided by the `Plots` package and understood by all of its backends.

For the examples in this section, any backend will work, but I suggest sticking with the default setup when you execute using Plots. This will always be a relatively stable and performant engine that displays color plots either in a new window when using the REPL, or on the page when using Pluto or VS Code. In all of the examples in this chapter, using Plots is assumed.

The plot() function accepts arguments of various kinds, and, as mentioned previously, usually does what we expect. It returns a result in the form of a plot object. In the REPL, a notebook interface such as Pluto, or another interactive environment, it immediately displays the plot, unless we suppress the output by following the call with a semicolon. We can display the plot later with a call to gui() or by storing the plot object in a variable and simply evaluating it.

Plotting from Vectors

We can call the function with a single Vector argument:

```julia
julia> gr()
Plots.GRBackend()

julia> plot([0, 3, 1, 4, 1])
```

This plots the numbers in the Vector, in order, against an independent variable that gives their index. Figure 4-1 shows the plot.

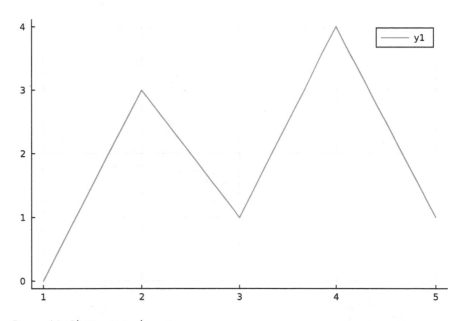

Figure 4-1: Plotting a single vector

We get a legend, which at the moment is not very informative. We'll learn shortly how to adjust this, and change other things about the graph, but first let's look at the different ways we can use plot().

I've created grayscale versions of all the examples in this chapter for printing, but the original color output from each plot command is available from the book's supplementary website at https://julia.lee-phillips.org.

The second form supplies both *x*- and *y*-variables, with two Vectors:

```
julia> plot([0, 0.13, 0.38, 0.88, 1.88], [0, 3, 1, 4, 1])
```

The result (Figure 4-2) shows the same *y*-values plotted at different horizontal locations.

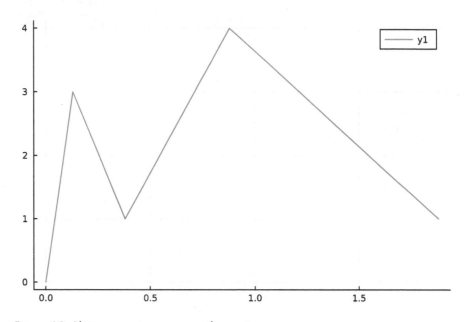

Figure 4-2: Plotting a vector versus another vector

Plotting Functions

To plot a function, we can supply a vector as the first argument and a second vector created by broadcasting the function over the first argument (see "Broadcasting" on page 51):

```
julia> f(x) = sin(1/x)
f (generic function with 1 method)

julia> x = π/1000:π/1000:π
0.0031415926535897933:0.0031415926535897933:3.14

julia> plot(x, f.(x))
```

In this example we first create a function, f(), using the succinct one-line function definition syntax. Next we define a range and store it in x; the range excludes 0 to avoid the singularity there. The `plot()` command has two `Vector` arguments, as before. The range is instantiated into a `Vector` and the dot after `f()` broadcasts the function over x, returning a `Vector` for the dependent variable. Figure 4-3 shows the result.

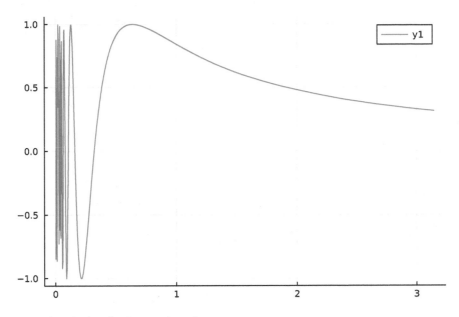

Figure 4-3: A plot of a function broadcast over a vector

We can see the plot becoming inaccurate as we approach the origin and the π/1000 resolution fails to keep up with the rapid oscillations in that region.

The `plot()` function and its comrades offer a convenient shorthand. Instead of supplying the second argument as a broadcast expression that explicitly creates a vector, we can simply write the name of a function, or construct an anonymous function. The `plot()` function will broadcast the function we name over the independent variable vector that we pass in the first argument.

In other words, we can write `plot(x, f.(x))` as simply `plot(x, f)`. If we had not already defined `f()`, we could insert an anonymous function directly as `plot(x, s -> sin(1/s))`. These three ways of calling `plot()` are all equivalent.

We can even leave out the independent variable and supply only a function name or an anonymous function. In this case, `plot()` will plot the function for us, choosing the locations of the independent variable and handling singularities automatically. We can supply a domain on the horizontal axis using a second and third argument, with default values of −5 and 5. If we use a `Vector` of functions in the first argument, we'll get a plot of all of them on the same axes. Using the same definition for `f`, executing `plot([sin, cos, f], -π, π)` produces Figure 4-4.

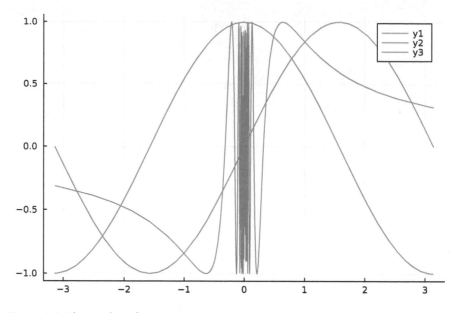

Figure 4-4: Plotting three functions

In this use of plot(), we supply the names of the functions. We're not *calling* these functions, so we omit the parentheses. Plotting is a common application for anonymous functions (see "Creating Anonymous Functions" on page 51). This is their purpose: to pass a function as an argument to another function, in this case plot().

Plotting Vectors of Vectors or Functions

If we supply vectors of vectors in the first two argument positions, plot() will cycle through both arguments, reusing elements as necessary. For example, if we call plot([x1, x2], [y1, y2]), we'll get a plot of y1 versus x1 and y2 versus x2, both on the same set of axes. But if we call plot(x1, [y1, y2]), we'll get a plot of y1 versus x1 and y2 versus x1. If we call plot([x1, x2], y1), we'll see y1 versus x1 and y1 versus x2.

We'll get the same results if we use horizontal concatenation; in other words, plot([x1, x2], [y1, y2]) produces the same plot as plot([x1 x2], [y1 y2]). When given Matrix arguments, plot() plots by columns. We can even call plot([x1, x2], [y1 y2]), mixing a vector of vectors with a matrix, and plot() will know what we mean and draw the same graph as in the two preceding examples.

If we use *vertical* concatenation, we will simply create longer vectors. We can use this to plot different functions over different ranges:

```
julia> x = 0:5π/1000:5π
julia> plot([x; 5π .+ x], [sin.(x); -exp.(-x .* 0.2) .* sin.(x)])
```

In this example, we join the x vector to itself shifted to the right by 5π and supply the result as the independent variable. Against that, we plot a sin function joined to the same function multiplied by a decaying exponential (note the use of broadcast notation throughout). Figure 4-5 shows the result.

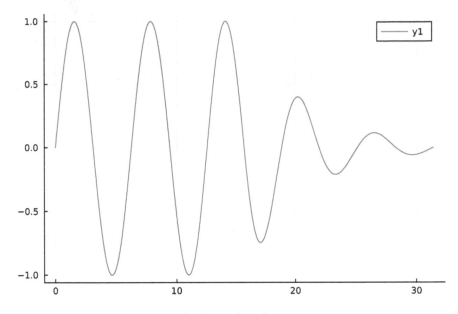

Figure 4-5: Joining vectors to model a damped oscillation

The graph can be interpreted as an initially frictionless oscillation with damping applied at $x = 5\pi$.

Displaying and Mutating

I mentioned earlier that we cause the display of a plot in a program file with the call gui(). But how does the gui() function know what plot to display? The plotting system maintains a *current plot* in the global namespace, along with other settings and state related to the display of graphics. This is convenient during interactive plotting, as it allows us to incrementally adjust and add things to the current plot by mutating it. The mutating version of plot() is plot!(), following the convention (see "Functions That Mutate Their Arguments" on page 56).

Using mutation, we can produce Figure 4-4 with these three lines:

```
julia> plot(sin, -π, π)

julia> plot!(cos)

julia> plot!(f)
```

The plot!() function maintains the domain established in the first call. We can use the mutating form to change many aspects of the plot, in addition to adding curves.

The plot() and plot!() functions return plot objects, which we can assign to variables. The reason we see a plot when we call the function in the REPL or in a notebook is that Julia calls gui() automatically in interactive contexts whenever a plot object is returned from an expression. If we've assigned some plots to variables, anytime we want to see one, we can simply type its name in the REPL and press RETURN. In a program file, we can supply the plot object as an argument to gui().

If we give plot!() a plot object as its first argument, it will mutate that plot instead of the current plot. For example, if we execute ps = plot(sin), then ps is a plot of the sin() function. A call to plot!(ps, cos) will do two things: it will mutate ps, adding a cos() curve to it, and it will return the result, so that the altered plot pops up on the screen. Making the same call using the non-mutating version, plot(), will display the plot with both curves, but won't alter ps.

We can supply any number of plot objects as arguments to plot(), and it will arrange them automatically into a grid. See "Layouts" on page 117 for details on how to get more control over this arrangement.

This REPL session creates several plots and then combines them:

```
julia> parabola = plot(x -> x^2);

julia> ps = plot(sin, 0, 2π);

julia> plot!(ps, cos);

julia> plot(ps, plot(f), plot(s -> s^3), parabola)
```

All the lines end with a semicolon except the last, where we want to see the plot. First we give the variable parabola the value of a plot object depicting a parabola, constructed with an anonymous function. The value of the variable is now a data type representing a complete plot, with axes, tick marks, and so on. We don't specify a domain, so the parabola is plotted from −5 to 5.

Then we assign ps to a plot of the sin function, this time with a domain from 0 to 2π.

Next we decide we would like ps to also contain a cos curve, so we change it; plot!() will keep the existing domain.

The final line creates the plot shown in Figure 4-6.

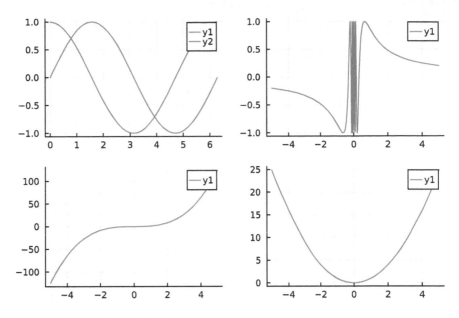

Figure 4-6: Plotting four plot objects

We call plot() with four plot-object arguments. The first and last are the two plot-holding variables, the second is a plot object created directly with a plot() function on the previous f function, and the third uses an anonymous function.

Creating Parametric Plots

Parametric plots in the plane are also classified with 2D plots because there is one independent variable, now called the *parameter*. In this type of plot, x and y both depend on the parameter. If we pass two arguments that are both functions to plot(), it recognizes this as the signature for a parametric plot and produces a graph with the x-dependence given by the first function and the y-dependence given by the second (where, as usual, x is plotted on the horizontal axis and y on the vertical). We must specify the domain for the parameter with two additional arguments; however, there is no default as when plotting non-parametric functions.

Parametric plotting allows us to render various complex shapes and such plots as circles and spirals, as shown in Figure 4-7.

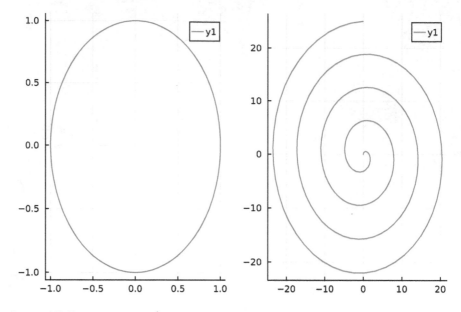

Figure 4-7: Two parametric plots

The left-hand plot is produced with the call `circle = plot(sin, cos, 0, 2π)` and the spiral in the right-hand plot is created by `spiral = plot(r -> r*sin(r)`, `r -> r*cos(r), 0, 8π)`. We draw the composite figure by calling `plot(circle, spiral)`.

As in the case of regular function plotting, the independent variable, in this case the parameter, can be implicit, as in the call we used to draw the circle. When the functions to be plotted are too complex to allow this, as in the spiral example, we must employ a dummy variable, which we named r in this case.

Making Polar Plots

A polar plot uses the conventional polar coordinate system rather than a rectangular coordinate system. The independent variable is the angle, measured counterclockwise from the horizontal axis, and the dependent variable is the distance from the origin.

Figure 4-8 shows two simple plots in polar coordinates. The `plot()` function renders the coordinate grid to reflect the symmetry of the polar geometry.

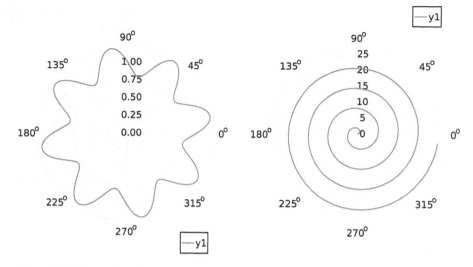

Figure 4-8: Two polar plots

We created the plot on the left with plot(0:2π/500:2π, t -> 1 + 0.2*sin(8t); proj=:polar) and the spiral on the right with plot(0:8π/200:8π, t -> t; proj=: polar). The first arguments in these calls are arrays of angular coordinates, and the second arguments are functions mapping the angle to the distance from the origin, using t as a dummy variable. The argument proj=:polar tells plot() to make a polar plot. This is a keyword argument, as explained in "Optional and Keyword Arguments" on page 96.

Making Scatterplots

The 2D plots we've seen so far draw a continuous line through a set of points. Sometimes we need to plot a collection of dots or other markers, each at a particular (x, y) position: a *scatterplot*. The scatter() function works identically to the plot() function, but it draws point collections rather than curves.

As an example application, suppose we wanted to visualize the output of the iterated map:

$$x_{i+1} = 1 - y + a|x_i|$$
$$y_{i+1} = x_i$$

This simple map produces a fascinating variety of patterns with an unpredictable dependence on a. The Julia version is:

```
julia> function ginger(x, y, a)
           x2 = 1.0 - y + a*abs(x)
           y2 = x
           x2, y2
       end
```

I've named it after the common nickname for the map: the *gingerbread man*.

We'll store the sequence of values in two vectors, x and y, initialized with the starting coordinates, and iterate 4,000 times:

```
julia> x = [20.0]; y = [9.0];
julia> for i in 1:4000
❶     x2, y2 = ginger(x[end], y[end], 1.76)
          push!(x, x2)
          push!(y, y2)
      end
```

The listing uses a form of *destructuring* ❶. The ginger() function returns a tuple with its first member stored in x2 and its second in y2.

After running this loop, we can see what's in x and y with a scatterplot. The call scatter(x, y; ms=0.5, legend=false) produces the plot shown in Figure 4-9.

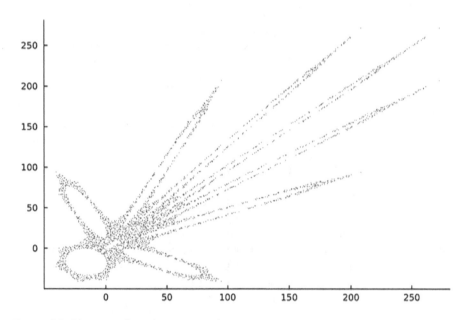

Figure 4-9: The gingerbread man iterated map

In the call to scatter(), after the x and y arguments, we add something new after a semicolon. These two *optional keyword arguments* affect the plot's appearance, as explained in the next section.

Optional and Keyword Arguments

In a function definition, we can supply default values for arguments. Doing so makes those arguments *optional*, as the user can call the function without using them:

```
julia> g(x, y=2) = x + y
g (generic function with 2 methods)
```

```
julia> g(4)
6

julia> g(4, 9)
13
```

In this example, the definition of g() includes the default value of 2 for y. If we call it with no second argument, it returns x + 2. When we do supply a second argument, it uses that instead.

So far we've learned how to define and call functions with *positional arguments*. Values are assigned based on the order in which we put them in the argument list when calling the function, whether they're optional or not.

Julia also has *keyword arguments*, identified by name rather than position. Unlike some other languages, we must make a distinction when defining a function between its positional and keyword arguments; we separate them with a semicolon, as in this example:

```
julia> p(x; y=2) = x + y
p (generic function with 1 method)

❶ julia> p(4)
6

julia> p(4, 5)
ERROR: MethodError: no method matching p(::Int64, ::Int64)
Closest candidates are:
  p(::Any; y) at REPL[346]:1

julia> p(4; y=5)
9
```

Here we define p() to have one positional argument and one keyword argument, named y, with the default value of 2. We can call p() omitting the keyword argument ❶, because the default makes it optional. If we supply two positional arguments, that returns an error because the function takes only one. Make sure you understand the difference between the functions g() and p(): they differ only in their function signatures.

NOTE *When calling a function we have the option to use a comma instead of a semicolon because there's no chance of ambiguity; however, the semicolon is required in function definitions.*

The plotting functions in the Plots ecosystem use positional arguments for data or functions and keyword arguments for setting plot options. Because all the plot options have default values, we haven't had to use them until now.

Basic Plot Settings

To adjust a plot's appearance, we use keyword arguments. There are four components that can make up a visualization made with the `Plots` package, and each one has a collection of settings that applies to it.

These four components are *plot*, *subplot*, *axis*, and *series*. Plots can contain subplots, and either of those can contain axes or series.

The overall illustration is called the plot; it contains other plots, the subplots, when there are more than one, as in Figure 4-6. Settings such as an overall title and background color apply to the plot.

Within a plot, each subplot can have its own title, background color, margin, and many other settings.

The actual curves or other visualizations of functions or data are the series, and a subplot can contain many series.

Each subplot contains an axis object. Its settings determine such things as whether the coordinate axes are drawn with arrows, the color of tick labels, or the numbers on the coordinate axes.

For the most part, we can simply use the appropriate keyword to set the desired *attribute* of our visualization, and the plotting system will apply it where it makes sense. But when designing complicated visualizations, we sometimes need to target specific components.

The official plotting system documentation at *https://docs.juliaplots.org/ stable/* contains the complete list of attributes for all components, as well as which attributes are supported by which backends. The following list provides the most important ones and gives examples of their effects:

Titles

- Overall title: `plot_title`
- Title for subplot: `title`
- Title for legend: `legendtitle`

Other labels

- Legend text: `label`
- Legend existence and position: `legend`
- Axis labels: `[x,y]guide`
- Label anywhere: `annotation=(x, y, "Text")`

Font colors

- Overall title: `plot_titlefontcolor`
- Subplot title: `titlefontcolor`
- Legend: `legendfontcolor`
- Axis labels: `[x,y]guidefontcolor`

Area colors

- Margin area: `background_outside`
- Plot area only: `background_inside`

Curves

- Line color: `lc`
- Line width: `lw`
- Line style: `ls`

Scatterplots

- Marker shape: `shape`
- Marker color: `mc`
- Marker size: `ms`

Contour plots

- Give contours labels (Boolean): `clabels`
- Contour levels: `levels`

Axes and ticks

- Reverse axis (Boolean): `[x,y]flip`
- Rotation of tick labels: `[x,y]rotation`
- Draw axis: `showaxis [x,y]ticks`
- Frame style: `framestyle`

Grid

- Draw a grid (Boolean): `grid`
- Gridline opacity: `gridalpha [0,1]`
- Gridline style: `gridstyle`

Coordinate system

- Use polar coordinates: `:proj=polar`

Sizes and margins

- Margin around subplot: `[left,right,top,bottom]margin`
- Overall plot size: `sizes(a, b)` (in px)
- Subplot aspect ratio: `ratio`

Each of the keywords in these lists has a set of abbreviations and alternative spellings, all listed in the official documentation. I've picked one version in each case; it's not always the briefest alternative, but a choice designed to be memorable and to avoid confusion.

The purposes of a few of these settings will not be clear until we discuss them later, but I've listed them all here for easy reference.

Font Attributes

To form the keyword for setting a font attribute such as the font size or family, look up the corresponding name for setting the font color in the attribute list shown earlier, and substitute the desired attribute, such as fontsize or fontfamily in place of fontcolor. For example, to make the plot title have a size of 30pt, use the setting plot_titlefontsize=30.

The font *families* are dependent on which backend is in use. A list for the GR backend is at *https://gr-framework.org/fonts.html*. Some of the more useful families, which also may be available in other backends, are Times (Roman, Italic, Bold), Courier, Bookman, DejaVu Sans, and Computer Modern. Supply the setting as a string. If we set the attribute fontfamily, that will apply to all or most of the text on the plot. For example, to get the ticks, axis labels, and other annotations in Computer Modern, but the title in Times, we'd call plot(...; fontfamily="Computer Modern", legendfontfamily="Times").

If we mutate a plot that contains subplots, and we're adding or changing attributes that apply to subplots, we must specify which subplot to mutate, unless we want our changes to apply to all of them. This is the purpose of the subplot keyword. Set it to an integer indexing the subplots as they appear in the plot() statement. For example, for two graphs displayed side by side with plot(p1, p2), we can put a label on the horizontal axis of p2 with plot!(; xguide ="Time", subplot=2). Without the subplot keyword, both plots would get the label.

The Frame Styles

The framestyle setting determines the type of axis. Figure 4-10 displays the six possibilities.

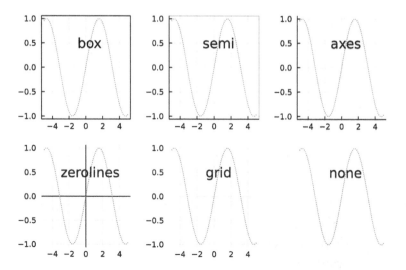

Figure 4-10: The six possible frame styles

We set the attribute to the symbol version of the term printed on the graph. For example, to get the style in the lower-left corner, we'd use the setting `framestyle=:zerolines`.

Working with Plot Settings

Now we can understand the call to `scatter(x, y; ms=0.5, legend=false)` that produced Figure 4-9. After the first two positional arguments, the arrays holding the points to be plotted, we have a semicolon indicating the start of the keyword arguments. The first sets a small marker size and the second turns off the legend.

Let's use some combinations of the basic attributes listed in "Basic Plot Settings" on page 98 to solve some other visualization problems.

Aspect Ratio and Title Font Size

The following program creates a simple plot with two subplots displaying a circle and a parabola:

```
julia> p1 = plot(sin, cos, 0, 2π; title="A Circle", ratio=1,
             grid=false, ticks=false, legend=false)

julia> p2 = plot(x -> x^2, -1, 1; title="A Parabola",
             gridalpha=0.4, gridstyle=:dot, legend=false)

julia> plot(p1, p2; plot_title="Two Shapes", plot_titlefontsize=20)
```

Here we use the `ratio` keyword to set the aspect ratio in the first line. You may have noticed that what is supposed to be a circle in Figure 4-7 is rendered as a noncircular ellipse. The default size of Julia's plots is not square, but is instead longer than it is tall, so the circle is stretched horizontally. If it matters, as it does in this case, we can use `ratio` to fix the problem. We also turned off the grid and ticks on this plot.

The default grid in most backends is quite light, so we made it more prominent by increasing the `gridalpha` in the plot of the parabola. The default for this is `0.1`.

The last line creates the combined plot with an overall title set a little larger than the default. Figure 4-11 shows the result.

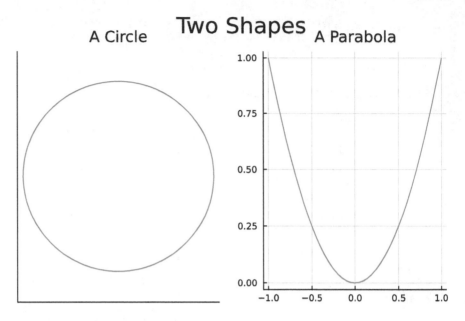

Figure 4-11: A plot with two subplots

To get more space between the two subplots, we can, for example, set a rightmargin on the left subplot. Before setting margins, execute **using Plots .PlotMeasures**, which lets us use literal dimensions in margin settings; for example, rightmargin=10mm. Other available dimensions are inch, cm, px, and pt.

NOTE *The plot_title is a recent addition to the plotting system, and its implementation is incomplete. If we choose larger font sizes for the title, it will overlap the titles of the subplots, and there is no straightforward way to fix that.*

Labels and Legend Positioning

For our next example, let's make a plot of x^n for a few values of n:

```
julia> plot()

julia> for n = 1:5
           plot!(x -> x^n; lw=3, ls=:auto, label=n)
       end

julia> plot!(; legend=:topleft, legendtitle="Exponent")
```

First we'll clear any existing plots with an empty plot() command, and then mutate the empty plot once for each function. Since the for loop doesn't return a result, we won't see anything until the final call after the loop, which simply makes some plot settings. In the plotting statements, the label setting defines the text associated with that plot in the legend. It expects a string (or symbol), but can convert the integer n. The lw setting makes the lines thicker than the default. The `ls` setting is for the line style. It can take the values `:auto`, `:solid`, `:dash`, `:dot`, `:dashdot`, or `:dashdotdot`. The option used here, `:auto`, cycles through the other five styles, reusing them if the plot has more than five curves. It's a good choice for print when we can't use color. Figure 4-12 shows the results.

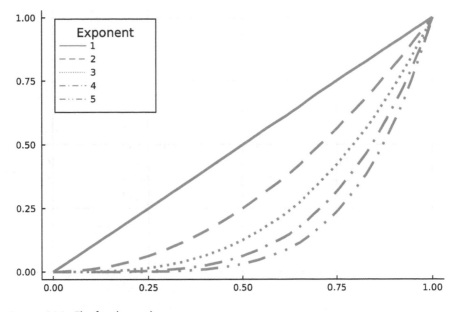

Figure 4-12: The five line styles

The final `plot()` statement sets `legend` to place it at the top left of the plot. We can use other similar positioning symbols, optionally preceded by `outer` to place the legend outside the axes. For more precise positioning we can use an `(x, y)` tuple specifying the coordinates of the legend box. Finally, we can set `legend=false` to omit the legend.

LaTeX Titles and Label Positioning by Data

Let's plot the same functions with a different style of labeling. We'll use annotations to place labels indicating each exponent on top of each corresponding curve, as shown in Listing 4-1.

```
julia> plot()

julia> for n = 1:5
           xlabel = (0.2 + 0.12n)
         ❶ ylabel = xlabel^n
           plot!(x -> x^n; lw=3, ls=:auto,
                 annotation=(xlabel, ylabel, n),
                 annotationfontsize=25)
       end
```

```
julia> using LaTeXStrings

julia> plot!(; legend=false, xguide="x", yguide="y", guidefontsize=18,
    ❷ title=L"x^n \textrm{~labeled~by~}n", titlefontsize=30)
```

Listing 4-1: Using calculated labels and a LaTeX title

Here we calculate coordinates for each of the five labels within the loop.
The x-coordinate increases to the right with the exponent, to space out the
labels so they don't overlap. The label's y-coordinate ❶ is the same function of x as the curves we're plotting, to ensure that they lie precisely on the
curves that they're labeling.

The setting for the annotation has n, a variable holding an integer, where
there should be a String, but the plot() function converts it for us.

We then import a package we haven't seen before: LaTeXStrings (note
the capitalization) lets us put math in our plot titles and annotations using
LaTeX syntax. Even non-LaTeX users may still need equations in graphs
occasionally, and LaTeX's math syntax is straightforward. Check "Further
Reading" on page 121 for a link to a guide. After importing this package, we
can prepend L to any string to turn it into a LaTeX string. In a context where
typesetting is possible, such as in a plot, Julia will typeset the string appropriately. The entire string is in LaTeX math mode, where all letters are treated
as mathematical symbols. Therefore, if we need some normal text, as we did
in this example ❷, we must wrap it in a LaTeX command to force it to be set
as such. Within these text segments, indicate spaces with a tilde (~). The plot
in Figure 4-13 shows the result of this REPL session.

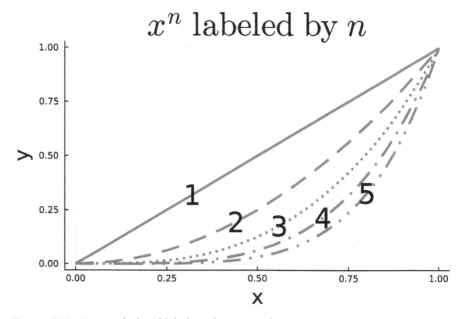

Figure 4-13: Using calculated labels and a LaTeX title

In addition to the settings for individual plot elements, two others make larger-scale changes. The thickness_scaling setting is useful for creating a version of the plot with better legibility for presentation. It thickens everything, including tick labels. It affects the margins as well, however, and can change the positioning of plot elements. Setting the values between 1 and 1.7 produces useful results. Use values less than 1 to create a spindly version of the plot.

Regression Lines

The smooth setting draws a line of best fit, calculated by linear regression, through each curve or dataset on the plot.

Let's return to the gingerbread map and, using the same initial conditions, calculate 20,000 iterations with $a = 1.6$, again storing the results in the x and y Vectors. We'll make two subplots. The first will be a scatterplot similar to Figure 4-9, but with a regression line showing the average orientation of the points. The second will plot the first 100 values of x versus iteration number, with a regression line showing the trend of a gradually increasing distance from the origin:

```
julia> sc = scatter(x, y; smooth=true, ms=1, legend=false,
                     xguide="x", yguide="y", guidefontsize=18)

julia> pl = plot(x[1:100]; smooth=true, legend=false)

❶ julia> pl = plot!(x[1:100]; lc=:lightgray, legend=false,
                     xguide="iteration", yguide="x", guidefontsize=18)

julia> plot(sc, pl, plot_title="Gingerbread map with a = 1.6",
            plot_titlefontsize=22)
```

First we create a scatterplot of the map as before, adding the trend line with the setting smooth=true, and assign the result to sc. Then we plot the initial 100 x-values, also with a trend line. Plotting the two subplots together with a title gives us Figure 4-14.

Gingerbread map with a = 1.6

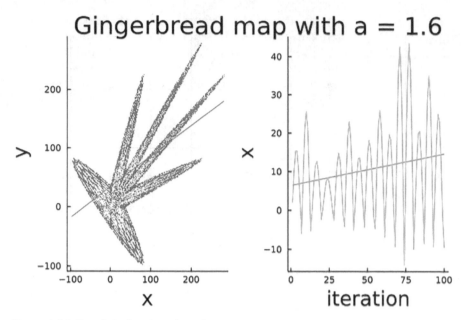

Figure 4-14: Trends in the gingerbread map

As before, the `plot_title` attribute creates an overall title for the two plots. We wanted the plotted curve and the calculated trend line to have different styles, but there's no setting for this, so we resorted to a trick, over-plotting the curve in a different style but without a trend line ❶.

Saving Plots

When you're ready to save your creation to disk, call **savefig(p, path)** where *p* is the variable holding the visualization and *path* is the location where you would like the image file stored. The filename extension to *path* determines the format, but different backends support different types of images. PDF and PNG should always be available, and SVG is also widely supported.

If we omit p, it defaults to the current plot. A common workflow is to repeatedly mutate a plot, making adjustments until it's satisfactory, and then call savefig(*path*).

Detail Insets

An inset plot is a small plot inside the frame of a larger one. It's often used to provide a magnified view of a section of the outer plot. Julia's plotting system has a built-in function for creating this type of detail inset, called `lens!()`. It exists only in a mutating form because the inset plot makes sense only as an addition to an existing plot.

The first argument to `lens!()` either is an existing plot or is omitted to indicate the current plot. The next two arguments are vectors defining the rectangular region to be magnified. The required argument inset specifies which subplot gets the inset as well as the inset's position and size. The diagram in Figure 4-15 shows how to use these arguments.

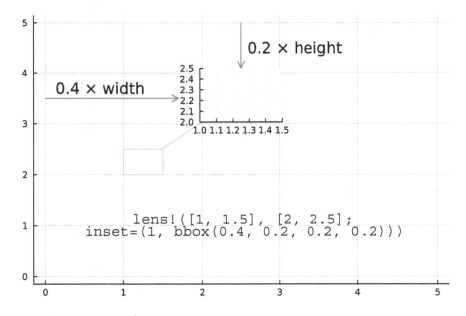

Figure 4-15: How to make an inset

Figure 4-15 uses a blank plot with a grid for illustration. The annotations "width" and "height" refer to the width and height of the outer plot. The complete command that created the inset is shown near the bottom of the plot.

As an application for lens!(), I constructed another instance of the gingerbread map, this time with a = 1.4 and 100,000 iterations to produce more detail. The following two lines first create the scatterplot and then add the inset:

```
scatter(x, y; ms=0.1, legend=false)

lens!([-26, -22], [31, 38];
      inset=(1, bbox(0.1, 0, 0.3, 0.3)),
    ❶ ticks=false, framestyle=:box, subplot=2,
      linecolor=:green, linestyle=:dot)
```

In the call to lens!(), the settings ❶ for the ticks and Framestyle apply to the inset plot, while the linecolor and linestyle settings apply to the drawing of the magnifying glass that delineates the expanded area. A full frame style is a good choice for an inset plot.

Figure 4-16 shows the result. I've used the inset plot to magnify one of the corners of the gingerbread map, showing the pattern of points within it.

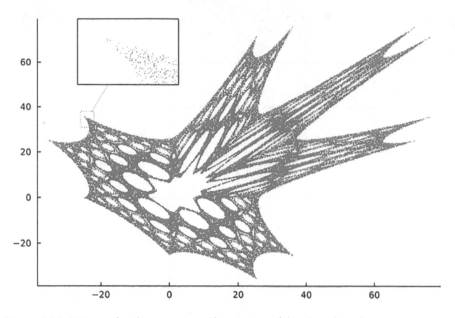

Figure 4-16: Using a detail inset to magnify a section of the gingerbread map

The setting `subplot=2` in the call that creates the inset ensures that the other graph settings in that call apply only to the inset, which becomes the second subplot. By referring to the number of the subplot, we could create an inset within the inset, if we were so inclined.

3D Plots

Several types of plots visualize a quantity that depends on two independent variables. When in rectangular coordinates, the dependent variable is conventionally called z, and the two independent variables are called x and y. The three common ways to represent such a relationship are with a surface plot, a heatmap, or a contour plot. Which is most effective depends on the nature of the data and the features we're trying to clarify.

Surface Plots

After importing the plotting package with `using Plots`, we have access to several 3D plotting routines. For a *surface plot*, we use the `surface()` function to create a perspective rendering of a 2D surface embedded in a 3D space, with the height and coloring of the surface indicating the z-value.

Here are a few additional settings that apply to surface plots:

- Draw a colorbar: `colorbar` (`true` or `false`)
- Opacity of the surface: `fillalpha`
- Angle of view: `camera` (azimuth, elevation) (in degrees)

- Colorbar title: cbtitle
- Surface palette: c

Let's put some of these settings to use in making a surface plot of a Gaussian distribution of two variables. After defining a vector *x* to go from −1 to 1, we can use anonymous function syntax to plot the surface with the following:

```
surface(x, x, (x, y) -> exp(-(0.05x^2 + y^2)/.1);
        fillalpha=0.5, camera=(45, 50), c=[Gray(0), Gray(0.8)],
        xrotation=45, yrotation=-45)
```

We use an alpha less than 1 in order to see through the surface, and rotated the axis tick labels to make them easier to read and to keep them from colliding where the axes meet. Figure 4-17 shows the surface plot.

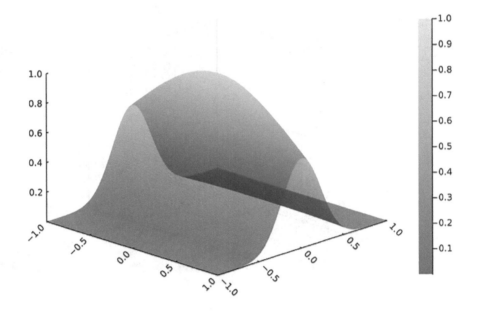

Figure 4-17: A surface plot

The c setting defines the palette used to color the surface. There are several ways to define the palette; the one used earlier, with a number of colors in a Vector, creates a palette by smoothly interpolating between them. Gray(0) is black, Gray(1) is white, and so on. We can also define colors with RGB(r, g, b), where r, g, and b are the red, green, and blue components, also ranging from 0 (absent) to 1 (fully saturated). Over 600 color names are available as symbols, including both memorable names such as :red and :blue and meaningless ones such as :seashell3 and :oldlace.

Instead of a Vector of colors, we can supply a symbol giving the name of a predefined palette, of which there are scores listed at *https://docs.juliaplots .org/latest/generated/colorschemes/*. The more useful ones have names such as

`:blues` or `:grays` that use one hue and vary the saturation and lightness, but there are plenty to choose from for special purposes.

Heatmaps

A heatmap also visualizes a mapping of two independent variables to one dependent variable, but the values of the independent variable are indicated by a color or gray value. The call is similar to a surface plot, but uses the `heatmap()` function:

```
heatmap(x, x, (x, y) -> exp(-(0.05x^2 + y^2)/.1);
            c=:grays)
```

This call creates the heatmap shown in Figure 4-18.

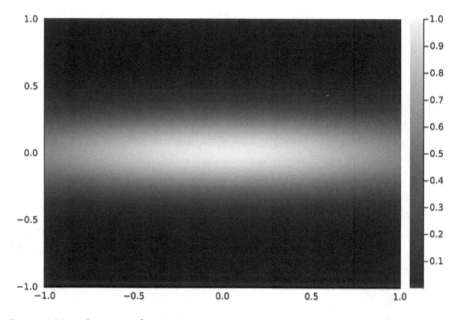

Figure 4-18: A heatmap of a 2D Gaussian

Color palettes for heatmaps work the same way as for surface plots.

Contour Plots

Contour plots are similar to heatmaps, but they use isolines rather than color to indicate the values of the independent variable. Here are a few important attributes specific to contour plots:

- Number of contours or specific contour levels: `levels` (integer or vector of levels)
- Draw contour labels (Boolean): `clabels`
- Fill areas between contours (Boolean): `fill`

If we supply an integer for levels, Julia will draw that many contours. If we also set clabels to true, it will label the contour lines with the values they represent. Unfortunately, these numerical labels are printed with too many digits and often become crowded. If we set levels to a Vector of numbers, the plot will have contours at just those values, and their labels will be printed using the same precision used for the levels. The following example shows this use of levels and clabels:

```
contour(x, x, (x, y) -> exp(-(0.05x^2 + y^2)/.1);
            clabels=true, levels=[0.1, 0.3, 0.5, 0.7, 0.9, 1.0],
            colorbar=false, framestyle=:box)
```

This call uses the same x vector and plots the same function as the surface plot and heatmap examples shown in Figures 4-17 and 4-18. The result, in Figure 4-19, shows the labels with one digit of precision.

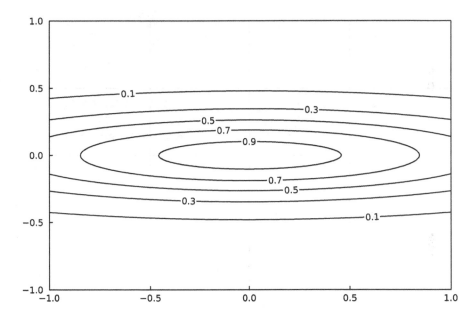

Figure 4-19: A labeled contour plot

The :box framestyle works well with contour plots. Eliminating the color bar is also a good idea. We can color the lines by setting a c, but this doesn't always work well with every backend. If we find stray colors creeping into the contour lines, we can fix it with c=:black.

Line styles such as :dot work, but not :auto.

NOTE   *When using filled contours with some backends, including GR, and manually set contour levels, we must include a level greater than or equal to the maximum of the data, or the graph will not be properly drawn.*

The fill attribute, when set to true, adds colors between the contour lines, resulting in a kind of discrete heatmap with contours. The c attribute defines the palette for these colors. The `contourf()` function is an alias for `contour()` with `fill=true`.

Let's repeat the previous contour plot (Figure 4-19), but this time leave the color bar in, turn on the `fill`, and use a grayscale palette:

```
contour(x, x, (x, y) -> exp(-(0.05x^2 + y^2)/.1);
                clabels=true, levels=[0.1, 0.3, 0.5, 0.7, 0.9, 1.0],
                fill=true, c=[Gray(0.4), :white])
```

Figure 4-20 shows the filled contour plot.

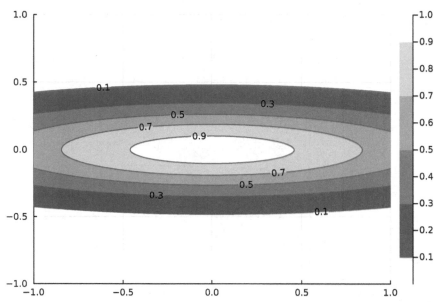

Figure 4-20: A filled contour plot

In this case, having both contour labels and a color bar is somewhat redundant, as they carry the same information, but this may make the plot easier to interpret. There is an art to scientific visualization in creating a result that is both intuitively clear and quantitatively precise.

3D Parametric Plots

Parametric plots in 3D work just as they do in 2D, but they trace a path through 3D space, with three functions of the single parameter giving the x-, y-, and z-coordinates. Unlike in 2D parametric plots, we must supply three vectors, and it doesn't work with functions. Here is an example:

```
julia> t = 0:2π/100:2π;

julia> xp = sin.(3 .* t);

julia> yp = cos.(3 .* t);
```

```
julia> zp = t .* 0.2
```

```
julia> plot(xp, yp, zp; lw=3, gridalpha=0.4, camera=(30, 50))
```

The plot() function knows what to do when supplied with three vectors as positional arguments, producing the resulting 3D parametric plot shown in Figure 4-21.

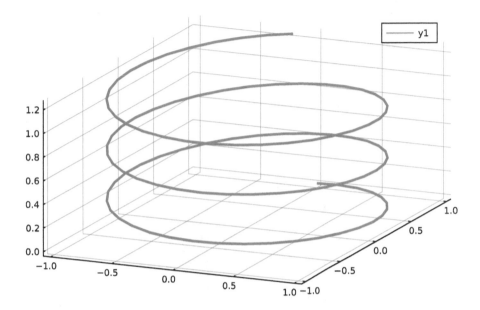

Figure 4-21: An example of a 3D parametric plot

We can use the attributes for lines as for ordinary 2D plots, and set the camera angle as for surface plots.

Vector Plots

A vector field maps every point in space to a vector, which can be represented by an arrow. The Plots package offers vector plots created with the quiver() function. Its first two arguments are x and y Vectors containing the coordinates of the start of the vectors. The displacements from those coordinates to the vectors' endpoints are stored in two other Vectors, placed in a Tuple, and assigned to a keyword argument also called quiver.

The following example shows how to use quiver():

```
julia> xc = 0:.3:π;
```

```
julia> yc = sin.(xc);
```

```
julia> quiver(xc, yc; quiver=(xc .- π/2, yc .- 0.25), lw=3)
```

These three lines produce the vector plot in Figure 4-22.

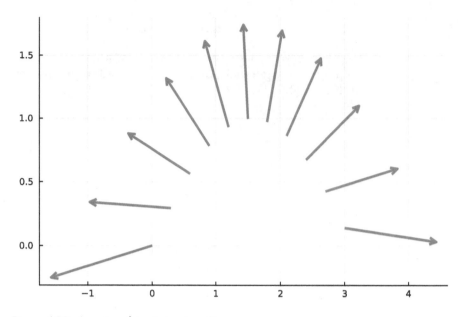

Figure 4-22: A vector plot using quiver()

The quiver() function accepts all the attributes for curves; here we set the line width to get thicker arrows.

3D Scatterplots

Plots can extend scatterplots into the third dimension. One way to visualize a 3D distribution of some quantity is to plot a regular 3D grid of markers while setting some marker attribute, such as size or opacity, to a function of the quantity. First we need to establish the grid by making x, y, and z Vectors:

```
x = []; y = []; z = [];

for i in 0:20, j in 0:20, k in 0:20
    push!(x, i/10 - 1)
    push!(y, j/10 - 1)
    push!(z, k/10 - 1)
end
```

This will create the coordinate arrays ranging from −1 to 1.

Let's imagine a planet sitting in the center of our grid. We could plot the shape of the gravitational potential due to the planet by first defining a potential function and then using it to set the marker size:

```
pot(x, y, z) = 1 / sqrt(x^2 + y^2 + z^2)
scatter(x, y, z;  ms=min.(pot.(x, y, z), 5), ma=0.4, legend=false)
```

The potential becomes large near the planet, so we need to limit the marker size with the min() function. It actually becomes infinite at $(0, 0, 0)$, but Julia handles that gracefully. The result is shown in Figure 4-23.

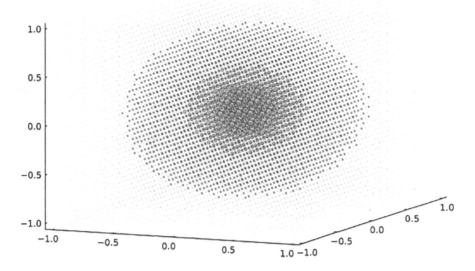

Figure 4-23: A 3D scatterplot

We set an opacity to allow us to see through the markers. This is the same scatter() function that we used in 2D, but Julia knows what to do if we give it three positional arguments.

Useful Backends

GR, the current default backend, has the merit of being fast and capable of producing most basic categories of visualization.

A few other backends are available for special purposes, but most of them require us to add them in the package manager before use.

UnicodePlots

The unicodeplots backend plots directly in the terminal. It's good for a quick look at some data, which it plots using characters. We can also use it to generate plots to paste into an email, but obviously it's not suited to making figures for publication, and it can't save plots.

To produce quick plots in the terminal, first execute **add UnicodePlots** in package mode, then call **unicodeplots()** to activate the backend.

The unicodeplots backend doesn't support every plot type. It can make 2D plots, including scatterplots, but not contour or surface plots. However, unicodeplots can render colored heatmaps in the terminal.

PyPlot

The pyplot backend uses Python's Matplotlib, so it may be a good choice for those already familiar with that system. Although it can sometimes be a bit slow, it creates better plots than the default in some cases.

PlotlyJS

With the plotlyjs backend we can create interactive graphs for the web. Saving the plot with the *.html* file extension creates a file containing an HTML fragment that we can paste into a web page. The fragment loads some third-party JavaScript that supplies interactive controls for panning, zooming, and, for 3D plots, rotating in 3D space. Other forms of interactivity vary appropriately with the plot type. Two-dimensional plots display data values as the user hovers over the curve, and surface plots draw contours on the surfaces at the z-value of the mouse pointer.

Plotting is not at all fast, although the results look good and interaction is impressively responsive. Contour plots are better with plotlyjs than with GR, especially for colored contours, but the attributes for linewidth or linestyle have no effect, and manual levels don't work.

When plotting from the REPL, a separate window pops up for each plot, using the same JavaScript interactivity as in the HTML files.

PGFPlots and PGFPlotsX

I won't say much about these, because they are useful only to those who have LaTeX installed and some knowledge of the LaTeX graphing system PGFPlots. Those who do use these systems should be aware of the two Julia interfaces to them. The difference between the two versions is that PGFPlotsX's syntax is closer to what's used directly in LaTeX. With PGFPlots, we can make extraordinary visualizations that are difficult to achieve through other means. LaTeX users who aren't familiar with the system may want to acquaint themselves. This backend does depend on a LaTeX installation—not a trivial requirement.

HDF5

HDF5 stands for Hierarchical Data Format, version 5. This backend does not display plots directly; its purpose is to bundle data and plots together into an HDF file. For anyone who uses HDF in their research, this package will be essential, but others will have no use for it.

The backend not only writes HDF files, it also can read them into the Julia session for display with other Plots backends.

Gaston

Gaston is an interface to gnuplot and depends on a gnuplot installation. This backend will be of interest to those already using that venerable and powerful graphics program.

Gaston is fast and powerful, because gnuplot is fast and powerful. If you routinely need to make complex 3D plots that the other backends can't handle, or need more fine control over plots for publication, installing gnuplot and using it with Gaston may be the best choice.

Layouts

Earlier in this chapter we saw that the plot() function will arrange graphs in a grid if we pass it a number of plot objects. Sometimes we need more control over the arrangement of subplots in an illustration. In such cases, we turn to the Layout system.

The plotting package's method for composing plots into larger illustrations is one of the jewels of the system. Considering the complexity that it allows, it's remarkably intuitive to use.

In the following demonstrations, the Vector s contains six plots, each displaying a prominent digit, from 1 to 6. This will make it clear where the layout engine positions each plot.

If you'd like to follow along, you'll need to create your own s vector, with plots of your choosing.

Making Simple Rectangular Layouts

To replace the default square grid of plots with a different rectangular arrangement, supply the desired number of rows and columns as a tuple assigned to the layout attribute:

```
plot(s[1], s[2], s[3], s[4]; layout=(1, 4))
```

As Figure 4-24 shows, this call arranges the plots using one row and four columns.

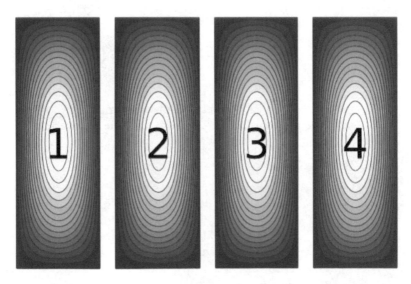

Figure 4-24: A one-row layout

The number of plots implied in the layout tuple must match exactly the number of subplots. The default in this case would be equivalent to layout=(2, 2).

Using grid()

The simple layouts in the previous example make all the subplots the same size. To control the heights and widths of the rows and columns, use the grid() function, as in the following example:

```
plot(s[1], s[2], s[3], s[4];
     layout=grid(2, 2; widths=(0.2, 0.8), heights=(0.7, 0.3)))
```

This call creates the layout in Figure 4-25. We can omit either the height or the width specification to get equalized lengths in that direction.

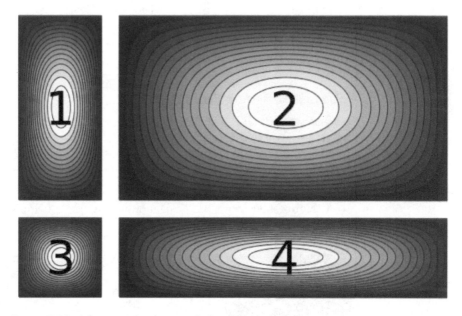

Figure 4-25: A layout using the grid() function

When using grid(), the dimensions can add up to less than 1, which will simply leave some blank space, but they should not add to greater than 1.

Creating Complex Layouts Using @layout

We can create layouts of arbitrary complexity. The next level requires the use of the @layout macro. We haven't seen macros yet; they're introduced in "Macros" on page 170. For now, I'll show how to use this particular macro to create graph layouts. We'll be better equipped to understand how it works under the hood after we learn a bit more about the language.

The @layout macro creates a layout that follows the shape of a matrix that we supply to the macro. We use spaces to place subplots horizontally and newlines or semicolons to place them vertically, as when constructing actual matrices. However, these @layout matrices don't need to have matching dimensions. As in the following example, the rows can have different numbers of elements. I use a to represent a subplot, but we can use any identifiers. They have no meaning, as the layout engine just uses the plots in the order we supply them in the plot() function. Here's a simple use of the macro:

```
plot(s[1], s[2], s[3], s[4], s[5], s[6];
    layout = @layout [ a a a
                       a a
                       a   ] )
```

Figure 4-26 shows the resulting layout. Observe how the arrangement of subplots follows the arrangement of the a placeholders used in the macro.

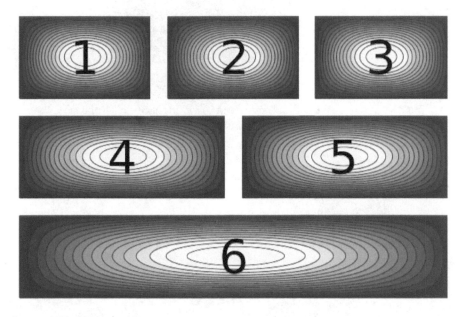

Figure 4-26: Using the @layout macro

The use of @layout in this form equalizes the space allotted to the subplots. To change the height or width of any of them, use the notation in the following example:

```
plot(s[1], s[2], s[3], s[4], s[5], s[6];
    layout = @layout [ a a a
                       a{0.68w} a
                       a{0.5h} ])
```

The specifications inside the curly brackets are width or height as a fraction of the entire plot. This call creates the layout in Figure 4-27.

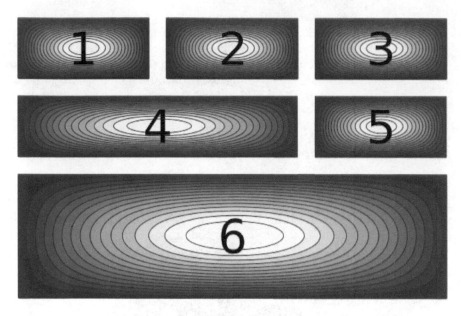

Figure 4-27: Using the @layout macro with dimension specifications

We can achieve even greater flexibility in layouts by using a call to grid() within the @layout argument, as in the following example:

```
plot(s[1], s[2], s[3], s[4], s[5], s[6];
    layout=@layout [ grid(2, 2) a{0.3w}
                           b{0.2h} ])
```

The number of subplots passed to the @layout macro must equal the number in the positional arguments to plots(). The grid(2, 2) call here accounts for four subplots, and the remaining two are represented by a and b. Figure 4-28 shows the result.

Figure 4-28: Using subgrids within a layout

"Detail Insets" on page 106 explained how to create inset plots that magnified a section of a main plot. We can use the `inset` and `subplot` attributes that we used there to make any kind of inset, not merely one using `lens!()`, and we can combine it with any layout.

After creating the layout in the previous example, we can add an inset to it with this call:

```
plot!(x -> sin(7x); inset=bbox(0.2, 0.2, 0.3, 0.3), subplot=7,
    background_inside=RGBA(1, 1, 1, 0.3), lw=5, framestyle=:box,
    legend=false, lc=:black)
```

The `inset` attribute is set to a `bbox`. Since we didn't supply it with a positional argument, the `bbox` parameters will position the plot relative to the entire layout, rather than any particular subplot. The `subplot=7` setting makes the inset into a new subplot, which is necessary to make this work as intended, as the layout already has six subplots. `RGBA` is similar to the `RGB` that we saw before, but with a final parameter for the opacity.

Figure 4-29 shows the result of adding the inset.

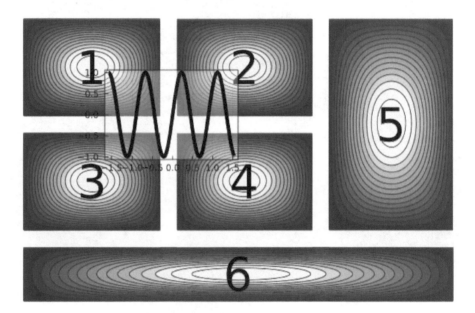

Figure 4-29: Adding a floating inset to a layout

Conclusion

This chapter covered everything about the `Plots` package that you'll need for most scientific graphics: the main types of plots, lenses and annotations, how to customize appearance, and how to lay out sets of graphs to form a composite illustration. In Chapter 7 we'll find out how to make animations and explore some packages to create diagrams, and in Chapter 8 we'll revisit the plotting system to learn about plot recipes.

FURTHER READING

- The official reference for the `Plots` package is available at *https://docs.juliaplots.org/latest/*.

- Here's where you can find a video about `Plots` by its creator: *http://www.breloff.com/plots-video*.

- For a useful guide to making publication-quality plots, visit *https://nextjournal.com/leandromartinez98/tips-to-create-beautiful-publication-quality-plots-in-julia*.

- More information on the HDF5 format is available at *https://www.hdfgroup.org/solutions/hdf5*.

- Documentation on using HDF5 files in Julia is available at *https://juliaio.github.io/HDF5.jl/stable/*.

- For more information on predefined palettes for plots, visit *https://docs.juliaplots.org/latest/generated/colorschemes/*.

- The Gaston headquarters, at *https://mbaz.github.io/Gaston.jl/stable*, contains a well-chosen illustration.

- Information and software downloads for gnuplot are available at *http://gnuplot.info*.

- The basics of LaTeX math syntax are available at *https://www.cs.princeton.edu/courses/archive/spr10/cos433/Latex/latex-guide.pdf* (see Section 7).

- Documentation on a Julia wrapper over the powerful *plotly.js* interactive plotting system is available through the `plotlyjs` package: *https://plotly.com/julia/*.

5

COLLECTIONS

I don't want to belong to any club that would accept me as one of its members.
–Attributed to Groucho Marx

A *collection* is a data structure that functions as a container. The values that it holds are its *elements*. Julia's collections are distinguished from each other by what they can contain, whether or not they are mutable, how their elements are accessed, whether their contents are ordered, and several other characteristics.

We've already worked with arrays, strings, and other kinds of Julia containers. In this chapter, we'll learn more about those collections and meet some new ones.

Controlling Loop Execution

There is an intimate relationship between loops and collections in Julia. The for loop, for example, depends on a collection or an iterable object whose elements are visited in turn.

We already know how to write loops using while and for blocks. In this section, we'll explore how to further control loop execution with the break and continue statements, and how to write compact loops with *comprehensions*, a concise way to create collections.

The break Statement

Sometimes we need to end a loop based on some condition and prevent it from reaching its "normal" termination. This is the purpose of the `break` command, which terminates both `while` and `for` loops.

For example, the following loop repeatedly asks the user for a number and prints its square root:

```
while true
    println("Enter a number, or 0 to quit.")
    x = readline()
    x = parse(Float64, x)
    if x ≤ 0
      ❶ break
    end
  ❷ println("The square root is ", sqrt(x))
end
```

The `while` condition is true, which never changes, so the loop would run forever were it not for the `break` statement ❶, which terminates the loop if the user enters 0 (or a negative number). This is a common pattern when intending a loop to run forever until halted by a condition arising with the loop.

The `readline()` statement reads a line of input from the terminal, terminated when the user presses ENTER, and puts the result into a string variable. We need to interpret this string as a number, which is what the `parse()` function does for us. The first argument to `parse()` specifies what data type to convert the string to. The multi-argument version of the `println()` function concatenates its arguments, converting numbers to strings as needed ❷.

The `break` statement also terminates `for` loops. In the following example, we loop through the numbers in a vector and stop if we get to one that's a perfect square:

```
n = [12, 53, 19, 64, 16, 8]

for x in n
    if round( √x ) == √x
        println("Found a perfect square in the list: ", x)
        break
    end
end
```

When this is run, it prints this:

```
Found a perfect square in the list: 64
```

A number is a perfect square if its square root is an integer. The code tests for that by comparing the number's square root with the same quantity rounded by the round() function. Since round() rounds a number to the near-est integer, the two will have the same value if the number is already an integer. The break statement terminates the loop when the first perfect square is found, so we never hear about 16.

The continue Statement

The continue statement skips further processing in the current loop iteration and proceeds to the next one. This program prints out the first 100 prime numbers (we'll skip the output):

```
for n in 1:100
    possibly_prime = true
    x = 2
    while x ≤ √n
    ❶ if n % x == 0
            possibly_prime = false
            break
        end
        x += 1
    end
    if !possibly_prime
    ❷ continue
    else
        println(n)
    end
end
```

The program tests the first 100 integers by checking for integer divisors up to the square root of the integer. If x is a divisor of n, there is no remainder when we calculate n/x; this is what n % x == 0 checks for ❶. If we find a divisor, n is not prime, so we set a flag indicating that and break out of the while loop over x. In the outer for loop, we want to continue ❷ to the next n if the current one is not prime, but print it if it is.

Comprehensions and Generators

We often can write for loops that create arrays more concisely as *array comprehensions*. As a simple example, suppose we wanted a Vector containing the first five perfect squares. We can construct this with a for loop, as in the following REPL session listing, but first we have to initialize an empty Vector:

```
julia> xs = [];

julia> for x in 1:5
           push!(xs, x^2)
       end
```

```
julia> xs
5-element Vector{Any}:
  1
  4
  9
 16
 25
```

We can accomplish the same thing with an array comprehension:

```
julia> xs = [x^2 for x in 1:5]
5-element Vector{Int64}:
  1
  4
  9
 16
 25
```

We don't need to initialize the xs vector, as the comprehension creates and populates it in one step. The types of the results in these examples are different, a subject that we'll examine in Chapter 8.

Array comprehensions typically contain two main parts, separated by the keyword for. The first part is an expression involving a dummy variable, in this case x. The second part, beginning with for, has the same form as the first line of the familiar for loop and uses the dummy variable from the first part. The first part becomes the body of the implied loop, adding a new element to the resulting array at each iteration.

The array that the comprehension creates will have the same shape as the container in its second part. Consider the following:

```
julia> [2x for x in [1 2
                     3 4]]
2×2 Matrix{Int64}:
 2  4
 6  8
```

Here, since the container iterates over a 2×2 matrix, that is the shape of the result as well.

An array comprehension can contain any number of implied loops. The shape of the result depends on whether the loops are separated by for or by a comma. The following examples illustrate the two possibilities:

```
julia> [x * y for x in 1:3 for y in 1:3]
9-element Vector{Int64}:
 1
 2
 3
 2
 4
```

```
6
3
6
9

julia> [x * y for x in 1:3, y in 1:3]
3×3 Matrix{Int64}:
 1  2  3
 2  4  6
 3  6  9
```

In the first case, the result is a Vector, as we might expect from two nested for loops. The second case, using a comma to separate the implied loops, produces a Matrix. We can add more comma-separated loop clauses to extend this to any number of dimensions.

Consider the following example that determines which even numbers in the multiplication table are divisible by 7:

```
julia> [x * y for x in 1:9, y in 1:9
       if x * y % 2 == 0 &&
       x * y % 7 == 0] |> unique
4-element Vector{Int64}:
 14
 28
 42
 56
```

An if statement at the end of a comprehension filters the results; the final result of the comprehension is a Vector. This example depends on the order of operations to avoid unnecessary parentheses: multiplication comes before (binds more tightly) than the modulus operator %. We pass the result of the comprehension to the unique() function, which removes duplicate entries from a collection.

A *generator expression* has the same form as an array comprehension, but without the enclosing square brackets. It creates an iterator, rather than a populated array. We can loop, or iterate, over this object to use its members one at a time, but it occupies almost no memory. In this way it should recall range expressions and their relationship to vectors.

In practice, we sometimes need to enclose the generator expression in parentheses to avoid ambiguity, as with any other expression. This is the case in the following example, where we create a generator version of our multiplication table:

```
julia> multiplication_generator = (x * y for x in 1:9, y in 1:9)
```

We need the parentheses because of the double for loop. Julia will not recognize this as a generator expression without them.

Now we can extract, as before, the even numbers in the table that are divisible by 7:

```
julia> [n for n in multiplication_generator
        if n % 2 == 0 && n % 7 == 0]
        |> unique
4-element Vector{Int64}:
 14
 28
 42
 56
```

If the table were large, rather than merely 9×9, using a generator rather than populating an array would provide significant memory savings. We can always use collect() to produce the realized table from the iterator.

More Ways to Join Strings

A string in Julia is a collection. Its elements are characters. We first met the String type in "Strings and Characters" on page 44, and here we'll explore the most important operations you can perform on strings.

We've seen how we can join strings using the * operator or using join() to form a string from a vector of strings. We can also use the string() function, which joins any number of literal strings and string-valued variables into a larger String:

```
julia> comma_space = ", ";
```

```
julia> string("Hello", comma_space, "François")
"Hello, François"
```

Since comma_space is a string, the string() function simply glues it to the other strings we supplied. If it were some other type of object, such as a number, the call would still work if the object had a string representation. In that case, the function first converts it to a string and then performs the join.

The repeat() function joins a string to itself a specified number of times:

```
julia> repeat("ABC ", 5)
"ABC ABC ABC ABC ABC "
```

In this example, the new string is formed from "ABC" repeated five times, as specified in the second argument.

We can also use this function to create arrays, as we'll see in "The repeat() Function" on page 139.

Nonstandard String Literals

A *string literal* is an expression such as "abc" that represents a String directly. Julia supports a variety of *nonstandard* string literals, represented by placing a keyword in front of the string literal with the prefix specifying what kind of special-purpose string the expression represents. Such objects carry a significance beyond their existence as strings.

We've already met an example of one of these objects. In "LaTeX Titles and Label Positioning by Data" on page 103, we described how to use LaTeX strings as graph labels. These are prefixed with an uppercase L, as in L"e^{iπ} + 1 = 0". When the graphing programs see an ordinary string used as a label, the string is printed on the graph verbatim, but if the label is a LaTeX string, the programs know to print its LaTeX-processed form. LaTeX strings are defined in the LaTeXStrings package. Some nonstandard string literals are defined in their own packages, which need to be imported before you can use them, while others are built in.

Under the hood, nonstandard string literals are implemented as macros (see "Macros" on page 170). The name of the macro is the tag of the string literal followed by _str. In other words, the name of the macro implementing LaTeX strings is @L_str. To see the documentation for a nonstandard string literal in the REPL, we enter either ?@L_str or ?L"" (for LaTeX strings).

Raw Strings

One useful built-in nonstandard string literal is the *raw string*, written by prepending raw. Most keywords for nonstandard strings are single letters, but raw is an exception. Raw strings are used to represent certain character sequences literally, where in standard strings they would have an interpretation as control characters or something else. For example, ordinarily the sequence \t is converted into a TAB character when printing a string, but in a raw string it's interpreted literally:

```
julia> print(raw"a\tb")
a\tb
julia> print("a\tb")
a       b
```

In the second print command, the non-escaped TAB character is rendered as a horizontal space.

Within raw strings, therefore, backslashes are interpreted literally, with one exception—they are still needed to escape double quotation marks:

```
julia> print("I said, \"No\".")
I said, "No".
julia> print(raw"I said, \"No\".")
I said, "No".
```

If a backslash appears anywhere in a raw string aside from directly before a double quotation mark, it's interpreted literally.

Semantic Version Strings

Versions of software releases are identified with tags such as v1.7.1. Different projects use different systems for version tags; one such system is called *semantic versioning*. The fields in the string refer to major and minor versions and, optionally, other versioning information. See "Further Reading" on page 151 for a link to the detailed specification.

Prepend a v to create a semantic version string. We can compare versions and extract the numerical value of fields, which are returned as hexadecimal numbers, indicated by a leading 0x:

```
julia> v"1.6.1" < v"1.6.2"
true

julia> version = v"1.7.2"
v"1.7.2"

julia> version.major, version.minor, version.patch
(0x00000001, 0x00000007, 0x00000002)
```

The Julia project itself uses an extended version of this scheme for numbering language and package releases, so semantic version strings are built into the language.

Byte Array Literals

Prepending a string with b creates a *byte array literal*: a sequence of unsigned, 8-bit integers representing the sequence of characters in the string in UTF-8 encoding. As described in "Strings and Characters" on page 44, characters can take up one to four bytes. Here's an example of turning a three-character string into a byte array:

```
julia> b"a2Σ"
4-element Base.CodeUnits{UInt8, String}:
 0x61
 0x32
 0xce
 0xa3
```

The characters a and 2 are each represented by a single byte, but the character Σ occupies two bytes.

We can enter the uppercase sigma as a character in the REPL to learn more about it:

```
julia> 'Σ'
'Σ': Unicode U+03A3 (category Lu: Letter, uppercase)
```

The response informs us that 03A3 is the Unicode *code point* for the character. The code point is a single, possibly large, hexadecimal integer that uniquely identifies the Unicode character.

NOTE *A Unicode character may not correspond to a single character when printed. Some of them combine with one or more neighboring characters to create accents or ligatures.*

We can use code points directly in strings with the escape code \u, where they'll be converted into the characters they represent:

```julia
julia> "a2\u03a3"
"a2Σ"
```

To avoid the conversion, we can escape the backslash or use a raw string.

String Searching and Replacing

The replace() function replaces a substring with a different one. It can take any number of replacements, which are applied left to right, with the proviso that no character undergoes more than one substitution. The following example demonstrates the syntax as well as the consequence of the proviso:

```julia
julia> s = "abc"
"abc"

julia> replace(s, "b" => "XX", "c" => "Z")
"aXXZ"

julia> replace(s, "c" => "Z", "Z" => "WWW")
"abZ"
```

The proviso means that the "Z" in the first replacement in the last example is not replaced by "WWW".

NOTE *Multiple replacements in the string replace() function first appeared in Julia v1.7. If you are using an earlier version, you can use the replace() function as described here, but with only one replacement.*

The occursin() function tests for the presence of a substring in a string:

```julia
julia> occursin("abc", "abcdef")
true

julia> occursin("abc", "abCdef")
false
```

This tests for the existence, in the second argument, of the string given in the first argument, and it's case-sensitive.

The occursin() function follows the tradition of other functions, such as iseven(), that test a condition and return true or false (see "The filter() Operator" on page 163).

The findfirst() and findlast() functions each search for the location of a character or string in another string. If we ask for the location of a character, the functions return the index of its first or last occurence:

```julia
julia> findfirst('a', "abcabc")
1
```

```
julia> findlast('a', "abcabc")
4
```

If, instead of a character, we supply a string in the first argument, the functions return a range giving the location of the string in the second string:

```
julia> findfirst("abc", "abcabc")
1:3
```

```
julia> findlast("abc", "abcabc")
4:6
```

These functions return `nothing` if the character or string we're searching for does not exist in the second string.

The `findnext()` function behaves similarly, but it accepts a third argument giving the location to begin the search:

```
q = "To be or not to be, that is the question"
i = 0
locations = []

❶ while i != nothing
    i = findnext('e', q, i + 1)
    push!(locations, i)
end

print("""The letter "e" was found at locations """,
        join(locations[1:end-1], ", ", " and "), ".")
```

This demonstrates a third optional positional argument for `join()`, which is inserted in place of the delimiter (given in the second argument) between the final two elements.

When we run this program, it prints:

```
The letter "e" was found at locations 5, 18, 31 and 35.
```

If `findnext()` or the other string search functions don't find what they're looking for, they return nothing, or, more specifically, a particular value called `nothing`. We take advantage of this in the `while` condition ❶ to end the loop when there are no further e characters to be found.

All of the searching and replacing functions described in this section work with regular expressions as well. Julia uses Perl-compatible regular expressions; consult "Further Reading" on page 151 for a link to the syntax.

To define a regular expression, we use a nonstandard string literal with the r keyword. For example, `r"A.*B"` is a regular expression matching A followed by any number of characters ending with B.

Here's a simple use of a regular expression to delete everything between a particular pair of characters:

```
julia> s = "abc<ABC>def"
"abc<ABC>def"

julia> replace(s, r"<.*>" => "")
"abcdef"
```

Parenthesized fragments in the regular expression become targets that we can refer to, in the replacement text, using escaped integers. These integers follow the order of the parenthesized fragments, so the first one is referenced by \1, and so on. In a normal string such escaped integers are interpreted as control characters; therefore, Julia has another nonstandard string literal for this purpose, using the s keyword:

```
julia> replace(s, r"(.*)<(.*)>(.*)" => s"\1\3, \2")
"abcdef, ABC"
```

This replacement moves the delimited string to the end, preceded by some punctuation, instead of deleting the string between the angle brackets.

String Interpolation

Julia happily borrows good ideas from other languages. Perl not only has powerful regular expressions, it also has a convenient syntax for *string interpolation*, which you can use in Julia.

We use string interpolation when we want to insert the values of variables or expressions into a string. The interpolation syntax tells Julia to create the string representations of these values and place them within a larger string. Interpolation lets us avoid messy sequences of string concatenations in favor of neater code:

```
julia> function name_length()
           println("Hi. What's your name?")
       ❶ name = readline()
       ❷ println("Hello, $name. Your name has $(length(name)) letters.")
       end
name_length (generic function with 1 method)

julia> name_length()
Hi. What's your name?
Emily
Hello, Emily. Your name has 5 letters.
```

This example demonstrates the two kinds of string interpolation, both in the argument to the println() call ❷. After the name entered by the user is stored in the variable name ❶, we can access its value using string interpolation. To interpolate the value of the variable, just use its name after a dollar sign (\$). To interpolate another type of expression, put it inside parentheses after the \$. We did this in order to interpolate the length of the user's name ❷.

We can interpolate any expression into a string. If we want to exclude spaces (because they are not letters) from the length of the name, we could use the following:

```
println("Hello, $name. Your name has $(length(replace(name, " " => ""))) letters.")
```

If you need an actual dollar sign, escape it with a backslash: \\\$. Naturally, raw strings do not partake of the interpolation process.

Additional Collection Types

This section describes additional types of collections that are all part of routine Julia programming: dictionaries, sets, structs, and named tuples.

Dictionaries

Julia's Dict type is similar to dictionaries in Python or associative arrays in Bash. It's a one-dimensional collection like a vector that's indexed by *key* rather than position. Listing 5-1 shows one of two ways to initialize a dictionary.

```
julia> bd = Dict("one"=>1, "two"=>2)
Dict{String, Int64} with 2 entries:
  "two" => 2
  "one" => 1
```

Listing 5-1: Creating a dictionary from key-value pairs

After this initialization, the new dictionary contains two key-value pairs. Each key in this dictionary happens to be the name of the number that it indexes.

In addition to supplying the key-value pairs as separate arguments, we can supply any iterable object that yields key-value pairs when iterated over. We can initialize the dictionary from Listing 5-1, for example, with Dict(["one"=>1; "two"=>2]).

The keys and values in a dictionary can be of any type. In bd both of the keys are strings, and the values they point to are integers.

The syntax for indexing dictionaries is the same as for indexing vectors, but the indices are the keys, not the positions:

```
julia> bd["one"]
1

julia> bd[2]
ERROR: KeyError: key 2 not found
```

We initialize the bd dictionary with two key-value pairs; as 2 is not one of the keys, our attempt to index it with 2 produces an error.

The keys(bd) function returns a list of the keys in bd; a corresponding values() function returns a list of values.

The keys in a Dict must be unique. If we define an entry with a key that already exists, the later definition replaces the existing one:

```
julia> bd["one"] = 9;

julia> bd
Dict{String, Int64} with 2 entries:
  "two" => 2
  "one" => 9
```

In the first line we reuse the "one" key. Displaying the dictionary shows that the new value has replaced the earlier one.

The other way to initialize dictionaries is to pass a single argument to Dict(). The argument can be any iterable that yields tuples; each tuple generates a key-value pair:

```
julia> Dict([("one", 1) ("two", 2)])
Dict{String, Int64} with 2 entries:
  "two" => 2
  "one" => 1
```

Notice that the dictionary is printed in what appears to be a random order. This is normal, as dictionaries are *unordered* collections, unlike vectors.

Sets

Julia's Set data type implements many of the properties of mathematical sets. A set in Julia is a collection defined by what elements are contained within it. The elements have no order, and the set can't be indexed. If you add an element that's already there, the set doesn't change because it already contains the element, which can appear only once.

Let's define two simple sets that we'll use to illustrate some of the operations we can perform on them:

```
julia> s1 = Set(1:5)
Set{Int64} with 5 elements:
  5
  4
  2
  3
  1

julia> s2 = Set(4:8)
Set{Int64} with 5 elements:
  5
```

```
    4
    6
    7
    8
```

The Set() function, which takes any iterable object, initializes sets. The sets' members are listed in the REPL in an arbitrary order, as order is meaningless within a set.

Let's ask for the intersection and union of the two sets we just created:

```
julia> intersect(s1, s2)
Set{Int64} with 2 elements:
    5
    4

julia> union(s1, s2)
Set{Int64} with 8 elements:
    5
    4
    6
    7
    2
    8
    3
    1
```

The results in both examples are also sets. The intersection is the set of elements common to both sets, while the union is the set of elements existing in either set.

We can test for a subset relationship between sets with the issubset() function, which has a Unicode synonym that we also can use as a binary operator:

```
julia> issubset(4:7, s2)
true

julia> 4:7 ⊆ s2
true
```

❶ julia> 4:7 ⊇ s2
false

To create the subset or superset ❶ characters, we enter \subseteq or \supseteq, respectively, followed by TAB. The functions converted the range 4:7 into a set automatically and told us that Set(4:7) is a subset of s2, because every member of the former is a member of the latter.

We can find the *difference* between two sets, which are the elements of one set that are not in another set, using the setdiff() function:

```
julia> s1
Set{Int64} with 5 elements:
  5
  4
  2
  3
  1

julia> setdiff(s1, 3:5)
Set{Int64} with 2 elements:
  2
  1
```

The result shows us what remains after removing 3, 4, and 5 from s1.

The mutating form of this function removes the members of the second set from the first. To add new elements to a set, use push!():

```
julia> push!(s1, 999);

julia> setdiff!(s1, 1:3)
Set{Int64} with 3 elements:
  5
  4
  999
```

In this example, first we enlarge s1 with the member 999, and then we remove the elements in Set(1:3).

Structs

A struct is a collection of named values packaged together under one identifier. For an example, Listing 5-2 creates a struct to hold two pieces of information identifying a web page.

```
julia> struct Website
           url
           title
       end

julia> google = Website("https://google.com", "google")
Website("https://google.com", "google")
```

Listing 5-2: Defining a struct

First we define a new struct called Website, and then we create a variable, google, that holds a particular instance of Website with specific values for url and title.

Conventional style is to capitalize the names of structs. A struct's name is used as a *constructor* that creates *composite objects* with the struct's type.

Therefore, making a struct extends Julia by adding a new type to the language. Asking Julia for the type of google with typeof(google) returns Website. See "User-Defined Types" on page 234 for more about the utility and power of user-defined types.

We can reference the fields of composite objects such as structs and the named tuples (described next) using *property notation*:

```julia
julia> google.title
"google"
```

```julia
julia> google.title = "Google"
ERROR: setfield!: immutable struct of type Website cannot be changed
```

After noticing that we forgot to capitalize the title of the website, we try to correct it, but Julia doesn't allow the change because, by default, structs are immutable.

We can fix our error by defining google anew, but if we plan to mutate Website objects routinely, we can define them as *mutable structs*:

```julia
julia> mutable struct MutableWebsite
           url
           title
       end
```

```julia
julia> google = MutableWebsite("https://google.com", "google")
MutableWebsite("https://google.com", "google")
```

```julia
julia> google.title = "Google"
"Google"
```

Now we can change the values of google's fields whenever we want.

Named Tuples

A named tuple is just like Julia's ordinary Tuple, except we can give names to its values:

```julia
julia> nt = (a=1, b=2, c=3);
```

```julia
julia> nt.c
3
```

Now we have a new named tuple called nt, with three fields called a, b, and c. As this example shows, we extract values from a named tuple using property notation, just as with structs.

Named tuples are immutable, just as (immutable) structs and ordinary tuples:

```julia
julia> nt.a = 17
ERROR: setfield!: immutable struct of type NamedTuple cannot be changed
```

The attempt to assign to a field of an immutable data type is not allowed.

Tuples and named tuples are intimately related to function argument lists, as we'll explore in "Functions and Their Arguments" on page 154.

Initializing Arrays with Functions

Julia provides a handful of functions to initialize arrays. Using one of these is often more convenient and concise than the literal array definitions that we've been using up to now.

The repeat() Function

The repeat() function repeats an array a given number of times along each dimension corresponding to the arguments you supply:

```
julia> repeat(['a' 'b' '|'], 4, 3)
4×9 Matrix{Char}:
 'a'  'b'  '|'  'a'  'b'  '|'  'a'  'b'  '|'
 'a'  'b'  '|'  'a'  'b'  '|'  'a'  'b'  '|'
 'a'  'b'  '|'  'a'  'b'  '|'  'a'  'b'  '|'
 'a'  'b'  '|'  'a'  'b'  '|'  'a'  'b'  '|'
```

In this example, the elements of the one-row array ['a' 'b' '|'] are replicated four times in the first (column) direction and three times in the second (row) direction.

We've already met repeat(), as a function that replicates a string, in "More Ways to Join Strings" on page 128.

The fill() Function

The fill() function takes the value supplied in its first argument and creates an array with a shape given by its subsequent arguments, filling it with the value. Listing 5-3 shows how it works.

```
julia> XY = fill(['X' 'Y'], 3, 4)
3×4 Matrix{Matrix{Char}}:
 ['X' 'Y']  ['X' 'Y']  ['X' 'Y']  ['X' 'Y']
 ['X' 'Y']  ['X' 'Y']  ['X' 'Y']  ['X' 'Y']
 ['X' 'Y']  ['X' 'Y']  ['X' 'Y']  ['X' 'Y']
```

Listing 5-3: Filling an array

Here the value ['X' 'Y'] is used to fill a 3×4 array. Unlike repeat(), fill() can accept the dimensions as a tuple as well as separate arguments, so we can write the above as fill(['X' 'Y'], (3, 4)).

The most important difference beteen repeat() and fill() is that the former concatenates the elements of the array supplied in the first argument into the requested shape, whereas the latter concatenates the array itself. This can be seen in the results of the two examples just shown.

Mutability with the fill() and repeat() Functions

Let's try to change one of the elements of the matrix XY defined in Listing 5-3. We'll try to change the 'X' to an 'O' in the top-right element:

```julia
julia> XY[1, 4][1] = 'O';

julia> XY
3×4 Matrix{Matrix{Char}}:
 ['O' 'Y']  ['O' 'Y']  ['O' 'Y']  ['O' 'Y']
 ['O' 'Y']  ['O' 'Y']  ['O' 'Y']  ['O' 'Y']
 ['O' 'Y']  ['O' 'Y']  ['O' 'Y']  ['O' 'Y']
```

The result is surprising to many who encounter it for the first time. In altering one of the elements of XY, we've altered them all. This happens because fill() doesn't *copy* its first argument into multiple locations in the result. Each element of XY is the identical one-row matrix; the output here shows the result of mutating this matrix.

If, instead of mutating the element, we *replace* it, something different happens:

```julia
julia> XY = fill(['X' 'Y'], 3, 4);

julia> XY[1, 4] = ['O' 'Y'];

julia> XY
3×4 Matrix{Matrix{Char}}:
 ['X' 'Y']  ['X' 'Y']  ['X' 'Y']  ['O' 'Y']
 ['X' 'Y']  ['X' 'Y']  ['X' 'Y']  ['X' 'Y']
 ['X' 'Y']  ['X' 'Y']  ['X' 'Y']  ['X' 'Y']
```

Now XY contains two different matrices, one of them appearing 11 times.

We would observe exactly the same behavior using repeat() if we placed the first argument within an extra set of square brackets:

```julia
julia> XY = repeat([['X' 'Y']], 3, 4);
```

In this way, after repeat() extracts the contents of the first argument and concatenates them, we still have an array of arrays.

To get an array of *different* arrays, rather than the array of references to a single array that fill() constructs, we can use a comprehension:

```julia
julia> xy = [['X' 'Y'] for i in 1:3, j in 1:4]
3×4 Matrix{Matrix{Char}}:
 ['X' 'Y']  ['X' 'Y']  ['X' 'Y']  ['X' 'Y']
 ['X' 'Y']  ['X' 'Y']  ['X' 'Y']  ['X' 'Y']
 ['X' 'Y']  ['X' 'Y']  ['X' 'Y']  ['X' 'Y']

julia> xy[1, 4][1] = 'O';
```

```
julia> xy
3x4 Matrix{Matrix{Char}}:
 ['X' 'Y']  ['X' 'Y']  ['X' 'Y']  ['O' 'Y']
 ['X' 'Y']  ['X' 'Y']  ['X' 'Y']  ['X' 'Y']
 ['X' 'Y']  ['X' 'Y']  ['X' 'Y']  ['X' 'Y']
```

Now altering one of the arrays has no effect on the other elements of xy because each element is a separate array.

The zeros() and ones() Functions

The zeros() and ones() functions act as special cases of fill() with 0.0 or 1.0 as a first argument. Like fill(), they accept either tuples or separate numbers for dimensions:

```
julia> zeros(4, 5)
4x5 Matrix{Float64}:
 0.0  0.0  0.0  0.0  0.0
 0.0  0.0  0.0  0.0  0.0
 0.0  0.0  0.0  0.0  0.0
 0.0  0.0  0.0  0.0  0.0
```

The zeros() function creates a 4×5 matrix and fills it with 0.0.

Using zeros() or ones() is common when we need to initialize an array of floating-point numbers that's going to be populated by direct indexing. This method is faster than using push!() to enlarge the array as it's populated because the compiler knows the size of the array at the start, so reallocating memory isn't needed. However, push!() may be a better choice if you don't know the size of the array ahead of time and prefer not to allocate memory that the array won't need.

The reshape() Function

You can transform an array into a new shape with reshape():

```
julia> a1 = collect(1:6);

julia> a2 = reshape(a1, (3, 2))
3x2 Matrix{Int64}:
 1  4
 2  5
 3  6

julia> reshape(a1, 2, 2)
ERROR: DimensionMismatch("new dimensions (2, 2) must
        be consistent with array size 6")
```

The first two examples show how to use reshape(): give the array as a first argument and its new dimensions either in a tuple or as a series of individual arguments. The last example produces an error because `reshape()` will not change the total number of elements.

The `reshape()` function does not create a new array, but returns the original array molded into a different shape. You can see the consequence of that when mutating either incarnation of the array:

```julia
julia> a1[5] = 0;

julia> a2
3×2 Matrix{Int64}:
 1  4
 2  0
 3  6
```

Changing the fifth element of a1 also changes the fifth element of a2, where, as always, the elements are in column-major order.

The behavior of `reshape()` should call to mind the remarks in "Scalar Indexing" on page 38: arrays are stored contiguously in the computer's one-dimensional memory, which is reflected in their scalar indexing. The multidimensional forms of arrays that we use in our programs are abstractions, without which algorithms would be far more cumbersome to express in code.

Array Manipulations Useful in Numerical Algorithms

Arrays are the most important data type, aside from numbers, in scientific and numerical computing. Our algorithms often take the form of a series of transformations and operations upon vectors, matrices, and higher-dimensional arrays. Julia's powerful array handling helps us to express these computations in terms of high-level operations on entire arrays, rather than verbose loops over their elements. This style of programming, when we can use it, is conceptually clearer and less prone to error. This section surveys several array operations that arise repeatedly in scientific code.

General Concatenation

We've discussed the semicolon as a concatenation operator along the first dimension, as in this example:

```julia
julia> m = [[1 2]; [3 4]]
2×2 Matrix{Int64}:
 1  2
 3  4
```

As an alternative, we can replace the single semicolon with a newline, making the input resemble the way Julia prints the matrix in the REPL.

NOTE *The use of repeated semicolons described in this section arrived with Julia v1.7. In earlier versions, repeated semicolons were treated as a single semicolon.*

A series of n semicolons concatenates along the nth dimension, adding new dimensions as needed, so two semicolons concatenate along the second dimension, which is also how a space concatenates:

```
julia> m = [[1 2];; [3 4]]
1×4 Matrix{Int64}:
 1  2  3  4

julia> m = [[1 2] [3 4]]
1×4 Matrix{Int64}:
 1  2  3  4
```

Both examples perform the same operation: [1 2] is concatenated with [3 4] along the second, or column, dimension, increasing the number of columns.

Using three semicolons creates a new third dimension and joins along it:

```
julia> m = [[1 2];;; [3 4]]
1×2×2 Array{Int64, 3}:
[:, :, 1] =
 1  2

[:, :, 2] =
 3  4
```

In this example, the [3 4] array is put "on top" of the [1 2] array, in what is sometimes called a new *plane*.

Logical Indexing

Julia can store an array of Boolean values in a space-efficient manner with its BitArray data type. In a BitArray, or the subtypes BitVector and BitMatrix, true and false are represented by 1 and 0. These logical arrays are used for indexing, where they act as filters, selecting elements corresponding in position to the 1 values and rejecting the ones corresponding to the 0 values. When used for indexing, the array being indexed and the BitArray must have the same number of elements.

We create a BitArray with a logical condition broadcast into an array. For example, the following creates a BitArray that picks out which elements of 1:9 are divisible by 3:

```
julia> s3 = (1:9) .% 3 .== 0
9-element BitVector:
 0
 0
 1
 0
 0
 1
 0
```

```
0
1
```

In order to return the result, Julia instantiates the range expression into an array. Each location that gives a zero remainder when divided by 3 is indicated by a `1`, and the others by a `0`.

We assigned the `BitArray` to a variable so we can use it in other expressions. We can use it on the `1:9` range itself:

```julia
julia> (1:9)[s3]
3-element Vector{Int64}:
 3
 6
 9
```

The 1s in `s3` pick out the elements in `1:9` that are divisible by 3.

We can also use it to select every third element from any collection with nine elements:

```julia
julia> ('a':'i')[s3]
3-element Vector{Char}:
 'c': ASCII/Unicode U+0063 (category Ll: Letter, lowercase)
 'f': ASCII/Unicode U+0066 (category Ll: Letter, lowercase)
 'i': ASCII/Unicode U+0069 (category Ll: Letter, lowercase)
```

Although the collection we're indexing and the `BitArray` must have the same number of elements, the collection can have any shape if the `BitArray` is a `BitVector`; otherwise, the array and the `BitArray` must have the same shape.

Here's an example of using `BitArray` indexing, also called logical indexing, as a concise way to print out all the integers in [1, 100] that are divisible by 17:

```julia
julia> (1:100)[(1:100) .% 17 .== 0]
5-element Vector{Int64}:
 17
 34
 51
 68
 85
```

The only difference here is that we create the bit index and use it in an indexing expression in one step, rather than storing it in a variable for later use.

Adjoints and Transposes

The transpose of a matrix is the matrix formed by flipping it across its diagonal, so that $M'_{ij} = M_{ji}$ when M' is the transpose of M. The adjoint of a matrix is formed by taking its transpose and replacing each of its elements by its complex conjugate (the terminology is consistent with the concept of the adjoint of a linear operator, if matrices are regarded as linear transformations applied to vectors through conventional matrix multiplication).

To flip a matrix `MR` containing real numbers across its diagonal, we can use three notations: `MR'`, `adjoint(MR)`, or `permutedims(MR)`. Listing 5-4 shows that they all give the same results.

```
julia> MR = [[1 2]; [3 4]]
2×2 Matrix{Int64}:
 1  2
 3  4

julia> MR'
2×2 adjoint(::Matrix{Int64}) with eltype Int64:
 1  3
 2  4

julia> MR' == adjoint(MR) == permutedims(MR)
true
```

Listing 5-4: Matrix adjoint notations

Since the elements of `MR` are their own complex conjugates, its adjoint is just its transpose.

However, if the matrix's elements are almost anything else, `adjoint()` and `permutedims()` generally give different results; the ' operator is a synonym for `adjoint()`. The `permutedims()` function flips the matrix around the diagonal and does nothing else, as shown here, and `adjoint()` does the same flip, called a *transpose*, but also takes the complex conjugate of each element. This operation is also known as the *Hermitian adjoint*. Consider this example:

```
julia> M = [[1+im 2+2im]; [3+3im 4+4im]]
2×2 Matrix{Complex{Int64}}:
 1+1im  2+2im
 3+3im  4+4im

julia> M'
2×2 adjoint(::Matrix{Complex{Int64}}) with eltype Complex{Int64}:
 1-1im  3-3im
 2-2im  4-4im
```

The matrix is flipped, as before, but now with each element replaced by its complex conjugate. Note that we can't use the `adjoint()` function on non-numerical matrices, where the complex conjugate of the elements has no meaning.

In addition to `adjoint()` and `permutedims()`, we have the `transpose()` function:

```
julia> Mt = transpose(M)
2×2 transpose(::Matrix{Complex{Int64}}) with eltype Complex{Int64}:
```

```
1+1im   3+3im
2+2im   4+4im
```

The result looks like the simple transposition of M, with no complex conjugates taken, but this is what `permutedims()` is supposed to do. Why do we have two functions that seem to do the same thing?

The `adjoint()` and `transpose()` functions, on the one hand, and `permutedims()`, on the other, behave quite differently. The first two functions mentioned act recursively: if the elements of M are themselves matrices, `adjoint()` and `transpose()` will first act on M, then on the elements of M, and so on, all the way down. In contrast, `permutedims()` just flips M and stops.

The second difference is that, like `reshape()`, `adjoint()` and `transpose()` return the same array in a different form, so mutating the result mutates the original, unlike `permutedims()`, which returns a new array.

In general, to flip around tables of numbers, we turn to the `permutedims()` function. The other two functions are intended for more specialized linear algebra applications.

The `conj()` function, which takes the complete conjugate of a number, can of course be broadcast to work on each element of an array by using the dot operator. However, unlike most other math functions, it acts elementwise on arrays without broadcasting:

```
julia> conj(M)
2×2 Matrix{Complex{Int64}}:
 1-1im   2-2im
 3-3im   4-4im
```

Here we've taken the complex conjugate of each element to transform the matrix.

Matrix Multiplication

The multiplication operator (*) performs matrix multiplication when supplied with a pair of matrices or a matrix and a vector. As an example, we'll make a rotation matrix and matrix-multiply to rotate a vector:

```
julia> a = π/2
1.5707963267948966

julia> RM = [[cos(a) -sin(a)]; [sin(a) cos(a)]];

julia> RM * [1, 0]
2-element Vector{Float64}:
 6.123233995736766e-17
 1.0
```

The exact result should be [0, 1]: the rotation of a unit vector pointing "to the right" when rotated $\pi/2$ radians counterclockwise. The answer we get is the result of roundoff in floating-point arithmetic.

For serious work with matrices, systems of linear equations, and related fields, you should import the LinearAlgebra package, which we'll visit in "The LinearAlgebra Package" on page 399. That package has a function for calculating the *inverse* of a matrix, but we can calculate matrix inverses without importing the package with an intuitive notation:

```julia
julia> MR^-1
2×2 Matrix{Float64}:
 -2.0   1.0
  1.5  -0.5

julia> MR^-1 * MR
2×2 Matrix{Float64}:
 1.0          0.0
 2.22045e-16  1.0
```

In this example we use the matrix MR defined in Listing 5-4. The result of multiplying a matrix by its inverse (with matrix multiplication) should be the identity matrix (1s along the diagonal and 0s elsewhere), which, within floating-point roundoff, is what we get.

Enumeration and Zipping

Julia comes with several functions, common in modern high-level languages, for enumerating and zipping arrays. The former refers to the association of indices with the elements of a collection, while the latter refers to the joining, element by element, of two collections. All the functions in this section return iterators, either over a collection of tuples or over a collection of key-value pairs.

The enumerate() Function

The enumerate() function takes a collection and returns an iterator into a collection of tuples that contains the number of the iteration as their first elements and the member of the collection retrieved as their second elements. Listing 5-5 shows that the collection of tuples has the same shape as the original collection.

```julia
julia> collect(enumerate([10 20; 30 40]))
2×2 Matrix{Tuple{Int64, Int64}}:
 (1, 10)  (3, 20)
 (2, 30)  (4, 40)
```

Listing 5-5: Using enumerate()

Since enumerate() returns an iterator, we need to collect() it to see it. These iterators, like ranges and other iterators, such as the ones created by generators (see "Comprehensions and Generators" on page 125), take up almost no space until we use them to loop over a collection or turn them into an actual array with the collect() function.

The array that collect() returns in Listing 5-5 is laid out as specified in the argument to enumerate(), and the iteration numbers, the first elements of the tuples, reflect the column-major order in which the array was traversed.

The iteration numbers that enumerate() returns aren't guaranteed to be legal indices of the array. Even when they are, they don't necessarily return the element that they index. In other words, if one of the tuples enumerate(A) returns is (i, e), A[i] may be an error. If it's not an error, it may be the case that A[i] does not equal e.

In the case of a numerical array, such as in Listing 5-5, the first elements of the tuples *can* be used as scalar indices into the array, and enumerate() is sometimes used for this purpose.

An example of where the iteration number *cannot* be used as an index involves our old friend François:

```
julia> for letter in enumerate("François")
           println("Letter number $(letter[1]) is $(letter[2]).")
       end
Letter number 1 is F.
Letter number 2 is r.
Letter number 3 is a.
Letter number 4 is n.
Letter number 5 is ç.
Letter number 6 is o.
Letter number 7 is i.
Letter number 8 is s.
```

The iteration number tells us where each character appears in the string, but, as we saw in "Strings and Characters" on page 44, not all of these character positions are legal indices:

```
julia> "François"[5]
'ç': Unicode U+00E7 (category Ll: Letter, lowercase)
```

```
julia> "François"[6]
ERROR: StringIndexError: invalid index [6], valid nearby indices [5]=>'ç', [7]=>'o'
```

In summary, don't confuse iteration numbers with indexing.

The pairs() Function

The pairs() function is similar to enumerate(), except it creates an iterator over key-value pairs rather than over tuples:

```
julia> collect(pairs("François"))
8-element Vector{Pair{Int64, Char}}:
 1 => 'F'
 2 => 'r'
```

```
3 => 'a'
4 => 'n'
5 => 'ç'
7 => 'o'
8 => 'i'
9 => 's'
```

The indices returned by pairs() are legal indices into the collection rather than iteration numbers as with enumerate().

The objects in the iterator returned by enumerate() are tuples; those in the iterator returned by pairs() are key-value pairs. Such pairs have their own data type: Pair. If p is a Pair, we can access its key with p.first and its value with p.second. Therefore, if we need a vector of indices into the name of our French friend, we can get it this way:

```
julia> [p.first for p in pairs("François")]
8-element Vector{Int64}:
 1
 2
 3
 4
 5
 7
 8
 9
```

We can create a Pair with a constructor like Pair(9, 's'), or by using the => operator—for example, 9 => 's'.

In Listing 5-1, we created a dictionary from a series of key-value pairs entered directly. Each of those literal key-value pairs is a Pair; here's another way to construct the dictionary:

```
julia> p1 = "one" => 1
"one" => 1

julia> p2 = Pair("two", 2)
"two" => 2

julia> Dict([p1, p2]) == Dict("one"=>1, "two"=>2)
true
```

We make the pair p1 using the => operator and p2 using the Pair() constructor. Passing them to the Dict() function creates the same dictionary as in Listing 5-1.

A dictionary is an unordered collection of Pairs. Iterating through a dictionary produces each Pair in turn, but in an unpredictable order:

```
julia> Dict(pairs("François"))
Dict{Int64, Char} with 8 entries:
```

```
5 => 'ç'
4 => 'n'
7 => 'o'
2 => 'r'
9 => 's'
8 => 'i'
3 => 'a'
1 => 'F'
```

The zip() Function

The zip() function takes any number of collections and returns an iterator into a collection of tuples that combines the elements of the collections.

When the collections passed in have the same shape, the returned iterator will have that shape as well:

```
julia> zip([1 2; 3 4], ['a' 'b'; 'c' 'd']) |> collect
2×2 Matrix{Tuple{Int64, Char}}:
 (1, 'a')  (2, 'b')
 (3, 'c')  (4, 'd')
```

The first elements of each collection are paired together, followed by the second, and so on. In this use of zip(), the shapes of the arguments must match.

If one of the collections is a list, the other can have any shape. The elements of the list are paired with the elements of the other collection in column-major order:

```
julia> zip([1, 2, 3, 4], ['a' 'b'; 'c' 'd']) |> collect
4-element Vector{Tuple{Int64, Char}}:
 (1, 'a')
 (2, 'c')
 (3, 'b')
 (4, 'd')
```

Here a one-dimensional list is zipped with a 2×2 matrix; each has four elements.

When using a vector, the numbers of elements need not match; zip() will continue until it runs out of elements:

```
julia> zip(1:3, ['a' 'b'; 'c' 'd']) |> collect
3-element Vector{Tuple{Int64, Char}}:
 (1, 'a')
 (2, 'c')
 (3, 'b')
```

```
julia> zip(1:5, ['a' 'b'; 'c' 'd']) |> collect
4-element Vector{Tuple{Int64, Char}}:
 (1, 'a')
```

```
(2, 'c')
(3, 'b')
(4, 'd')
```

In the first example, the three-element vector is exhausted before we run out of elements in the 2×2 matrix. In the second example, the second argument is exhausted before we use up all the elements in 1:5.

Conclusion

Julia is a somewhat "big" language: it has a lot of syntax and a large stable of data types. These features have a purpose, and they contribute to Julia's power and convenience. Fortunately, you don't have to use everything in the language in every program. In this chapter, we've encountered some new syntax that makes working with collections more concise and intuitive. In the next chapter, we'll explore some new concepts that afford the Julia programmer higher levels of flexibility and control.

FURTHER READING

- The specification for semantic versioning is available at *https://semver.org*.

- For more information on Perl-compatible regular expressions, visit *http://www.pcre.org*.

6

FUNCTIONS, METAPROGRAMMING, AND ERRORS

A small error at the beginning of something is a great one at the end.
–Thomas Aquinas

In this chapter, we'll explore three topics that afford greater power, control, and flexibility when writing programs. We'll delve deeper into the central subject of functions, and further explore function arguments and higher-order functions. We'll see how metaprogramming and macros let us create new syntax and bend Julia to our will in a way that's not possible with most programming languages. Finally, we'll see how to take control of the error system and use it to manipulate program execution.

Functions and Their Arguments

In Chapter 4, we learned about positional and keyword arguments to functions. In this section we'll extend our knowledge of functions and learn additional ways to supply them with arguments.

Concise Syntax for Keyword Arguments

Keyword arguments tend to have names that reflect their purposes, which means when calling a function using variables for some of the keyword arguments, the names of those variables often are the same as their names in the function definition. This is even more likely to happen if we've defined these variables with their eventual use in calling the function in mind.

Under such circumstances our function calls look something like this:

```
somefunction(pos1, pos2; keyword1=keyword1, keyword2=keyword2)
```

Julia has a syntax option that reduces this visual noise and unnecessary typing. We can replace the previous call with:

```
somefunction(pos1, pos2; keyword1, struct.keyword2)
```

As the example shows, we can use either a variable with the same name as the keyword or a composite object that has a property name matching a keyword name.

The Splat and Slurp Operators

The ... operator (three dots) is either a *splat* or a *slurp*, depending on context. When we're supplying arguments to a function, we can *splat*, and when we're defining a function, we can *slurp*.

Splatting

Suppose we make a function that takes three arguments and adds them together:

```
julia> function addthree(a, b, c)
           return a + b + c
       end;

julia> addthree(1, 2, 3)
6

julia> v3 = [1, 2, 3];

julia> addthree(v3)
❶ ERROR: MethodError: no method matching addthree(::Vector{Int64})
```

When we supply three arguments, as the function definition demands, the sum is returned. However, if the three values are part of a vector, we get an error ❶ if we call the function with the vector as an argument. That's because its definition includes no method that accepts a single `Vector` argument; the only option is three separate values.

We could handle this situation by extracting the values within v3 into three separate variables and passing those to addthree(), but, since this situation arises frequently, Julia provides an easier way, through an operator spelled as three dots and called *splat*:

```
julia> addthree(v3...)
6
```

Here the splatting operator unpacks the values in a collection and supplies them as separate arguments to the called function.

Listing 6-1 shows how we can also splat keyword arguments stored in a named tuple.

```
julia> function addthreeWithCoefficients(a, b, c; f1=1, f2=1, f3=1)
           return f1 * a + f2 * b + f3 * c
       end;

julia> coeffs = (f1=100, f2=10)
(f1 = 100, f2 = 10)

❶ julia> addthreeWithCoefficients(1, 2, 3; coeffs...)
123
```

Listing 6-1: Splatting a named tuple

In this example, we create a new function, addthreeWithCoefficients(), that takes the three keyword arguments f1, f2, and f3 and multiplies the positional arguments by them before returning the sum. We then create a named tuple, coeffs, that has two properties with names matching two of the keyword arguments. When we call the function with a splat applied to the named tuple ❶, f1 and f2 get values assigned from the corresponding properties of the tuple. The argument f3 does not exist in the tuple, so it gets its default value of 1.

Although structs also have properties, we can't use them for splatting in this way. This limitation is related to the fact that we can't iterate over a struct as we can over a named or ordinary tuple.

However, dictionaries will work, as long as the keyword names appear as symbols:

```
julia> csd = Dict(:f1=>100, :f2=>10);

julia> addthreeWithCoefficients(1, 2, 3; csd...)
123
```

Here the dictionary keys :f1 and :f2 correspond to the arguments f1 and f2 in the function definition in Listing 6-1.

Slurping

In a function definition, the three dots indicate the *slurp* operator. Slurping is a kind of inverse operation to splatting: instead of unpacking a collection into separate arguments, it packs any number of separate arguments into a single iterable object. If we want a function to accept an unknown, or variable, number of positional arguments, we can use slurping:

```julia
julia> function addonlythreeWithNote(a, b, c, more...)
           if length(more) > 0
               println("Ignoring $(length(more)) additional arguments.")
           end
           return a + b + c
       end;

julia> addonlythreeWithNote(1, 2, 3, 99, 100, 101)
Ignoring 3 additional arguments.
6
```

The addonlythreeWithNote() function returns the sum of the first three arguments we supply, just as the addthree() function did. This version, however, accepts any number of additional arguments, which it packs into a tuple called more.

We can also slurp keyword arguments. The function defined in the following example performs two optional tests on the string supplied as its positional argument. If it gets a keyword called palindrome, it tests for the thusly named property, and if it gets one called onlyascii, it uses the isascii() function to check for the presence of non-ASCII characters in the string:

```julia
julia> function examine_string(s; checks...)
           if :palindrome in keys(checks)
               if s == reverse(s)
                   println("\"$s\" is a palindrome.")
               end
           end
           if :onlyascii in keys(checks)
               if isascii(s)
                   println("\"$s\" contains only ASCII characters.")
               else
                   println("\"$s\" contains non-ASCII characters.")
               end
           end
       end;
```

❶ julia> examine_string("step on no pets"; kw1=17, palindrome=1, onlyascii=1)
"step on no pets" is a palindrome.
"step on no pets" contains only ASCII characters.

```
julia> examine_string("step on no pets"; palindrome=1)
"step on no pets" is a palindrome.
```

Because we define examine_string() using slurping for keyword arguments, it doesn't matter if it's called with extra arguments ❶; they will be ignored. Since we supply default values for the keyword arguments in the function definition, it also doesn't matter if some are missing. Finally, since the program checks only for the presence of the keyword arguments, the values assigned in the call are arbitrary.

We can also call the function with a splatted value as before. The difference now is that the object we splat into the call may contain superfluous keywords without creating an error condition. Here's an example:

```
julia> kws = Dict(:palindrome => 1, :anyOtherKeyword => 17)
julia> examine_string("step on no pets"; kws...)
"step on no pets" is a palindrome.
```

Defining functions with slurped keyword arguments can be convenient for users. For example, some of the functions in the Plots package work this way. We can call them with keywords that they don't use; they'll use the ones they can handle and ignore the others. This might happen in the REPL if we create a plot using one plotting function supplied with a list of keywords and then decide we want to use a different one. We can press the up arrow and change the function's name without having to consult its documentation to see whether it understands all the keywords we used previously.

Julia allows one more way to supply keyword arguments to such functions. We can list them separately in the form :kw=>value, with keywords appearing as symbols, or we can splat a dictionary, but all of its keys must be symbols.

Destructuring

Destructuring refers to the unpacking of a tuple of values into named variables with a single assignment:

```
julia> x, y = (3, 4);

julia> x
3

julia> y
4
```

This feature is especially convenient in unpacking tuple return values from functions. As mentioned previously, tuples need not be written with parentheses as long as omitting them doesn't create an ambiguity, so we can write the assignment in the example just shown as x, y = 3, 4.

Listing 6-2 shows another form of destructuring that unpacks keyword arguments from a struct, using the following syntax:

```
julia> (; url, title) = google
Website("https://google.com", "google")

julia> url
"https://google.com"

julia> title
"google"
```

Listing 6-2: Destructuring a struct

In this example, the definition of google from Listing 5-2 is in force. In this type of destructuring, the variable names on the left-hand side of the assignment must match the field names of the composite type on the right-hand side.

NOTE *Keyword destructuring from structs first appeared in Julia v1.7. In earlier versions, (; a, b) is a syntax error.*

The utility of this form of destructuring may not be immediately obvious. After all, without this peculiar syntax, we can still do this:

```
julia> url, title = google.url, google.title
```

It's not much more verbose than the form in Listing 6-2 and has the same effect.

However, one advantage of this destructuring syntax is in providing a succinct way to define functions that take keyword arguments extracted from structs. In the following example, we first define a struct with three fields and create an object from the struct:

```
julia> struct Fco
           f1
           f2
           f3
       end

julia> someco = Fco(100, 10, 1)
Fco(100, 10, 1)
```

❶ ```
julia> function addthreeWithCoefficients(a, b, c, (; f1, f2, f3))
           return f1 * a + f2 * b + f3 * c
       end;

julia> addthreeWithCoefficients(1, 2, 3, someco)
123
```
```

Then we make a different version of the `addthreeWithCoefficients()` function that we created in Listing 6-1 ❶. Instead of a list of keyword arguments, this version takes a fourth positional argument that has the syntax of a struct destructuring. When we call the function, supplying the composite object as the fourth positional argument, the function makes the assignment(; f1, f2, f3) = someco. Referring to the syntax in Listing 6-2, we can see that this will assign 100 to f1, 10 to f2, and 1 to f3. The struct used as an argument may contain fields that are not extracted by the function, as the destructing syntax doesn't require all fields to be unpacked.

Operators Are Functions Too

Binary operators in Julia, such as * and +, also called *infix operators*, are functions of two arguments. Each one has a more explicit functional form:

```
julia> +(1, 2, 3)
6

julia> *(8, 2)
16
```

In the first example, the + function operates on the arguments 1, 2, and 3, adding them up to return 6. The functional form of infix operators can be more concise when we have many arguments.

Since binary operators are functions, we can pass them as arguments to higher-order functions (see Listing 6-5 for an example).

In an expression involving infix operators, the order of operations, or *precedence rules* for operators, determines the result. For example, the expression 3 + 2 * 5 evaluates to 13 because multiplication happens before addition.

When using the functional forms of operators, there are no precedence rules, because the function application syntax makes the order of operations explicit. For example, the expression 3 + 2 * 5 is equivalent to +(3, *(2, 5)). The syntax shows that the multiplication occurs before the addition.

Julia allows us to use certain characters to define our own binary operators. If we create a function and give it one of these characters for its name, we can use the function in an infix position.

We can't create an infix operator from any character, however. The source code for Julia's interpreter provides a complete list of available characters (see "Further Reading" on page 187). The source also indicates the precedence of each character by grouping them in classes with equal precedence. When deciding on a symbol for an infix operator, it's not enough to pick one that looks right. We must decide how the operator is to fit within the hierarchy of precedence and choose a symbol in the appropriate group.

The three major precedence groups are multiplication, addition, and comparison. Figure 6-1 shows a small selection of characters from each group.

Multiplication precedence: ∩ ∧ ⊗ ⊘ ⊙ ⊚ ⊛ ⊠ ⊓ ◇

Addition precedence: ⊕ ⊖ ⊞ ⊟ ⊻ ∪ ⋁ ⊔ ± ∓

Comparison precedence: ∷ ∻ ~ ≃ ≈ ≠ ≅ ≇ ≜ ⊏ ⊐

Figure 6-1: A few operator characters

Comparison operators have the lowest precedence of these three types, so the expression 2 * 3 + 2 > 7 is equivalent to ((2 * 3) + 2) > 7 and returns true.

Let's use one of these characters to create a new infix operator that extends the idea of subtraction to give us the Euclidean distance between two vectors. We want it to have the same precedence as addition and subtraction operators, so we'll pick a symbol from that group that looks like it has something to do with subtraction (enter **\boxminus** followed by TAB to enter the function's name in the REPL).

```julia
julia> function ⊟(a, b)
           return sqrt((b[1] - a[1])^2 +
                       (b[2] - a[2])^2)
       end;
```

NOTE   *To learn the shortcut for any other special character, paste it in after entering help mode.*

After this definition, we have a new function with a single-character name.

Since the character is in the list of characters blessed for use as infix operators, it should work:

```julia
julia> v1 = [0, 1];

julia> v2 = [1, 0];

julia> v1 ⊟ v2
1.4142135623730951
```

This result is correct.

Let's use the new operator in an expression containing a higher-precedence operation to check that it follows the desired precedence rules:

```julia
julia> 3 .* v1 ⊟ 4 .* v2
5.0
```

The multiplications were taken before the vector subtraction, as expected (the result may remind you of the 3-4-5 right triangle from high school trigonometry).

We can transform infix operators we create ourselves into broadcast versions using the dot prefix, just like built-in operators:

```julia
julia> v1a = [v1, v1, v1]
3-element Vector{Vector{Int64}}:
 [0, 1]
 [0, 1]
 [0, 1]

julia> v2a = [v1, v2, [0, 0]]
3-element Vector{Vector{Int64}}:
 [0, 1]
 [1, 0]
 [0, 0]

julia> v2a .⊟ v1a
3-element Vector{Float64}:
 0.0
 1.4142135623730951
 1.0
```

The broadcasting operation applies our function to all corresponding elements of the pair of vectors (of vectors). The result is a vector containing the Euclidean distance between each pair of corresponding vectors.

The Mapping, Filtering, and Reduction Operators

A *higher-order function* is a function that takes one or more functions as some of its arguments. Usually they either transform functions into other functions or apply them to data supplied as further arguments. The three operators map(), filter(), and reduce() are higher-order functions that apply a supplied function to a collection.

The map() Operator

The map() operator applies a function to each element of a collection and returns another collection:

```julia
julia> double(x) = 2x
double (generic function with 1 method)

julia> map(double, [2 3; 4 5])
2×2 Matrix{Int64}:
 4   6
 8  10
```

Here map() applies double() to each element of the matrix individually, returning a result with the same shape as the matrix.

In the case of an infix operator, map applies it between corresponding elements of all the collections supplied:

```
julia> map(+, [2 3], [4 5], [6 7])
1×2 Matrix{Int64}:
 12  15
```

The result has the same shape as the collections that map() is operating on. The result's first element comes from applying + to the first elements of all the collections; the second element, 15, is 3 + 5 + 7.

The key to understanding map() is understanding zip() because the map() operator combines the elements of the arrays we give it using zip():

```
julia> map(+, 20:10:40, [2 3; 4 5])
3-element Vector{Int64}:
 22
 34
 43
```

```
julia> map(+, 20:10:90, [2 3; 4 5])
4-element Vector{Int64}:
 22
 34
 43
 55
```

In these examples, map() applies the + operator between the elements of the vector and the 2×2 matrix in column-major order. In both cases, it stops when it runs out of elements in one of the collections.

In some cases, map() returns the same result as an equivalent broadcast using the dot. The map of double() earlier could have been written this way:

```
julia> double.([2 3; 4 5])
2×2 Matrix{Int64}:
 4   6
 8  10
```

However, mapping and broadcasting are not the same. We can see this clearly in the case of an infix operator:

```
julia> [20 30] .+ [2 3; 4 5]
2×2 Matrix{Int64}:
 22  33
 24  35
```

In this example, the array on the left-hand side has a different shape from the one on the right-hand side. However, its shape fits the shape of the *rows* of the right-hand array. The broadcasting operator .+ extends, or broadcasts, the array [20 30] over the rows of the other array.

If we make the left-hand array a single column instead of a single row, it's broadcast over the columns of the other array:

```
julia> [20, 30] .+ [2 3; 4 5]
2×2 Matrix{Int64}:
 22  23
 34  35
```

Examining the examples in this section should make the difference between mapping and broadcasting clear. Unlike broadcasting, map() does not perform operations on entire arrays, but goes element by element, using zip() under the hood. Using map() in this last example yields a different result:

```
julia> map(+, [20, 30], [2 3; 4 5])
2-element Vector{Int64}:
 22
 34
```

The [3, 5] column of the last argument is never used because map() runs out of elements before it gets there.

The filter() Operator

The filter() operator takes a function of one variable as its first argument; this function should return true or false. It applies this function to each element of its second argument, which should be a collection. It returns a new collection with the elements for which the function returned false *filtered* out, or removed.

As with map(), Listing 6-3 shows how filter() is often used with anonymous functions.

```
julia> filter(x -> x % 17 == 0, 1:100)
5-element Vector{Int64}:
 17
 34
 51
 68
 85
```

Listing 6-3: Using filter() with an anonymous function

Here we've created a list of the integers from 1 to 100 that are divisible by 17.

Julia provides a collection of test functions that can be convenient to use with filter(), such as isodd(), iseven(), isfinite(), and isfile(), which answer the questions indicated by their names.

The isascii() function tells you whether a character is part of the old ASCII character set; we can use it on a string to filter out non-ASCII characters:

```
julia> filter(isascii, "François")
"Franois"
```

We get the string back with "ç" filtered out. We can also invert the condition to filter out the ASCII characters with filter(!isascii, "François"), which returns "ç".

The reduce() Operator

We've used the sum() function several times. It adds up all the numbers in an array, reducing it to a single number. The reduce() higher-order function generalizes this concept. It applies a function of two variables, supplied as its first argument, to a collection supplied as its second argument.

Let's consider an example to visualize how it works. If there were no sum() function, we could use reduce() instead. We can calculate the sum 1 + 2 + 3 with sum([1, 2, 3]), but also with reduce(+, [1, 2, 3]).

We can use any binary operator, or any function of two variables, with reduce(). For example, Listing 6-4 shows a function that divides its first argument by its second and uses it in reduce().

```julia
julia> q(a, b) = a/b
q (generic function with 1 method)

julia> reduce(q, 1:3)
0.16666666666666666

julia> (1/2)/3
0.16666666666666666
```

Listing 6-4: The reduce() function

The last line shows how reduce() inserts the function between elements, accumulating partial results as it goes.

However, reducing with division introduces a complication. While the + and * operators are *associative*, division and subtraction are not. Associativity means that it doesn't matter how we group: (1 + 2) + 3 gives the same result as 1 + (2 + 3). Division is not associative: 1/(2/3) is equal to 1.5.

NOTE *In fact, addition and multiplication are associative when operating on real numbers (and other number systems in the realm of mathematics), but they are not truly associative when applied to floating-point numbers in a computer. Although the numerical effect of association, the difference between (a + b) + c and a + (b + c), is usually small, it's better to use the folding operators, which we'll introduce next, when numerical accuracy or reproducibility are important.*

In cases where the function or operator is not associative, the result of using reduce() is undefined: we cannot assume that it works from left to right. In such cases, we should use foldl() or foldr(), which work just like reduce(), but associate from the left or the right:

```julia
julia> foldl(q, 1:3)
0.16666666666666666
```

```
julia> foldr(q, 1:3)
1.5
```

Listing 6-5 shows how the reduce() operator, but not foldl() or foldr(), accepts the keyword argument dims to reduce along the specified dimension.

```
julia> reduce(+, [1 2; 10 20]; dims=2)
2×1 Matrix{Int64}:
  3
 30

julia> reduce(+, [1 2; 10 20]; dims=1)
1×2 Matrix{Int64}:
 11  22
```

Listing 6-5: Reducing along a specified dimension

Here dims=1 causes a reduction along the rows, while dims=2 reduces along the columns. If we omit the dims argument, the result is a reduction over all elements, giving the single number 33.

All three reducing functions accept another keyword argument that acts as a default in case they encounter an empty collection. This argument is called init:

```
julia> reduce(+, []; init=0)
0
```

In this example, when faced with the empty collection [], reduce() returns the specified value 0.

If a reducing function encounters an empty collection, no default neutral element exists, and no init argument has been supplied, it returns an error. Some reducing functions *may* use the value of init as a starting value for the reduction when the collection is not empty, but this behavior is formally unspecified and may change in future implementations of these functions. For that reason, to assure correct results, when init is present it should be the correct *neutral element* for the applied operation. For addition, this is 0, and for multiplication, the neutral element is 1.

Some reducing operations arise so frequently in programs that Julia has purpose-built versions for them. We've already seem sum(); prod() is similar but multiplies rather than adds:

```
julia> prod(1:7)
5040

julia> factorial(7)
5040
```

The first expression in this example multiplies together all the integers from 1 to 7 inclusive; as this is the definition of 7!, we get the same result returned from the second expression.

The `maximum()` and `minimum()` reducers find the largest or smallest element of a collection:

```julia
julia> maximum(sin.(1:.01:2π))
0.9999996829318346

julia> minimum(sin.(1:.01:2π))
-0.999997146387718
```

In this example, we create the collections by broadcasting the `sin()` function over an interval.

The `any()` and `all()` reducing tests apply a test over a collection:

```julia
julia> any(iseven, 3:2:11)
false

julia> all(isodd, 3:2:11)
true
```

These two operations answer the questions: do *any* or *all* elements of the collection satisfy the test in the first argument?

The mapreduce() Function

The powerful `mapreduce()` function does what its name suggests: it combines a `map()` and a `reduce()`. For example, here are two ways to add up the first 100 squares:

```julia
julia> mapreduce(x -> x^2, +, 1:100)
338350

julia> reduce(+, map(x -> x^2, 1:100))
338350
```

The second method shows exactly what a `mapreduce()` call does. However, it's almost always better to use `mapreduce()` instead of combining a `map()` and a `reduce()` because the former uses far less memory and is much faster; the gain in efficiency grows dramatically as the collection gets larger. The main reason is that combining `map()` and `reduce()` creates an intermediate collection to reduce over, whereas `mapreduce()` performs the calculation in one go, without allocating a collection.

do Blocks

Many functions in Julia take functions as their first arguments, and we often want to supply an anonymous function, as we have no need to reuse the function elsewhere. We've seen this with `plot()` and related plotting routines, and with the mapping and reducing functions described in this chapter.

Constructing an anonymous function can be cumbersome or impossible using the x -> ... syntax. For example, we might want it to contain loops or if blocks. In those situations, we can resort to first creating a named function and then passing it to the higher-level function, but Julia provides another way.

The do block is a type of function definition block solely for the purpose of creating anonymous functions. The function is inserted as the first argument of the function call immediately preceding the do block.

Let's revisit reducing using our q() function from Listing 6-4. If any of the denominators taken from the collection is 0, the reduction will return Inf. But what if we want to simply skip those denominators?

```julia
julia> foldl(q, 3:-1:0)
Inf

julia> foldl(3:-1:0) do x, y
           if y == 0
               return x
           else
               return x/y
           end
       end
1.5
```

The do block defines an anonymous function of two variables that returns the first divided by the second, handling 0 denominators as a special case. The call to foldl() looks wrong because it passes only a single argument, but the function defined by the do block is inserted as the missing first argument.

Symbols and Metaprogramming

We've used the Symbol type in several places—for example, when setting attributes in plotting functions—but we've deferred a thorough discussion of what symbols in Julia actually are until now.

To grasp the meaning of symbols, we must introduce the concept of *metaprogramming* in Julia. Metaprogramming refers to a general class of language facilities and associated techniques for writing code that examines itself, modifies itself, and can even modify or add to the syntax of the language. In this section, we'll introduce the basic concepts and apply them to the code-transforming programs called *macros* described in the next section.

Scientific code does not typically use much metaprogramming. However, Julia, and many of its packages, provides some indispensable macros, such as the @layout macro that we used in "Creating Complex Layouts Using @layout" on page 118. Even if you never write a macro yourself, having a basic understanding of how they work is worthwhile. Programming in Julia routinely uses a handful of indispensable macros, so it's important to be able to use them intelligently and debug them if something goes wrong.

Expression Objects

Julia has the ability to manipulate Julia code. That's possible because Julia code itself is expressible as a data type that the language can operate on, just as it operates on numbers, strings, and arrays. This data type is called Expr. Objects with this data type are referred to as Expr objects or *expression objects*. Expression objects are different from *expressions*, which are language forms that return results, such as 3 * 5.

Expression objects often involve Julia Symbols. We can create a Symbol by prepending a colon to a name, as with the attributes, such as :red, that we used when making plots. We can convert a string to a symbol with the Symbol() function as well: Symbol("red") == :red.

We can also use colons to construct expression objects by following the colon with an expression in parentheses. To reiterate: 3 * 5 is an expression, while :(3 * 5) is an expression object. If we enter 3 * 5 in the REPL, Julia evaluates the expression and returns 15. If we enter :(3 * 5), or any other expression object, it simply returns what we entered.

In order to evaluate the expression that the Expr object represents, the part inside the parentheses, we use the eval() function. If we enter eval(:(3 * 5)) in the REPL, Julia returns 15.

NOTE *We can turn a string into an expression using Meta.parse()—for example, Meta.parse("3 * 5") returns :(3 * 5).*

Sometimes putting the entire expression object on one line is inconvenient. Julia has a block called quote for defining such objects:

```
julia> ex = quote
           a = 3
           a + 2
       end;

julia> typeof(ex)
Expr

julia> a
ERROR: UndefVarError: a not defined

julia> eval(ex)
5

julia> a
3
```

The assignment beginning the example assigns the result of the quote block to ex. Since quote blocks create expression objects, that's the type of ex, as we confirm in the following line. Evaluating the expression performs the operations within the block, as the next two lines confirm.

The block gets its name from the concept of *quoting*, which means turning an expression into an expression object, whether we accomplish that by surrounding an expression with :(...) or using the quote block.

In English, sometimes we need to distinguish between *using* a word or expression and talking *about* the word or expression. We do this by surrounding the terms we are discussing with quotes. Quoting in Julia serves the same purpose. We quote an expression so that we can act on it as an expression; the expression object is simply the quoted expression.

Most languages have no way to talk about themselves. All those that do, such as Julia, all Lisps, and Elixir, have a way to quote expressions.

Expression Object Interpolation

We can interpolate values into an expression object similarly to how we can interpolate into a string. As a simple example, let's define a variable and create two expression objects, one that uses the variable and one that uses the interpolated value of the variable:

```
julia> w = 3
3

julia> ex = :(w * 5)
:(w * 5)

julia> ey = :($w * 5)
:(3 * 5)
```

In the definition of ey, the value of w was interpolated into the expression object at the time of its creation. The expression object ex contains the *variable* w instead. Applying eval() to those expression objects, before and after changing the value of w, clarifies the consequences of this:

```
julia> eval(ex)
15

julia> eval(ey)
15

julia> w = 4
4

julia> eval(ex)
20

julia> eval(ey)
15
```

Changing the value assigned to w does not change the result of evaluating ey because that expression does not contain w as a variable. Instead, it uses the *value* of w in its definition.

With just these few simple metaprogramming tools, we can already perform a whole category of programming tricks that are impossible without them. For example, suppose we want to create a function that, given a string and a value, creates a variable from the string and assigns the value to it. Listing 6-6 shows a function that performs this task.

```
mkvar(s, v) = eval(:($(Symbol(s)) = $v))
```

Listing 6-6: Putting expression objects to work

The mkvar() function converts the s string into a Symbol. It then creates an expression object that assigns to the interpolated value of that symbol the value of v. Finally, it applies eval() to the expression object. The result of this eval() is a new variable with a name identical to the supplied string s, and with the value v.

Here it is in action:

```
julia> mkvar("Arthur", 42);

julia> Arthur
42
```

This kind of functionality requires metaprogramming. In particular, we can't do "Arthur" = 42, because we can't assign to a string.

The previous example makes clear exactly what symbols are: they are the way Julia represents variables within expression objects. In other words, symbols are how Julia represents variables to itself. They are also, as we've shown, often drafted for service as keyword arguments and for other purposes, but that usage is tangential to their fundamental identity. Symbols are popular for these purposes simply because they're more efficient than strings.

The mkvar() function is more than just a magic trick. The strings it consumes may be taken, for example, from the headings of a table of data read from a file. In that case, mkvar(), or something like it, could create variables named after those headings and assign them to the columns of data underneath them. We'll explore applications of these ideas in Chapter 10.

Macros

A *macro* is a function that accepts expressions, symbols, and literals as arguments and returns an expression object. The expression object is automatically evaluated at runtime.

There is a crucial difference between macros and the other functions that we've studied up to now, including functions that manipulate expression objects. Functions are evaluated at runtime, using the current values of any global variables.

The processing inside a macro, in contrast, happens during a separate compilation stage *before* the program runs. The expression object returned by the macro is inserted into the code at the location of the macro and eval()ed. This property allows us to use macros to alter or add to the syntax of the language.

How to Create Macros

The following is a macro version of the mkvar() function that we defined in Listing 6-6:

```
julia> macro mkvarmacro(s, v)
           ss = Symbol(s)
        ❶ return esc(:($ss = $v))
       end
@mkvarmacro (macro with 1 method)

❷ julia> @mkvarmacro "color" 17
17

julia> color
17
```

Normally, to avoid collisions with names in the calling context, macros change the names of all the variables they contain into private versions. In cases where we want these variables to refer to variables of the same name when we use the macro, we use esc() ❶ to bypass the private naming process. This is one of those cases because the purpose of this macro is to create a variable from the string we supply and to assign it a value.

We invoke a macro by prepending an @ sign to its name ❷. The syntax for supplying arguments is more flexible than in the case of functions. We can list the arguments separately using spaces, as in this example, or place a comma-separated list inside parentheses, as we do with functions: @mkvarmacro("color", 17). If the argument is a literal array, we can dispense with the space and the parentheses and call the macro as @macroname[1 2 3].

As soon as the macro is invoked, the Expr object ($ss = $v), with interpolation substituting a literal color for ss and 17 for v, is evaluated, so 17 is assigned to the variable color.

As an example of how we can use macros to add new syntax to Julia, suppose we don't like using the end keyword in while loops. In Listing 6-7 we'll create a simple macro that accepts a condition and a loop body, with no end required. We're not allowed to reuse the while keyword, so we'll call our macro @during.

```
macro during(condition, body)
    return quote
```

```
        while $condition
        ❶ $(esc(body))
        end
    end
end
```

Listing 6-7: Creating new syntax with a macro

We use the esc() function ❶ because we want the loop body to be able to use variables defined outside the macro.

Here's how to use this macro:

```
julia> i = 0
0

julia> @during i < 10 (println(i^2); i+=1)
0
1
4
9
16
25
36
49
64
81

julia> i
10
```

The last two lines show that the macro indeed references the variable i in the global scope.

With our new powers, we can invent a kind of loop that doesn't exist in the language. Let's create an "until" loop that repeats a block *until* a condition is met. This is the same thing as a while loop that continues while the condition is *not* met. With this insight, our new macro is a simple modification of the one in Listing 6-7:

```
macro until(condition, body)
    return quote
        while !$condition
            $(esc(body))
        end
    end
end
```

Let's test it in the REPL to see if it does what we expect:

```
julia> i = 0
0
```

```
julia> @until i == 11 (println(i^3); i+=1)
0
1
8
27
64
125
216
343
512
729
1000
```

Our @until loop works as intended, incrementing i until i == 11.

Writing macros is inherently more difficult than writing normal functions, partly due to the necessity to keep track of levels of quoting and self-reference. Fortunately, you'll never need to write a single macro to perform scientific calculations or numerical work. However, if you find you're repeating "boilerplate" code often, and this repeated code can't be expressed using a normal function, you may have a situation where the code-writing powers of macros can save you some work.

Useful Macros

Although you may never write your own macros, you'll use them often. Both the standard library and many packages provide useful functionality through various macros. This section surveys several convenient macros for general use.

The Broadcast Macro

We've described how Julia's dot operator can extend functions and operators to act element-wise over entire arrays (see "Broadcasting" on page 51). We often want to write long expressions in which all, or the great majority, of the functions need to be broadcast over their array arguments. The broadcast macro frees us from having to sprinkle dots everywhere in such an expression—for example:

```
julia> r = 1:10

julia> [r (@. exp(r) > r^4) (exp.(r) .> r.^4)]
10×2 BitMatrix:
  1  1  1
  2  0  0
  3  0  0
  4  0  0
  5  0  0
  6  0  0
```

```
 7  0  0
 8  0  0
 9  1  1
10  1  1
```

This example constructs a three-column matrix showing when the exponential function becomes larger than its argument to the fourth power (exp(x) is the Julia function for e^x). The second column is made from an expression using the broadcast macro, while the third is an expression with the identical meaning, but with explicit dots. The two columns are identical.

To exclude a function from the macro's automatic broadcasting, precede it with a dollar sign ($). As an example, here is the sum of the first 10 squares:

```
julia> sum((1:10).^2)
385
```

The sum() function, which adds all the numbers in an array, does not have a dot because it acts on the array as a whole, rather than element by element.

If we rewrite the expression using the broadcast macro, we should exempt sum() from the auto-dotting:

```
julia> @. $sum((1:10)^2)
385
```

Without the prepending dollar sign, sum() would be applied to each element individually; however, this is not what we want, as sum(n) is simply equal to n when n is a single number.

The @chain Macro

The @chain macro, which is not part of the standard library and must be imported from the Chain package, is a more convenient alternative to the pipe operator (|>) for transforming data through a series of expressions. The pipe operator has certain limitations. For example, it's designed to work only with functions that have a single argument. The @chain macro is one of several approaches in the Julia ecosystem that creates a more flexible pipelining mechanism.

First, let's look at the syntax of the built-in pipe with a simple example:

```
julia> "hello" |> uppercase |> reverse
"OLLEH"
```

We've passed the string "hello" through two functions to transform it.

Suppose we want to continue the pipeline, adding occursin() as a third function, to check for the occurrence in the result of the string "OL". The occursin() function takes the string to search in as the *second* argument, so there's no obvious way to extend the pipeline to use it.

Instead of the pipe operator, we can use the @chain macro to accomplish this task:

```
julia> @chain "hello" begin
           uppercase
           reverse
       ❶ occursin("OL", _)
       end
true
```

The @chain macro creates a pipeline from a series of expressions without the use of any extra operators. It handles functions of any number of arguments. By default, the result of each expression is fed into the first argument of the following function. To insert the result into an argument in a position other than the first, indicate its slot with an underscore ❶.

The @time Macro

The @time macro tells how much machine time a computation consumes, plus some information about memory allocations:

```
julia> @time sum((1:1e8).^2)
  0.661141 seconds (2 allocations: 762.940 MiB, 1.01% gc time)
3.333333383333333e23
```

First the REPL prints a line with information about the resources used, and then the result of the computation.

NOTE   *The @time macro is handy for getting a rough idea of timings, but for more systematic benchmarking or profiling, I recommend importing the BenchmarkTools package and using the @btime macro and other tools therein. The BenchmarkTools macros can run an expression multiple times and take an average, separate run time from compilation time, and more.*

Macros for Performance

Julia comes with several macros we can use to alter the behavior of the compiler, sometimes leading to more efficient code. They need to be used with care, as their use is not without risk. The two macros discussed in this section can provide significant speedups in some circumstances; in others, they have little or no effect. One usually has to experiment to find out if they'll provide any benefit. These two macros, and similar strategies, should be explored at the final stages of performance tuning. During the development of an algorithm or a program, such attempts at optimization would likely be a counterproductive distraction.

Normally the compiler checks our indexing expressions to make sure we're not indexing array elements that don't exist, returning a BoundsError if we index beyond the end of an array, or wind up using a nonpositive index.

In some routines, this bounds checking can affect performance. If we're sure that an area of code cannot contain an indexing error, we can instruct the compiler to skip the bounds checking for that location using the @inbounds macro:

```
x = (1:1e6).^2; s = 0
@inbounds for i in 1:2:1000
    s += x[i]
end
```

The @inbounds instruction at the start of the for loop tells the compiler not to worry about x[i] being an illegal access during the loop. We're responsible for ensuring that i stays within the bounds of x.

The utility of inbounds is much reduced in recent versions of Julia; there's no longer a good reason to use it for versions more recent than 1.8. However, we'll encounter it in much existing code, so it's important to know what it's supposed to do.

NOTE *A common error is to try to generate the indices for the array A with 1:length(A). This does not create legal indices for every type of array, and, if used to access A within an @inbounds section, it can create silent bounds errors. Instead, we should use eachindex(A), which always returns an iterator over legal indices of A.*

As mentioned earlier in this chapter, addition and multiplication on floats are not associative: the results can depend on the order in which we add or multiply numbers. For this reason, the Julia compiler will normally perform arithmetic exactly the way we spell it out, even if it would be faster to change the order of operands or rewrite expressions to "real number equivalents" that would be more efficient. This ensures that running a program on different versions of the compiler will produce the same numerical results, as all the arithmetic will occur in the same order.

In situations where the last few decimal places of a result are not important, we can sacrifice some of this reproducibility to gain speed by allowing the compiler to rearrange our expressions. The instruction is provided by the @fastmath macro:

```
julia> const d = 1.0045338347428372e6
1.0045338347428372e6

julia> @time sum(i/d for i in 1:1e9)
  5.248617 seconds
4.9774331456739935e11

julia> @time @fastmath sum(i/d for i in 1:1e9)
  3.856526 seconds
4.977433145673994e11
```

Here we've performed the same sum

$$\sum_{i=1}^{10^9} (i/d)$$

twice, the second time using the @fastmath directive. Our expression needlessly performs an extra billion divisions. One obvious optimization available for @fastmath is to factor out the constant d. The macro gets us a speedup of about 26 percent. It also changes the result slightly in the two final digits. Neither result is more "correct." This is an example of how arithmetic on floats depends on the details of the calculation.

Macros for String Formatting

The Printf package provides two macros that format strings using the C-style specifications that have become a de facto standard across multiple programming languages. The following example shows how a macro makes our code neater, allowing us to list the variables to be formatted without parentheses and commas:

```
julia> using Printf

julia> @printf "10! is about %.2e and √2 is approximately %.4f" factorial(10) √2
10! is about 3.63e+06 and √2 is approximately 1.4142
```

The format specifiers are the fragments in the string beginning with %; the digit after the decimal point determines the number of digits after the point printed in the result. For a list of all the format specifiers and a guide to their syntax, see "Further Reading" on page 187.

A companion to this macro is sprintf, which behaves the same way but returns the formatted string as a result rather than printing it. Use sprintf to store the generated string in a variable.

Macros for Information

Several macros that provide information about the environment in which they are invoked are always available. The @__MODULE__, @__DIR__, @__FILE__, and @__LINE__ macros return the module, directory, filepath, and line number, respectively, where they are called. These macros can be useful for debugging, writing build scripts, code formatting, testing, and other purposes. (Each of the macro names in this paragraph begins and ends with a double underscore.)

One essential aid when debugging macros is a macro called @macroexpand. Simply prepend it to your macro call, and it will show you what the macro is using for each variable and reference.

Error Handling

Like most modern languages, Julia has methods for handling, manipulating, and creating errors (also called *exceptions*). We've seen plenty of examples of errors in this book so far: they occurred in REPL sessions or as a result of running programs when Julia encountered a situation that prevented it from continuing with the computation. These situations have included calling functions with arguments that they were not designed to accept, indexing arrays outside their bounds, using an undefined name, and others. Each one was introduced in order to illustrate a characteristic of the language, but in practice we encounter errors when something unexpected happens, or something happens that we need to guard against.

In this section we'll explore how to handle errors and some methods for making them part of our programs' flow control. Julia's type system and its method of function dispatch, covered in Chapter 8, provide a cleaner way to accomplish some of what relies on exception handling in other languages. These more idiomatic Julia techniques should be preferred because they allow the compiler to perform more optimizations. Nevertheless, sometimes the methods described in this section are the most convenient way to accomplish a programming task.

Types of Errors

Julia uses about 25 distinct kinds of exceptions. Some occur rarely, while others we may only wish were rare. Here are the most common ones:

```
julia> 1 + "1"
ERROR: MethodError: no method matching +(::Int64, ::String)

julia> [1, 2, 3][4]
ERROR: BoundsError:
  attempt to access 3-element Vector{Int64} at index [4]

julia> notdefined
ERROR: UndefVarError: notdefined not defined

julia> 'abc'
ERROR: syntax: character literal contains multiple characters

julia> [1 2] * [3 4 5] ❶
ERROR: DimensionMismatch:
  matrix A has dimensions (1,2), matrix B has dimensions (1,3)

julia> log(-1)
ERROR: DomainError with -1.0:
log will only return a complex result if called with a complex argument.
Try log(Complex(x)).
```

```
julia> 1 ÷ 0 ❷
ERROR: DivideError: integer division error

julia> Int(2.1) ❸
ERROR: InexactError: Int64(2.1)

julia> Dict(["a" => 1, "b" => 2])["c"]
ERROR: KeyError: key "c" not found

julia> factorial(55)
ERROR: OverflowError: 55 is too large to look up in the table;
consider using `factorial(big(55))` instead ❹

julia> "François"[6]
ERROR: StringIndexError: invalid index [6], valid nearby indices [5]=>'ç', [7]=>'o'
```

The identifier immediately following the word ERROR: is the name of the error. It's usually followed by some explanation and even occasionally some advice.

Most of the error messages are self-explanatory. A MethodError means that someone tried to call a function with argument types that it doesn't support. Operators such as + are functions written with an infix syntax. (See "Creating Multiple Methods" on page 230 for more information on methods and the precise meaning of the error message.)

The * operator, when applied to arrays, performs matrix multiplication, which requires that the second dimension of the first argument match the first dimension of the second argument ❶.

We're allowed to divide by a floating-point 0, which results in Inf or -Inf, which means that we can do 1/0 because the / operator converts to floating point. However, dividing by 0 using the integer division operator (÷) results in a DivideError ❷.

If we try a conversion between numerical types that would lose information, an InexactError is the result ❸.

The usual types of integers aren't large enough to hold the result of factorial(55), but, as the advice following the error message ❹ suggests, we can turn to another type of number. We'll cover big numbers in "'Big' and Irrational Types" on page 216.

The Call Stack

Suppose we have a series of function calls, where a function calls a second function, which calls a third, and so on. When the final function in this chain finishes its job, the compiler needs to know what to do next. In order to know what the next instruction should be, the compiler keeps track of "how we got here." That information, which includes the details of the chain of function calls, is called the *call stack*. It forms the sometimes lengthy part of error messages that I usually omit from the listings in this book to save space.

In practice, the compiler optimizes nested function calls through "inlining" when possible. This optimization replaces the nested calls with direct insertion of the called function's code into the calling function. But there is still the logical notion of the call stack, and the error report prints this logical stack, noting any inlining.

To illustrate how the call stack works, Listing 6-8 sets up a series of five functions, each one defined to call the next one by name, except the last, which calls the log() function.

```
function a(n)
    b(n)
end

function b(n)
    n -= 1
    c(n)
end

function c(n)
    n -= 1
    d(n)
end

function d(n)
    n -= 1
    e(n)
end

function e(n)
    return log(n)
end
```

Listing 6-8: A chain of functions

Function a() calls b(), passing the supplied argument n. Function b() decrements that argument and calls c(), passing its new value, then c() calls d() similarly. Finally, e() calls log(n), where now n is 3 less than the original n.

Listing 6-9 shows calling a() a couple of times.

```
julia> a(5)
0.6931471805599453

julia> a(2)
ERROR: DomainError with -1.0:
log will only return a complex result if called with a
complex argument. Try log(Complex(x)).
Stacktrace:
  [1] throw_complex_domainerror(f::Symbol, x::Float64)
    @ Base.Math ./math.jl:33
```

```
  [2] _log(x::Float64, base::Val{:e}, func::Symbol)
    @ Base.Math ./special/log.jl:292
  [3] log
    @ ./special/log.jl:257 [inlined]
  [4] log
    @ ./math.jl:1350 [inlined]
  [5] e
    @ ./REPL[215]:2 [inlined]
  [6] d
    @ ./REPL[214]:3 [inlined]
  [7] c
    @ ./REPL[213]:3 [inlined]
  [8] b
    @ ./REPL[212]:3 [inlined]
  [9] a(n::Int64)
    @ Main ./REPL[211]:2
 [10] top-level scope
    @ REPL[217]:1
```

Listing 6-9: A call stack when an error occurs

First we call a(5), which ultimately leads to a call to log(5-3), or log(2), and returns the expected result. When we call a(2), that results in log(2-3), or log(-1), and the attempt to take the logarithm of a negative number produces the expected DomainError. What follows is the stacktrace: information about the call stack at the moment that the error occurred. This data, which can become far lengthier than in this artificial example, is an aid to debugging, informing us about the state of the program that led to an error condition.

The numbers in square brackets are part of the trace as printed in the REPL, showing the sequence of function calls, beginning with the most recent, where the error was raised, and proceeding up the chain. The first entry is the function that actually handles the error. This is followed by the log functions themselves, and then our functions e() up through a(). The final entry informs us that a() was called from the REPL. The stacktrace also tells us which functions were inlined by the compiler.

try...catch Blocks

Instead of allowing errors to simply stop our program, we can intercept them. We do this in Julia with the try...catch block, another form of flow control like the if block. Here's an example:

```
function friendly_log(n)
    try
        return log(n)
    catch oops
        if oops isa DomainError
            @warn "you may have supplied a negative number: $n"
```

```
        ❶ @info "Trying with $(-n)."
            log(-n)
        elseif oops isa MethodError
            ❷ @error "please supply a positive number."
        end
    end
end
```

The `friendly_log()` function wraps the built-in `log()` function in some error handling. The normal `log()` rejects negative arguments with a `DomainError`, but this version tries again with the argument's absolute value, warning the user about what it's doing. The `try` part of the block contains the code whose errors we want to intercept; the `catch` part intercepts them, optionally assigning the error itself to a variable, here `oops`. Inside the `catch` block we put an ordinary `if` block, using `isa` to test for the type of error ("Types in Practice" on page 214 explains more about `isa` and types). If `oops` happens to be a `DomainError`, the `@warn` macro prints a warning to the terminal, after which we issue another message, using the `@info` macro, explaining how the program plans to change the faulty argument ❶. We then call `log()` with the argument made positive.

If the error is not a `DomainError`, but instead is a `MethodError`, something else is wrong with the argument. In this case, we don't know what to do and the program should halt. The `@error` macro ❷ prints an error message, *after which the program continues*. Since there's nothing else for it to do, it exits. The `@error` macro, like the `@warn` macro, simply prints an appropriately formatted message; neither macro creates an error condition nor has any effect on flow. On a color device, warnings are signaled in yellow and errors in red, and both attempt to indicate where in the program the problem occurred. Messages generated by `@info` appear in blue in the REPL, and don't include a program location. All three macros are part of Julia's logging system. See the link to the documentation in "Further Reading" on page 187 for information about more of what you can do with this logging information.

Since we "handle" the errors in the `catch` block, they won't stop the program or lead to a stacktrace:

```
julia> function call_fl(n)
           friendly_log(n)
       end

julia> call_fl(-3)
 Warning: you may have supplied a negative number: -3
 @ Main REPL[222]:6
[ Info: Trying with 3.
1.0986122886681098
```

If we had not intercepted the error in the `catch` block, it would have led to a stacktrace as in the previous section, with `call_fl()` as part of the call stack.

Using throw()

The REPL's help mode explains that throw() throws an object as an exception. Most Julia tutorials describe it as a way for the programmer to create errors. Both of these descriptions are true, but they tell only part of the story. Before delving into the full power of throw(), let's look at a simple example of where we might want to create an error where there otherwise would not be one.

Creating Errors

The log() function allows us to call it with an argument of 0, returning -Inf as the result. Suppose we wanted to have a logarithm function that did *not* allow 0 as an argument because we wanted to exclude infinities from its results. The finite_log() function would be one way to accomplish this:

```
function finite_log(n)
    if n == 0
        throw(DomainError(n, "please supply a positive argument; log(0) = -Inf."))
    end
    return log(n)
end
```

An if block checks for the 0 input and calls throw() if it finds one. The argument of throw() is the name of an error turned into a function; each of Julia's errors has such an associated function for constructing the error. The finite_log() function raises a DomainError if it gets 0 as an argument. We can raise any error we want, but as the idea here is to exclude a value from the domain, a DomainError makes sense:

```
julia> finite_log(2)
0.6931471805599453

julia> finite_log(0)
ERROR: DomainError with 0:
please supply a positive argument; log(0) = -Inf.
Stacktrace:
 [1] finite_log(n::Int64)
   @ Main ./REPL[230]:3
 [2] top-level scope
   @ REPL[234]:1

julia> log(0)
-Inf
```

Here finite_log() behaves like log() unless it gets a 0, when it halts with a DomainError. The message that we included in throw() is printed out with the error message.

Most of the error constructors accept arguments for information for Julia to include in the error message. To see what arguments are permitted, ask the REPL:

```
help?> DomainError
search: DomainError

  DomainError(val)
  DomainError(val, msg)

  The argument val to a function or constructor is outside the valid domain.
```

The documentation informs us that there are two versions, one with just the offending value, and the version that we used, with an explanatory message as well.

Combining throw() with try...catch Blocks

Combining throw() with try...catch blocks unleashes its full power. In combination, they create a new form of flow control that allows us to pass *any value* up the call stack until it is intercepted by a catch, at which point we can halt the program or do something else.

As an example, Listing 6-10 modifies the chain of functions from Listing 6-8.

```
function a(n)
    try
        b(n)
    catch oops
        if oops[1] == 0
            @warn "$(oops[2]) Attempted to call log(0) = Inf."
        else
            @error "$(oops[2]) Attempted to call log($(oops[1]))."
        end
    end
end

function b(n)
    n -= 1
    c(n)
end

function c(n)
    n -= 1
    d(n)
end

function d(n)
    n -= 1
```

```
        e(n)
end

function e(n)
    if n < 0
    ❶ throw((n, "Got a negative number."))
    elseif n == 0
        throw((0, "Got 0."))
    end
    return log(n)
end
```

Listing 6-10: Throwing and catching

Looking at the e() function first, we've added an if block above what used to be its only line. Before trying to calculate the logarithm, it checks the argument n. If this argument is not positive, it calls throw() with a Tuple as an argument ❶. In both cases, the tuple's first element is n and its second element is a string. The throw() function sends this tuple up the call stack and returns from e() without attempting to calculate the logarithm. If n == 0, we send a different message up the call stack.

The message sent by throw() travels from function call to function call until it's intercepted by the try...catch block in function a(). The catch statement assigns the message, in this case a Tuple, to the variable oops, where it's examined in the if block, which prints the appropriate warning or error message.

Here it is in action:

```
julia> a(5)
0.6931471805599453

julia> a(3)
 Warning: Got 0. Attempted to call log(0) = Inf.
 @ Main REPL[1]:6

julia> a(2)
 Error: Got a negative number. Attempted to call log(-1).
 @ Main REPL[1]:8
```

This exhibits a dramatic difference from the error reporting shown in Listing 6-9. Here we see no call stack, but merely the messages constructed in our try...catch block. The throw()...catch mechanism lets us toss a message "over the heads" of any number of functions in a call stack, directly to the first one ready with the appropriate catch statement. Listing 6-9 had no catch in place to intercept the error, so Julia halted the program and printed out the complete call stack for our diagnostic use.

The finally Clause

The try...catch block can optionally end with a finally clause, which is executed before the program exits. We typically use this for "cleanup," such as releasing external resources or file handles that an error condition otherwise might leave in an uncertain state.

Let's add a finally clause to a() from Listing 6-10:

```
function a(n)
    try
        b(n)
    catch oops
        if oops[1] == 0
            @warn "$(oops[2]) Attempted to call log(0) = Inf."
        else
            @error "$(oops[2]) Attempted to call log($(oops[1]))."
        end
    finally
        @info "Calculation completed with input n = $n."
    end
end
```

Calling it as before, we'll see the following:

```
julia> a(5)
[ Info: Calculation completed with input n = 5.
0.6931471805599453

julia> a(2)
 Error: Got a negative number. Attempted to call log(-1).
 @ Main REPL[11]:8
[ Info: Calculation completed with input n = 2.
```

This example shows how the finally clause is always executed, whether there is a message to catch or not.

Conclusion

With the more advanced language features discussed in this chapter, we've attained a higher level of Julia mastery. We're now better prepared for the detailed applications in Part II, where we'll see how to apply our skills to address problems across a variety of fields.

7

DIAGRAMS AND ANIMATIONS

Tell me, Steed. Is everything to scale?
–Mrs. Peel

Diagrams are an essential form of scientific communication and education. The type of diagram treated in this chapter is distinct from the plots of data or mathematical functions we worked with in Chapter 4. *Diagrams* in this context refers to illustrations of mathematical structures, drawings of experimental setups, flowcharts describing algorithms or processing pipelines, and similar graphical descriptions.

Animations now frequently accompany scientific papers reporting on simulations, as supplementary material offered online. They're also a valuable tool in education and have a myriad of uses in scientific and mathematical communication. In this chapter, we'll explore several Julia packages that can help you create a variety of types of diagrams and animations.

Diagramming with Luxor

The Luxor package is sophisticated and highly versatile, allowing you to create almost any type of diagram. To install it, enter **add Luxor** in the package manager.

The package uses an imperative style to build up a picture in stages. You enter a series of commands that manipulate a global state, each command potentially adding something to the drawing. The effect of each drawing command depends on the state at the time it is entered. For example, to draw a blue circle, first set the color to blue and then enter the circle-drawing command, with arguments giving its position, size, and whether it should be "stroked" (an outline drawn) or filled. The outline or fill will use the currently set color. Each element—circles, polygons, lines, text, or any of a variety of objects—requires a separate command, and colors, styles, opacities, and other settings are set globally before each command is issued.

For a concrete example, let's create a simple diagram (shown in Figure 7-1) of the relative sizes of the planets in the solar system, arranged in order of their distance from the Sun.

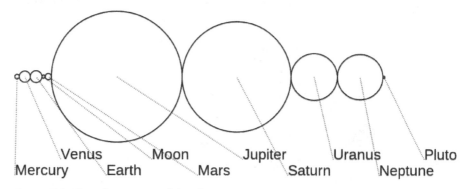

Figure 7-1: The relative sizes of the planets

Listing 7-1 shows the complete REPL session that creates the diagram in Figure 7-1.

```
julia> using \captionlst{Luxor}

❶ julia> planet_diameters = [4879 12104 12756 ;;
   3475 6792 142984 120536 51118 49528 2370];

julia> planet_names = ["Mercury", "Venus", "Earth", "Moon",
   "Mars", "Jupiter", "Saturn", "Uranus", "Neptune", "Pluto"];

julia> dimenx = 1000;

julia> dimeny =  500;

❷ julia> @png begin
            dscale = 500.0
```

```
❸ origin(Point(planet_diameters[1]/(2*dscale), dimeny/2))
  ledge = 0.0
  diameter = 0
❹ fontface("Liberation Sans")
  fontsize(32)
  for i in 1:10
      ledge += diameter/2.0
      name = planet_names[i]
      diameter = planet_diameters[i]/dscale
❺    ledge += diameter/2.0
      setcolor("black")
      setdash("solid")
      circle(Point(ledge , 0), diameter/2.0, :stroke)
      txtstart = Point(100*(i-1), 180 + 35*(i%2))
      text(planet_names[i], txtstart)
      setcolor("blue")
❻    setdash("dot")
      line(txtstart, Point(ledge, 0), :stroke)
  end
❼ end dimenx dimeny "planets.png"
```

Listing 7-1: Creating a diagram of the solar system using Luxor

The program gets its planetary diameters, which are in kilometers, from a NASA website (see "Further Reading" on page 211). When copying and pasting from the NASA table there, the numbers are space separated. This creates a 1×10 array (Earth's moon and Pluto are included), which is fine; we just need a list we can iterate over.

The double semicolon at the end of the line ❶ breaks the literal input of the array over two lines (this feature was added in Julia v1.7). Although spaces and double semicolons both signify concatenation along the second dimension, normally you may not mix them in a single literal array definition. The usage here is an exception just for this purpose.

The two variables dimenx and dimeny hold the dimensions of our diagram. Dimensions in Luxor are points, which are 1/72 of an inch.

Luxor supplies several macros for conveniently setting up the drawing environment. The @png macro ❷ initializes a PNG illustration, defines the origin of the coordinate system to be the center of the picture, and displays the result upon reaching the end of the block ❼. After the final end statement, we give the dimensions of the image and its filename (you can leave this out, but probably won't want to). The default size is 600×600, and the default filename is *luxor-drawing-* followed by a timestamp and the file extension. This can lead to a profusion of files on your disk as you develop your drawing code, so you probably want to specify a filename, which will get overwritten on each run. The file extension is optional and Luxor will supply one if you leave it out.

We need a scaling factor to deal with the large planetary diameters, which we assign to dscale.

The macro sets the origin of the coordinate system to the center of the diagram, which, using our variables, would be (dimenx/2, dimeny/2). The code will be neater if we set the origin ❸ in the *x*-direction such that the left edge of the first planet starts at the left boundary.

I discovered that, on my system, if I don't set a fontface ❹, I get ugly bitmapped fonts in the output. This particular font may not exist on your system, so adjust as needed. If you ask for a font that Luxor can't find, it will carry on, making a substitution.

The x-coordinate of the current circle's center is assigned to ledge, which is updated twice ❺ for each planet: once to increase it by the radius of the previous planet and once by the planet about to be drawn. The result is a series of osculating circles.

The color is set to blue and the dash style to dot ❻ before each label is printed. As with other diagrams in this chapter, you can find color versions in the online supplement at *https://julia.lee-phillips.org*.

If you run the code from Listing 7-1 in the REPL, your default image viewing application will open a window displaying the diagram file when you run the code. The REPL will hang until you quit the application. If you run this in Pluto or Jupyter, the diagram will be embedded in the cell below the code.

Other options for macros are @svg and @pdf, which create files of the respective types. However, PDFs will not be embedded into notebooks.

In addition to lines, circles, and text, Luxor has commands for drawing several other shapes, and even such geometrical constructions as tangent lines to circles. (See "Further Reading" on page 211 for a link to the manual.)

The Graphs Package

With enough patience, you can use Luxor to create any type of diagram. However, it's usually easier to use a specialized package for diagrams of a specific, standard type.

This section is about graphs in the mathematical sense and their visualization. The word *graph* is often used synonymously with the types of plots that were the subject of Chapter 4, but to a mathematician, a graph is a set of nodes connected by edges, and that's the type of graph we consider here. Graphs of this type are used to represent a huge variety of systems. Anytime you have a collection of objects that are connected together in a network of relationships, you have a graph. Examples include a taxonomy of plants or animals, call sites in a computer program, grammatical structures in a sentence, organizational charts, and the relationships among characters in a novel. In such a graph, the objects (parts of the organization or characters in the novel) are called *nodes* and the connections between nodes are called *edges*.

The Julia `Graphs` package contains functions for making several types of graphs. It depends upon `Plots` and `GraphRecipes` to actually draw the pictures representing the graphs. The first of these we're familiar with from Chapter 4; the second is a collection of *plotting recipes* that, in turn, use `Plots` to draw pictures. The recipe mechanism allows users and package authors to extend `Plots` so that it can visualize new data types or make new types of plots. To understand how these recipes work, we need to know more about the type system, so plot recipes are covered in "Plot Recipes" on page 252.

As an introduction to the `Graphs` package, we'll build a program to create a diagram of the predator–prey relationships among 14 species living in the Chesapeake Bay in the eastern United States:

```
using Plots
using Graphs
using GraphRecipes

creatures = ["Striped bass", "Atlantic croaker", "White perch",
             "Summer flounder", "Clearnose skate", "Bay anchovy",
             "Worms", "Mysids", "Amphipods", "Juvenile weakfish",
             "Sand shrimp", "Mantis shrimp", "Razor clams",
             "Juvenile Atlantic croaker"]

foodchain = SimpleDiGraph(14)
```

First, we import the three necessary libraries (`Plots`, `Graphs`, and `Graph Recipes`) and create a vector of the names of the creatures. These names will become labels in the diagram and will also serve as references for the graph's nodes.

The final line of the program so far creates an empty *directed graph* with 14 nodes (called "vertices" by `Graphs.jl`). A directed graph is one where the edges have a direction, usually represented visually as an arrowhead. For this example, the direction of the edge will represent what creature eats what. In an *undirected graph*, the edges simply represent connections, with no hierarchy involved.

The next step is to add edges to `foodchain` representing information about the predator–prey relationships. The `add_edge!(foodchain, a, b)` function mutates the graph in its first argument by adding an edge going from node a to node b. That's what we want, but it's not convenient, because a and b need to be integers representing the orders of the nodes in the list. To enter these arguments, we would have to count through the list of `creatures` for each relationship. For example, to enter an edge representing the fact that striped bass eat worms, we would have to call `add_edge!(foodchain, 1, 7)`.

Let's make the process more convenient by defining a dictionary and a function that will allow us to refer to the creatures by name:

```
food_dict = Dict([creatures[i] => i for i in 1:14])

function ↪(predator, prey)
    add_edge!(foodchain, food_dict[predator], food_dict[prey])
end
```

The food_dict dictionary simply associates each creature string with its order in the list, for easy reference. The new function allows us to add edges by naming the predator and its prey. We're using a name for this function that can serve as an infix operator (see "Operators Are Functions Too" on page 159). The REPL shortcut (and LaTeX command) for that character is \hookrightarrow.

With the hooked arrow function in place, we can list a set of predator-prey relationships taken from a study of the ecology of the Chesapeake Bay:

```
"Striped bass" ↪ "Worms"
"Striped bass" ↪ "Amphipods"
"Striped bass" ↪ "Mysids"
"Striped bass" ↪ "Bay anchovy"
"Atlantic croaker" ↪ "Mysids"
"Atlantic croaker" ↪ "Worms"
"White perch" ↪ "Worms"
"White perch" ↪ "Amphipods"
"Summer flounder" ↪ "Bay anchovy"
"Summer flounder" ↪ "Mysids"
"Summer flounder" ↪ "Juvenile weakfish"
"Summer flounder" ↪ "Sand shrimp"
"Summer flounder" ↪ "Mantis shrimp"
"Clearnose skate" ↪ "Mantis shrimp"
"Clearnose skate" ↪ "Razor clams"
"Clearnose skate" ↪ "Juvenile Atlantic croaker"

graphplot(foodchain; names=creatures, nodeshape=:rect, fontsize=5,
          nodesize=0.14, method=:stress)
```

The add_edge!() function mutates the foodchain graph by adding edges. The last call produces the illustration shown in Figure 7-2. In the diagram, the arrows point from predator to prey, reflecting the directions of the edges we defined.

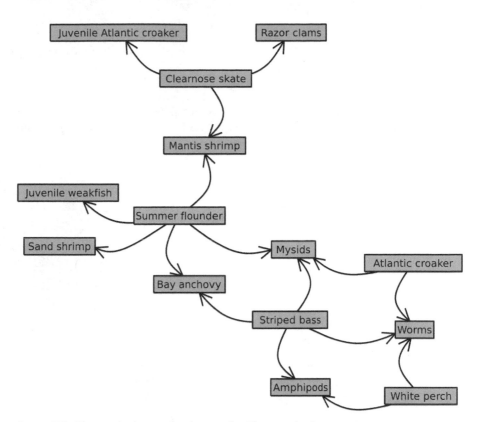

Figure 7-2: The predator–prey food net in the Chesapeake Bay

If you run this program, you will find that your picture looks somewhat different. In fact, each time you run it the diagram will be arranged differently in space, although the *structure* will always be the same—the same creatures being eaten by the same predators. This happens because of a random element in how the nodes and edges are arranged. In fact, I had to run the program about five times before I got a result that I liked. Some of the generated graphs were rather poor, with overlapping nodes.

The final argument in the call to graphplot(), method, selects an algorithm for laying out the graph: for turning the structure into a picture by deciding where to place the nodes. The stress algorithm does this by trying to maximize a global measure of how far the distances between nodes differ from a theoretical optimum. The random element comes in because the algorithm finds this maximum by deforming a random initial state.

The Adjacency Matrix

Internally, the list of edges established by calls to add_edge!() gets transformed into an *adjacency matrix*. We can see the adjacency matrix as shown in Listing 7-2.

```
julia> foodchain_matrix = adjacency_matrix(foodchain)
14×14 SparseArrays.SparseMatrixCSC{Int64, Int64} with 16 stored entries:
 ·  ·  ·  ·  ·  1  1  1  1  ·  ·  ·  ·  ·
 ·  ·  ·  ·  ·  1  1  ·  ·  ·  ·  ·  ·  ·
 ·  ·  ·  ·  ·  1  ·  1  ·  ·  ·  ·  ·  ·
 ·  ·  ·  ·  ·  1  ·  1  ·  1  1  1  ·  ·
 ·  ·  ·  ·  ·  ·  ·  ·  ·  1  1  1  ·  ·
 ·  ·  ·  ·  ·  ·  ·  ·  ·  ·  ·  ·  ·  ·
 ·  ·  ·  ·  ·  ·  ·  ·  ·  ·  ·  ·  ·  ·
 ·  ·  ·  ·  ·  ·  ·  ·  ·  ·  ·  ·  ·  ·
 ·  ·  ·  ·  ·  ·  ·  ·  ·  ·  ·  ·  ·  ·
 ·  ·  ·  ·  ·  ·  ·  ·  ·  ·  ·  ·  ·  ·
 ·  ·  ·  ·  ·  ·  ·  ·  ·  ·  ·  ·  ·  ·
 ·  ·  ·  ·  ·  ·  ·  ·  ·  ·  ·  ·  ·  ·
 ·  ·  ·  ·  ·  ·  ·  ·  ·  ·  ·  ·  ·  ·
 ·  ·  ·  ·  ·  ·  ·  ·  ·  ·  ·  ·  ·  ·
```

Listing 7-2: The adjacancy matrix is a sparse array.

The result is returned as a *sparse array*, one of a collection of data types defined in the SparseArrays package, which the Graphs package loads automatically. A sparse array behaves similarly to a normal array, but is specialized to be efficient when only a small proportion of its elements are defined. The REPL displays them as shown in Listing 7-2, with dots representing undefined locations.

The elements of an adjacency matrix are set to 1 to record the existence of edges in the graph. For example, foodchain_matrix[1, 6] has a 1, because there's an edge going from node 1 to node 6 (established by "Striped bass"↪ "Bay anchovy"). The adjacency matrix encodes the structure of the graph, and therefore contains its complete definition, because a graph is identical to its structure. We can plot the graph with a call to graphplot(foodchain_matrix); the remaining arguments simply supply details, such as names for labeling the nodes, for its display. If the adjacency matrix is symmetrical (M[i, j] == M[j, i]), it represents an undirected graph. Otherwise, as in the food chain example, it represents a directed graph, and graphplot() will draw it using arrows rather than simple lines. The adjacency matrix must have at least one nonzero element, or at least one edge defined with add_edge!(), before plotting a graph.

The package uses sparse matrices for efficiency, but, if we're constructing an adjacency matrix directly, as in the next example, we have the option of using normal matrices. In this case, a 0 element indicates the absence of an edge and nonzero elements show where the edges are.

Factor Trees

At the risk of awakening bad memories from high school algebra class, our next example, found in Listing 7-3, will be a program to draw factor trees: graph diagrams showing the division of a number into ever-smaller factors, ending with its unique prime factors. It will show how to build a graph by constructing its adjacency matrix and provide an example of an undirected graph with a tree structure. Here's the complete program that produces the factor tree.

```
using Primes: factor
using Plots
using Graphs
using GraphRecipes
function factree(n)
❶  factors = factor(Vector, n)
    lf = length(factors)
    if lf == 1
        println("$n is prime.")
❷      return
    end
    names = [n; n ÷ factors[1]; factors[1]]
    for f in factors[2:end-1]
        push!(names, names[end-1] ÷ f, f)
    end
    nel = length(names)
❸  a = zeros(nel, nel)
    println("Prime factors: $factors")
    j = 1; i = 1
    a[1, 2] = 1
    a[1, 3] = 1
    for i in 2:2:nel-3
        a[i, i+2] = 1
        a[i, i+3] = 1
    end
    graphplot(a;
            nodeshape=:circle,
❹          nodesize=0.12 + log10(n) * .01,
            axis_buffer=0.3,
            curves=false,
            color=:black,
            linewidth=2,
            names=names,
            fontsize=10,
❺          method=:buchheim)
end
```

Listing 7-3: A program to create a factor tree

The new import, the first line of the program, gets us the factor() function ❶, which returns the prime factors of its argument. The program works only for integers n greater than 1. The first argument supplied to factor() tells it to return the results in a vector, the form that we need to construct the factor tree. The default is to return the results in a special-purpose type that lists factors and multiplicities. If there is only one of those, n is a prime number, so we stop immediately ❷, announcing why. The program proceeds through the list of primes, dividing and concatenating the results onto the names vector. We then initialize the adjacency matrix a ❸ and record the links between each pair of factors and their product up the tree. The final call to graphplot() takes the adjacency matrix as its first argument; the keyword arguments set details for the illustration. The nodesize argument sets the extra size of the circles beyond what is required for them to contain their labels. The algorithm for enlarging them does not quite succeed in making them grow big enough, so we add something extra proportional to the number of digits in the label ❹. Calling factree(14200) produces Figure 7-3.

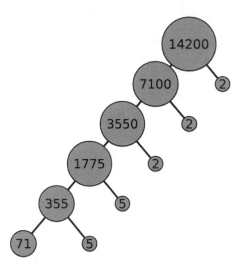

Figure 7-3: A factor tree for the number 14,200

The package provides two layout methods for creating tree-like graphs. The :tree method works, but the results are a bit free-form. The :buchheim method ❺ produces the regular tree shown in Figure 7-3. Although the prime factorization is unique, the factor tree that leads to it, and thus the result of the program, may not be.

Animations with Javis

The widely used Javis package is a good choice for making almost any type of animated diagram. It's built on top of Luxor (see "Diagramming with Luxor" on page 190), which means you can build on your knowledge of that package to create animations. A Javis program creates objects from Luxor drawing commands and turns them into videos by means of a fairly intuitive set of calls to rotate, translate, or move them along paths, as well as by changing shape parameters in time.

Closures

To use Javis effectively, it helps to be familiar with a programming technique called a *closure*. Experienced programmers who know how to use closures can safely skip this section.

A closure is a function that is created and returned by another function. We'll refer to the returned function as the *inner function* and the one that creates it as the *outer function*. Most modern languages allow the programmer to create closures, but some are more convenient for this than others. Julia, because of its lexical scoping and convenient syntax for function definition, makes closures easy and intuitive.

The key aspect to closures is that the inner function can access variables defined in the outer function. We say that they are *closed over*, hence the name. The outer function becomes a function factory, returning a function whose behavior depends on the arguments passed to the outer function, but with, potentially, a completely different function signature.

Listing 7-4 shows a simple example of a closure that we'll find a useful application for shortly.

```
function power(n)
    return function(x)
        x^n
    end
end
```

Listing 7-4: Defining a closure

With this definition, when we call, for example, power(5), we get a function of a single variable that raises that variable to the fifth power and returns the result. In other words, if we define two functions this way:

```
p = power(5)
```

```
q = x -> x^5
```

then p and q have the same behavior:

```
julia> p(4) == q(4) == 1024
true
```

The function power() returns is anonymous, but we can assign it to a variable, in this case p, as we can any other function.

Now power() is a function factory that makes functions that raise their arguments to any desired exponent. As mentioned in "Plotting Functions" on page 88, one version of the plot() function from the Plots package accepted the simple names of functions of one variable to plot. We can plot such functions without mentioning variables or defining arrays.

It would seem that this convenience could not be exploited to plot, say, functions that depend on a parameter in addition to the independent variable, and that we would need to use named functions or the anonymous function syntax to pass such functions to plot(). For example, if we want to plot f(x, n) = x^n, we can't just call plot(f), because f() needs two arguments, but we could call plot((x) -> x^n) if n were already defined. Closures are an alternative to passing anonymous functions in cases such as this.

Once we have the closure defined in Listing 7-4, we can make the following plotting call:

```
plot([power(1), power(2), power(3)]; legend=:top)
```

This produces the plot in Figure 7-4.

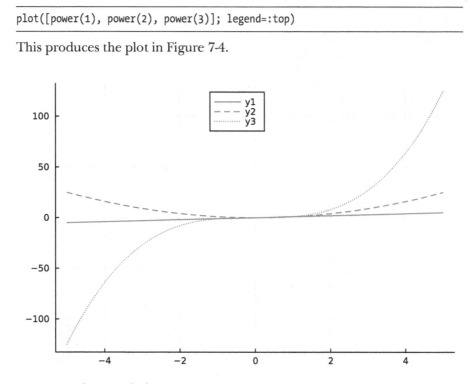

Figure 7-4: Plotting with closures

This plotting example is simply one application of closures. They are a powerful technique for generating functions that capture the state under which they are defined.

Epicycle Animation

The pattern for using Javis is to define functions that produce each of the objects you intend to animate, and then call a series of statements that refer to those objects and animate them, changing their positions or other properties in time.

Since Javis *is built on* Luxor, *it imports* Luxor *itself and re-exports that package's functions. The consequence is that a program that contains using* Javis *must not also contain using* Luxor, *because that would lead to name conflicts. If you've been using* Luxor *in the REPL, you must start a new REPL before using* Javis.

The object-creating functions use one or more Luxor functions for circles, lines, text, or other graphical entities available through Luxor, and optionally return information about the object for use in the animation calls.

The Luxor documentation describes three methods for passing the object-creating functions into the animation functions. We'll learn another method, based on closures, that's more general and leads to neater and easier-to-read code.

The goal for this example is to create a program that produces animations of models of the solar system in the style of Ptolemy. This ancient cosmology put our Earth at the center of the universe and explained observations of planets as caused by their circular orbits, which themselves circled around larger orbits. These circular orbits are called *epicycles*; any one planet's motion might be modeled by one or more epicycles, ending with a large circle around a point somewhat displaced from Earth by a distance called the *eccentricity*.

To build the program, we'll start with functions that create the planets and orbits. Here's the one for a planet:

```
function planet(radius=15, color="green"; action = :fill, p=0)
    return function(video, object, frame)
        sethue(color)
        circle(p, radius, action)
        return p
    end
end
```

This is a closure. A call to planet() returns a function that accepts three positional arguments and draws a circle with a radius, color, and position determined not by the arguments passed to the returned function, but by the original arguments passed to planet().

This indirection is necessary because the Javis functions that do the animation expect a function as their first and only required argument. They don't accept a shape as an argument, but a function that draws a shape. They pass the three values (video, object, frame) to this function: data types representing the video, the object being animated, and the integer frame number. The function can use any of them, or as in the case of the function created by planet(), none of them.

The closure returns the circle's position. We must do this if other animation functions need to know that position, as is the case in our video.

The function for drawing orbits will be almost the same:

```
function orbit(radius, color="orchid1"; p=0)
    return function(video, object, frame)
        sethue(color)
```

```
        circle(p, radius, :stroke)
        return p
    end
end
```

Orbits will have an outline, but won't be filled in.

With these two functions, we can draw animatable planets and orbits, which is most of what we need. But it would also be nice to show how the wandering of the planet around the solar system translates into changes in its observed location in the sky relative to the fixed stars as the days go by. We'll approximate this movement by the projection of the planet's position along the horizontal coordinate. The pos() function supplied by Javis returns an object's position, and it has convenient x and y fields for extracting the respective coordinates.

The following function accepts an object and draws another circle that shares its horizontal coordinate, close to the top of the video:

```
function observed_position(orbiter; radius=10, color="orangered")
    return function(video, object, frame)
        sethue(color)
    ❶  y = 0 - video.height/2 + 50
        x = pos(orbiter).x
        circle(Point(x, y), radius, :fill)
    end
end
```

Here observed_position() uses the video argument's height field ❶ automatically supplied by the animation functions.

We would like to draw one more object: a curve in space visualizing the path taken by the planet. We'll record this path as a series of points in a global positions vector. At every frame, this function pushes the new position onto the vector and draws a series of tiny circles tracing the path:

```
function track!(positions, orbiter)
    return function(video, object, frame)
        sethue("cadetblue1")
        push!(positions, pos(orbiter))
        circle.(positions, 2, :fill)
    end
end
```

We need one more drawing function, used in nearly all Javis animations, for defining the background:

```
function ground(args...)
    background("black")
    sethue("white")
end
```

This definition for ground() creates a drawing canvas with a black background and uses white as the default drawing color.

With functions for each object we want to draw, we can create the animation:

```
using Javis

function epicycles(inputcycles; eccentricity=0.1, file=nothing)
    box = 200
    eccentricity *= -box
    cycles = [(box*s, f) for (s,f) in inputcycles[1:end-1]]
    R = sum(c[1] for c in cycles)
    # Some encoders require a multiple of 2:
    box_length = 1.5*(2box + R) ÷ 2 * 2
❶   solar_system = Video(box_length, box_length)
    positions = []
❷ Background(1:500, ground)
    earth = Object(planet(), Point(0, eccentricity))
    origin = Object(planet(2, "white"))
    inner_orbit = Object(orbit(box))
    for (radius, frequency) in cycles
        outer_orbit = Object(orbit(radius), Point(0, box))
        box += radius
❸     act!(outer_orbit, Action(anim_rotate_around(frequency * 2π, inner_orbit)))
        inner_orbit = outer_orbit
    end
    wanderer = Object(planet(6, "bisque"), Point(0, box))
    act!(wanderer, Action(anim_rotate_around(inputcycles[end] * 2π,
        inner_orbit)))
❹ Object(track!(positions, wanderer))
    Object(observed_position(wanderer))
    if file == nothing
❺     render(solar_system; liveview=true)
    else
        render(solar_system; pathname=file, framerate=30)
    end
end
```

The epicycles() function accepts one required positional argument, inputcycles, in the form [(s1, f1), (s2, f2), ..., fp]. Each (s, f) pair gives the size s as a fraction of the main orbit radius of an epicycle with an orbital frequency of f. Frequencies here refer to the number of cycles completed during the animation. The final fp is the planet's frequency.

After some calculations to scale the orbits according to the video's overall size, and to adjust this size to account for the epicycles input by the user, we have the one statement ❶ that all Javis animations require: defining the Video and its dimensions.

The first animation command ❷ establishes the background to be drawn for the first 500 frames. The next three animation commands are calls to Object(); this is the Javis command that places the graphical element on the background. The Object() function accepts a range of frames as a first argument, but uses the range supplied to the most recent Background() or Object() command as a default. Javis is an imperative system that maintains a state to which animation statements apply, containing the current Video and range of frames.

Next we have a loop that adds orbits for each epicycle supplied in the argument. The act!() function ❸ is how we create most types of motion in Javis. Its first argument is the object we want to animate, and the second argument is a function defining the motion. The only such motion we use in this program is anim_rotate_around(), which takes an angle (in radians) and the object that becomes the center of rotation. The complex, compound motions in the epicycle model are easy to construct because the object rotated around can itself be in motion.

The final two Object() calls ❹ create the path tracking the planet and the projection showing its approximate observed position. Although these are animated objects, they don't need an act!() call because they're defined with reference to other animated objects.

The epicycles() function also accepts two optional keyword arguments. The eccentricity gives the displacement of Earth from the center of the main orbit. If file is supplied, the program creates a video file and saves it there; if not, it displays the result in an interactive viewer.

As an example, to produce an animation with a planet that goes around once during the movie, with two epicycles going around two and three times as fast, the first with a diameter half of the orbit's diameter, and the second with a diameter half the first's, make the following call:

```
epicycles([(0.5, 2), (0.25, 3), 1]; file="ptolemaic.mp4")
```

This call saves the rendered animation in an MP4 file.

The type of viewer depends on the coding environment. In the REPL, Javis opens a window with controls to step or scrub through the animation frames. In a Pluto notebook, the frames appear in a horizontal list with a scroll bar. A change to the rendering call when using a notebook, setting liveview=false ❺, will embed an animated GIF directly in the notebook instead. The Javis package can save animations as GIFs or MP4 files; the choice is controlled with the file extension. As GIFs can become quite large, the MP4 format is a good option; however, either one requires significant time to render compared with the liveview option, which is remarkably fast.

Figure 7-5 shows one frame from the rendered video. (See the book's online supplement at *https://julia.lee-phillips.org* for the full video.)

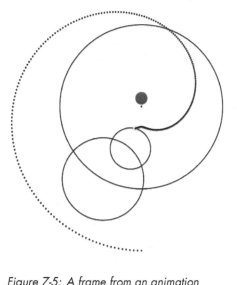
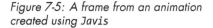

*Figure 7-5: A frame from an animation
created using Javis*

We are able to create this visualization using only one type of motion, the anim_rotate_around() call. To make an object spin around its origin, the call is anim_rotate().

Some of the other motions that we can create by supplying them as arguments to Action() include the following:

appear() and disappear()   Accept any of the arguments :fade, :scale, and :fade_line_width, and make the object come into or out of existence by changing the specified property. Using :draw_text makes text appear with a typing effect.

follow_path()   Causes an object to follow a path given as a series of points.

anim_scale()   Shrinks or grows an object.

anim_translate()   Moves an object along a line.

change()   Changes any property of an object.

Animations with Reel

The Reel package, like Javis, creates animations, but it serves a different purpose. While Javis makes it easy to create animations by programmatically describing objects and their motions, Reel lets us create a video from any function that creates images depending on a parameter (typically time).

We use an exported function from Reel, called roll(), to which we pass an image-creating function of two positional arguments: the duration that we want for the video and the frames per second (fps). The two aforementioned positional arguments are time (t) and timestep (dt); roll() calculates both of these, setting dt = duration/fps, and passes them to the function, calling it repeatedly, each time with an updated t. It returns a video object that we turn into either a GIF or an MP4 file with a call to write(). Arranging for a function to accept t and dt and create the desired video frame is our responsibility.

NOTE *The Reel package is not updated frequently, and may not work properly in every computing environment. An alternative, that only creates GIFs but is simple and convenient, is built into recent versions of Plots. See "Further Reading" on page 211 for documentation of the @animate and @gif macros.*

Listing 7-5 calculates the displacement of one axisymmetric mode of a vibrating drumhead and creates a video visualizing the motion as a heatmap.

```
using SpecialFunctions
using Plots
using Reel
R = 1.0 # Drum radius
z2 = 5.52008 # 2nd zero of J0
λ2 = z2/R
c = 1
A = 1; B = 1

function vibe(r; t=0)
    if r > R
        return 0
    else
❶     return (A * cos(c*λ2*t) + B * sin(c*λ2*t)) * besselj0(λ2*r)
    end
end
r = 0:R/100:R
theta = 0:2π/100:2π
❷ function drum_frame(t, dt)
    heatmap(theta, r, (theta, r) ->
        vibe(r; t=t); colorbar=false, clim=(-1, 1),
        c=:curl, proj=:polar, ticks=[], size=(100, 100))
end
```

```
drum_video = roll(drum_frame, fps=30, duration=2)
write("drum_video.mp4", drum_video)
```

Listing 7-5: Animating the vibration of a circular drum head

First we import three packages. The vibrating circular drumhead has a radial dependence described by a Bessel function, available from the SpecialFunctions package. We use a plotting function from Plots to create our movie frames, and then use Reel to stitch the animation together.

After defining a few constants for the solution, we define the vibe() function, which takes the radial coordinate and a keyword argument t and returns the solution at that time and coordinate. The Bessel function J_0 from the SpecialFunctions package is named besselj0() ❶.

The next two lines define the coordinate arrays for plotting. A polar coordinate system is most natural in this circular geometry: r is the radial coordinate and theta is the angular coordinate. We have to wrap ❷ the plotting function in a function of t and dt so that roll() can generate the animation frames. For this application, we don't use dt for anything, but the function still needs to accept two arguments. The call to heatmap() uses the :curl color spectrum, which has a thin white region near 0, letting us see the nodal lines and clearly distinguishing the positive and negative regions. The proj argument selects the polar geometry.

Figure 7-6 shows one frame from the resulting animation. (See the online supplement at *https://julia.lee-phillips.org* for the complete video.)

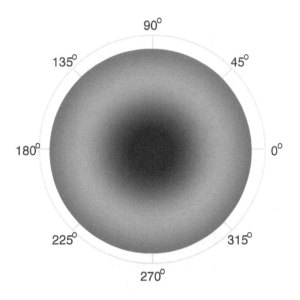

Figure 7-6: One frame from a vibrating drumhead animation

After we create the video with the roll() function, we save the result to a file using write(). The file extension specifies the video format; the other two choices are GIF and WEBM.

The write() function is Julia's standard for writing data to files. The Reel package defines a version of it that converts the video to the requested format when it sees a Reel video in its second argument. Chapter 8 explains how this is possible and how you can make your own specialized versions of functions activated by the types of their arguments.

Interactive Visualizations in Pluto

The Pluto notebook (see "Pluto: A Better Notebook" on page 17) provides an easy way to create interactive animations through its @bind macro. This macro binds the output of any of the standard HTML input controls to a Julia variable. When we execute a cell containing a @bind macro call, Pluto creates the control in the output area for the cell. When the user manipulates the control, Pluto instantly updates the value of the variable to which the control is bound. Because of the reactive nature of the notebook, any cells that depend on that value are automatically re-executed. If any of those cells produce a graph or other visualization, the graphic will change in response to the user interaction. Input controls in HTML include sliders, numerical or text input boxes, file choosers, color pickers, checkboxes, selection menus, and more.

We don't need to actually write any HTML (or know anything about it) thanks to the PlutoUI package, which provides a convenient Julia interface to the HTML input controls. For HTML experts, however, the option to use the web's markup language directly is supported. It's even possible to create custom controls using JavaScript. See "Further Reading" on page 211 for links to more information and for PlutoUI documentation.

Let's look at a few examples of how to use the @bind macro with PlutoUI controls. The following uses the browser's date-picker widget:

```
@bind some_date DateField()
```

This command assigns the date the user selected to some_date, which will have Julia's Dates.DateTime data type.

This example uses the HTML checkbox:

```
@bind a_setting CheckBox()
```

Here a_setting becomes a Boolean: true if the user clicks the box and false otherwise.

The following uses an HTML text field:

```
@bind label TextField()
```

This call will assign whatever the user types into a text box as a String to the variable label.

There are many more. All of these functions accept a default keyword argument, and some accept other arguments as well. For example, TextField() accepts an optional tuple argument; if supplied, it creates a multiline textarea with the number of columns and rows taken from the tuple's first and second elements.

As an example of an interactive visualization, let's return to the vibrating drumhead problem from Listing 7-5. The goal is to create a notebook containing a plot of the drumhead where the user can move in time by manipulating a slider.

We'll make a few small changes to the code from Listing 7-5. First, we need one additional import, using PlutoUI, to be able to use the HTML widgets, and we won't need to import Reel.

The vibe() function needs no changes, but let's alter the plotting function to make a surface plot rather than a heatmap and to show the time in a title. The surface() function from Plots doesn't understand polar coordinates, so we need to use x and y and convert manually:

```
function drum_frame(t)
    surface(x, y, (x, y) ->
        vibe(sqrt(x^2 + y^2); t=t); colorbar=false, clim=(-1, 1),
        c=:curl, zrange=(-1.2, 1.2), title="t = $t")
end
```

We want the interactivity to be responsive, so we'll sacrifice some smoothness in the plot by using a coarser gridding:

```
x = -1:0.05:1
y = -1:0.05:1
```

We're not making a movie, so we don't need the last two lines of Listing 7-5. To make the notebook, we import Pluto in the REPL and execute Pluto.run(), which opens a new tab in the default web browser with the Pluto start page. After clicking the link to create a new notebook, we can enter all these variable and function definitions into cells. The final cell will contain the line:

```
@bind t Slider(0:0.01:1.1382)
```

The range supplied as an argument will become the starting, step size, and ending values for the slider. The ending value is the time for one complete vibration cycle.

A picture in a book can't convey the experience of using the notebook. For that, there is no substitute for trying it yourself. But Figure 7-7 shows a screenshot of the plot and slider.

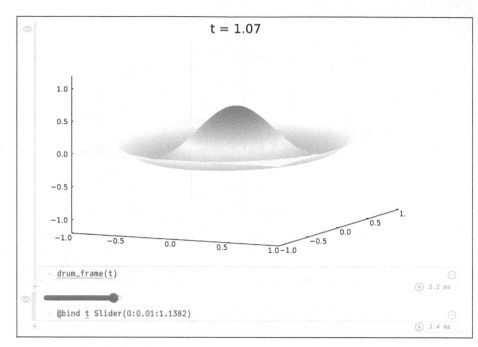

Figure 7-7: The vibrating drumhead in a Pluto notebook

Interactive Pluto notebooks are a powerful means to create explanatory documents and educational material. The fact that they're stored as text files makes them easy to share, at least with other Julia users.

Conclusion

The packages we've explored in this chapter make it easy to create a wide variety of diagrams and animations. This facility is a boon to the community of Julia users, as many of the scientists and engineers who form a large segment of its audience are also teachers, conference presenters, and creators of online educational materials. All of these activities are enhanced by having tools at hand to construct explanatory visualizations. The ability to create complex visualizations within Julia is important: much of the time they will require computations that we're already performing in our Julia programs. Indeed, often they will be part of the dissemination of the results of those computations. Packages such as Luxor and Javis free us from the need to reach for external programs and from becoming mired in another "two language problem."

In the next chapter, we'll return to the language itself and learn about the type system. This is the final piece required for Julia mastery; putting it in place will unlock a new level of programming power.

FURTHER READING

- Videos and color images are available in the online supplement at *https://julia.lee-phillips.org*.

- The Luxor documentation is available at *http://juliagraphics.github .io/Luxor.jl/stable/*.

- The Javis documentation is available at *https://juliaanimators.github .io/Javis.jl/stable/*.

- For GraphRecipes attributes, including a complete list of available layout algorithms, visit *https://docs.juliaplots.org/stable/generated/ graph_attributes/*.

- Documentation for the NetworkLayout package that supplies the different graph layout algorithms, where you can see interesting animations of the workings of the various layout strategies, is available at *https://juliagraphs.org/NetworkLayout.jl/stable/*.

- For details on how to use the @gif and @animate macros, visit *https:// docs.juliaplots.org/latest/animations/*.

- A tutorial on making custom interface components for Pluto using JavaScript is available at *https://cotangent.dev/how-to-make-custom -pluto-ui-components/*.

- The creator of Pluto explains how to create custom interactions using JavaScript in this video: *https://www.youtube.com/watch?v=SAC _RCjyRRs*.

- For documentation on the functions available in PlutoUI, visit *https:// docs.juliahub.com/PlutoUI/*.

8

THE TYPE SYSTEM

Object-oriented programming is an exceptionally bad idea
which could only have originated in California.
–Edsger Dijkstra

Up to now we've been using and creating a lot of functions. We can think of functions as the verbs of the Julia language. And just as in natural languages, verbs act on nouns. The nouns in Julia are numbers, collections, strings, and other instances of types.

We've encountered many data types in our journey up to this point: different varieties of numbers, strings, characters, and collections such as arrays and maps. Although our focus hasn't been on types, it's impossible to talk much about Julia programming without making some reference to them. Julia is unusual in that it allows us to create very fast code without having to specify the types of variables, unlike other fast languages such as Fortran (where the specifications can be implicit) and C. However, effective Julia programming requires some knowledge of its type system. The main reason for this is that Julia programs are organized around functions and methods through its dispatch system, which relies on argument types. A secondary reason has to do with those occasions where an awareness of types allows us to write more efficient programs. This chapter covers both of these concerns.

Types in Practice

Rather than delve into the abstract theory of type systems, let's approach types from a practical point of view.

To find the type of any value, Julia provides the typeof() function:

```
julia> typeof(17)
Int64

julia> typeof(17.0)
Float64

julia> typeof(17//1)
❶ Rational{Int64}

julia> typeof("7")
String

julia> typeof('7')
Char
```

We've already considered the difference between strings and characters, and the related difference between single and double quotes; however, it's important to have some understanding of the various numeric types. Although, for example, 17, 17//1, and 17.0 have the same values, they are different types of objects, and their behavior is potentially different. The difference in their types reflects this reality.

The curly brackets used in reporting the type of a rational number ❶ indicate that this is a *parametric type*, a topic we'll return to in "Parametric Types" on page 248. For now, it's sufficient to understand that this is a Rational made up of Int64 pieces.

The type reported for the floating-point literal is Float64, which means it's a floating-point number, or a number with a decimal point, and that it's stored in a 64-bit segment of memory. The 64 bits are apportioned as follows: 1 for the sign, 11 for the exponent, and 52 for the "fraction." The maximum absolute value of a Float64 is about 10^{300}, and it has 17 significant digits, or 16 digits of precision beyond the decimal point. (This agrees with the observation that it takes three binary digits to represent a decimal digit.) We can see this using the @printf macro, supplied by the Printf package:

```
julia> using Printf

julia> @printf "%.16f" 1/3
0.3333333333333333
```

```
julia> @printf "%.17f" 1/3
0.33333333333333331

julia> @printf "%.18f" 1/3
0.333333333333333315
```

This shows incorrect digits appearing if we ask for more than 16.

We'll see more incorrect digits if we use floating-point types with lower precision:

```
julia> @printf "%.16f" Float32(1/3)
0.3333333432674408
julia> @printf "%.16f" Float16(1/3)
0.3332519531250000
```

Here we used the names of the types as functions to cast their arguments to the named types. Without the cast, expressions like 1/3 are Float64 by default on most systems.

The default integer type on typical systems, Int64, ranges between -2^{63} and $2^{63} - 1$, with one bit used for the sign.

Julia supplies built-in functions for finding the maximum and minimum values representable with each numeric type:

```
julia> typemax(Int32)
2147483647

julia> typemin(Int32)
-2147483648

julia> typemax(Int16)
32767

julia> typemin(Int16)
-32768
```

But typemax() and typemin() aren't very helpful if we ask them about floats:

```
julia> typemax(Float64)
Inf

julia> typemax(Float16)
Inf16

julia> Inf64 === Inf
true
```

Apparently infinity is a floating-point number, and Julia has infinities for each size float. This is consistent: since nothing is larger than infinity, if Inf16 is a Float16 it must be the largest possible Float16.

Julia has another function that comes to the rescue here:

```julia
julia> floatmax(Float64)
1.7976931348623157e308

julia> floatmin(Float64)
2.2250738585072014e-308

julia> floatmax(Float16)
Float16(6.55e4)

julia> floatmin(Float16)
Float16(6.104e-5)
```

The functions floatmax() and floatmin() return the maximum *finite* float and the minimum positive float of the requested type.

Usually we should perform arithmetic in our programs using these *native types*, which are the most efficient choices. If needed, and if possible, we can use smaller numbers to save space—for example, Int16—and we can get larger integers using Int128. However, if the native types are not adequate for our purposes, it's usually because we need a lot of precision—in other words, many digits—in our computation. This is the subject of the next section.

To check whether a particular value has a certain type, use the isa() function. We can use it as a normal function or in infix position:

```julia
julia> isa(17, Int64)
true

julia> 17 isa Number
true

julia> 17 isa String
false
```

This function returns a Boolean value. The first two calls return true because 17 is both an Int64 and a Number. The former implies the latter (see "The Type Hierarchy" on page 222).

"Big" and Irrational Types

Julia makes it easy to perform *arbitrary precision arithmetic* using types whose precision grows as needed: where the number of digits can grow without bound. Arithmetic with these types is slower than normal computation with native types, but for some jobs it's the only choice.

Arbitrary Precision

As a simple example of where we would need arbitrary precision types, suppose we want to graph the factorial function. This is the function usually spelled with an exclamation mark:

$$n! = n \times n - 1 \times n - 2 \ldots 1; \qquad 0! = 1$$

The corresponding Julia function is factorial(n). The function grows extremely quickly:

```
julia> factorial(20)
2432902008176640000

julia> factorial(21)
ERROR: OverflowError: 21 is too large to look up in the table;
    consider using `factorial(big(21))` instead
```

This shows that 20 is the largest factorial that fits in an Int64. We can go up to 33! if we use Int128, but what if we want to go bigger?

The error message provides a hint. The big() function converts its argument to a corresponding type with unlimited size and precision. For integers, this is called BigInt, and for floats it's BigFloat.

Let's use BigInt to make a plot of the factorial function:

```
julia> plot(factorial.(big.(1:50)), yscale=:log10,
            legend=:topleft, label="Factorial")
```

Here we're plotting up to 50!, which is far beyond what can fit in a native integer. Figure 8-1 shows the result.

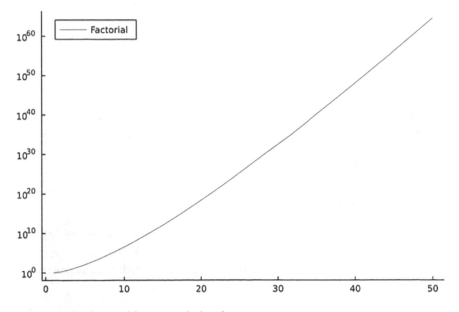

Figure 8-1: The factorial function calculated using BigInt

We'll revisit the factorial in "Factorials" on page 312, where it appears as the number of ways to permute n objects.

The `BigFloat` type also offers unlimited magnitude. Its default precision is 256, giving us about 80 significant digits. We can set the `BigFloat` precision to be anything we need, using the `setprecision()` function:

```julia
julia> big(1.0)/3
0.3333333333333333333333333333333333333333333333333333333
  33333333333333333333333333333348

julia> setprecision(512);

julia> big(1.0)/3
0.3333333333333333333333333333333333333333333333333333333
  33333333333333333333333333333333333333333333333333333333
  33333333333333333333333333333333333333333333333333333333
  333333346
```

To retrieve the precision, we have the `precision()` function, which accepts the type that we're asking about:

```julia
julia> precision(big(1.0))
512

julia> precision(float(1.0))
53
```

The number of digits used for a `BigInt` grows as needed, so it doesn't come with the concept of a fixed precision applicable to the floating-point numbers.

Irrationals

An unusual attribute of Julia is the existence of the *irrational type*:

```julia
julia> π
π = 3.1415926535897...

julia> typeof(π)
Irrational{:π}
```

The number represented by the Greek letter π is printed with three dots appended to suggest that there is more to the story. Although it appears to be a floating-point number, its type is not given as `Float64`, but as something new: `Irrational`. That's because in Julia, π represents *not* a floating-point number, but the *exact value* of the ratio of a circle's circumference to its diameter. The three dots remind us that the digits presented are simply the first few in an endless, nonrepeating series.

Julia calculates and presents more digits as and when needed:

```julia
julia> big(π)
3.141592653589793238462643383279502884197169399375
  1058209749445923078164062862898
```

The number is not printed with trailing dots, as it's no longer a representation of an exact value, but an approximation to it.

Several other irrational numbers are built into Julia; the most important of these for general purposes is *e*, the base of the natural logarithms. To insert this character, which is the Unicode codepoint 212F (Script Small E), enter \euler and press TAB in the REPL:

```
julia> e
e = 2.7182818284590...

julia> big(e)
❶ 2.718281828459045235360287471352662497757247093699995957496696762772407663035
    3555

julia> log(e)
❷ 1

julia> log(2.71828182845904)
0.9999999999999981

julia> log(2.718281828459045)
1.0
```

As with π, Julia displays the value of *e* with three trailing dots to indicate that it's showing us a few digits of an exact value.

We can see an approximation to *e* ❶ to any desired number of digits by converting it to a BigFloat. By definition, the value of the natural logarithm of *e* is exactly the integer 1 ❷, but if we take the logarithms of approximations to *e*, we get an approximate, or floating-point, result.

Type Promotion

When performing arithmetic on a mixture of different numerical types, Julia will silently *promote* types as needed:

```
julia> 1 + 1
2

julia> 1 + 1.0
2.0
```

The addition of two integers provides no reason to leave integer land, so the result is also an Int64. But if one of the numbers is a Float64, the other is promoted to that type, which is also the type of the result.

Julia will not promote nonnumerical types to numbers:

```
julia> 1 + "1"
ERROR: MethodError: no method matching +(::Int64, ::String)
```

Its treatment of types and promotion is therefore similar to Python and dissimilar from JavaScript.

The promote() function takes any number of numerical arguments and returns a tuple with (possibly) some of them promoted as necessary to give them all a common type so they can be used in subsequent calculations without further promotion. It performs the same promotions as would be performed automatically when doing arithmetic:

```
julia> promote(big(2.0), 3.5, 3.4)
(2.0, 3.5, 3.39999999999999991118215802998747676610
 9466552734375)

julia> typeof(promote(big(2.0), 3.5, 3.4))
Tuple{BigFloat, BigFloat, BigFloat}

julia> typeof(promote(2, 3.5, 3.4))
Tuple{Float64, Float64, Float64}
```

The promotion in the first line shows how some numbers (2.0, 3.5) have an exact binary representation, but others (3.4) do not. The two following commands provide examples of how promote() converts its arguments to a common type.

Collections

Julia prints the types of collections in the REPL when printing their values more often than it announces simple numerical types, so we've seen more of the former:

```
julia> [1 2]
1×2 Matrix{Int64}:
 1  2

julia> [1.0; 2]
2-element Vector{Float64}:
 1.0
 2.0

julia> [[1 2];;; [3 4]]
1×2×2 Array{Int64, 3}:
[:, :, 1] =
 1  2

[:, :, 2] =
 3  4
```
❶

Julia prints the type of collection (Matrix, Vector, or Array) and its dimensions. A Vector is one-dimensional, and a Matrix is two-dimensional. For the more general Array type, Julia prints an integer showing the number of dimensions: here it's a three-dimensional array ❶.

It also indicates the types of the collection's elements inside curly brackets. We can extract this information separately using the eltype() function:

```
julia> eltype([1 2])
Int64

julia> eltype([1.0 2])
Float64

julia> eltype([1.0 "2"])
❶ Any

julia> [1.0 "2"]
1×2 Matrix{Any}:
 1.0  "2"
```

In the first example, the result, Int64, is the type of both elements of the array. The second example shows how Julia promotes numerical types when possible to create homogeneous arrays, which are more efficient to calculate with. However, when confronted with types where no promotion is possible ❶, the element type becomes Any: a type that literally means any type.

These results follow the behavior of the promote() function:

```
julia> promote(1.0, 2)
(1.0, 2.0)

julia> promote(1.0, "2")
ERROR: promotion of types Float64 and String failed to change any arguments
```

If elements can be promoted to a common type, that type is used for the eltype of the collection; otherwise, the Any type is used.

The collection types Vector, Matrix, and Array have some behaviors in common: for example, they can all be indexed. This is not true of all collections, however. The Set type has no ordering, hence no ability to be indexed. These three collection types share certain behaviors because they're special cases of a more general type, a concept that we'll explore in the next section.

The Type Hierarchy

All types in Julia are *subtypes* of types that are their *supertypes*. The one type that has no strict supertype is the Any type, which is its own supertype. The concepts of supertypes and subtypes are connected with the inheritance of behaviors, and the configuration of the type hierarchy is usually intuitive when applied to particular cases. For example, we expect that any kind of number will support some notion of addition. Exactly what addition means may vary among various species of numbers—addition of complex numbers is a generalization of addition of real numbers, for example—but when we encounter a type that is a subtype of the Number type, we can be confident that, at least, the + operator is defined for it.

As shown in Listing 8-1, the supertype() function, when supplied a type, returns its supertype.

```
julia> typeof(17)
Int64

julia> supertype(Int64)
Signed

julia> supertype(Signed)
Integer

julia> supertype(Integer)
Real

julia> supertype(Real)
Number

julia> supertype(Number)
Any

julia> supertype(Any)
Any
```

Listing 8-1: Walking up the type hierarchy

The typeof() function returns the type of a literal value or variable. The types that we actually compute with, such as Float64 and Int64, are called *concrete types*. Concrete types are leaves at the tips of the tree of types; they can not subtype each other.

Listing 8-1 shows a series of calls to supertype() to find where the default integer type, Int64, lies in the type hierarchy. All of the types that concrete types such as Int64 inherit from are *abstract types*. The purpose of abstract types, such as Number, is simply to create nodes in the tree of types to enable the definition of methods. The function of these abstract types, and the type hierarchy that they constitute, is not to make things more complicated, but to make the life of the Julia programmer easier. Because of the tree of types, we can define functions and methods that operate at the ideal level of abstraction, as we'll see in "Functions and Methods: Multiple Dispatch" on page 229.

The final two lines in Listing 8-1 show that Number is at the top of the hierarchy of numerical types, and its supertype, Any, is the root of the entire hierarchy, and, as the last line shows, is its own supertype.

By making more calls to supertype(), we can explore more of the type tree. Listing 8-2 shows a modification of the program in Listing 7-3 to visualize a section of it.

```
using Plots
using Graphs
using GraphRecipes

sometypes = [Any, Complex, Float64, Int64, Number, Signed,
             Irrational, AbstractFloat, Real,
             AbstractIrrational, Integer, String, Char,
             AbstractString, AbstractChar, Rational,
             Int32, Vector, DenseVector, AbstractVector,
             Array, DenseArray, AbstractArray]

type_tree = SimpleDiGraph(length(sometypes))

for t in sometypes[2:end]
❶ add_edge!(type_tree, indexin([supertype(t)], sometypes)[1],
             indexin([t], sometypes)[1])
end

graphplot(type_tree; names=[string(t) for t in sometypes], nodeshape=:rect,
          fontsize=4, nodesize=0.17, nodecolor=:white, method=:buchheim)
```

Listing 8-2: Visualizing part of the type hierarchy

We've collected a handful of mostly numeric types in the sometypes vector. These are a subset of the total number of types that come with Julia and its standard library, and many more are defined in various packages.

Listing 8-2 uses the supertype() function to create the edges ❶ of the tree graph, connecting each type to its supertype. Figure 8-2 shows the result.

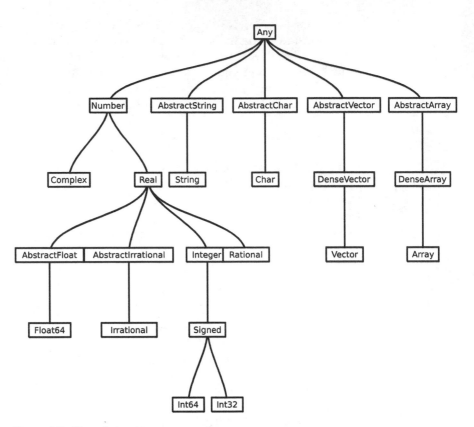

Figure 8-2: The relationships among a few types

Figure 8-2 makes it clear that Any is the root of the tree and reminds us that, for example, characters and strings are distinct types. But it also obscures certain relationships, such as that some types are aliases of others. This is a topic we'll explore later in this chapter (see "Type Aliases" on page 247).

Two additional functions that are handy for exploring the type hierarchy are subtypes(), which returns a vector of all the *immediate* subtypes of the type supplied as an argument, and supertypes():

```
julia> supertypes(Irrational)
(Irrational, AbstractIrrational, Real, Number, Any)
```

This example shows that supertypes() returns a tuple containing the type supplied and all of its supertypes.

Type Assertions and Declarations

Now we know how to discover the type of any variable and the supertype of any type. On occasion, we also need to tell Julia that a variable is of a particular type (a *type declaration*), or that the value of an expression should have a specified type (a *type assertion*). The :: operator performs either operation, depending on where it occurs.

Type Assertions

Sometimes in our programs we reach a point where it is important to ensure that the value of a particular expression has a certain type. If it does not, we want to generate an error, which we can either handle or allow to halt the program.

The simplest expression in Julia is a literal value. Let's use 17 as our first example:

```
julia> 17::Number
17

julia> 17::Integer
17

julia> 17::Int64
17

julia> 17::String
ERROR: TypeError: in typeassert, expected String, got a value of type Int64
```

The first line is an assertion that 17 has the Number type, which of course it does. An expression with a type assertion attached returns the value of the expression if the assertion is true, so here Julia simply returns 17. The following two lines are also true assertions. A type assertion is true if it specifies any supertype of the type of the expression.

The final type assertion returns an error because 17 is neither a String nor a subtype of the String type.

Here's an example of how we might use a type assertion in a program:

```
function greetings()
    println("Who are you?")
    yourname = readline();
    greeting = ("Hello, " * yourname * ".")
❶  return greeting::String
end
```

The program asks the user a question, receives the reply using readline(), and joins it with two other strings to construct a greeting, which it returns. We used a type assertion ❶ to ensure that the type returned by the function is what is expected.

Type Declarations

We also use the :: operator for type declarations. Its meaning is determined from its position within a statement.

We can declare that a variable has a particular type in two ways. One way is to supplement the usual assignment statement with a declaration, as in this example:

```
julia> a::Int16 = 17
17

julia> typeof(a)
Int16
```

Here the assignment and the type declaration happen simultaneously.

NOTE *Julia v1.8 was the first version that allowed type declarations of global variables; this makes working in the REPL more convenient. In earlier versions, all type declarations must occur in a local scope.*

Once we declare the type of a variable, we are committed:

```
julia> a = "Paris"
ERROR: MethodError: Cannot `convert` an object
  of type String to an object of type Int16

julia> a::Int32 = 17
ERROR: cannot set type for global a. It already
  has a value or is already set to a different type.
```

As this example shows, an attempt to assign a value of the wrong type to a declared variable, or to explicitly change its type, results in an error.

Any value assigned to a must be convertible to a's type, Int16:

```
julia> a = 32767
32767

julia> a = 32768
ERROR: InexactError: trunc(Int16, 32768)
```

The second assignment failed because 32,768 is larger than the largest value that an Int16 can hold, which is $2^{15} - 1 = 32,767$, returned by typemax(Int16).

Listing 8-3 shows the other way to declare a type: as part of a local or global definition.

```
julia> global gf::Float64

julia> gf = 17
17

julia> gf
17.0 ❶
```

```
julia> typeof(gf)
Float64

julia> gf = "London"
ERROR: MethodError: Cannot `convert` an object
  of type String to an object of type Float64 ❷

julia> function weather_report(raining)
           if !(raining isa Bool) ❸
               println("Please tell us if it's raining with \"true\" or \"false\".")
               return
           else
               if raining
                   n = ""
               else
                   n = "not "
               end
               local gf::String ❹
               gf = "London"
               return("It is $(n)raining in $gf today.")
           end
       end
weather_report (generic function with 1 method)
```

Listing 8-3: Type declarations

We define gf to be global and to have the Float64 type. Julia seems happy to let us assign a literal integer to it, but it has converted the value to a Float64 as part of the assignment ❶. Because there is no way to convert a literal string to a Float64, our attempt to assign a string to the variable failed ❷.

We can use a variable of the same name, declared to be local, inside a function ❹; this local variable has no relationship with the global gf. The function weather_report() expects a Bool from the user (true or false), and uses it to construct a sentence about the weather. It uses the isa operator to check that it's received the correct type ❸.

The following short program illustrates an important behavior of type declarations:

```
function type_dec_demo()
    a = 17
    println("a = $a and has the type $(typeof(a)).")
    local a::Int16
end
```

Running this function produces the output:

```
a = 17 and has the type Int16.
```

The line that prints the type of a comes *before* the type declaration; so why is a already an `Int16`? After all, this is what happens in the REPL:

```julia
julia> a = 17
17

julia> typeof(a)
Int64
```

This output is what we expect, as the concrete type `Int64` is the native integer on a 64-bit machine, which is the most common architecture. The explanation is that a type declaration within a scope block, in this case a function definition, enforces an unchangeable type for the entire block. The declaration can occur anywhere within the block.

In the absence of a declaration, a variable *can* change type within a block as a consequence of arithmetic operations:

```julia
function changing_type_demo()
    a = 17
    println("a = $a and has the type $(typeof(a)).")
    a = a + 1.0
    println("a = $a and has the type $(typeof(a)).")
end
```

This function produces the output:

```
a = 17 and has the type Int64.
a = 18.0 and has the type Float64.
```

Allowing this to happen can interfere with performance, a topic we return to in "Vanquish Type Instability" on page 242.

The :: operator can also declare the type of the value returned by a function. For example, we can change the first line of the definition of `weather_report()` in Listing 8-3 as follows:

```julia
function weather_report(raining)::String
```

This asserts that the function must return a `String` value.

The purpose of such declarations is the same as type declarations for variables: they are never required, and usually not needed, but in some cases they can provide extra information to the compiler that helps with performance. We'll see some examples of this in "Performance Tips" on page 242. When we construct expressions using functions, it's helpful to know the types returned by each function call; using type declarations in function definitions assists in writing correct and efficient programs.

Functions and Methods: Multiple Dispatch

When we define a function in the REPL, if there are no errors, we'll see a message like the one we saw after the definition of weather_report() in Listing 8-3:

```
weather_report (generic function with 1 method)
```

A generic function is defined by its name, in this case weather_report(). Each generic function can have any number of *methods* associated with it, which are distinguished by their method *signatures*. The signature is the part that goes inside the parentheses when you define the method. Up until now, these signatures have included the names of positional and keyword arguments and their default values, if any. If we make a second definition of weather_report() with a different set of arguments in its signature, we will have created a second method.

A further use of the :: operator is within method signatures, to specify the types that the arguments therein are supposed to have. Two definitions, both with the same arguments, define different methods if any of these type specifications are different, even if the signatures are otherwise the same.

When the compiler sees a function call, it invokes the method with the most specific definition that matches the arguments supplied in the call. Here is where we see the real purpose of the abstract types that we learned about in "The Type Hierarchy" on page 222. With all else being equal, a method defined using a particular type for one of its arguments is more specific than one defined for a supertype for the same argument.

To determine which method to call, the compiler examines *all* of the arguments. This procedure for method selection, or *dispatch*, is called *multiple dispatch* for this reason. It is an unusual, but not unique, feature in the landscape of programming languages, and it's a major reason for Julia's power and success.

In contrast, object-oriented languages dispatch solely on the first argument of a method, often supplied implicitly as the object the method is part of and represented within the procedure with variables such as this or self.

Functional languages have no real dispatch mechanism at all. All specialization must take the form of alternative code paths within one large function.

Julia's multiple dispatch paradigm means that it is neither an object-oriented nor a functional language, but something more general and flexible than either of them.

Creating Multiple Methods

Our definition of weather_report() included a check that the supplied argument was the correct type and a measure to take in case it wasn't, implemented in an if block. We can eliminate that check by restarting the REPL and replacing the definition of weather_report() with two other methods with different signatures:

```julia
julia> function weather_report(raining::Bool)
           if raining
               n = ""
           else
               n = "not "
           end
           gf = "London"
           println("It is $(n)raining in $gf today.")
       end

weather_report (generic function with 1 method)

julia> function weather_report(raining)
           println("Please tell us if it's raining with \"true\" or \"false\".")
           return
       end

weather_report (generic function with 2 methods)
```

After the first definition, the REPL replies with the same message as before, but after the second, we are informed that weather_report() now has two methods. The only difference between our two methods is that the first has a type specification for the single argument, raining, in its signature, whereas the second does not. The absence of a type specification means that the compiler will accept an argument with any type, or, said another way, with the Any type. The rule is that the compiler will always select the most specific method for the arguments supplied. If we supply a Bool (true or false), the first method is selected, because it's more specific than the second, as Bool is a subtype of Any. Any other type dispatches the second method, and the request to supply true or false.

Let's verify that the two methods work the way we expect:

```julia
julia> weather_report(true)
It is raining in London today.

julia> weather_report(17)
"Please tell us if it's raining with "true" or "false"."
```

This technique of creating a collection of methods rather than cramming a bunch of type-checking code into one larger function is more idiomatic to

Julia and leads to better-organized projects that are easier to maintain and extend.

Suppose we wanted to extend the function by giving it the ability to comment on the weather in a city supplied by the user. The power of multiple dispatch allows us to simply add another method without changing anything we've already written:

```julia
julia> function weather_report(raining::Bool, city::String)
           if raining
               n = ""
           else
               n = "not "
           end
           println("It is $(n)raining in $city today.")
       end

weather_report (generic function with 3 methods)

julia> weather_report(true, "Tegucigalpa")
It is raining in Tegucigalpa today.
```

If we try to call weather_report() with arguments that don't match the signature of any existing method, we get an error message:

```julia
julia> weather_report(true, 17)
ERROR: MethodError: no method matching weather_report(::Bool, ::Int64)
Closest candidates are:
  weather_report(::Bool) at REPL[1]:1
  weather_report(::Bool, ::String) at REPL[7]:1
  weather_report(::Any) at REPL[4]:1
```

The error message tells us that none of the methods of weather_report() have the right signature and lists some of the available methods, showing the types we can use for their arguments. We'll get a similar error if we, for instance, try to add two things that can't be added, such as 1 + "1", but the three or so possible methods mentioned in the error message will be a small fraction of the over 200 methods defined for the + operator. To see a list of all the methods defined for any function, call methods():

```julia
julia> methods(weather_report)
# 3 methods for generic function "weather_report":
[1] weather_report(raining::Bool) in Main at REPL[1]:1
[2] weather_report(raining::Bool, city::String) in Main at REPL[7]:1
[3] weather_report(raining) in Main at REPL[4]:1
```

Here we see the list of methods we've defined for weather_report() with their method signatures.

Extending Built-in Functions with New Methods

Suppose we had a program that reads numbers from a file, or from user input, and adds them to an existing number. The read-in values would be strings, and the program would have to convert them to numbers before performing the addition. Listing 8-4 shows a case like this, where we might decide to eliminate the explicit conversion step from the program by adding a method to + that does the conversion automatically.

```
import Base.+
function +(a::Number, b::String)
    if Meta.parse(b) isa Number
        return a + Meta.parse(b)
    else
        return a
    end
end
```

Listing 8-4: Extending addition with a new method

We're not allowed to extend certain basic functions, such as +, unless we first explicitly import them, which is accomplished in the first line. After defining this method, it will be dispatched on any attempt to add a string to a number, something that normally results in a `MethodError`. If the `String` argument can be parsed as a `Number`, that number is added to the first argument and the method returns the result. If it can't, the method simply returns the first argument. This method definition is an example of the use of abstract types in signatures. It will work for any type of number in the first argument, without the need to write definitions for each subtype of `Number`.

Let's check that this method works as intended:

```
julia> 1 + "16"
17

julia> 1 + "16.0"
17.0

julia> 1 + "sixteen"
1

julia> 1//2 + "3"
7//2

julia> π + "1"
4.141592653589793
```

We've added to the language by extending the behavior of one of its basic operators. Multiple dispatch gives us the power to do this without altering any existing methods.

Specialized methods are not only useful for creating new behaviors, they're sometimes created for efficiency. For example, operations such as matrix multiplication or matrix inverse produce mathematically well-defined results (when they exist); however, for matrices with certain properties, specialized algorithms for computing that result may be more efficient than a general algorithm. The SparseArrays package (see "The Adjacency Matrix" on page 196) provides methods for these matrix operations that are more efficient when one or both of the arguments is a sparse array. Multiple dispatch will automatically select the ideal method when a matrix operator is passed a sparse array, without any intervention needed on the part of the user.

Although we can create new methods to do anything we want, it makes sense that their behavior be conceptually related to the purpose or meaning of the generic function that they are a part of. Each of the over 200 methods for + has something to do with the idea of addition, as does the new method that we've defined here. Multiple dispatch should be seen as a paradigm for code organization rather than a license for chaos. The language does nothing to enforce this principle, which depends on the discipline of the programmer.

Understanding Union Types and the <: Operator

Sometimes, when constructing a method, a single abstract type is not general enough for our purposes. In such cases, we can declare an argument to have any one of several types using Union{}. This is an operator that accepts a list of types and constructs a new type that includes all of them. A value that has the type of anything in the list belongs to the new union type. Also, a type that is a subtype of any of the types in the list is a subtype of the union.

The <: infix operator is a test that acts on types and returns true if the type on its left is a subtype of the type on its right. This example illustrates the creation of a union type and the use of the <: operator:

```
julia> 17 isa Union{Number, String}
true
```

```
julia> Real <: Union{Number, String}
true
```

Because 17 is a Number, the first expression returns true.

Suppose we want to write a function that acts on real numbers other than integers: numbers with a decimal point. We might consider using a type declaration in the function signature such as n::AbstractFloat, which would include all the concrete floating types, such as Float64 and Float32. However, examining Figure 8-2 reminds us that this declaration would exclude any number supplied as an Irrational. If the user stuck in a literal π as an argument, a MethodError would be the result. We can use a union type to handle this scenario: n::Union{AbstractFloat, Irrational}. We might also consider adding Rational to the union, depending on the purpose of the function.

User-Defined Types

Just as we can create our own verbs (functions and methods) for our own purposes, we can create our own nouns (data types) as well. The purpose of user-defined types in Julia is the same as the main purpose of types in general: to organize projects around methods that can be dispatched based on the types of their arguments.

Creating Abstract Types

Sometimes, rather than simply adding a leaf to the tree of types we will want to add a branch and then create types as leaves attached to that branch. As we mentioned earlier, these branches are *abstract* types, and we can make our own with the abstract type declaration. As an example of its use, here is how to create a new abstract type descended from the Number type:

```
julia> abstract type MyNumber <: Number end
```

After executing this statement, the new type MyNumber will be a subtype of the existing abstract type Number (recall that concrete types cannot be subtyped).

If the new type is something really new that won't share methods with existing types, there's no need for it to inherit from any existing type. However, if it is a new type of number, string, or other existing type, it makes sense to place it appropriately in the type hierarchy. This way, existing methods that act on the Number type, for example, will be able to handle the new subtype of number.

Creating Composite Types

The purpose of creating a new abstract type is to be able to define new types as its subtypes, types that actually hold values and that we manipulate in calculations. These new types can either descend directly from Any or descend from an abstract type that we create.

In almost all cases, these new types will be *composite types*, defined in a struct block:

```
struct EarthLocation
    latitude::Float64
    longitude::Float64
    timezone::String
end
```

Composite types typically have several fields (but may have only one). The new EarthLocation type is intended to represent a location on Earth by its latitude and longitude and includes a field for the location's time zone. The type declarations on the fields are optional; a field without a declaration will be of the Any type.

The following creates a variable with this type:

```
julia> NYC = EarthLocation(40.7128, -74.006, "ET")

julia> typeof(NYC)
EarthLocation
```

This function, created by Julia using the same name as the type, is called a *constructor*. As the second interaction shows, it creates values with the EarthLocation type.

We can access a composite type's field values using property notation:

```
julia> NYC.latitude
40.7128

julia> NYC.timezone
"ET"
```

The fields are assigned in the order in which they appear in the type's definition.

Since a constructor is a function, we can define multiple methods for it. Here is one that handles the case where the caller supplies coordinates but no time zone:

```
julia> EarthLocation(a, b) = EarthLocation(a, b, "Unknown")
EarthLocation

julia> someplace = EarthLocation(59.45607, -135.316681)
EarthLocation(59.45607, -135.316681, "Unknown")

julia> someplace.timezone
"Unknown"
```

The method dispatched when the caller uses only two arguments calls the original method with "Unknown" as the time zone. This method could have done anything, but naming it the same as the constructor for EarthLocation types and having it return something other than an instance of that type would be confusing. As mentioned in "Parametric Types" on page 248, we should exploit the type system and multiple dispatch to make our code easier to understand, rather than the opposite.

Suppose we decide to use a different convention for recording time zones, and try to make some changes to existing variables:

```
julia> NYC.timezone = "America/New_York"
ERROR: setfield!: immutable struct of type EarthLocation cannot be changed
```

Julia objects to what seems like a reasonable attempt to assign a new value to one of the fields of NYC. By default, composite types are immutable, which permits the compiler to generate more efficient code in some circumstances. If a program requires types whose field values can be changed, we need to explicitly define our type using the mutable keyword:

```
mutable struct MutableEarthLocation
    latitude::Float64
    longitude::Float64
    timezone::String
end
```

With this definition, we can alter variables with the MutableEarthLocation type:

```
julia> NYC = MutableEarthLocation(40.7128, -74.006, "ET")
MutableEarthLocation(40.7128, -74.006, "ET")

julia> NYC.timezone = "US/Eastern"
"US/Eastern"

julia> NYC
MutableEarthLocation(40.7128, -74.006, "US/Eastern")
```

We can change the values of fields of mutable composite types at will. However, when this isn't necessary, such as when the type represents a permanent object that should not be mutated, it's generally better to define it without the mutable keyword.

Using Composite Types

Let's explore a simple example that shows the usefulness of creating our own types, along with methods designed to operate on them. The idea is to define a couple of types representing circles. They'll be somewhat different from each other, but since they both represent circles, they will have some commonality. We plan to write some methods that are specialized to our two circle types, and at least one that should be applicable to both (or more, if we extend the project in the future). This situation calls for the creation of an abstract type to represent circles in general, from which we'll derive each composite circle type:

```
abstract type Circle end
```

If we're not concerned *where* a circle is, we can define it completely by its radius. With this in mind, let's define our first composite circle type to have only one field:

```
struct FloatingCircle <: Circle
    r::Real
end
```

Here r represents the circle's radius, which can be any Real number. The type FloatingCircle is a subtype of our abstract Circle type:

```
julia> supertypes(FloatingCircle)
(FloatingCircle, Circle, Any)
```

Our next circle type also contains information about the shape's position in space:

```
struct PositionedCircle <: Circle
    x::Real
    y::Real
    r::Real
end
```

Of course, PositionedCircle is also defined as a subtype of Circle. The real numbers x and y are intended to hold the coordinates of its center. The abstract Circle type now has two subtypes:

```
julia> subtypes(Circle)
2-element Vector{Any}:
 FloatingCircle
 PositionedCircle
```

What we have so far might be the beginnings of a package to perform some geometrical calculations.

Suppose the next step is to write a function that calculates the area of a circle. This area doesn't depend on where the circle happens to be, only on its radius. Therefore, it should accept either subtype of the abstract Circle type and any future subtype that we might come up with:

```
function circle_area(c::Circle)
    return π * c.r^2
end
```

The `circle_area()` function's signature demands that the type of its argument is a subtype of Circle. If it is, it will have a radius, which, by convention, we call r in all of our circular composite types:

```
julia> c1 = FloatingCircle(1)
FloatingCircle(1)

julia> c1.r
1
```

❶
```
julia> circle_area(c1)
3.141592653589793

julia> c2 = PositionedCircle(2, 2, 1)
PositionedCircle(2, 2, 1)

julia> c2.x, c2.y
(2, 2)

julia> c2.r
1
```

❷
```
julia> circle_area(c2)
3.141592653589793

julia> circle_area(17)
ERROR: MethodError: no method matching circle_area(::Int64)
```

After confirming that the new function calculates areas correctly for both FloatingCircles ❶ and PositionedCircles ❷, we forget that `circle_area()` deals only with subtypes of Circle and try to hand it a number, which results in a MethodError.

Let's add one more function to this geometry project: a routine that takes two circles and tells us if the second circle is entirely within the first.

```
function is_inside(c1::PositionedCircle, c2::PositionedCircle)
    d = sqrt((c2.x - c1.x)^2 + (c2.y - c1.y)^2)
    return d + c2.r < c1.r # true if c2 is inside c1
end
```

The function calculates the distance between the centers of the two circles using their x- and y-coordinates, and then checks whether one lies inside the other by referring to their radii. Of course, the concept of a circle being "inside" another makes sense only if we can say where the circles are, so the new function accepts only PositionedCircles and will have only one method.

Let's try it:

```
julia> a = PositionedCircle(2, 2, 2)
PositionedCircle(2, 2, 2)

julia> b = PositionedCircle(1, 1, 0.5)
PositionedCircle(1, 1, 0.5)

julia> is_inside(a, b)
true

julia> c = PositionedCircle(3, 3, 1)
PositionedCircle(3, 3, 1)

julia> is_inside(a, c)
false
```

It seems to be working, but to be sure, it will help to make a diagram. We can draw our three circles using Luxor in a program similar to the one in Listing 7-1:

```
using Luxor
@pdf begin
    origin(Point(30, 30))
❶   scale(100, 100)
    fontsize(0.32)
    fontface("Liberation Sans")
    setdash("solid")
    setcolor("black")
    circle(Point(2, 2), 2, :stroke)
    text("a", Point(1, 3))
    setcolor("blue")
    circle(Point(1, 1), 0.5, :stroke)
    text("b", Point(1, 1))
    setcolor("green")
    circle(Point(3, 3), 1, :stroke)
    text("c", Point(3, 3))
end 500 500 "circles.pdf"
```

The Luxor package uses points as its unit of length, so we expand our dimensions ❶ to make a reasonably sized illustration. The labels on the circles are the same as the names we gave them before. Figure 8-3 shows the diagram that this program creates, where we can see that the is_inside() function calculates the "inside" relationship correctly.

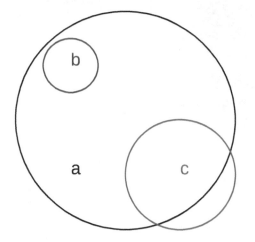

Figure 8-3: Circle b is inside a, but c is not.

We know how to enforce types used in constructors for user-defined types. But what if we want to constrain the allowed values passed to the constructors? Here's how to make a type like our FloatingCircle that demands a positive radius:

```
struct ReasonableCircle <: Circle
    r::Real
❶ ReasonableCircle(r) =
        if r >= 0
            new(r)
        else
            @error("It's not reasonable to make a circle with a negative radius.")
        end
end

julia> ReasonableCircle(-12)
 Error: It's not reasonable to make a circle with a negative radius.
 @ Main REPL[4]:7

julia> ReasonableCircle(12).r
12
```

As with functions, constraints on the values passed as arguments must be enforced in the body. The method inside the body ❶ is called an *inner constructor*; the other constructors we've been using up to now are *outer constructors*. The function new() creates the instance. It's used only inside inner constructors.

Those who have experience with a class-based object-oriented language, such as Python, are sometimes at a temporary disadvantage when trying to absorb the concept of a user-defined composite type in Julia. We all have a tendency, when confronting a new concept, to relate it to concepts that are familiar to us. Composite types in Julia are not classes; Julia has no classes and, obviously, no class inheritance. In an object-oriented language, the next step would be to define methods as part of the class: the nouns and verbs are bound together. The more flexible multiple dispatch paradigm decouples nouns and verbs. Julia programmers are free to write methods that act upon any combination of types and to create new types at will, without friction.

Defining structs with Base.@kwdef

The default method for defining composite types leaves a bit to be desired. Its main deficiency is that the constructor it creates requires the programmer to remember the order in which a type's fields appear in its definition. The `Base.@kwdef` macro improves on this limitation by creating constructors that we can use with field names. For repeated use, it's convenient to import this macro and rename it: `import Base.@kwdef as @kwdef`.

Let's expand our geometry package with a new type representing ellipses as shown in Listing 8-5. This time we'll use `@kwdef`.

```
@kwdef struct Ellipse
    axis1::Real = 1
    axis2::Real = 1
end
```

Listing 8-5: Defining an Ellipse type with @kwdef

This definition shows the second convenient feature of `@kwdef`: we can supply default values for fields. We also have the option to define a mutable struct with `@kwdef mutable struct`.

Let's make an ellipse and assign it to a variable:

```
julia> oval = Ellipse(axis2=2.6)
Ellipse(1, 2.6)

julia> oval.axis1, oval.axis2
(1, 2.6)
```

This example shows how we can supply a subset of the type's keyword arguments, and the ones we omit will get their default arguments. As with functions, any keyword argument without a default in the type definition must be supplied when using the constructor. Also, similarly to functions, we may not mix positional and keyword forms:

```
julia> Ellipse(2, 3)
Ellipse(2, 3)

julia> Ellipse(2, axis2=3)
ERROR: MethodError: no method matching Ellipse(::Int64; axis2=3)
```

As there is no drawback to using @kwdef when defining composite types, it's convenient to use it routinely.

Because of the way Julia's JIT compiler works with the type system, computing with user-defined types is as fast as using native types. We can work at a higher level of abstraction, creating a set of types that naturally conform to the objects in our problem, without any compromise in performance.

Performance Tips

Speed and efficiency are often of great concern in scientific programming. While Julia generally produces performant code without requiring extreme expertise or knowledge of internals, good performance does sometimes depend on an awareness of the compilation process.

I've included topics related to performance in various places throughout this book. Here we'll learn about several such issues specifically related to types.

Vanquish Type Instability

Type stability is perhaps the single most important performance-related concept in Julia. Its central principle is that the return values of functions should have types we can predict based on the types of the arguments supplied to the function. The returned type should not depend on the *values* of the arguments. A secondary issue is that the local variables used within a function should not change type.

Suppose we want to have a function for dividing two numbers that would return 0 when the denominator is 0, rather than Inf. Listing 8-6 shows one way to write such a function.

```
function safe_divide(a, b)
    if b == 0
        return 0
    else
        return a/b
    end
end
```

Listing 8-6: This function needs improving.

It certainly seems to work as intended:

```
julia> safe_divide(1, 2)
0.5

julia> safe_divide(1, 0)
0
```

However, the sharp-eyed programmer may notice that in the first case, the function returns a Float64, whereas in the second case it returns an Int64:

```
julia> typeof(safe_divide(1, 2))
Float64

julia> typeof(safe_divide(1, 0))
Int64
```

The types of the arguments in both cases are integers, but the types of the results depend on their values. This type instability may not matter. However, an insidious problem is lurking, as one day we may pull out our safe_divide() function to use within some other program where its varying return type affects performance.

In more complicated functions, the type instability may not be so obvious. In situations where performance or memory consumption makes us wonder whether one of our functions may have such an issue, Julia provides a convenient tool for ferreting out type instability: the @code_warntype macro. Let's use it on our safe_divide() function:

```
julia> @code_warntype safe_divide(1, 2)
MethodInstance for safe_divide(::Int64, ::Int64)
  from safe_divide(a, b) in Main at REPL[7]:1
Arguments
  #self#::Core.Const(safe_divide)
  a::Int64
  b::Int64
Body::Union{Float64, Int64}
1 - %1 = (b == 0)::Bool
--       goto #3 if not %1
2 -      return 0
3 - %4 = (a / b)::Float64
--       return %4
```

This is one of several macros and functions available for use in the REPL that display a translated version of a Julia function. The @code_warntype macro prints a *lowered form* of the code: a representation of the computation in terms of a smaller set of operations. It is one of four stages of code transformation beginning with our Julia source and ending with machine code specific to the processor we're running on. This lowered form is similar to the version that is sent to the compiler, but it contains the type information that we can examine when debugging performance issues. Other than that, it's not particularly useful and not intended for routine human consumption.

When printed in the REPL, type information that indicates a possible type stability issue is displayed in red type, which I've converted to bold for printing in the book. The bold fragment indicates that the return type can be either a `Float64` or an `Int64`: in other words, it's not determined from the types of the input arguments. This is the signature of a type-unstable function.

Fortunately, this case has a simple fix:

```
function safe_divide2(a, b)
    if b == 0
    ❶ return 0.0
    else
        return a/b
    end
end
```

Since `a/b` is always a float, even if `a` and `b` are integers, we can ensure that the function always returns a float by replacing the integer `0` with `0.0` ❶.

To confirm whether we've fixed the type instability problem, let's turn to `@code_warntype` again:

```
julia> @code_warntype safe_divide2(1, 2)
MethodInstance for safe_divide2(::Int64, ::Int64)
  from safe_divide2(a, b) in Main at REPL[5]:1
Arguments
  #self#::Core.Const(safe_divide2)
  a::Int64
  b::Int64
❶ Body::Float64
1 - %1 = (b == 0)::Bool
--       goto #3 if not %1
2 -      return 0.0
3 - %4 = (a / b)::Float64
--       return %4
```

This time, there are no red (bold) warnings, and the macro confirms ❶ that the return type is always a `Float64`.

NOTE   *The output from @code_warntype often also includes yellow warnings involving unions with the Nothing type, which is used when a function does not return a result. These are not usually considered type instabilities.*

We can also correct this type stability problem by defining the function using a type declaration:

```
function safe_divide_typed(a, b)::Float64
    if b == 0
        return 0
    else
        return a/b
    end
end
```

This version, when called with b = 0, will convert its return value to 0.0. It will always return a Float64; @code_warntype will verify its type stability.

Although the form of the code returned by @code_warntype can be difficult to parse, it's fairly simple to use it to scan for type stability problems.

Avoid Changing the Types of Variables

Let's write a function to approximate π using the Leibniz sum:

$$\pi = 4 \left(1 - \frac{1}{3} + \frac{1}{5} - \frac{1}{7} + \dots \right)$$

This is not a good way to get the digits of π, as it converges quite slowly, but it'll be useful for our demonstration. One version of the function might be:

```
function leibπ(N)
    s = 0
    for n in 1:N
        s += (-1)^(n+1) * 1/(2n-1)
    end
    return 4.0s
end
```

This works as intended; Figure 8-4 shows its output gradually converging to the correct value for π.

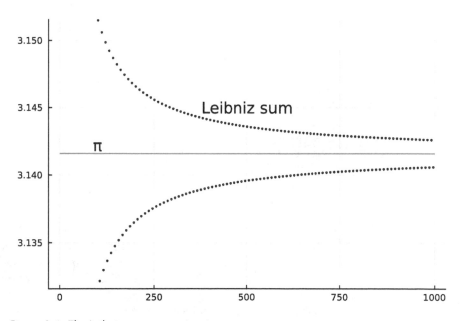

Figure 8-4: The Leibniz sum approximation to π

This function is clearly not type-unstable in the sense used earlier: the output is always a Float64, regardless of the number supplied as an argument.

Nevertheless, taking a look at the output of @code_warntype indicates a problem:

```
julia> @code_warntype leibπ(100)
MethodInstance for leibπ(::Int64)
  from leibπ(N) in Main at REPL[33]:1
Arguments
  #self#::Core.Const(leibπ)
  N::Int64
Locals
  @_3::Union{Nothing, Tuple{Int64, Int64}}
  s::Union{Float64, Int64}
  n::Int64
Body::Float64
1 -       (s = 0)
|   %2  = (1:N)::Core.PartialStruct(UnitRange{Int64}, Any[Core.Const(1), Int64])
|         (@_3 = Base.iterate(%2))
|   %4  = (@_3 === nothing)::Bool
|   %5  = Base.not_int(%4)::Bool
--        goto #4 if not %5
2   %7  = @_3::Tuple{Int64, Int64}
|         (n = Core.getfield(%7, 1))
|   %9  = Core.getfield(%7, 2)::Int64
|   %10 = s::Union{Float64, Int64}
|   %11 = (n + 1)::Int64
|   %12 = ((-1) ^ %11)::Int64
|   %13 = (%12 * 1)::Int64
|   %14 = (2 * n)::Int64
|   %15 = (%14 - 1)::Int64
|   %16 = (%13 / %15)::Float64
|         (s = %10 + %16)
|         (@_3 = Base.iterate(%2, %9))
|   %19 = (@_3 === nothing)::Bool
|   %20 = Base.not_int(%19)::Bool
--        goto #4 if not %20
3 -       goto #2
4   %23 = (4.0 * s)::Float64
--        return %23
```

Once again, the warnings are rendered in bold. They inform us that the local variable s is a union of the types Float64 and Int64, rather than a single numerical type. This happens because we initialize it as a literal integer, 0, but then use it in a loop that causes Julia to promote it to a float.

Changing the type of a local variable may prevent the compiler from optimizing our code as well as it could otherwise. This is a common mistake, as the pattern of initializing variables and then using them in a for loop is routine. When doing so, we should take care to initialize them with types appropriate to the arithmetic in the loop.

This case is also easy to fix:

```
function leibπ2(N)
❶ s = 0.0
    for n in 1:N
        s += (-1)^(n+1) * 1/(2n-1)
    end
    return 4.0s
end
```

As before, we simply have to replace 0 with 0.0 ❶. I won't reproduce the (mostly redundant) output here, but checking with @code_warntype shows that the warnings are gone.

Type Aliases

Several types have alternative names, called *type aliases*. The use of aliases is for convenience; they are typically shorter names or dispense with the indication of the machine's pointer size. For example, on a 64-bit computer, Int is another name, or alias, for Int64, but on a 32-bit machine, Int means Int32:

```
julia> typeof(17)
Int64

julia> 17 isa Int
true

julia> Int === Int64
true
```

This shows that, at least on my computer, Int is another name for Int64.

We can create our own type aliases:

```
julia> const F64 = Float64
Float64

julia> typeof(3.14)
Float64

julia> 3.14 isa F64
true
```

Here we've created an alternative name for the default floating-point type. After this definition, we can use F64 and Float64 interchangeably.

Defining type aliases as const is not required, but it makes sense, as they are additional names for something that will not change.

Parametric Types

A parametric type is a type made from pieces that themselves can be of several possible types. The parameters are variables that vary with the types of the pieces.

Listing 8-7 shows an example of a parametric type that we've already encountered, the type used for complex numbers.

```
julia> typeof(2 + 2im)
Complex{Int64}

julia> typeof(2.0 + 2.0im)
ComplexF64 (alias for Complex{Float64})

julia> typeof(2.0 + 2im)
❶ ComplexF64 (alias for Complex{Float64})

julia> typeof(1//2 + 1//2im)
Complex{Rational{Int64}}
```

Listing 8-7: The types of some complex numbers

The curly brackets ({}) in the type names indicate that we're dealing with *parametric types*. In the first line, we've asked for the type of a complex number that's written using integer literals for each coefficient. The response indicates that the number is Complex with an Int64 parameter; this parameter is the type of the coefficients.

The second line tells us something similar, but this time the complex number has floating-point coefficients. In addition, we learn about an alias for the type.

The fact that there is only one parameter within the curly brackets suggests that both coefficients must have the same type. This is indeed true; mixing literal floats and integers causes an automatic conversion of the integer coefficient to a Float64 coefficient ❶.

In the final example, we've created a complex number with Rational coefficients. This time the parameter is itself a parametric type. Rational numbers can be composed of any integers. The Rational{Int64} notation means that the numerator and denominator are Int64s rather than, for example, Int32s.

Collection types, such as Array, are defined as parametric types because they can hold elements of various types:

```
julia> typeof([1,2])
Vector{Int64} (alias for Array{Int64, 1})

julia> supertype(Vector)
❶ DenseVector (alias for DenseArray{T, 1} where T)

julia> supertype(DenseVector)
AbstractVector (alias for AbstractArray{T, 1} where T)
```

The use of aliases is common for collection types, as in these examples. We see here that `Array` is a parametric type with two parameters: the first is the type of the array's elements, and the second is the number of dimensions.

The `where` keyword creates a `UnionAll` type, a union of many types, each defined by assigning a particular type to the type variable `T`. One example of this is the notation `AbstractArray{T, 1}`, where `T` denotes an abstract type that is the union of `AbstractArray{Int64, 1}`, `AbstractArray{Float64, 1}`, and so on.

We can create our own parametric types for the same reason we create any type: to organize our methods with the help of the type system and multiple dispatch.

Let's revisit our `Ellipse` type from Listing 8-5 and make a parametric version of it:

```
@kwdef struct CEllipse{T}
    axis1::T
    axis2::T
end
```

Now the fields can be any type, as long as they are both the same type:

```
julia> e1 = CEllipse(12.0, 17.0)
CEllipse{Float64}(12.0, 17.0)

julia> e2 = CEllipse(12.0, "Snails")
ERROR: MethodError: no method matching CEllipse(::Float64, ::String)
Closest candidates are:
  CEllipse(::T, ::T) where T at REPL[67]:2

julia> e2 = CEllipse("Clams", "Snails")
CEllipse{String}("Clams", "Snails")
```

After defining a new `CEllipse`, the REPL tells us the type, with `Float64` substituted in place of the parameter `T`. Our attempt to give the fields two different types failed because they are both `T` in the type definition. `T` can be anything, but the definition requires that both axes have the same type, so the final example is accepted. But what does it mean to have an ellipse with arbitrary strings for the axes? It's up to us. We are creating types for our own purposes, to organize our projects. If we prefer to limit the `CEllipse` type to have numerical values for the axes, we can use the subtyping operator:

```
@kwdef struct CEllipse{T<:Number}
    axis1::T
    axis2::T
end
```

Before defining this struct, if we're working in the REPL, we're obligated to begin a new session if the previous definition of `CEllipse` is still active. Another option would be to name it differently.

Now a `CEllipse` can have two axes of the same type, and that type can be anything, as long as it's a subtype of `Number`:

```
julia> e2 = CEllipse("Clams", "Snails")
ERROR: MethodError: no method matching CEllipse(::String, ::String)

julia> e2 = CEllipse(1//3, 1//5)
CEllipse{Rational{Int64}}(1//3, 1//5)
```

Since we make `T` a subtype of `Number`, rather than a subtype of the more specific `Real`, we are allowing the possibility of ellipses with complex-valued axes. In some cases, our functions for calculating properties of ellipses will need methods specialized for this case. For an example, let's write a function that returns the eccentricity of an ellipse. This is a measure of how elongated the ellipse is, where an eccentricity of 0 is a circle. If a is the longer of the two axes and b is the shorter, the eccentricity is given by:

$$ e = \frac{\sqrt{a^2 - b^2}}{a} $$

Here's a direct translation of this formula into a Julia function:

```
function eccentricity(e::CEllipse{<:Real})
    a = max(e.axis1, e.axis2)
    b = min(e.axis1, e.axis2)
    return sqrt(a^2 - b^2)/a
end
```

This definition works for real-valued axes, so to ensure that the function accepts only such ellipses, its type parameter specifies subtypes of `Real`.

We can visualize an ellipse with complex-valued axes as lying in the complex plane. We can define ellipses this way as long as we ensure that their axes are perpendicular.

Let's make a method of our eccentricity function that handles these ellipses:

```
function eccentricity(e::CEllipse{<:Complex})
    a = max(abs(e.axis1), abs(e.axis2))
    b = min(abs(e.axis1), abs(e.axis2))
    return sqrt(abs(a)^2 - abs(b)^2)/abs(a)
end
```

The `abs()` function, when handed a complex number, returns its length. We use the `<:` operator in the type parameter slot to include every possible kind of complex number.

We know a bit more about ellipses with complex axes: not merely their eccentricities, but their orientations. Figure 8-5 shows an ellipse in the complex plane.

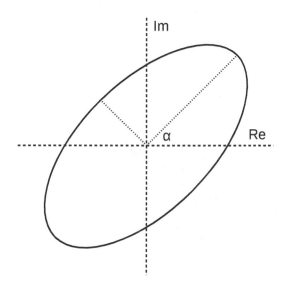

Figure 8-5: An ellipse in the complex plane

Its axes, represented by dotted lines, are $2 + 2i$ and $-1 + i$. We'll define the orientation as the angle that its major (longer) axis makes with the real axis, shown in the figure by α.

Here's the program that created the illustration in Figure 8-5:

```
using Luxor
@pdf begin
    scale(100, 100)
    fontsize(0.22)
    fontface("Liberation Sans")
    setdash("dash") # Coordinate axes
    line(Point(-2, 0), Point(2, 0), :stroke)
    line(Point(0, -2), Point(0, 2), :stroke)
    text("Re", Point(1.6, -0.1))
    text("Im", Point(0.1, -1.8))
    setdash("dot") # Ellipse axes
    line(Point(0, 0), Point(sqrt(2), -sqrt(2)), :stroke)
    line(Point(0, 0), Point(-1/sqrt(2), -1/sqrt(2)), :stroke)
    text("α", Point(0.25, -0.08))
    setdash("solid") # The ellipse
    rotate(-π/4)
    ellipse(0, 0, 4, 2, :stroke)
end 500 500 "ellipse.pdf"
```

Remember, in Luxor the vertical coordinate goes from the top down, opposite to the conventional direction in mathematical diagrams.

This function calculates the orientation of an ellipse with complex axes:

```
function orientation(e::CEllipse{<:Complex})
    if abs(e.axis1) > abs(e.axis2)
```

```
        a = e.axis1
    else
        a = e.axis2
    end
    return angle(a)
end
```

Since no orientation can be defined for an ellipse with axes given only by real-number lengths, orientation() will have just this one method. The angle() function returns a complex number's phase angle; it's equivalent to atan(imag(a)/real(a)).

Let's define an ellipse with complex axes and calculate its eccentricity and orientation:

```
julia> e45 = CEllipse(2 + 2im, -1 + im)
CEllipse{Complex{Int64}}(2 + 2im, -1 + 1im)

julia> eccentricity(e45)
0.8660254037844387

julia> orientation(e45)
0.7853981633974483

julia> orientation(e45) |> rad2deg
45.0
```

This ellipse corresponds to Figure 8-5. The orientation() function returns its result in radians, so for good measure, we've converted that to degrees in the final expression.

Parametric types make Julia's rich type system even more flexible and expressive. Like the other parts of the type system, we're not required to use any of it in our own programs, but a little bit can go a long way in helping with code organization, reuse, and efficiency. Finally, a basic knowledge of parametric types is essential in understanding the messages and information that Julia sends to us, and in reading language and package documentation.

Plot Recipes

As authors of programs, modules, and perhaps packages, we should expect to create our own data types routinely. There is no performance penalty for using custom data types in Julia, and they are essential for writing concise, well-organized code and for taking the best advantage of multiple dispatch.

In Part II of this book we'll explore various packages from the Julia scientific ecosystem. Many of these packages define one or a variety of data types that describe the objects they manipulate. These objects include audio signals, solutions to differential equations, images, measurements with uncertainties, entire environments housing interacting creatures, the creatures themselves, and much more. We'll discover that we can use the plotting commands from Chapter 4 to visualize these data structures directly, with no preprocessing needed on our part. How is it possible that Plots knows what to do with all these different data types?

Visualization is an essential part of scientific computation. The plot *recipe* system is how we hook our data types into Julia's plotting system, that is, how we teach it to handle and display our custom objects. The authors of the scientific packages that we use in Part II did not have to touch the code in the Plots package, which in turn doesn't need to know anything about the new data types. Plot recipes insert data transformations into the plotting *pipeline*, so existing plotting functions can handle our data types as if they were the familiar arrays of numbers.

The result is that users of our programs need simply call plot(), scatter(), or another plotting function on the new data type to get a reasonable visual representation. We can also define entirely new plotting functions for more elaborate visualizations.

We need a specific application in mind to make the operation of plot recipes clear. Let's imagine that we're creating a program that has something to do with the weather, and create some simple data types for representing daily temperature and rainfall data:

```
import Base.@kwdef as @kwdef
using Dates

@kwdef struct TempExtremes
    tempunit::String = "°C"
❶ temps::Vector{Tuple{Float64, Float64}}
end

@kwdef struct WeatherData
    temps::TempExtremes
    rainfall::Vector{Float64}
end

@kwdef struct WeatherReport
    notes::String
    location::Tuple{Float64, Float64}
    data::WeatherData
    start::Dates.Date
end
```

Our temperature data, we'll suppose, comes to us as two measurements per day, representing that day's minimum and maximum temperatures. We'll store these measurements in a vector of tuples ❶, one tuple per day, containing the temperature extrema. That vector of tuples, along with a string holding the temperature unit, are packaged together in the TempExtremes data type.

That data type is put next to a vector of rainfall measurements in another data type called WeatherData.

A third data type, WeatherReport, contains the WeatherData along with some notes, a pair of numbers (latitude and longitude) for the location of the measurements, and the date recording when the series of measurements begin.

Next we make instances of these three data types to have something to plot:

```
tmin = randn(60) .+ 15.0
tmax = tmin .+ abs.(randn(60) .+ 3.0)
td = TempExtremes(temps=collect(zip(tmin, tmax)))
wd = WeatherData(rainfall=abs.(randn(60) .* 5.0 .+ 4), temps=td)
wr = WeatherReport(notes="Rainfall and temperature extremes",
                   location=(-72.03, 45.47),
                   data=wd, start=Date(1856, 12, 31))
```

The randn() function produces normally distributed (see "The Normal Distribution" on page 323) fake random temperature and rain data. Earlier we imported the Date module so we can use one of its data types to define a starting date.

The Plotting Pipeline

The recipe system consists of a series of four recipe varieties that get processed in order in the plotting pipeline, as shown in Listing 8-8.

```
user recipes:
    user types => user types, numerical arrays

type recipes:
    user types => numerical arrays

plot recipes:
    numerical arrays => series
        and
    series => series

series recipes:
    numerical arrays => series
        and
    series => series
```

Listing 8-8: The plotting pipeline

Each recipe type transforms its input and passes it to the next stage in the pipeline; these transformations are indicated after the recipe names. The built-in plotting functions generally know how to plot arrays of numbers, so the plotting recipes have to transform our custom types into ordinary arrays. The first two recipe types, user recipes and type recipes, can do this. The final two recipe types take numerical arrays and produce *series*, which are the components of plots that represent individual vectors, which may be extracted from matrix columns (in one dimension).

The user and plot recipes can also create layouts and set overall plot properties. We don't need to define every one of these recipes, and generally won't require all of them for any particular plotting task. Any that we *have* defined we can use separately, or as part of the pipeline, for different purposes. In this discussion, we'll start at the end of the pipeline and work our way toward the beginning, defining recipes as we go. In this way, each example recipe will do something when we call it directly, passing information along to the previously defined recipes to produce a plot.

The Series Recipe

We define recipes with the `@recipe` macro, exported by the `RecipesBase` package. The macro decorates a function definition where the name of the function is arbitrary. The function's signature determines the type of recipe created. In the following listing, we create two series recipes. The signature, a type followed by three additional positional arguments x, y, and z, tells the pipeline that these are series recipes. As always, the keyword arguments are not part of the function signature for dispatch. Referring to Listing 8-8, we see that these recipes will accept numerical arrays and create series:

```
using RecipesBase

@recipe function f(::Type{Val{:ebxbox}}, x, y, z; cycle=7)
    if cycle <= 2; cycle = 7; end
    ymin = similar(y)
    ymax = similar(y)
    yave = similar(y)
❶ seriestype := :line
    for m = 1:cycle:length(y)
        nxt = min(m+cycle-1, length(y))
        ymin[m] = ymax[m] = yave[m] = NaN
        ymin[m+1:nxt] .= minimum(y[m:nxt])
        ymax[m+1:nxt] .= maximum(y[m:nxt])
        yave[m+1:nxt] .= sum(y[m:nxt]) / (nxt - m + 1)
    end
❷ @series begin
        y := ymax
❸       linecolor --> "#ff000049"
        linewidth --> 6
    end
    @series begin
        y := ymin
        linecolor --> "#0000ff49"
        linewidth --> 6
    end
```

```
    @series begin
        y := yave
        linecolor --> "#66666649"
        linewidth --> 6
    end
end

@recipe function f(::Type{Val{:temprange}}, x, y, z)
    seriestype := :line
    legend := false
    if plotattributes[:series_plotindex] == 1
      ❹ merge!(plotattributes[:extra_kwargs], Dict(:nextfr => y[:]))
        linecolor := :blue
        linewidth := 3
    elseif plotattributes[:series_plotindex] == 2
        fillrange := plotattributes[:extra_kwargs][:nextfr]
        linecolor := :red
        linewidth := 3
        fillcolor := "#45f19655"
    else
        x := []
        y := []
    end
    ()
end
```

To define recipes, we need only import `RecipesBase`. This is important because it means that packages can define plotting behaviors without a dependence on the large `Plots` package. `RecipesBase` is tiny, containing only about 400 lines of Julia.

Plot recipes defined using the `@recipe` macro use several special-purpose syntax conveniences. The `:=` operator ❶ makes a setting in the `plotattributes` dictionary, which holds attributes such as line color—all the options for the plot. Here we set the `seriestype` in the attribute dictionary to `:line`. This is the default series type, which creates a continuous line through the plotted points. Another option is `:scatter`, for plotting individual marks. In fact, the familiar `scatter()` function is a shorthand for `plot(; seriestype=:scatter)`.

The `-->` operator ❸ also makes settings in the `plotattributes` dictionary, but, in this case, defers to settings made in keyword arguments previously in the pipeline. In a sense, these are optional, whereas settings we make with `:=` are important for the series under construction.

Next we have a `for` loop that divides the input y vector into segments of cycle elements and calculates extrema and an average for each segment. It inserts NaNs after each segment to separate them in the plot.

Next come three blocks preceded by the `@series` macro ❷. Each `@series` block creates a new series for the plot. In this case, each will be a `:line` series, since we make that setting outside the blocks, but in general, they can be of different types. They can also create a series type unknown to `Plots`, in which case the pipeline will pass the data on to the recipe where the new series is defined. There can be a chain of series recipes of any length. The data will pass through each in turn until a recipe creates a series type known to the backend in use.

The next recipe is designed to accept an $N \times 2$ matrix. It will plot each of the two columns as lines, the first in blue and the second in red. It will fill the space between the two lines using the `fillrange` attribute. This presents a small problem, as we need to refer to the first column to define the `fillrange` when plotting the second, but the pipeline starts afresh for each column in the input data. However, we know which column we're on by referring to the `:series_plotindex` key in the attribute dictionary. One way to pass information between different columns is to stuff it into the `:extra_kwargs` entry in the attribute dictionary ❹. We call our new attribute `:nextfr`.

Although we have in mind the weather data types defined previously, these recipes don't know anything about that. Like all series recipes, they can plot any arrays of numbers. For actual plotting, we need to import `Plots`:

```
using Plots

@shorthands temprange
@shorthands ebxbox

tl = [t[1] for t in wd.temps.temps]
th = [t[2] for t in wd.temps.temps]

temprange([tl th])

ebxbox(wd.rainfall)
plot!(wd.rainfall)
```

The `@shorthands` macro, provided by `RecipesBase`, takes the names in the function signatures of recipes and makes function names that we can call directly to make plots. For each one, it makes two functions, one for creating a new plot and one for adding to an existing plot, just like `plot()` and `plot!()`.

After transforming the temperature data in `wd` to a matrix, we can use the shorthand on it directly, creating Figure 8-6.

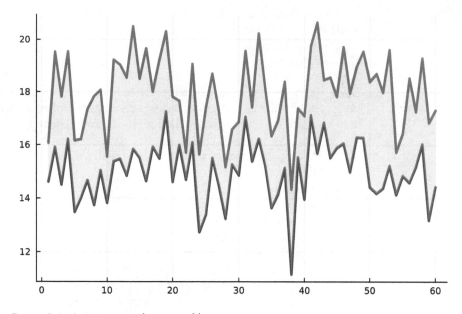

Figure 8-6: A fillrange plot created by a series recipe

For Figure 8-7, we call ebxbox() on the rainfall vector. It only plots the extrema and mean bars, so we add a normal plot of the vector using plot!().

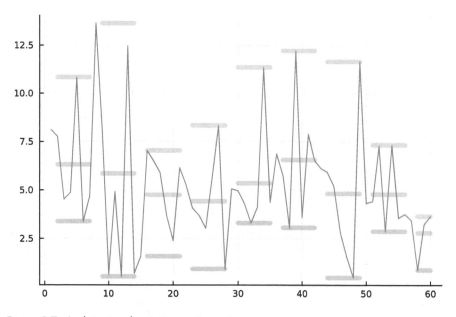

Figure 8-7: A plot using the ebxbox series recipe

We can use these series recipes in other programs and as components within other pipelines.

The Plot Recipe

The type of recipe called a *plot recipe* (not to be confused with the general concept) also transforms series into other series or numerical data into series, as do series recipes, but can create complete visualizations containing subplots and other elements as well. Like all recipes, it's identified by its particular function signature:

```
@recipe function f(::Type{Val{:weatherplot}}, plt::AbstractPlot; cycle=7)
    frames = get(plotattributes, :frames, 1)
    if frames > 1 layout := (2, 1) end
❶ cycle := cycle
    legend := false
    @series begin
      ❷ if frames > 1
            subplot := 1
            xguide := ""
            ylabel := "Temperature (°C)"
        end
      ❸ seriestype := :temprange
    end
    if plotattributes[:series_plotindex] == 3
        @series begin
            if frames > 1 subplot := 2 end
            seriestype := :ebxbox
        end
        @series begin
            if frames > 1
                subplot := 2
                title := ""
                ylabel := "Rainfall (mm)"
            else
                ylabel := "Rainfall (mm) / Temperature (°C)"
            end
            seriestype := :line
            linecolor := :aqua
            linewidth := 3
            linestyle := :dot
        end
    end
end
```

The recipe takes input data in the form of an $N \times 3$ matrix. It uses a `frames` attribute, which we invented for the purpose, to decide whether to place all the series in one plot or to use two subplots ❷, one with temperature and the other with rainfall. (As in the case of the series recipes, this recipe knows nothing of our weather-related data types, so we can repurpose it to plot other types of data as well.)

The cycle variable sets the length of the segments used for calculating extrema and averages in the third column of the input data, which we intend to use for the rainfall data. We use 7 as a default value for this keyword argument, for weekly summaries. If, however, we supply the parameter when calling the recipe directly or upstream in the pipeline, we override the default by reading its value from the plotattributes dictionary ❶.

The three @series blocks handle the first two columns, containing temperature minimums and maximums, and the rainfall in the third column. The temperature @series block sets the series type to temprange ❸, which won't work unless we've already defined a series recipe for it, as we did previously.

The purpose of this recipe, then, is to use the visualizations defined in our series recipes to create a graph with either one or two subplots, with labels appropriate for either case. We can also call it directly, as shown in Listing 8-9.

```
@shorthands weatherplot

weatherplot([tl th wd.rainfall])
```

Listing 8-9: Calling the plot recipe with array data

But we'll defer this for now.

Type Recipes

Referring back to Listing 8-8, we can see that *type recipes* are the first recipes in the pipeline that can accept user-defined types. They're the simplest class of recipe. They have one job: to transform user types into numerical arrays that the functions from Plots can plot directly, or that can be fed into the following steps in the pipeline.

The following listing defines two type recipes; they're recognized as such by their particular function signatures:

```
@recipe function f(::Type{TempExtremes}, v::TempExtremes)
    tmin = [t[1] for t in v.temps]
    tmax = [t[2] for t in v.temps]
    [tmin tmax]
end

@recipe function f(::Type{WeatherData}, wdt::WeatherData)
    tmin = [t[1] for t in wdt.temps.temps]
    tmax = [t[2] for t in wdt.temps.temps]
    [tmin tmax wdt.rainfall]
end
```

The first recipe takes instances of the TempExtremes type defined previously and returns a matrix with two columns; the second transforms WeatherData into a three-column matrix.

After defining these recipes, we can now plot either of these types directly by calling plot(td) or plot(wd). If we do so, we'll get simple line plots of the columns: two from the first call and three from the second, as in Figure 8-8.

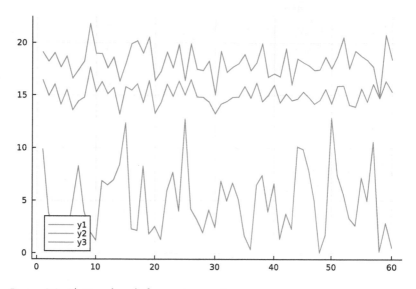

Figure 8-8: Plotting directly from a type recipe

We call plot(wd) to produce Figure 8-8. The top two lines are the temperature extrema and the bottom line is the rainfall.

If, instead, we call weatherplot(wd), we get the exact same plot that would result from the call in Listing 8-9 because the type recipe transforms wd into a three-column matrix. Figure 8-9 shows the result.

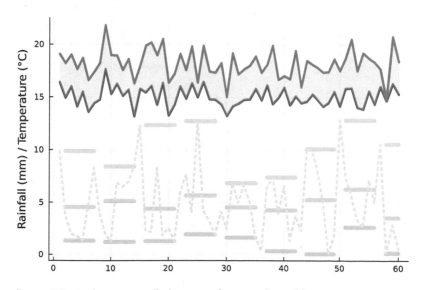

Figure 8-9: A plot recipe called on user data transformed by a type recipe

Here the plot recipe assembles the two types of visualizations, defined in series recipes, onto a single plot, and adds a label on the vertical axis. Since we don't define frames, we get the default single frame.

User Recipes

Now we've ascended to the top of the pipeline. The *user recipes* accept not only single user types, but any combination of types, with each different signature creating a new method for dispatch. They can emit array data or other types, but if they emit types other than array data we must have defined a type recipe to transform them.

Such is the case with the following user recipe:

```
@recipe function f(wr::WeatherReport; frames=1)
    title := wr.notes
    frames := frames
    xlabel --> "Days from $(wr.start)"
    @series begin
        seriestype := :weatherplot
        wr.data
    end
end
```

The pipeline will see this as a user recipe because of its signature. It takes an instance of the WeatherReport data type, creates a title from its notes field, and constructs a useful label for the x-axis by referring to the start field. It has a single @series block, to which it passes the data field. The series invoked is the plot recipe weatherplot, but the data field is not an array, it's WeatherData. The next step in the pipeline, the type recipes, handles any type conversions. Here the WeatherData instance is transformed into a three-column matrix that is handed off to the weatherplot recipe, which optionally sets up the subplots and passes the matrix columns to the series recipes. Calling plot(wr; frames=2) invokes this recipe and creates Figure 8-10.

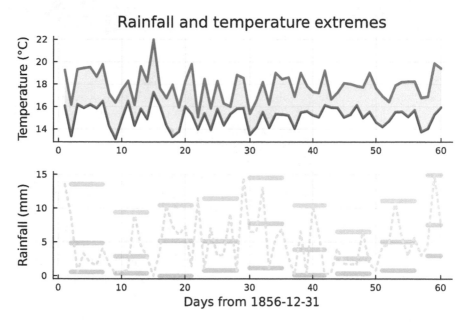

Figure 8-10: The result of calling the user recipe

Defining the user recipe teaches the plot() function how to handle a new data type. As we've seen throughout this section, we can enter the plotting pipeline at any point for a different result, or reuse any of these recipes as part of different pipelines for handling different types of data.

The @userplot Macro

The RecipesBase package also exports the @userplot macro, which is convenient for defining a visualization without having to define a new data type:

```
using SpecialFunctions

@userplot Risep

@recipe function f(carray::Risep)
    seriestype := :line
❶   x, y = carray.args
    @series begin
        label := "Real part"
        linestyle := :solid
        x, real.(y)
    end
    @series begin
        label := "Imaginary part"
        linestyle := :dot
        x, imag.(y)
    end
```

```
end

xc = 0.01:0.001:0.1
risep(xc, expint.(1im, xc); lw=2)
```

The first line after the import creates a new type and a shorthand using its lowercase name. The user recipe that we define using the name of the type is invoked using the shorthand name. Inside the recipe, we can access plot data using the `args` property ❶. The `@userplot` is useful when we want a shorthand name for a particular visualization for an existing type. In this case, we want to plot complex numbers by separating their real and imaginary parts, which may be more useful than the default treatment given them by `plot()`. After defining the recipe, we can invoke it directly using its name as in the last line. The `expint()` function is an exponential integral from the `SpecialFunctions` package, parameterized by its first argument. With the parameter here, it maps real numbers to complex numbers. The result appears in Figure 8-11.

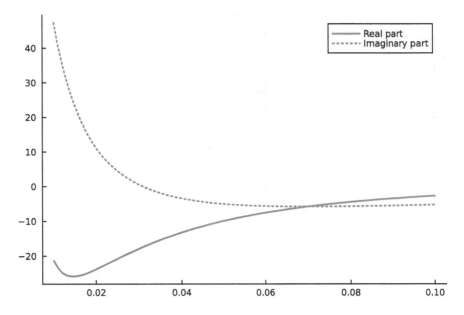

Figure 8-11: Using @userplot to render a vector of complex numbers

We can also use the `@userplot` macro to create alternative visualizations for user-defined types by using type aliases or subtyping.

Conclusion

With this survey of the most important practical aspects of the type system, our introduction to the Julia language is complete. The ideas in this chapter and the preceding ones will find concrete application in the chapters of

Part II, where we'll put Julia to work to solve real problems in a variety of fields.

This book's division into language learning and application sections isn't a strict one, however. We've seen several useful applications in the preceding chapters, and the chapters in Part II will introduce various programming techniques and Julia features in places where they can be immediately applied and more readily appreciated in the context of solving problems.

FURTHER READING

- Details on performance implications of one form of type instability are available at *https://docs.julialang.org/en/v1/manual/performance-tips/#Avoid-changing-the-type-of-a-variable*.

- Dr. Chris Rackauckas gives an example of when dynamic dispatch is a net win here: *https://discourse.julialang.org/t/why-type-instability/4013/8*. This is a case where type instability is beneficial.

- Interesting information about π in Julia is available at *https://julialang.org/blog/2017/03/piday/*.

- My attempt to explain multiple dispatch using an extended recipe analogy is available at *https://arstechnica.com/science/2020/10/the-unreasonable-effectiveness-of-the-julia-programming-language/*.

- For a detailed tutorial about optimization and the type system, visit *https://huijzer.xyz/posts/inference/*.

- Here is a package for nice visualization of type hierarchies: *https://github.com/claytonpbarrows/D3TypeTrees.jl*.

- Another approach to finding and fixing type instabilities is offered by the Cthulhu package: *https://docs.juliahub.com/Cthulhu/Dqimq/2.7.5/*.

PART II

APPLICATIONS

9

PHYSICS

Physics is not a religion. If it were, we'd have a much easier time raising money.
–Leon M. Lederman

Julia is a superb platform for physics calculations of all kinds. Various features of its syntax, such as the ability to use mathematical symbols and its concise array operations, make it a natural fit for programming algorithms that we use in physics. Julia's speed of execution makes it one of only a few languages used for the most demanding large-scale simulations (and the others in this club are all lower-level, statically compiled languages). Julia's physics ecosystem includes some state-of-the-art packages. Finally, Julia's unique ability to mix and match functions and data types from disparate packages to create new capabilities is especially powerful in physics calculations, as we'll see in detail in this chapter.

We begin with an introduction to two packages of general utility for dealing with units and errors. Both of these are potentially helpful in any physics project. We'll spend some time in the first section looking into various options for producing publication-quality plots including typeset units in axis labels. Then we'll turn to specific calculations, first using a package for fluid dynamics and then using a general-purpose differential equation solver. See "Further Reading" on page 304 for each major package's URL.

Bringing Physical Units into the Computer with Unitful

The traditional way to perform physics calculations on a computer is to represent physical quantities as floating-point numbers, subject those numbers to a long series of arithmetic operations, and then interpret the results again as physical quantities. Since physical quantities are usually not simply numbers, but have *dimensions*, we need to manually keep track of the *units* that are associated with these quantities, often with code comments to remind us what the various units are.

NOTE *A* dimension *is a fundamental physical idea encompassing something that can be measured, such as mass or time. A* unit *is a specific way of measuring a dimension. The dimensions are universal, but there are various systems of units. For example, for the dimension of length, some common units are centimeter (cm), meter (m), or, if we live in the United States, inches or football fields.*

In other words, the physical meanings of the numbers appearing in a program are not part of the quantities themselves, but are implicit. It may not be surprising that this can lead to confusion and errors. In 1999, NASA lost a spacecraft because two different contractors were contributing to the design, and their engineering programs used different systems of units.

In traditional languages for physics, such as Fortran, not much can be done about this issue directly. In Julia, because of its sophisticated type system, we are not limited to collections of dimensionless numbers; we can calculate with richer objects including units.

After importing the Unitful package, we can refer to many common physics units using a nonstandard string literal (see "Nonstandard String Literals" on page 128) with the prefix u:

```
julia> using Unitful

julia> u"1m" + u"1cm"
101//100 m

julia> u"1.0m" + u"1cm"
1.01 m

julia> u"1.0m/1s"
1.0 m s^-1
```

Here we add a meter and a centimeter, and receive the result as a rational number of meters. The package returns results as rational numbers, when possible, to preserve the ability to carry out exact conversions. But, as the second example shows, we can coerce a floating-point result by supplying a floating-point coefficient. The third example shows how we can construct expressions within the string literal.

You can find the complete list of units only in the source code, in its GitHub repository at *src/pkgdefaults.jl*, but most of them follow the usual physics conventions. Using the string literal syntax each time we want to refer to a unit can be cumbersome, so we can assign units to our own variables to ease our typing and make the code easier to read:

```
julia> m = u"m";

julia> 1m + u"1km"
1001 m
```

We add a meter to a kilometer, showing how we can use custom variables in combination with the string literals. The result is 1,001 meters.

We can parse a string as a Unitful expression with another function provided by the package (undocumented at the time of writing):

```
julia> earth_accel = "9.8m/s^2";

julia> kg_weight_earth = uparse("kg * " * earth_accel)
9.8 kg m s^-2
```

Here we use uparse() to convert a string, created by concatenating a string representing a mass with another representing the gravitational acceleration near the surface of Earth, into a unit expression representing the mass's weight. The forms in which unit expressions appear in the REPL are not themselves legal strings for converting with uconvert(). For example, we need to include the multiplication operator in the string in the second line.

Using Unitful Types

We can gain access to a large supply of standard SI units by importing the DefaultSymbols submodule rather than defining them one by one. This practice adds a profusion of names to our namespace, however, so it may not be a good idea if we're using only a few units:

```
julia> using Unitful.DefaultSymbols

julia> minute = u"minute"

julia> 2s + 1minute
62 s
```

Here we add 2 seconds to 1 minute, resulting in 62 seconds. The DefaultSymbols submodule supplies the s unit, but we need to define minute, as that's not an SI unit. We're using Julia's syntax for multiplication through juxtaposition; this expression is the same as `2 * s + 1minute`. However, these variables must be attached to numerical coefficients in arithmetic expressions; `2 * s + minute` is a `MethodError`.

We can find the reason for this error in the types of the two expressions:

```
julia> typeof(1minute)
Quantity{Int64, 𝐓, Unitful.FreeUnits{(minute,), 𝐓, nothing}}

julia> typeof(minute)
Unitful.FreeUnits{(minute,), 𝐓, nothing}
```

The type of `1minute`, which is the same as the type of `1 * minute`, is a `Quantity`, while the type of `minute` is a `FreeUnits`. Both of these types are defined in the package. The `Unitful` package defines methods for addition and other arithmetic operations that accept arguments of type `Quantity`, but not of type `FreeUnits`.

These types contain parameters appearing as boldface Unicode characters. The `Unitful` package uses these characters to represent dimensions, so these type specifications tell us that the `minute` unit has dimensions of time, represented by 𝐓.

The type of `minute` and other units is an abstract type (see "The Type Hierarchy" on page 222), while the types of quantified units such as `1minute` are concrete. For good performance, we should calculate with concrete types and define our own types with fields that have concrete types only.

Stripping and Converting Units

Sometimes we need to remove the units from the result of a calculation—for example, when passing a result to a function that doesn't understand units. We can do this with the `convert()` function:

```
julia> convert(Float64, u"1m/100cm")
1.0
```

The type of the result is `Float64`. The results returned by `Unitful` calculations may not always be what we expect, so we should use `convert()` when we require a simple number:

```
julia> u"1m / 100cm"
0.01 m cm^-1

julia> typeof(u"1m/100cm")
Quantity{Float64, NoDims, Unitful.FreeUnits{(cm^-1, m), NoDims, nothing}}
```

Here we divide a length by another length, so the result should be the simple number 1.0 (because the lengths are equal) with no dimensions. The actual result is equivalent to that, but it's expressed in an obscure form. Checking the type of the result, we find that it's the concrete `Unitful` type `Quantity`, with type parameters indicating that it has no dimensions.

If we use the same literal unit in the numerator and denominator, we get a result that may be closer to what we expect:

```
julia> u"1m / 2m"
0.5

julia> typeof(u"1m / 2m")
Float64
```

A further example shows that Unitful is consistent in retaining the units we use in expressions instead of making conversions that might seem obvious to a physicist:

```
julia> u"1m * 1m"
1 m^2

julia> u"1m * 100cm"
100 cm m
```

The two input expressions mean the same thing, but lead to equivalent results that are expressed differently.

The function upreferred() from Unitful converts expressions so they use a standard set of units. The user can establish preferred systems of units, but the default behavior uses conventional SI units:

```
julia> u"1m * 100cm" |> upreferred
1//1 m^2
```

In addition to converting to a number with convert(), we can use uconvert(), which is part of Unitful, to convert between units:

```
julia> uconvert(u"J", u"1erg")
1//10000000 J

julia> uconvert(u"kg", u"2slug")
29.187805874412728 kg
```

The function takes the unit to convert to in its first argument and the expression to convert in its second argument. In the first example we convert from ergs to joules. As both are metric units related by an exact ratio, uconvert() supplies the answer using a rational coefficient. The second example is a conversion from the US unit of mass, slugs, to kilograms, the standard SI unit used in physics. The conversion factor is a floating-point number.

Listing 9-1 shows another way to extract the purely numerical part of a Unitful expression with ustrip().

```
julia> vi = 17u"m/s"
17 m s^-1
```

```
julia> vf = 17.0u"m/s"
17.0 m s^-1

julia> ustrip(v), ustrip(vf)
(17, 17.0)
```

Listing 9-1: Stripping units with ustrip()

The ustrip() function preserves the numerical type in the expression.

To extract just the unit from a Unitful expression, the package provides the unit() function, as shown in Listing 9-2.

```
julia> unit(vi)
m s^-1
```

Listing 9-2: Extracting units with unit()

We'll find applications for ustrip() and unit() in "Plotting with Units" on page 276.

Typesetting Units

Using the UnitfulLatexify package, we can turn our Unitful expressions into LaTeX-typeset mathematics: either as LaTeX source ready to be dropped into a research paper or as a rendered image. Here is a simple example:

```
julia> using Unitful, Latexify, UnitfulLatexify

julia> 9.8u"m/s^2" |> latexify
L"$9.8\;\mathrm{m}\,\mathrm{s}^{-2}$"
```

The latexify() function transforms the Unitful expression for Earth's gravitational acceleration into a LaTeX string. We encountered LaTeX strings in Listing 4-1, when we used one to generate a title for a graph. The UnitfulLatexify package combines the LaTeX abilities in Latexify with Unitful, which is why we need to import all three packages, as we did at the start of this example.

When used in the REPL or another nongraphical context, latexify() produces LaTeX markup ready to be copied and pasted into a document. We can, instead, create a PDF image of the result by passing it to the render() function. To do that, you need to have the external program LuaLaTeX, which is part of standard LaTeX installations, installed. If that program is available, render() will use it to typeset the LaTeX string and immediately display it with the default PDF viewer. The render() process litters your temporary directory with files for every rendered expression, which is something to keep an eye on.

When using UnitfulLatexify in a graphical environment, such as a Pluto notebook, the output is rendered as LaTeX rather than LaTeX source. In most environments, typesetting uses a built-in engine rather than an external program, so no additional installations are required. For example, Pluto uses MathJax, a JavaScript library for LaTeX mathematical typesetting.

Figure 9-1 shows a Pluto session with Newton's Second Law of Motion.

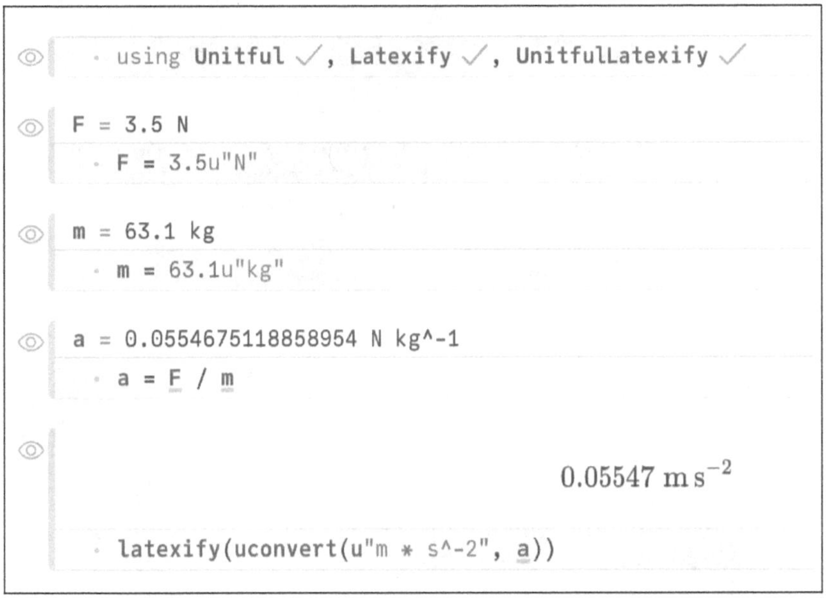

```
    · using Unitful ✓, Latexify ✓, UnitfulLatexify ✓

  F = 3.5 N
    · F = 3.5u"N"

  m = 63.1 kg
    · m = 63.1u"kg"

  a = 0.0554675118858954 N kg^-1
    · a = F / m


                                    0.05547 m s⁻²


    · latexify(uconvert(u"m * s^-2", a))
```

Figure 9-1: Using UnitfulLatexify in Pluto

In the final cell in Figure 9-1, we convert the acceleration to a more conventional combination of units and pass the result to `latexify()`. The typeset version appears as the result. MathJax provides a contextual menu when right-clicking on the result that gives us access to the LaTeX source.

If the use of negative exponents in unit expressions is not to our taste, we can pass the `permode` keyword to tell `latexify()` to use other styles. Here's an example that demonstrates the default and the two options for `permode`:

```
julia> a = 0.0571u"m/s^2"

julia> """
       a = $(latexify(a))

       or

       $(latexify(a; permode=:frac))

       or

       $(latexify(a; permode=:slash))
       """ |> println
a = $0.0571\;\mathrm{m}\,\mathrm{s}^{-2}$

or
```

`$0.0571\;\frac{\mathrm{m}}{\mathrm{s}^{2}}$`

or

`$0.0571\;\mathrm{m}\,/\,\mathrm{s}^{2}$`

The example uses the existing definition for a. The :frac option uses LaTeX fractions instead of negative exponents, and the :slash option uses a slash, which is usually better for inline math.

Pasting the output in the previous listing into the LaTeX source of this book shows the rendered result:

a = 0.0571 m s^{-2}
or
0.0571 $\frac{m}{s^2}$
or
0.0571 m / s^2

We can change the default mode for rendering units with the set_default(permode=:slash) command.

Plotting with Units

Listing 9-3 shows how Plots knows how to handle Unitful quantities.

```
julia> using Plots, Unitful
julia> mass = 6.3u"kg";
julia> velocity = (0:0.05:1)u"m/s";
julia> KE = mass .* velocity.^2 ./ 2;
julia> plot(velocity, KE; xlabel="Velocity", ylabel="KE",
       lw=3, legend=:topleft, label="Kinetic Energy")
```

Listing 9-3: Plotting Unitful arrays

Here we import Plots, which we need for plotting, and Unitful, to handle units. After defining a mass in kilograms and a range of velocities in meters per second, we create an array of kinetic energies, KE, from the fact that kinetic energy = 1/2 mass × velocity^2. The new package gives the plotting functions in Plots the ability to handle quantities with units and automatically appends the units to the axis labels. Figure 9-2 shows the result of the plot() statement.

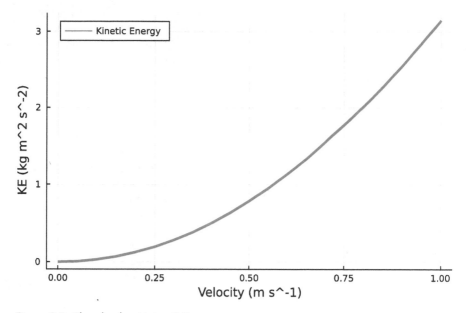

Figure 9-2: The plot that Listing 9-3 generates

I've left the energy units alone for this example, but more conventional physics usage would involve a conversion to joules using uconvert(), which we could have done before the plotting call or inline within plot().

We were able to create this graph with the same plot() call that we might have used to plot the same quantities stored in numerical arrays without units. All the plotting functions in Plots, such as scatter() and surface(), work with Unitful arrays to produce similar axis labels.

Making Plots for Publication

When attempting to make high-quality plots for publication, however, we encounter some shortcomings. While Plots aspires to create a unified interface to a variety of backends, each plotting engine works somewhat differently, with each having unique capabilities and limitations.

These differences among backends become more salient when we are making the final adjustments that accompany the preparation of graphs for publication. It is at this stage that, for example, the typographic details in labels and annotations become important. Figure 9-2 was created using the GR backend, which, as mentioned in "Useful Backends" on page 115, is the default at the time of writing, and is fast and capable.

Figure 9-2 may be acceptable as is, but for publication we may want to improve the appearance of its graph labels, especially to make the unit notations look like conventional mathematical notation. As we saw in "LaTeX Titles and Label Positioning by Data" on page 103, we can use LaTeX notation in graph annotations with mathematical content. This also works for the automatic labeling using units with the packages we've already imported:

```
julia> using Plots, Unitful, Latexify, UnitfulLatexify

julia> plot(velocity, KE; xlabel="\\textrm{Velocity}",
        ylabel="\\textrm{KE}", unitformat=latexroundunitlabel)
```

The example repeats the plot command from Listing 9-3, but with some alterations to create LaTeX strings for the plot labels. The unitformat keyword processes the unit annotations through latexify(), with the value latexroundunitlabel retaining the parentheses around the units. Since this triggers placing the entire label into a LaTeX string, we also need to wrap the non-math parts of the labels in LaTeX commands to set them as normal text instead of math.

The GR Backend

The results of this approach depend critically on what backend we're using. Obviously, it makes sense to use LaTeX strings only with backends that can do something with them. Although the default GR backend can interpret LaTeX, the results are not always adequate. This engine includes its own version of LaTeX processing, which often creates poor-quality typesetting with faulty kerning. The LaTeX engine in GR is the focus of some development activity, however, so its performance may improve.

Good-quality typesetting of labels in most cases requires processing by an external TeX engine, which involves a TeX installation such as TeXLive. As many physicists and other scientists have already made such an installation, we'll move on to considering options that take advantage of it.

The Gaston Backend

Gnuplot can optionally be compiled with support for the tikz terminal, which saves plots as text files containing TikZ commands. (TikZ is a graphics language that comes with most full-featured TeX installations.) Such files are processed with LaTeX and can contain TeX or LaTeX markup for the annotations on the plot. The result is of the highest quality, with fonts and styles that match the document in which the plot is included. Unfortunately, at the time of writing, the Gaston backend, which uses gnuplot, does not properly support the tikz terminal, so this option is off the table. It's being worked on, however, and once we can use Gaston with tikz, it will be the best option for complex plots for publication or when the best typographic quality is desired.

The PGFPlotsX Backend

Another backend that can make use of LaTeX strings is PGFPlotsX, which is invoked with the pgfplotsx() function. This backend creates plots by calling out to the LuaLaTeX TeX engine, which comes with most TeX installations, including TeXLive. Since LuaLaTeX does all the typesetting, the labels come out with TeX-level quality. This backend is, therefore, an excellent choice for publication-quality graphs. Gaston may still be the best future choice for complex plots because processing through LuaLaTeX can be far slower than through gnuplot if the plot contains a large number of elements, such as in a large scatterplot.

Handling Units Manually

Unfortunately, PGFPlotsX does not work properly with Unitful, not taking TeX processing into account. This limitation provides the opportunity to demonstrate a different way of plotting Unitful quantities and labeling axes with units—one that affords us complete control over the details.

The following listing contains the definition of a function that accepts two Unitful arrays for plotting, along with keyword arguments for labels:

```
using Plots, LaTeXStrings, Latexify, UnitfulLatexify

function plot_with_units(ux, uy; xl="", yl="", label="",
                          legend=:topleft, plotfile="plotfile")

    set_default(permode=:slash)
    x = ustrip(ux); y = ustrip(uy)
❶   xlabel = L"$\textrm{%$xl}$ (%$(latexify(unit(eltype(ux)))))"
    ylabel = L"$\textrm{%$yl}$ (%$(latexify(unit(eltype(uy)))))"

    plot(x, y; xlabel, ylabel, lw=2, label, legend)
❷   savefig(plotfile * ".tex")
    savefig(plotfile * ".pdf")

end
```

Using the ustrip() and unit() functions (see Listings 9-1 and 9-2), this code separates the arrays from their associated units, plotting the numerical parts and using the unit parts to construct labels with the LaTeXStrings package.

In order to interpolate values into a LaTeXStrings string, we need to use the two characters %$ rather than a simple $ ❶. When extracting the units from the arrays, we require the units of the elements of the array, which is why eltype() appears in the label assignment. The function saves both the stand-alone PDF version of the graph and its TeX version ❷ for including in a LaTeX document.

After selecting the desired backend, we call the function to create the *.pdf* and *.tex* files with the default names:

```
pgfplotsx()
plot_with_units(velocity, KE; xl="Velocity", yl="K. E.")
```

Figure 9-3 shows the result.

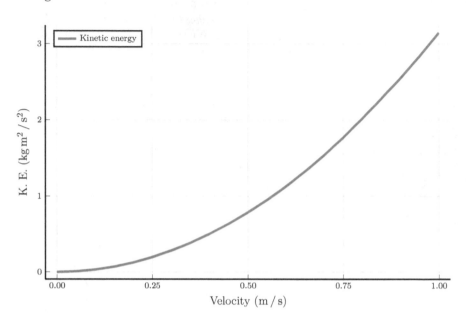

Figure 9-3: A PGFPlotsX plot with typeset unit labels

Typesetting by LuaTeX provides the excellent quality of the labels in Figure 9-3.

Error Propagation with Measurements

In the previous section we explored a package that extended the concept of numbers to include physical units. Here we'll meet Measurements, another package that defines a number-like object useful for calculations in physics or nearly any empirical science.

The Measurements package allows us to attach uncertainties to numbers. The number in question must be convertible to a float, so we can attach uncertainties directly to Float64 numbers, integers, and Irrational quantities. (We can also create complex numbers with uncertainties, if we really want to, by attaching errors to their real and imaginary parts.) The Measurements package defines a new data type, called Measurement{T}, where T can be any size float. We can perform any arithmetic operations on Measurement types that are allowed on floats, and the errors, or uncertainties, will be propagated to the result using standard linear error propagation theory.

Here are some examples of creating instances of Measurement types:

```
julia> using Measurements

julia> 92 ± 3
92.0 ± 3.0

julia> typeof(ans)
Measurement{Float64}
```

❶
```
julia> 92.0f0 ± 3
92.0 ± 3.0

julia> typeof(ans)
Measurement{Float64}

julia> 92.0f0 ± 3f0
92.0 ± 3.0

julia> typeof(ans)
Measurement{Float32}

julia> big(1227.0) ± 2
1227.0 ± 2.0

julia> typeof(ans)
Measurement{BigFloat}
```

We create Measurement objects using a notation that will be familiar to scientists. We can type the ± operator by entering \pm in the REPL and pressing TAB or by using the operating system's entry method for special characters.

In the REPL, the ans variable holds the most recently returned result. Since Measurement objects have only one type parameter, the base number and the error must be of the same type. As the typeof() calls show, Measurements promotes the smaller type as needed; the f0 suffix is a way to enter 32-bit float literals ❶.

The package treats significant digits intelligently:

```
julia> π ± 0.001
3.1416 ± 0.001

julia> π ± 0.01
3.142 ± 0.01
```

The digits made insignificant by the error are not printed.

When printing results in the REPL, the package displays only two significant digits in the error, to keep things neat:

```
julia> m1 = 2.20394232 ± 0.00343
2.2039 ± 0.0034
```

```
julia> Measurements.value(m1)
2.20394232
```

```
julia> Measurements.uncertainty(m1)
0.00343
```

However, it retains the full values internally for computations. We can access these components with the value() and uncertainty() functions shown here, which, as they are not exported, we need to qualify with the package namespace.

Scientists often use an alternative, convenient notation to express uncertainty by appending the error in the final significant digits within parentheses. The Measurements package understands this notation as well:

```
julia> emass = measurement("9.1093837015(28)e-31")
9.1093837015e-31 ± 2.8e-40
```

In order to use the notation, we need to employ the measurement() function and supply the argument as a string. We can also use measurement() as an alternative to the ± operator:

```
julia> m1 = measurement(20394232, 0.00343)
2.0394232e7 ± 0.0034
```

Arithmetic operations propagate errors correctly:

```
julia> emass
9.1093837015e-31 ± 2.8e-40
```

```
julia> 2emass
1.8218767403e-30 ± 5.6e-40
```

```
julia> emass + emass
1.8218767403e-30 ± 5.6e-40
```

```
julia> emass/2
4.5546918508e-31 ± 1.4e-40
```

```
julia> emass/2emass
0.5 ± 0.0
```

All these examples perform arithmetic as might be expected on the quantities and their errors. More interesting is the last example, where Measurements has recognized a ratio that has no error. The package maintains the notion of correlated and independent measurements, which is explained in its documentation. See "Further Reading" on page 304 for the URL.

Referring back to the example in Listing 9-3, we can add an uncertainty to the Unitful value for mass in two ways:

```
julia> using Measurements, Unitful

julia> mass = 6.3u"kg" ± 0.5u"kg"
6.3 ± 0.5 kg

julia> mass = 6.3u"kg"; mass = (1 ± 0.5/6.3) * mass
6.3 ± 0.5 kg
```

This example shows that the packages Measurements and Unitful can work together to create quantities with both units and uncertainties.

Let's continue with the example from Listing 9-3 using this new value for mass:

```
julia> using Plots

julia> velocity = (0:0.05:1)u"m/s";

julia> KE = mass .* velocity.^2 ./ 2;

julia> plot(velocity, uconvert.(u"J", KE); xlabel="Velocity", ylabel="K.E.",
       lw=2, legend=:topleft, label="Kinetic energy")
```

Although, as before, velocity has no uncertainty attached to it, mass does; therefore, KE should also contain uncertainties.

Figure 9-4 shows the result.

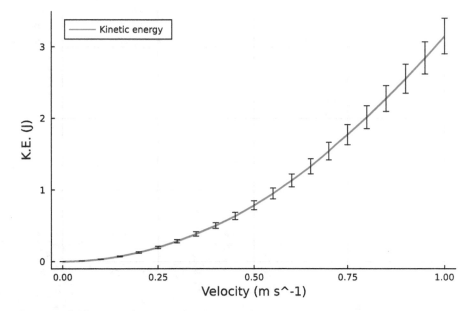

Figure 9-4: Plotting with units and errors

Figure 9-4 shows the `Unitful` arrays plotted as before with the axes labeled with their units. It also has error bars, showing how the error increases as the kinetic energy increases. We didn't have to change anything in the call to `plot()`. Somehow the type of the quantities to be plotted triggered the plotting function to use both unit labels and error bars. We would observe the same behavior with the other plotting functions in `Plots`, such as `scatter()` or `surface()`.

Fluid Dynamics with Oceananigans

The `Oceananigans` package for fluid dynamics simulations is especially well suited, as the name suggests, to the physics of the ocean. It provides a simulation construction kit that can include the effects of temperature and salinity variations, Earth's rotation, wind, and more. Its defaults usually perform well, but it's flexible enough that the user can specify one of several available solution methods. It has various physics models built in, including a linear equation of state, but makes it easy to substitute others of the user's devising.

The Physical System

We are setting out to simulate a two-dimensional layer of fluid in Earth's gravitational field. The bottom of the layer is maintained at a higher temperature than the top. This heating from below creates a convective motion, as can be seen in clouds or in a pan on the stove.

NOTE *Oceananigans depends on some compiled binaries in the standard library. If the precompilation of Oceananigans fails and you're using a recent or beta version of Julia, try it with an earlier Julia release (the previous major version number).*

The bottom and top simulation boundaries are impenetrable and freeslip, which means the fluid can slide across them. Horizontally, we impose a periodic boundary condition, requiring the solution to wrap around and be the same on the left and right boundaries. The horizontal direction is x and the vertical direction is z. We start the fluid at rest and are interested in the pattern of motion that the temperature difference creates.

Figure 9-5 shows the setup of the simulated system. The gray area represents the fluid, and the thick black horizontal lines indicate the constant-temperature boundaries.

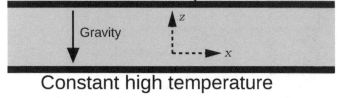

Figure 9-5: The simulation box

The Luxor program (see "Diagramming with Luxor" on page 190) that created this diagram is available in the Physics section of the online supplement at *https://julia.lee-phillips.org*.

A fluid dynamics simulation contains many pieces that we'll need to construct separately before we can begin the calculation. In the following subsections, we'll define the computational grid, the boundary conditions, the diffusivity models, and the equation of state, and establish the boundary conditions and the hydrodynamic model, in that order. After all the pieces are in place, we'll run the Oceananigans simulation and visualize the results.

The Grid

To put together an Oceananigans simulation, we'll define its various components using functions exported by the package, and then define a model using the model() function, passing in the components as arguments. For this example we'll use a grid, a buoyancy model that specifies the fluid's equation of state, a set of boundary conditions, the coefficients of viscosity and thermal diffusivity (material properties of the fluid), and initial conditions on the temperature within the fluid. We won't include the effects of Earth's rotation, salinity, or wind, but these ingredients are available for use in other Oceananigans models.

The grid is defined by its computational size (how many grid points exist in each direction), its extent (the physical lengths represented by these directions), and its topology, which is the term Oceananigans uses for what boundary conditions hold in each direction. For our problem we define the grid this way:

```
julia> using Oceananigans

julia> grid = RectilinearGrid(size=(256, 32);
           topology=(Periodic, Flat, Bounded),
           extent=(256, 32))
 256x1x32 RectilinearGrid{Float64, Periodic, Flat, Bounded} on CPU with 3×0×3 halo
|-- Periodic x ∈ [0.0, 256.0)     regularly spaced with Δx=1.0
|-- Flat y
-- Bounded  z ∈ [-32.0, 0.0]      regularly spaced with Δz=1.0
```

The RectilinearGrid() function that Oceananigans provides constructs grids as one of many data types defined in the package. We assign the grid to our own variable, grid, for use later when creating the model. We could have chosen any name for this variable, but grid is the name of the relevant keyword argument accepted by the model construction function; using the same names for our own variables will keep everything neat.

In the topology keyword argument, we list the boundary conditions in the x, y, and z directions, with z pointing upward. The boundary condition Flat means that we're not using (in this case) the y direction. This call defines a two-dimensional, x–z grid, with periodic boundaries in x and impenetrable boundaries in z. Oceananigans uses a kilogram-meter-second unit system.

Because we set the extent to be equal to the size, the grid spacing is one unit in length along each dimension, giving us a fluid layer 256 meters wide and 32 meters tall.

As the example shows, Oceananigans has useful forms for representing its data types in the REPL, summarizing the salient information for our inspection. Here the output provides us with a summary of the grid parameters and boundary conditions.

The Boundary Conditions

We define any boundary conditions on physical variables as a separate component, which is also eventually passed into model(). We want to impose constant values of temperature on the top and bottom boundaries; Oceananigans sets this type of boundary condition with the FieldBoundaryConditions() function, as it sets boundary conditions on, in this case, the temperature field. We can use Oceananigans's convenient definitions of top and bottom, which have their intuitive meaning (there are also north, south, east, and west, which we don't need in this problem):

```
julia> bc = FieldBoundaryConditions(
              top=ValueBoundaryCondition(1.0),
              bottom=ValueBoundaryCondition(20.0))
Oceananigans.FieldBoundaryConditions, with boundary conditions
|-- west: DefaultBoundaryCondition (FluxBoundaryCondition: Nothing)
|-- east: DefaultBoundaryCondition (FluxBoundaryCondition: Nothing)
|-- south: DefaultBoundaryCondition (FluxBoundaryCondition: Nothing)
|-- north: DefaultBoundaryCondition (FluxBoundaryCondition: Nothing)
|-- bottom: ValueBoundaryCondition: 20.0
|-- top: ValueBoundaryCondition: 1.0
-- immersed: DefaultBoundaryCondition (FluxBoundaryCondition: Nothing)
```

The immersed boundary refers to one that exists inside the fluid volume, but we're not using that one, nor any of the other myriad options, such as defined gradients or fluxes. The ValueBoundaryCondition that we use sets a constant value for a variable on the specified boundary.

The Diffusivities

We need to assign values to two constants that describe some of the fluid's material properties; this is part of the problem definition. The viscosity coefficient (ν) determines how "thick" the fluid is, and the thermal diffusivity (κ) determines how readily it conducts heat. These values are passed to the model in the closure keyword and can be set through the ScalarDiffusivity() function:

```
julia> closure = ScalarDiffusivity(ν=0.05, κ=0.01)
```

The symbol for viscosity is the Greek letter *nu* and that for thermal diffusivity is *kappa*. Like all Greek letters, we can precede their names with a backslash and then press TAB to enter them in the REPL.

The Equation of State

The equation of state is a function that describes how the density of the fluid at any point depends on the temperature and salinity there (the assumption of *incompressibility* usually used in Oceananigans models means that density has no dependence on pressure). Our model is salt free, but our fluid will be lighter when it's hotter. This is what will cause the fluid to move, as the lighter parts will rise and the heavier parts will sink, driven by gravity.

The model() function expects the keyword buoyancy, so we'll use that too:

```
julia> buoyancy = SeawaterBuoyancy(equation_of_state=
            LinearEquationOfState(thermal_expansion=0.01,
            haline_contraction=0))
SeawaterBuoyancy{Float64}:
|-- gravitational_acceleration: 9.80665
-- equation of state: LinearEquationOfState(thermal_expansion=0.01, haline_contraction=0.0)
```

Oceananigans offers many other options, including the ability to define our own equation of state, but we'll keep the model simple. The SeawaterBuoyancy component deals with buoyancy by combining gravity (with the default Earth value given here) with density variations. As we're not interested in salinity effects for this calculation, we set haline_contraction to 0 ("haline" is essentially a synonym for saline used by oceanographers).

The Model and Initial Conditions

Now that we have all the pieces set up, we can put them together into a *model*, the Oceananigans term for the definition of the computational problem, including all the physics along with the grid and the boundary conditions:

```
julia> model = NonhydrostaticModel(;
                grid, buoyancy, closure,
                boundary_conditions=(T=bc,), tracers=(:T, :S))
NonhydrostaticModel{CPU, RectilinearGrid}(time = 0 seconds, iteration = 0)
|-- grid: 256×1×32 RectilinearGrid{Float64, Periodic, Flat, Bounded}
   ❶ on CPU with 3×0×3 halo
|-- timestepper: QuasiAdamsBashforth2TimeStepper
|-- tracers: (T, S)
|-- closure: ScalarDiffusivity{ExplicitTimeDiscretization}
   (ν=0.05, κ=(T=0.01, S=0.01))
|-- buoyancy: SeawaterBuoyancy with g=9.80665 and
   LinearEquationOfState(thermal_expansion=0.01, haline_contraction=0.0)
   with -ĝ = ZDirection
-- coriolis: Nothing
```

The package prints a nice summary of the result, including a reminder of some (but not all) of the features we're not using, such as the coriolis force from Earth's rotation.

The `NonhydrostaticModel()` function creates a model using the approximation appropriate to our problem. Oceananigans offers several other choices, including a hydrostatic model to simulate surface waves.

We use the abbreviated form of passing keyword arguments explained in "Concise Syntax for Keyword Arguments" on page 154.

Our boundary condition `bc` doesn't refer to any particular physical variable; it simply defines a constant field value on the boundaries. The named tuple assigned to `boundary_conditions` enforces them on T, the variable used in Oceananigans for the temperature.

The printed result refers to the CPU ❶, which means that this model is intended for "normal" machine architectures. The other option is to calculate on GPUs (graphics processing units). The `halo` refers to the several points outside the physical grid that the numerical algorithm uses to enforce the boundary conditions or other constraints.

The final keyword argument, `tracers`, tells the model to keep track of the temperature and salinity as those scalar fields are advected around the fluid. We're required to include `:S` even though our equation of state means it will have no effect.

The fluid layer heated from below defined by our model is physically *unstable*, which means that a small perturbation to its initial, motionless state will be magnified and develop into a state with some form of persistent motion, driven by the temperature difference and the gravitational field. It is the development of the instability that we want to study. We need to add the small perturbation, or else, even though the system is unstable, it will never move.

The `set!()` function lets us create any desired initial condition on any of the fields. We'll use it to add a small, random perturbation to the temperature field throughout the fluid volume:

```
julia> tper(x, y, z) = 0.1 * rand()
tper (generic function with 1 method)

julia> set!(model; T = tper)
```

The function is spelled with an exclamation point to remind us that it mutates its arguments: it alters the T field in place, and the model as well.

The Simulation

Next we need to create a *simulation*, using the `Simulation()` function. This object will receive the model as its positional argument, along with keyword arguments for the timestep and when to stop the calculation. It will keep track of how much simulation time and wall-clock time has elapsed and the state of all the physical fields. This allows us to continue the simulation after the requested start time if we want, save the progress of the simulation in files, and retrieve the fields for examination and plotting.

```
julia> simulation = Simulation(model; Δt=0.01, stop_time=1800)
Simulation of NonhydrostaticModel{CPU, RectilinearGrid}(time = 0 seconds, iteration = 0)
|-- Next time step: 10 ms
|-- Elapsed wall time: 0 seconds
|-- Wall time per iteration: NaN years
|-- Stop time: 30 minutes
|-- Stop iteration : Inf
|-- Wall time limit: Inf
|-- Callbacks: OrderedDict with 4 entries:
|    |-- stop_time_exceeded => Callback of stop_time_exceeded on IterationInterval(1)
|    |-- stop_iteration_exceeded => Callback of stop_iteration_exceeded on IterationInterval(1)
|    |-- wall_time_limit_exceeded => Callback of wall_time_limit_exceeded on IterationInterval(1)
|     -- nan_checker => Callback of NaNChecker for u on IterationInterval(100)
|-- Output writers: OrderedDict with no entries
-- Diagnostics: OrderedDict with no entries
```

This is a simple call, as model already contains all the details of the problem. We get a summary of various options for the simulation, most of which we didn't use. If you want to use the *delta* for the time interval in the REPL, enter **\Delta** and press TAB.

Before running the simulation, let's arrange for the velocity and temperature fields to be stored on disk at regular intervals so we can see its development over time (if we don't do this, we'll see only the final state of the simulation), as shown in Listing 9-4.

```
julia> simulation.output_writers[:velocities] =
            JLD2OutputWriter(model, model.velocities,
            filename="conv4.jld2", schedule=TimeInterval(1))
 JLD2OutputWriter scheduled on TimeInterval(1 second):
|-- filepath: ./conv4.jld2
|-- 3 outputs: (u, v, w)
|-- array type: Array{Float32}
|-- including: [:grid, :coriolis, :buoyancy, :closure]
-- max filesize: Inf YiB

julia> simulation.output_writers[:tracers] =
            JLD2OutputWriter(model, model.tracers,
            filename="conv4T.jld2", schedule=TimeInterval(1))
 JLD2OutputWriter scheduled on TimeInterval(1 second):
|-- filepath: ./conv4T.jld2
|-- 2 outputs: (T, S)
|-- array type: Array{Float32}
|-- including: [:grid, :coriolis, :buoyancy, :closure]
-- max filesize: Inf YiB
```

Listing 9-4: Setting up output writers

Adding elements to the `output_writers` property of the `simulation` causes it to store the results periodically. The `JLD2OutputWriter` uses the `JLD2` file format, which is a compact way to store multiple Julia data structures in a single file. It's a version of the `HDF5` format widely used in computational science. The `schedule` causes a data dump every 1 second, which, using our timestep, will be every 100 steps. The information in the result shows which quantities will be saved: `T` and `S` are the temperature and salinity.

With this, we're ready to run the calculation:

```
julia> run!(simulation)
[ Info: Initializing simulation...
[ Info:     ... simulation initialization complete (6.850 ms)
[ Info: Executing initial time step...
[ Info:     ... initial time step complete (80.507 ms).
```

The REPL will not have anything more to say until it reaches the final timestep, which in this case will take several hours on a typical personal computer. Then it will indicate that the calculation is complete and return to the interactive prompt. Chapter 15 explores ways to speed up such calculations by using parallel processing.

The Results

When an Oceananigans simulation ends, the final state of the fields (the velocity components and the temperature, in this case) is available as properties of the `model`. Listing 9-5 shows how to retrieve them.

```
julia> using Plots

julia> uF = model.velocities.u;

julia> TF = model.tracers.T;

julia> heatmap(interior(TF, 1:grid.Nx, 1, 1:grid.Nz)';
               aspect_ratio=1, yrange=(0, 1.5grid.Nz))
```

Listing 9-5: Examining the results of a simulation

The velocity and temperature fields are properties of the model. The `heatmap()` call will plot the two-dimensional temperature field, but first we need to turn it into an array with the `interior()` function. This function converts the Oceananigans field into a numerical array and trims away the `halo` points. Its arguments, following the field to convert, are the extents of the grid in each of the three directions; we enter a `1` to indicate an unused coordinate. In setting the `yrange`, we've accessed another property of the field, its grid shape. The prime after the array to plot transposes it so that it appears in its natural orientation, with a vertical gravity.

We would normally run a simulation for just a few timesteps and examine the fields in this way before running a long calculation, to make sure we've set it up correctly. If we want to take another look after a few more timesteps, we can do this:

```julia
julia> simulation.stop_time+=10;

julia> run!(simulation);
```

These commands advance the simulation an additional 10 timesteps, after which we can repeat the steps in Listing 9-5 to see how things are going.

Returning now to the quantities stored in files, as set up in Listing 9-4, Listing 9-6 shows how to retrieve the entire history of a field.

```julia
julia> uF = FieldTimeSeries("conv4.jld2", "u")
256×1×32×1030 FieldTimeSeries{InMemory} located at
    (Face, Center, Center) on CPU
|-- grid: 256×1×32 RectilinearGrid{Float64, Periodic, Flat, Bounded}
    on CPU with 3×0×3 halo
|-- indices: (1:256, 1:1, 1:32)
-- data: 256×1×32×1030 OffsetArray(::Array{Float64, 4},
    1:256, 1:1, 1:32, 1:1030) with eltype Float64 with
 indices 1:256×1:1×1:32×1:1030
    -- max=7.66057, min=-7.88889, mean=2.79295e-11
```

Listing 9-6: Retrieving a field from the JLD2 file

The summary of the result shows that the FieldTimeSeries has dimensions of 256×1×32×1,030, which means that it's defined on a 2D, 256×32 grid and evolves over 1,030 timesteps.

After this call the entire history of the *x*-velocity field and its various properties are conveniently available. The data structure uF itself takes up almost no space:

```julia
julia> sizeof(uF)
544
```

The sizeof() function returns the amount of storage, in bytes, occupied by its argument. The actual data occupies $256 \times 32 \times 1{,}030 \times 8 = 67{,}502{,}080$ bytes.

We can plot the horizontal velocity field at any timestep:

```julia
julia> using Printf

julia> i = 50;

julia> h50 = heatmap(interior(uF[i], 1:grid.Nx, 1, 1:grid.Nz)';
            aspect_ratio=1, yrange=(0, 1.5grid.Nz),
            colorbar=:false, ylabel="z",
            annotations=[
               (0, uF.grid.Nz+15,
                  text("Horizontal velocity at timestep $i", 12, :left)),
```

```
(0, uF.grid.Nz+5,
  text((@sprintf "Max = %.3g" maximum(uF[i])), 8, :left)),
(100, uF.grid.Nz+5,
  text((@sprintf "Min = %.3g" minimum(uF[i])), 8, :left))],
grid=false, axis=false)
```

We've added some labeling to the version in Listing 9-5, annotating the plot using properties read out from the field. Creating similar plots for timesteps 100 and 500, adding an xlabel to the last one, and putting them together with plot(h50, h100, h500; layout=(3, 1)) creates the plot in Figure 9-6.

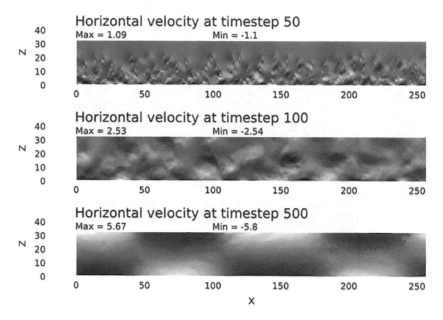

Figure 9-6: Results of an Oceananigans simulation

The system evinces the regime called *turbulent convection*; it's interesting to observe the emergence of large-scale order from randomness and its persistent coexistence with the turbulent flow.

In order to make an animation of the simulation, we need to generate plots at equally spaced time intervals and stitch them together into a video file. Our simulation used a constant timestep, so in this case, equal time intervals translates into equal numbers of timesteps. However, that won't always be the case. Oceananigans has options for automatically adjusted timesteps, and we may perform a simulation in stages with differently sized Δt. It's convenient, therefore, to have a function that creates a plot given a *time*. Since a given time may not correspond to any particular stored field, but may fall between two consecutive data dumps, we'll need a function that determines which stored field is closest to the time requested. The Julia program shown in Listing 9-7 retrieves the simulation output and produces a movie of a specified duration.

```
using Oceananigans, Reel, Plots

function heatmap_at_time(F, time, fmin, fmax, duration)
    ts = F.times
    time = time * ts[end]/duration
    i = indexin(minimum(abs.(ts .- time)), abs.(ts .- time))[1] ❶
    xr = yr = zr = 1
    if F.grid.Nx > 1
        xr = 1:F.grid.Nx
    end
    if F.grid.Ny > 1
        yr = 1:F.grid.Ny
    end
    if F.grid.Nz > 1
        zr = 1:F.grid.Nz
    end
    heatmap(interior(F[i], xr, yr, zr)'; aspect_ratio=1, yrange=(0, 1.5F.grid.Nz),
            clim=(fmin, fmax)) ❷
end

uF = FieldTimeSeries("conv4.jld2", "u")
const fmin = 0.5minimum(uF) ❸
const fmax = 0.5maximum(uF)
const duration = 30

function plotframe(t, dt)
    heatmap_at_time(uF, t, fmin, fmax, duration)
end

uMovie = roll(plotframe; fps=30, duration)

write("uMovie.mp4", uMovie)
```

Listing 9-7: Creating an animation of an Oceananigans simulation

The heatmap_at_time() function does what's needed, creating a heatmap at the time closest to the time in its argument. In this function, F is a field retrieved with a call to FieldTimeSeries(), as in Listing 9-6. It makes use of the times property of these objects, which is an array holding all the times at which the field has been saved. The index i holds the dump corresponding to the time closest to the supplied time ❶. When making an animation of a heatmap, we want to use the same mapping from values to colors in each frame, so our call to heatmap() uses the clim keyword ❷.

With this function in place we can create an animation using the Reel package introduced in "Animations with Reel" on page 206. To work with that package, we need to define a function of time t and (an unused) dt that returns a plot corresponding to t: the plotframe() function. The three constants ❸ in the script set the palette limits based on the data and the desired total duration of the animation. The palette limits are scaled so that more details are visible near the beginning of the run, but we can adjust it based on the features of interest.

NOTE   *See the online supplement at* https://julia.lee-phillips.org *for the resulting animation, along with full-color versions of the figures.*

The final call saves the animation as an MP4 file. Other options that will work with Reel are gif and webm. To create these file types, we merely need to use the appropriate file ending.

Solving Differential Equations with DifferentialEquations

Since the 18th century, differential equations have been the language of physical science and engineering, and of the quantitative aspects of other sciences as well. Julia's DifferentialEquations package is a massive, state-of-the-art facility for solving many types of differential equations using a multitude of methods. It incorporates recent research on the use of machine learning to apply the best line of attack for solving a given equation.

This section introduces the use of DifferentialEquations by solving an example problem. Interested readers can delve into its detailed documentation for more information (see "Further Reading" on page 304).

Defining the Physics Problem and Its Differential Equation

As an example, let's investigate the pendulum. Figure 9-7 diagrams the problem and defines the string length (L) and the angle (θ).

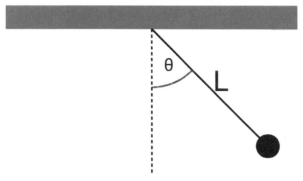

Figure 9-7: The pendulum system

We measure θ counterclockwise from the vertical reference line, which is dotted in the diagram, and the gravitational acceleration points down.

NOTE   *The Luxor program that produced the diagram is available in the code section of the Physics chapter on the online supplement at* https://julia.lee-phillips.org.

A straightforward analysis of the forces on the pendulum bob (the black circle in the diagram) and Newton's Second Law leads to the differential equation

$$\frac{d^2\theta}{dt^2} = -\frac{g}{L}\sin(\theta)$$

which is derived in any introductory general physics text. Here t is time and g is the gravitational acceleration. The usual next step is to confine the problem to small angles ($\lesssim 5°$), where $\sin(\theta) \approx \theta$, and solve the resulting differential equation for simple harmonic motion. We're going to solve the "exact" pendulum equation numerically, using the DifferentialEquations package. We'll be able to examine the solution for any initial θ, up to π radians.

The package works with systems of first-order equations, which means differential equations limited to first derivatives of the unknown function. To handle the pendulum equation, therefore, we first need to cast it into the form of two coupled first-order equations. This first step is also part of many analytic solution methods. We can proceed easily by defining a new variable:

$$\frac{d\theta}{dt} = \omega$$

$$\frac{d\omega}{dt} = -\frac{g}{L}\sin(\theta)$$

Now we're solving for two functions of time, the angle $\theta(t)$ and the angular velocity $\omega(t)$.

Setting Up the Problem

The first step in translating the mathematical problem into a form that DifferentialEquations can digest is to define a Julia function of four positional arguments:

du An array for the derivatives of the solutions

u An array for the solution functions

p An array of parameters

t The time

Listing 9-8 is the version for the pendulum problem.

```
function pendulum!(du, u, p, t)
    L, g = p
    θ, ω = u
    du[1] = ω
    du[2] = -g/L * sin(θ)
end
```

Listing 9-8: The Julia version of the pendulum equation

This is a mutating function, as indicated by the exclamation point, because as the calculation progresses, the solution engine mutates the u and du arrays to hold the results. Here L and g are set through destructuring the array p, and θ and ω are read from the array u. The solver from DifferentialEquations will repeatedly call pendulum!() as it builds up the solution, passing in p, t, and the developing solution arrays themselves.

Solving the Equation System

To calculate the solution, we first define the computational problem and then pass that problem to the solve() function. The components of the computational problem are the parameter array, the initial conditions, the time span over which we want the solution, and the function that defines the differential equations to be solved, in this example pendulum!(). Other options include such things as the numerical method to be employed, but in this simple example we'll leave those options unspecified. The package generally does an excellent job of choosing the solution method best suited to the nature of the equations we present to it. Listing 9-9 shows the problem set up and initiated.

```
using DifferentialEquations

p = [1.0, 9.8]
 #    L    g    <- Parameters

u0 = [deg2rad(5), 0]
 #      θ     ω    <- Initial conditions

tspan = (0, 20)

prob = ODEProblem(pendulum!, u0, tspan, p)
sol5d = solve(prob)
```

Listing 9-9: Solving differential equations using DifferentialEquations

The only two functions in this section from the DifferentialEquations package are ODEProblem() and solve(). ODEProblem() takes four positional arguments: the function defining the equation system, an array of initial conditions, the time span, and the parameter array. We defined the function in Listing 9-8 and we define the other three arguments here. Allowing the solver to pass the parameters as arguments makes it convenient to generate families of solutions with a range of parameters.

The result returned by ODEProblem() contains the complete solutions of all functions (in this example, two) bundled into a data type defined in the package. This data type is designed to make it easy to examine and plot the solutions, and it contains, in addition to the computed functions, information about the problem and the calculation.

Examining the Solutions

For small angles, the analytic solution to our pendulum problem is

$$\theta(t) = \theta_0 \cos\left(\sqrt{\frac{g}{L}}\, t\right)$$

where θ_0 is the initial angle. The initial conditions in Listing 9-9 have the pendulum at rest with a starting angle of $5°$, so the small angle approximation should be valid.

Since we know the analytic solution, we can check the numerical result against it. Listing 9-10 shows how we can plot one against the other.

```
using Plots

plot(sol5d; idxs=1, lw=4, lc=:lightgrey, label="Numeric",
    legend=:outerright, title="Pendulum at θ₀ = 5°")

L, g = p

plot!(t -> u0[1]*cos(sqrt(g/L)*t); xrange=(0, 20),
    ls=:dash, lc=:black, label="Analytic")
```

Listing 9-10: Solving for the small angle case

The first `plot()` call uses only one data argument, the solution itself, assigned to `sol5d` in Listing 9-9. This is neither an array nor a function, yet `plot()` seems to know how to display it. The first keyword argument, `idxs`, requests that (in this case) the first function, θ, is plotted. `idxs` does not appear in the documentation for the `Plots` package, and in fact is not defined in that package. Thus, it has no effect unless we first import `DifferentialEquations`.

The plot, shown in Figure 9-8, gives us confidence that we've set up the problem correctly and that the numerical solution methods are working.

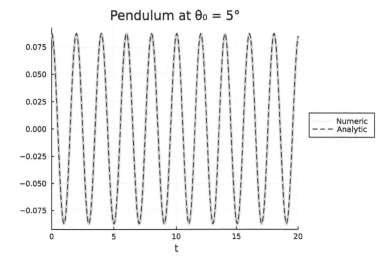

Figure 9-8: Checking the small angle solution of the pendulum equation

Plotting the solution as we did here does not simply plot the solution arrays. It also interpolates between calculated values in order to generate a smooth plot. In this case, the solution contains only 83 points, which, if plotted directly, would make a coarse graph.

Although the solution objects are not arrays, the package defines methods for indexing that make it convenient to extract the data. If we do want access to the uninterpolated solution data, we can get it by indexing. Here, sol5d[1, :] returns a Vector of the 83 points for the first variable, θ, and sol5d[2, :] for the second, ω. To get the times at which these values are defined, we use a property: sol5d.t.

Using the solution objects as functions returns the result interpolated to the time passed as an argument. (We're using time in this section, but in other problems the independent variable may be something else.) The sol5d(1.3) function call returns a Vector of two elements, one for each variable, interpolated to the time 1.3. These functions accept ranges and arrays as well, so sol5d(0:0.1:1) returns the interpolated solution data at 11 times from 0 to 1. To extract just the angle variable at these times, we can call sol5d(0:0.1:1)[1, :]. Controlling the density of the interpolation by using the functional form of the solution objects can be helpful when making, for example, scatterplots, where we need to control the density of plotted points.

How does the solution depend on the initial angle? Redefining u0 to try two larger initial angles, and proceeding as in Listing 9-10 to generate two new solutions, we get the results shown in Figure 9-9.

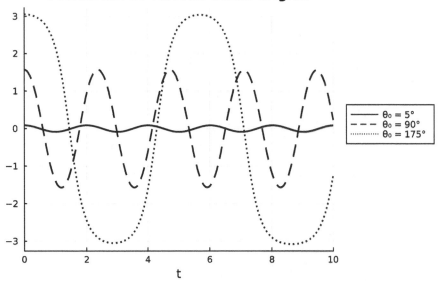

Figure 9-9: The pendulum with larger initial angles

The 90° solution, with the pendulum string initially horizontal, appears approximately sinusoidal, but with the frequency around 25 percent lower than the small angle case. When the initial angle is 175°, the period is nearly three times the small angle period, and the solution is clearly far from sinusoidal. In generating Figure 9-9, we limit the range of the independent variable by passing another DifferentialEquations-defined keyword to plot(): tspan=(0, 10).

Defining Time-Dependent Parameters

By replacing one or more of the constant parameters in the p array with functions of time, we can study the system's response to time-dependent parameters. In this way we can include inhomogeneous terms in the differential equations, forcing functions, and time-varying parameters in general.

Let's find out what happens if we pull up on the string steadily as the pendulum oscillates. We'll start at 45° and calculate the solution over 10 seconds, replacing the constant L by a linearly decreasing function of time:

```
tspan = (0, 10)
u0 = [π/4, 0]
Lt(t) = 1 - 0.999t/10
```

We need to create a slightly different version of our pendulum() function, shown in Listing 9-11, that can use the time-dependent string length.

```
function pendulum2!(du, u, p, t)
    L, g = p
    θ, ω = u
    du[1] = ω
❶   du[2] = -g/L(t) * sin(θ)
end
```

Listing 9-11: The pendulum function with a time-dependent L

The only change we made to the previous function is replacing L with L(t) ❶. We proceed just as before. The ODEProblem() function needs a new parameter array, shown in Listing 9-12, to pass in to pendulum2().

```
p = [Lt, 9.8]
prob = ODEProblem(pendulum2!, u0, tspan, p)
solLt = solve(prob)
```

Listing 9-12: Getting the numerical solution with a time-varying L

The ease of generalizing the problem to include a time-varying parameter clarifies the advantages of the parameter-passing approach in Differential Equations. The result, in Figure 9-10, shows a steadily decreasing period and amplitude with an increasing angular velocity (ω).

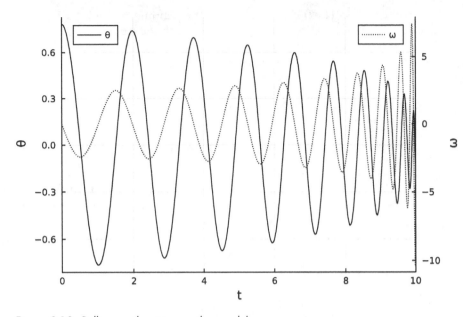

Figure 9-10: Pulling up the string on the pendulum

We create Figure 9-10 with the following calls:

```
plot(solLt; idxs=1, label="θ", legend=:topleft, ylabel="θ",
  ❶ right_margin=13mm)
plot!(twinx(), solLt; idxs=2, label="ω", legend=:topright,
    ylabel="ω", ls=:dot)
```

In the call to plot!(), the first argument, twinx(), creates a subplot overlay that shares the horizontal axis with the first plot and draws a new vertical axis; we use it so the two curves don't have to share the same scale. We need some extra room on the right ❶ for the labels on the second vertical axis. This margin setting requires the import of Plots.PlotMeasures, as explained in "Working with Plot Settings" on page 101.

Parametric Instability

A child "pumping" a swing in the playground to get it moving is exploiting a *parametric instability*. The driver of this instability is the periodic change in the effective length of the pendulum string. The results of linear theory (the small angle version of the differential equation that we're attacking in this section) tell us that a resonance occurs when the forcing frequency is twice the natural frequency of the pendulum, which, using our $L = 1$, is $2\sqrt{g}$. If the string length is perturbed sinusoidally at this frequency, the amplitude of small oscillations will increase exponentially.

Since we know how to insert any time-dependent function $L(t)$ into the numerical solution, we can investigate the response of the pendulum to parametric excitation beyond the small angle approximation. We'll start with a small initial angle, follow the evolution for a longer span, and define a new function of time for the string length:

```
const g = 9.8
tspan = (0, 400)
u0 = [π/32, 0]
Lt(t) = 1.0 + 0.1*cos(2*sqrt(g)*t)
```

Lt(t) will perturb the nominal length of 1 meter by 10 percent at the frequency of parametric resonance.

Our work proceeds exactly as before, with one adjustment. We use pendulum2(), defined in Listing 9-11, and set up the problem as in Listing 9-12. The adjustment is that we need to supply a keyword argument to the solving function:

```
solLt = solve(prob; reltol=1e-5)
```

The reltol parameter adjusts the adaptive timestepping as needed to limit the local error to the value that we supply. Its default of 0.001 led to a solution that seemed suspicious, as it was not quite periodic. I generated solutions with reltol = 1e-4, 1e-5, and 1e-6. The 1e-4 solution looked reasonable, but the 1e-5 solution was slightly different. As the solution with reltol = 1e-6 looked identical to the one at 1e-5, they're probably accurate. Figure 9-11 shows the resulting graph of θ versus time.

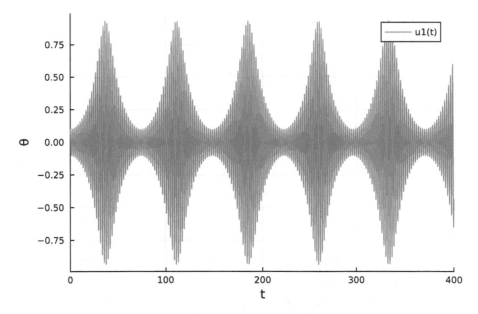

Figure 9-11: Parametric instability of the finite-angle pendulum

Initially, the amplitude increases exponentially, as predicted by the linear theory. But we know from our previous solutions that the frequency of the pendulum decreases with amplitude; therefore, it moves continuously out of resonance with the forcing function, and the amplitude decreases back to close to its initial value. At that point it's closer to resonance, and the amplitude again grows exponentially. As the solution shows, the process repeats.

Combining DifferentialEquations with Measurements

Suppose we want to verify the predictions of our pendulum solutions with an experiment. There will be some error inherent in the setting of the initial angle. If we estimate that uncertainty to be one degree, we might think to state the initial conditions this way (see "Error Propagation with Measurements" on page 280):

```
using Measurements

u0 = [π/2 ± deg2rad(1), 0]
```

The function `deg2rad()` converts from degrees to radians.

We can proceed exactly as before, repeating the procedure shown in Listings 9-8 and 9-9. A plot of the solution for $\theta(t)$ now looks like Figure 9-12.

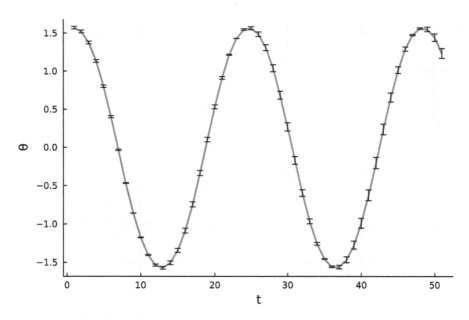

Figure 9-12: Combining DifferentialEquations *with* Measurements

Although we don't tell the `plot()` function anything about drawing error bars, they appear in the plot. The plot shows how the error in the angular position grows, on average, over time. The error doesn't grow monotonically, however. It decreases when the exact solution and those at the limits of the error bound happen to be in phase.

We generate the solution and plot it in Figure 9-12 as follows:

```
prob = ODEProblem(pendulum!, u0, tspan, p)

solM = solve(prob)

plot(solM(0:0.1:5)[1, :]; legend=false, lw=2, ylabel="θ", xlabel="t")
```

Since `DifferentialEquations` places an error on every point of the solution, including the points interpolated when creating a plot, we have to use the technique described in "Examining the Solutions" on page 297 to limit the number of points plotted; otherwise, the plot becomes too crowded with error bars and is impossible to interpret.

Conclusion

Although we delved into several physics packages at some length in this chapter, we really only scratched their surfaces. I hope, however, that the introductions here are sufficient to help you assess whether any of the packages explored in this chapter might be a good choice for your projects and to show you how to get started.

Another purpose of this chapter is to serve as an introduction to a superpower of Julia and the Julia ecosystem. In several examples we were able to combine the abilities of two or three packages without making any particular arrangements to do so. We made plots and typeset expressions that contained units, and saw that they were handled sensibly. We handed the output of a differential equation solver to a plotting function from a different package, and it extracted the relevant data and plotted it. We solved differential equations with error estimates in their initial conditions, and the error was propagated through the solution correctly. We plotted *this* result, and, as if by magic, the solution displayed error bars.

We wrote scripts and programs that combined the abilities of five packages in various combinations, giving them capabilities neither envisioned nor planned by their authors. Most of these packages were written without any knowledge of the others that we combined them with. The authors of these packages wrote their code in a generic way that allows Julia's type system and its method of multiple dispatch to enable its functions to work with data types defined in other packages.

Julia initially attracted attention as a language that was as easy to pick up and be productive in as a high-level interpreted language, but one that was fast enough for the most demanding scientific work: "as easy as Python and as fast as Fortran." The second reason for Julia's increasing adoption in the sciences is its ability to combine the abilities of disparate packages with no additional work on the part of the application programmer. Julia creators and package authors refer to this property as the *composability* of packages, in analogy with the composition of functions.

FURTHER READING

- The GitHub community "Julia's Physics Ecosystem" (*https://julia physics.github.io/latest/ecosystem/*) maintains a convenient list of packages related to all areas of physics, and includes related packages for mathematics and plotting.

- The Unitful package is available at *https://github.com/Painter Qubits/Unitful.jl*.

- See *https://www.simscale.com/blog/2017/12/nasa-mars-climate -orbiter-metric/* for details on how a mixup in units destroyed the Mars Climate Orbiter.

- The documentation for UnitfulLatexify is at *https://gustaphe .github.io/UnitfulLatexify.jl/dev/*.

- The Measurements package resides at *https://github.com/Julia Physics/Measurements.jl*.

- To get started with Oceananigans, see *https://clima.github.io/ OceananigansDocumentation/stable/quick_start/*.

- The DifferentialEquations.jl documentation is available at *https://diffeq.sciml.ai/stable/*.

- Animations, color images, and supplementary code for this chapter are available at *https://julia.lee-phillips.org*.

- You can find simple examples of the use of DifferentialEquations.jl at *https://lwn.net/Articles/835930/* and *https://lwn.net/Articles/ 834571/*.

- The parametric instability of a pendulum is demonstrated in the video at *https://www.youtube.com/watch?v=dGE_LQXy6c0*.

- The theory of parametric resonance for the general harmonic oscillator is treated at *https://www.lehman.edu/faculty/dgaranin/Mechanics/ Parametric_resonance.pdf*.

10

STATISTICS

The true Logic for this world is the Calculus of Probabilities.
–James Clerk Maxwell

 Many readers of this book are likely to skip one or more chapters in Part II. A biologist may not be interested in physics applications, for example. But *this* particular chapter has something in it for everyone, because sooner or later, all scientists must deal with the subject of statistics.

Anyone conducting experiments knows that the treatment and analysis of experimental data is a direct application of statistical methods and concepts. Every scientific calculator features buttons for calculating means and standard deviations of rows of numbers. In this chapter, you will learn how to apply Julia and its statistical libraries to manipulate, plot, and analyze all kinds of data. Julia is generally faster, more flexible, more extensible, and more powerful than R, the near-standard language in this field. But if you have R programs that you are already working with, I'll explain how to use them from within your Julia environment.

The concepts of probabilities and distributions are ubiquitous in physics, from the classical theories of statistical mechanics to quantum theory, in which probability plays a fundamental role. But statistics, and its basis in the language of probabilities, has its fingerprints all over science, even apart from experiments and observations. One of the detailed examples in this chapter involves probabilistic modeling in biology: an application of these ideas outside of both analysis of experiments and physics.

Probability

We don't have the space here for a complete course in probability and statistics, but fortunately, we can do everything we need to do without a detailed mathematical development. Almost all scientists have some familiarity with the basic concepts and methods of the discipline, but I will not assume any special knowledge.

To understand and use statistics, we first need a clear grasp of *probability*. For our purposes, we can understand a probability as a number between 0 and 1, inclusive, that represents the likelihood of an event. A probability of 0 means that the event is impossible, and a probability of 1 means that it must occur. Any other probability can be interpreted as the frequency, or proportion of times, with which the event will occur in a large number of experiments. For example, if we say that the probability of heads when you flip a coin is 1/2, this means if you flip the coin a large number of times, the ratio of times that it comes up heads divided by the total number of flips will be close to 0.5.

How many times is a large number of times? What we really mean is that there is a limit

$$P(x) = \lim_{N \to \infty} \frac{n_x}{N}$$

which just says that as we do more and more experiments, the number of times that we observe the event x, n_x, divided by the total number of experiments, N, gets closer and closer to a certain ratio. We call this ratio the probability. In probability theory, *experiment* means a process, such as flipping a coin or rolling a die.

The preceding paragraph describes a particular view of probability called the *frequency interpretation*. There are other ways to look at probability and its meaning, but in some sense, they are all equivalent. The frequency interpretation is practical, serves our purposes well, and is what most people think of when they need to pin down their idea of what probability means in practice. For more formal approaches to the subject, see "Further Reading" on page 359.

We'll often want to simulate events in our computer programs that are supposed to occur with certain probabilities. This could be part of the simulation of a system, such as the molecules of a gas bouncing around in a box, which we may want to initialize with random positions and velocities, or it could be part of a statistical test. But this presents a problem: if probability represents chance, the outcome of some kind of random process, and what goes on inside our computers is (we certainly hope) deterministic, how can we use computers to generate random events?

For the purposes of the examples in this book, we actually don't want our random events to be random, because we may want to repeat simulations or check to see whether we get identical results after changing a computational technique. We need to be able to repeat particular sequences of "random" events. Surely this is a contradiction. If we know what's going to happen, it can't be random.

The random numbers we generate in our programs are called *pseudorandom* numbers. They look like sequences of random numbers, satisfy certain tests of randomness, and adhere to given *distributions* (explained next). However, naturally, they are not really random. Again, we don't actually want them to be.

Except when we do. In some cryptography applications, we really need actual, unpredictable random numbers. Because the bad guys know the various algorithms for generating pseudorandom numbers, being able to predict such sequences can lead to defeating cryptographic systems. For such purposes, computer security systems exploit sources of real unpredictability available on any computer (known as *entropy sources*). These sources can be stored data derived from the timing of key presses on the keyboard, for example. The search for entropy has led to some creative solutions, such as pointing cameras at a wall of lava lamps.

Julia actually provides a way to tap into the entropy provided by your operating system. However, in this book, we are not interested in cryptography, but in science, so we want our random numbers to be not so random, and we'll be using Julia's pseudorandom number generators. I'll follow common practice for the rest of this chapter and just call these pseudorandom numbers "random numbers."

Random Numbers in Julia

Julia has functions for generating random numbers with all kinds of numerical types, even complex numbers. The basic random number generators are part of Base, so you can use them without any import statements.

NOTE   *I mentioned earlier that one reason to use pseudorandom numbers is so we can repeat a sequence of random numbers when developing code. This sequence repeatability is not guaranteed to work forever, however. The random sequence returned by a particular function can change when upgrading Julia, so you can't depend on this for code development over the long term. See "Further Reading" on page 359 if you need long-term reproducible number sequences.*

The simplest use is just calling rand(), which returns a random Float64 *uniformly distributed* in the interval [0, 1). This means that the number might be equal to 0, but it will be less than 1, and all numbers in this interval are equally likely.

We can check that the rand() function is doing what we expect by generating a bunch of random numbers and plotting them with a scatterplot. We could do this by calling rand() many times, storing its returned values in an array, and plotting the array. But rand() makes it even easier: if we give it an integer argument, it will oblige us by returning an array of random values whose length will be determined by the argument. If we give it more than one, we'll get back a higher-dimensional array. The little program shown in Listing 10-1 fills a length-10^5 array with random floats and visualizes their distribution with a scatterplot.

```
using Plots

ra = rand(100000)
scatter(ra, markersize=1, label=nothing)
```

Listing 10-1: Testing random number generation

In the resulting plot, shown in Figure 10-1, each of the 10^5 numbers is represented by a tiny dot. All the numbers lie within the correct interval, and they appear to be randomly and uniformly distributed, as they are supposed to be. A plot like this is a useful visual check to ensure that a pseudo-random number generator is behaving correctly and not introducing any unwanted patterns in the distribution of values.

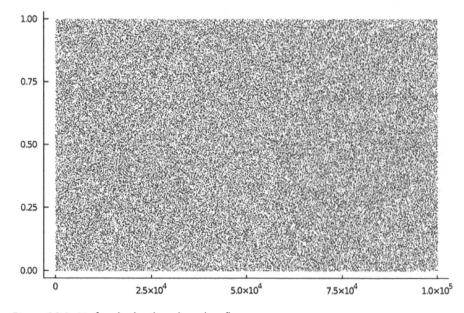

Figure 10-1: Uniformly distributed random floats

To get random integers, or some type other than floats, simply pass the type as an argument. The call rand(Int), which is the same as rand(Int64), returns a random integer within the range defined by the lowest and highest possible integers of that type. This is rarely what you want in applications, however. You'll probably want a random integer within some specified range that is relevant to your problem. In that case, simply pass the range as an argument: rand(1:6) represents the roll of a die, for example.

In fact, that argument can be a tuple or list as well, from which rand() will pick a random element, all with equal likelihood. You can even do something like rand([1, 3, "abc"]), and get either 1, 3, or the string "abc", each with a probability of 1/3. If you pass in a single string, it will be considered a collection of characters, and you will get a random character back.

The simple call rand() is useful in simulations where you want events to occur with a certain probability. If the probability of the event is supposed to be P, in your code, you'll have something like the following, which is a way to make something happen with a specified probability:

```
if P > rand()
    event()
end
```

The call to rand() works because it generates *uniformly distributed* random numbers in the interval [0, 1). Imagine repeatedly throwing a dart at a square dartboard one meter on a side (and assume it lands in a random place on the board). In the long run, the dart will land within the rightmost 90 centimeters 90 percent of the time. The rand() function is the dart.

Keeping in mind that, over the long term, you can't count on being able to repeat a particular sequence generated by one of Julia's random number functions, you'll need to know how to do it in the short term when debugging code or developing an algorithm. You'll often want to rerun a program after changing something that you believe should not change the results. If the program uses random numbers, and the sequence is truly unpredictable, such tests become impossible.

By passing a *seed* to a random number generator, you can generate a sequence of high-quality pseudorandom numbers and also repeat the same sequence in subsequent runs of your program. To do this, you need to import the Random package, as you'll need to use at least one function that's not in Base. But Random has a few other goodies, as you'll see shortly.

The following listing shows the three lines of code that illustrate the basic procedure:

```
using Random

rgen = MersenneTwister(7654);
rand(rgen)
```

After importing Random, the MersenneTwister() function, which is a random number–generating algorithm, will be available. The name comes from the mathematical library from which the function is taken. Its argument, in this case 7654, is called a *seed*. The purpose of the seed is to generate a particular sequence that we can repeat if needed. The rand() function, and all the other random number functions in Julia, accept an optional first argument that specifies the particular instance of the generator to use. As before, every time we call rand(), we get a random number between 0 and 1. But now we can restart the sequence anytime we want by reinitializing rgen using the same seed. We can generate a different, unpredictable sequence by simply changing the seed. Except for the most casual use, you should always specify a generator and supply it with a seed rather than using the simpler form of rand() as we did in the previous example.

The Monty Hall Problem

The ability to generate random numbers opens up a whole world of possibilities for interesting simulations. First, let's consider the *Monty Hall problem*, which is named after the longtime host of the game show *Let's Make a Deal*. This problem is guaranteed to generate lively debate in statistics classes and is something that experienced mathematicians, even statisticians, often get wrong—or they used to, before the problem became famous. For us, it will serve as an example of how a probabilistic computer simulation can verify a result that we believe we have calculated analytically. Simulations can supply some additional confidence in the solutions to tricky probability problems, where it is so easy to go astray analytically.

Imagine three doors. Behind one is a prize, say, a fancy car, and behind the other two are joke prizes. Monty often used goats for these "loser" prizes. You want the car. Monty asks you to choose a door. He knows where everything is, but you know nothing.

Let's say, to be definite, that you choose door #1. Before revealing what's behind that door, Monty opens one of the other ones, say, door #3, to reveal a goat. He offers you the chance to switch to door #2 if you like.

Here is the question: should you stick with your original choice or switch to door #2? Does it matter?

The correct answer is that you should switch. Nevertheless, many people have a strong initial intuition that it must not make any difference. After all, now two doors are available: door #1 and door #2. Surely they have an equal chance of leading to the prize, so it's the same as flipping a coin: heads or tails are equally likely.

However, this thinking is wrong. Initially, the probability that your choice was a winner was 1/3. Everyone agrees with that. That means that the probability that the prize was in *one of the other doors* is 2/3. Since the prize is guaranteed to be somewhere, the total probability must add up to 1. These initial probabilities still hold. The probability that door #1 is the winner is still 1/3. The probability that one of the others is, instead, is still 2/3. But now the set of "one of the others" consists of just door #2, since Monty has eliminated door #3. You should switch to increase your chances of winning from 1/3 to 2/3.

This analysis is just one of many ways to approach the problem, but they all (if done correctly) lead to the same conclusion. Nevertheless, at this point many people remain unconvinced. Sometimes actually doing the experiment can persuade people who don't believe in math.

The following program performs just such an experiment—a simple example of a simulation using a random process:

```
N = 3000

stay = zeros(Int32, N)
switch = zeros(Int32, N)

for game in 1:N
    prize = rand(1:3)
    choice = rand(1:3)
    if choice == prize
        stay[game] = 1
    end
end

for game in 1:N
    prize = rand(1:3)
    choice = rand(1:3)
    if choice != prize
        switch[game] = 1
    end
end

❶ stayra = [sum(stay[1:i]) / i for i in 1:N]
  switchra = [sum(switch[1:i]) / i  for i in 1:N]

using Plots

plot(1:N, [stayra, switchra, ones(N)*1/3, ones(N)*2/3],
    label=["Stay" "Switch" "" ""])
annotate!(2700, 1/3 + 0.05, "1/3")
annotate!(2700, 2/3 + 0.05, "2/3")
```

This program plays the game N times, where N is set to 3,000. It stores the record of wins or losses in two arrays, one for the set of 3,000 plays where the player stays with the initial choice of door and one for the round where the player decides to switch. The arrays are initialized to be all 0s. If the player wins game number game, that array element is changed to 1.

The two arrays ❶ hold the running average of each strategy, defined using list comprehensions. These are the arrays we want to look at.

The plot in Figure 10-2 shows that in the long run the switching strategy wins 2/3 of the time, while the player who stubbornly sticks with the initial choice wins only 1/3 of the time.

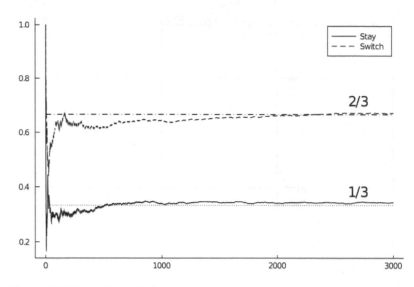

Figure 10-2: Two Monty Hall strategies

These ratios agree with the argument if we remember the meaning of the frequency interpretation of probability: over the long run, the ratio of events (wins, in this case) to the total number of experiments should approach the probability. Note that if you run this code yourself, the graph may look slightly different, because you'll get a different sequence of random numbers, but the *long-term behavior* should be the same.

Counting

After probability, the next most important idea in statistics is *counting*, also called *combinatorics*. Counting has to do with answering questions about how many ways an event can happen. If you roll a pair of dice, in how many ways can the sum of the two numbers that come up equal six? If there are 30 people on the squad, how many nine-person baseball teams are possible?

When simulating systems involving probability on a computer, to calculate correctly the probabilities of various events, we often *count* the number of ways a given event can happen and divide by the total number of all possibilities. If all of the ways are equally likely, this gives us the probability.

In the dice example, there are 10 ways to get a sum of six, so the probability is 10/36.

Two additional counting concepts arise frequently when dealing with probabilistic situations, and often in other places as well: *permutations*, calculated using factorials, and *combinations*, which involve binomial coefficients.

Factorials

The first counting concept is the idea of *permutations*: the number of distinct ways to arrange a collection of objects. If you have eight *Scrabble* tiles, all bearing different letters, how many different eight-letter strings can you make out of them?

The answer is $8 \times 7 \times 6 \times 5 \times 4 \times 3 \times 2 \times 1 = 40,320$.

Here's a quick argument to show why this is true: there are eight ways to choose the first tile; once that is chosen, there are seven ways to choose the next tile; and so on. This pattern comes up so often that we have a special name and mathematical notation for it. It is called the *factorial*, and it's written as 8! in this case. Julia also has a built-in function for it, but since ! is used for other purposes, we need to spell it out: `factorial(8)`.

The factorial function grows insanely quickly, so above `factorial(20)`, you need to supply the argument as a `BigInt`, and you'll get a `BigInt` back. How quickly does the factorial grow? The number of ways to arrange a standard 52-card deck is far larger than the number of stars in the universe. It's so large that, after shuffling a deck, there is almost no chance that the particular arrangement of cards you are holding in your hand has existed before in the history of the world.

Binomial Coefficients

The second combinatorial concept we'll be using is the *binomial coefficient*. This comes up in many mathematical contexts, and Julia has a built-in function called `binomial()` that deals with it. In the context of counting, the binomial coefficient answers the baseball teams question mentioned earlier. If there are 30 players available, the number of ways to form nine-member teams is written as:

$$\binom{30}{9} = 14,307,150$$

The baseball problem is calculated with `binomial(30, 9)`. The combinatorial term for these problems, involving binomial coefficients, is *combinations*.

See "Further Reading" on page 359 to learn more details about binomial coefficients: why they are so named, how to calculate them using factorials, and their connections to other areas of mathematics.

Modeling a Pandemic

We now have enough tools to perform a significant calculation. Listing 10-2 is a simulation that models the spread of an infection through a population. It's similar to models epidemiologists use to perform computational experiments with different scenarios for the spread of COVID-19. This model is a bit simplified relative to those, as my purpose is to illustrate an application of the tools and ideas from the chapter so far. For a pointer to similar models being used now in research, see "Further Reading."

```
using Plots
using Printf
using JLD
```

```
    worldgrad = cgrad([:blue, :red, :black, :green], [0.25, 0.50, 0.75],
            categorical=true)
    n = 16
❶  initial = Dict("infected"=>0.5, "isolated"=>0.15)
    transition = Dict("infected"=>0.05, "dead"=>0.1, "dud"=>7)
    include("plotworld.jl")
    """Simulate pandemic growth.
        n: length of side of world array;
        initial: starting proportions of infected and isolated subpopulations;
        transition: probabilities of infection and of death after dud days of
                infection;
        days: number of days before stopping;
        seeding: selects spatially random or centered initial distribution of
                infected individuals;
        plotmode: display or save plots of simulation while running, or save
                only the final state.
    """
    function pandemic(n::Int, initial, transition, days::Int; seeding=:normal,
                plotmode=:display)
        noi = [] # Number of infected people
        nod = [] # Number of dead people
        function finish()
            if plotmode == :last
                plotfilename = @sprintf "%d.png" days
                savefig(plotworld(world, noi, nod, worldgrad), plotfilename);
            end
            @save "pandata.jld" world noi nod
        end
        function nif(I, J) # Number of infected neighbors of an uninfected cell
            return sum(world[I-1:I+1,J-1:J+1] .== infected)
        end
        tpi = zeros(8)
❷      for N in 1:8
            tp = 0
            for i in 1:N
                tp += (-1)^(i-1)*binomial(N, i)*transition["infected"]^i
            end
            tpi[N] = tp # The total probability of infection with N infected neighbors
        end
        ok::Int32 = 1
        infected::Int32 = 2
        dead::Int32 = 3
        isolated::Int32 = 4
        world = fill(ok, n, n)
        if seeding == :normal
            world[rand(n, n) .< initial["infected"]] .= infected
        end
```

```
        world[rand(n, n) .< initial["isolated"]] .= isolated
        if seeding == :center
            world[n ÷ 2, n ÷ 2] = infected
        end
❸   next = copy(world)
❹   aoi = fill(0, n, n) # Age of infection
    dud = transition["dud"]
    for day in 1:days
        for j in 2:n-1 for i in 2:n-1
            if world[i, j] == ok
                if nif(i, j) > 0
                    if tpi[nif(i, j)] >= rand()
                        next[i, j] = infected
                        aoi[i, j] = day
                    end
                end
            end
            if (world[i, j] == infected) && ((day - aoi[i, j]) == dud)
                if rand() < transition["dead"]
                    next[i, j] = dead
                end
            end
        end; end
        world = copy(next)
❺       push!(noi, sum(world[2:n-1, 2:n-1] .== infected))
        push!(nod, sum(world[2:n-1, 2:n-1] .== dead))
❻       if day > 4dud
            if noi[end] == noi[end - dud] && nod[end] == nod[end - dud]
                return finish()
            end
        end
        if plotmode == :save
            plotfilename = @sprintf "%05d.png" day
            savefig(plotworld(world, noi, nod, worldgrad), plotfilename);
        elseif plotmode == :display
            display(plotworld(world, noi, nod, worldgrad))
        end
    end
    finish()
end
days = 2000
pandemic(n, initial, transition, days; seeding=:normal, plotmode=:display)
```

Listing 10-2: A pandemic simulation

The strategy is to represent the population as a square matrix. Each cell represents one person and can be in one of four possible states: infected, dead, isolated, or ok. An isolated person can't become infected. An ok person is not infected, but may become so. An infected person may die after a certain number of "days," or iterations, a number assigned to dud; if the person survives past this period, immortality is achieved. A dead person is no longer infectious. Thus, an ok person can never be infected (is "protected") if surrounded by dead or isolated people. Death and lockdown prevent the spread of the disease.

The simulation is initialized with probabilities, to establish both the starting state and its evolution. The state at day = 1 is set up using the probabilities in the initial dictionary ❶. At every iteration, the state of each person is updated according to the probabilities in the transition dictionary on the following line and the value of dud in that dictionary, which is the number of days during which someone needs to be infected before the disease may become fatal.

The population matrix is called world, and the length of its side is stored in n. Don't take the matrix geometry too literally. It does not assume that people stand in one spot while the disease runs its course. The matrix world represents a network of contact rather than a spatial arrangement.

After importing some libraries that you have seen before and including a file with the plotting function, which we'll get to later, the pandemic() function, which does the actual calculation, is defined. This function gets two keyword arguments: seeding should be either :normal or :center. In the former case, infection is seeded randomly, according to initial["infected"]; but if seeding is set to :center, a single infected individual is placed at the center of the world.

The second keyword, plotmode, controls whether daily plots are created, and if so, whether they are displayed or saved to files. At the end of the calculation, the finish() function is called, which saves a plot of the final state if the plotmode = :last. This function also uses the @save macro to save the world and the infection and death histories to a *.jld* file (introduced in Chapter 9).

At every iteration, the program has to decide, for each ok person, whether to change that person to the infected state. This is determined randomly, based on the probability of infection by each infected neighbor each day, given in transition["infected"], and on the number of infected neighbors.

But, we need to be careful here. The probability of infection with two infected neighbors is not twice the probability of infection with only a single sick neighbor. We need to subtract the probability of becoming infected by both neighbors. We won't provide a full treatment of the combination of events in probability theory here, but you likely can easily see why we can't simply add the probabilities.

Imagine you are flipping two coins and want to find the probability of getting at least one head. You know that the probability of a head with either coin alone is 1/2. If you add those, you get a probability of 1. But that can't be right, because it would mean a head *must* appear, and you know there's a good chance you'll get two tails. The correct calculation includes subtracting the probability of *two* heads: 1/2 + 1/2 - 1/4 = 3/4. You will get at least one head three-fourths of the time in the long run. At this point, you are in a good position to write a little Julia program to verify this, if you have any doubts.

The coin problem corresponds exactly to the case where you are in contact with two infected people and the probability of infection = 1/2. On the grid, however, each person can have up to eight neighbors. It's a bit more complicated than the case of two neighbors, but the idea is the same. For each new neighbor, you have to add the probability of infection by that neighbor, but subtract all the combinations it can make with the other neighbors. The word *combinations* suggests that we might have to reach for a binomial coefficient, and indeed we do. The formula for the total probability of infection by n neighbors, if the probability of infection by a single neighbor is p, is:

$$\text{Total probability} = \sum_{i=1}^{n} (-1)^{i-1} \binom{n}{i} p^i$$

See "Further Reading" on page 359 for more about this formula and related matters. This probability is pre-calculated for all possible numbers of neighbors, 1:8, and the results are stored in the tpi ❷ array.

It is necessary, before each iteration's calculations begin, to make a copy of the world array, which is called next in the program ❸. We update the cells in next, and then copy it back into world. If world is updated in place, cells will be transitioned based on the partially updated information in neighbor cells, which would be inconsistent. A copy is required, as we've encountered in previous chapters, because a simple next = world would create a second reference to the array rather than an actual copy.

An array aoi is initialized to 0s ❹; it will record the day on which each person becomes infected, so that the survival probability can be applied at the appropriate time.

The subsequent loops over persons within the loop over days, given all the foregoing, should be self explanatory. After the sweep of the matrix, we push!() ❺ new values for the current total number of infected and dead people onto the vectors noi and nod, respectively. Julia's neat and succinct syntax calculates these totals using a sum over a binary array.

Here, and in the previous loops over the world, the program treats only elements in 2:n-1 rather than the entire array, to implement the boundary condition. In keeping one row or column of cells on the boundaries "frozen," the updating logic is simplified, as the expression, for example, for calculating the number of each person's infected neighbors is identical for each nonfrozen person.

As in a physics problem, there are other possibilities for boundary conditions. The people on the edges could be updated based on their reduced numbers of neighbors, but doing so can induce artifacts. Periodic boundary conditions are another possibility, where the neighbor-ness wraps around the matrix to the opposite side. Any choice is to some degree arbitrary.

The conditional block ❻ checks to see whether the calculation has reached a steady state. If it has, there is no point in continuing, and the cleanup operation is called. The final line in the program starts the calculation by calling pandemic().

This simple algorithm can produce interesting behavior, and it can be used to explore questions such as the effect of lockdown conformity on the spread of the infection, and how a higher fatality rate can slow the growth of a pandemic.

Figure 10-3 shows the output of a 512×512 simulation with these initial and transition probabilities:

```
initial = Dict("infected"=>0.001, "isolated"=>0.5)
transition = Dict("infected"=>0.08, "dead"=>0.25, "dud"=>5)
```

The simulation stops after 1,064 iterations when reaching a steady state. The notation on the figure means that 5.48 percent of the population was protected from infection due to the isolation of others and the effects of mortality interrupting disease transmission.

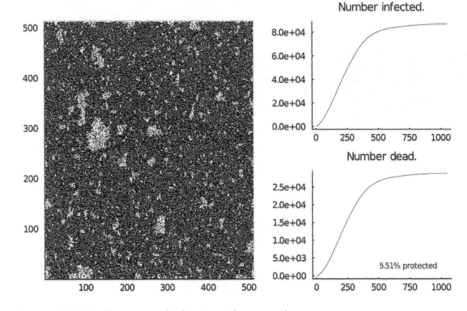

Figure 10-3: Steady state reached in a pandemic simulation

See the book's supplementary website (*https://julia.lee-phillips.org*) for a color version of the plot and an animation of a similar simulation. In the printed grayscale version, the darkest shades on the heatmap plot represent dead or infected people, white represents people who remained protected from infection, and the middle tone corresponds to isolated people.

Listing 10-3 shows the simple function that calculates the protected percentage and makes plots as in Figure 10-3.

```
using Plots
using Printf
"""Plot a heatmap of the current state of the pandemic with the histories
```

of the number of infected and dead people; calculate and display the
proportion of people protected from infection."""
function plotworld(world, noi, nod, worldgrad)
    ok::Int32 = 1
    day = length(noi)
    protected = sum(world[2:n-1, 2:n-1] .== ok) / n^2 * 100
❶ prot = @sprintf("%.2f%% protected", protected)
    p1 = heatmap(1:n, 1:n, world, c=worldgrad, clims=(1, 4), legend=nothing);
    p2 = plot(1:day, noi, label=nothing, yformatter=y -> @sprintf("%.1e", y),
            titlefontsize=10);
    p3 = plot(1:day, nod, label=nothing, annotate=
            (0.7day, 0.1nod[end], text(prot, :blue, 7)), yformatter=
            y -> @sprintf("%.1e", y), titlefontsize=10);
❷ layout=@layout [a{0.6w} grid(2, 1)];
    return plot(p1, p2, p3, layout=layout,
            title=["" "Number infected." "Number dead."]);
end
```

*Listing 10-3: Visualizing the pandemic*

The plotworld() function uses the @sprintf macro ❶, introduced in "Macros
for String Formatting" on page 177, to format the variable protected and the
y-axis label for display. After creating three plots and storing them in p1,
p2, and p3, the @layout macro, described in "Creating Complex Layouts Us-
ing @layout" on page 118, arranges them ❷ into a summary display of the
simulation.

## Common Statistics Functions

Julia provides functions to calculate all of the common statistical parameters,
as well as special plotting functions for statistical visualization of data.

Some reorganization of the Julia statistics packages is underway, so ev-
erything may not be where you might expect it. This section describes where
the packages are at the time of writing, but, when you try things out, you
may discover that a function or two have moved.

If you are analyzing data of any kind, you will make heavy use of at least
some of the functions described in this section, most of which are in the
Statistics package, which is part of the standard Julia library. In the re-
mainder of this chapter, I will assume you've imported the package with the
using Statistics command.

The package provides the basic functions that summarize datasets with
statistical parameters. For the *mean*, or arithmetic average, use mean(*data*),
where, here and below, *data* is some vector of observations.

For the *median*, which is the middle value in the data, use median(*data*).
If there are an even number of data points, none of them can be the middle
value. In this case, median() returns the mean of the two middle values:

```
julia> median([1, 2, 3])
2.0
```
```

```
julia> median([1, 2, 3, 4])
2.5
```

At the time of writing, Statistics does not contain a *mode* function. The mode is the most common value, or the maximum of a continuous distribution, if it exists. From this idea come the terms *bimodal* and *multimodal* to describe distributions with more than one local maximum. The height distribution in Figure 10-4 is an example of a bimodal distribution.

If you need a mode function, you can import it from another package called StatsBase, which you will need to add. StatsBase contains some other less commonly used statistical functions that are not in the standard Statistics package, but you may want to import only the ones you plan to use. If you just need to add a mode function to your toolbox, you can enter import StatsBase.mode.

Here are a few examples showing how the mode() function behaves:

```
julia> mode([1, 3, 2, 9, 9])
9

julia> mode([1, 3, 2, 9, 9, 4, 4])
9

julia> mode([1, 3, 2, 9])
1
```

If there is more than one mode, the function returns the first one. Consequently, if each value appears only once, they are all modes, so the function returns the first value.

The standard Statistics package contains most of the other basic statistical functions, including the following:

std   Standard deviation

stdm   Standard deviation with specified mean

var   Variance

varm   Variance with specified mean

cor   Pearson correlation

cov   Covariance

middle   (max + min) / 2

quantile   Quantile

These commands work on vectors or pairs of vectors of data in the way you would expect. In addition, the cor() function will accept a matrix and return a correlation matrix, and the cov() function can work similarly.

The mean() function takes an optional first argument that can be a unary operator or a function of one numeric variable. The function then maps the operator or function over the data vector before calculating the mean. This can be convenient if you need to scale or otherwise process the data, but, for the case of a simple vector, it gives the same result as broadcasting the function over the array:

```
julia> mean([1, 2, 3])
2.0

julia> mean(x -> 2x, [1, 2, 3])
4.0

julia> mean(2 .* [1, 2, 3])
4.0
```

There are two versions of the standard deviation and the variance used in statistics. The formula the var() function uses by default is

$$\sigma^2 = \frac{\sum_{n=1}^{N}(x_n - \mu)^2}{N - 1}$$

where μ is the mean, the x_n values are individual data points, N is the total number of data points, and σ^2 is the *sample variance*, or the variance with Bessel's correction applied. The standard deviation std() is just the positive square root of this.

In order to calculate the *population variance* and *population standard deviation*, supply the keyword argument corrected with a value of false to either of these functions. This will replace the $1/(N-1)$ term in the formula with $1/N$. Explaining the origin of the correction would take us too far into the arcana of statistical theory, but for most purposes, the defaults are what you want, and it makes little difference for reasonably large N in any case.

In either incarnation, the standard deviation is a measure of the average distance from the mean of a set of observations or of a theoretical distribution. It tells us how "spread out" the distribution is.

Distributions

We've looked at several examples of how we can do a lot with simple, uniformly distributed random numbers. However, not every random occurrence is uniformly distributed. Most things in nature display other types of distributions.

Consider the heights of adults in a particular city. Obviously, you don't expect that the probability of finding a 7-foot-tall adult is the same as finding one with closer to average height: heights are not uniformly distributed. If you make a graph, dividing the horizontal axis into height ranges covering, say, intervals of 2 inches, and collect the heights of a sample of residents, you can plot how many heights fall into each interval. After collecting a large number of measurements, this plot will start to look like a smooth curve, something like Figure 10-4. It has two peaks, because the average height of men is a little higher than women, and it shows that there are more people close to the average than very tall or very short.

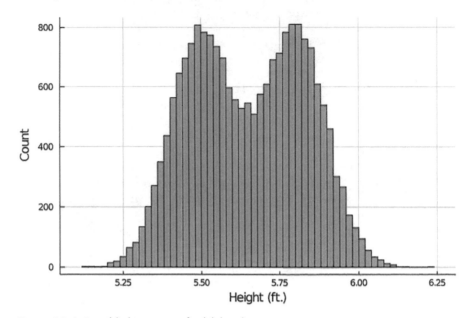

Figure 10-4: Possible histogram of adult heights

This type of graph is called a *histogram*; it is one way to represent a *distribution*. Probability distributions are the mathematical objects at the center of statistics, just as a probability forms, naturally, the central idea of probability theory. A distribution simply tells you how much of your data, or what proportion of your data, falls within different ranges. As a description of actual data it's called an *empirical distribution*, whereas if it comes from a model it's a *theoretical distribution*.

You can think of the discipline of statistics this way: probabilities tell us how likely something is to happen, and the mathematics of probability theory lets us elaborate this, telling us the likelihood of combinations of events and answering related questions. Statistics is the reverse: it starts with observations, and lets us systematically infer the probabilities that led to those observations. With these probabilities, we can make predictions about future observations.

Julia provides several packages and a great number of functions for helping out with statistics, including functions for statistical graphing. To produce a histogram like the one shown in Figure 10-4, simply call (after using Plots) histogram(data, bins = 100). The data in this call is the actual series of observations; the bins tells the routine to use that number of intervals to construct the histogram. For each interval, it will count the number of observations in data and draw the rectangle at the appropriate height. The area of each rectangle represents the number of observations in the horizontal axis interval that it covers. Beware that the same dataset may produce very different plots when choosing different numbers of bins; some choices will better reflect the underlying distribution than others. If you leave out the bins argument, the `histogram()` routine will attempt to choose the "best" value, using a formula from statistical theory that is designed to best represent the data. This formula does not always work perfectly, so the careful scientist or statistician will always be aware of the nature of the data being plotted, and intervene manually if necessary.

The Normal Distribution

Consider the `rand()` function described earlier in this chapter. Since it generates a floating-point number that is equally likely to be anywhere in the interval from 0 to 1, the mean value of the numbers it returns should be 0.5. The number is just as likely to be greater than 0.5 as to be smaller than that midpoint.

This means if you call `rand()` many times, and calculate the mean of the results, you should get something fairly close to 0.5: `mean(rand(1000))` should be approximately 0.5. I did it just now and got 0.49869515604579906. Intuitively, you may expect if you use a number smaller than 1,000, the mean is more likely to be farther from 0.5, and that is correct.

But even using 1,000 numbers, the mean will rarely be exactly 0.5. Since (unless you reset the seed) you will get a different set of random numbers each time, the mean will be different each time, as well. The numbers themselves, as you know, are uniformly distributed in $[0, 1)$. If you call `mean(rand(1000))` many times, how will the *means* be distributed?

You know they can't be distributed uniformly, because they are more likely to be near 0.5 than far from it. But what exactly is the distribution of the means?

Let's write a little program to find out. Even those who have studied statistics and know what to expect may find the numerical experiment in Listing 10-4 interesting.

```
using Plots
using Statistics
N = 10000
averages = zeros(N)
for i in 1:N
    averages[i] = mean(rand(1000))
end
histogram(averages, label="Empirical")
```

Listing 10-4: Exploring the distribution of the mean

The program is a straightforward calculation of the N means of 1,000 random numbers. To see how these means are distributed, we turn to the `histogram()` plotting function introduced earlier in the chapter. The purpose of this function is exactly to display distributions. The `"Empirical"` label indicates that the histogram is the result of a numerical experiment. Figure 10-5 shows the result.

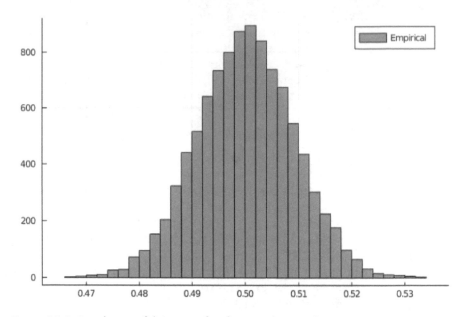

Figure 10-5: Distribution of the mean of uniform random numbers

Obviously, the distribution of the means is not uniform. As we expect, it shows that means closer to 0.5 are more frequent.

In fact, from a central result in probability theory, we can predict the precise mathematical form of this distribution. It should be

$$\phi(x) = \frac{1}{\sigma\sqrt{2\pi}} e^{-\frac{1}{2}\left(\frac{x-\mu}{\sigma}\right)^2}$$

where x is the random variable whose distribution we are describing, σ is the standard deviation, and μ is the mean.

This is the equation for the famous *normal distribution*, also called the *Gaussian*. Does it describe the empirical distribution from the program? We don't need to translate the equation into code to find out. This distribution is so crucial, it's included in the second most important Julia package for statistical work, `Distributions`.

Once you import this package into your namespace, the function `Normal(μ, σ)` creates a normal distribution with a mean of μ and a standard deviation of σ. You can interact with the distribution by sampling from it using the `rand()` function. For example, if you create a normal distribution with a mean of 10 and a standard deviation of 2 with d = `Normal(10, 2)`, you can draw 10 samples from it with `rand(d, 10)`. Calling `rand()` without supplying an explicit distribution, as we've been doing up to now, uses the uniform distribution by default.

One way to see if the empirical distribution shown is predicted by the normal distribution is to take a healthy sample from the normal distribution and plot its histogram with the previous one. To make the plot easier to see, instead of trying to plot two `histogram()` plots on the same graph, we can plot the second one using a different type of histogram display by supplying the :scatterhist series type to the normal plot() command. Adding the four additional lines shown in Listing 10-5 to the program in Listing 10-4 makes the graphical comparison that we want.

```
using Distributions
σ = std(averages)
nd = Normal(0.5, σ)
plot!(rand(nd, 10000), seriestype=:scatterhist, label="Normal sample")
```

Listing 10-5: Sampling from the normal distribution

Figure 10-6 shows that the two distributions are close, as theory predicts.

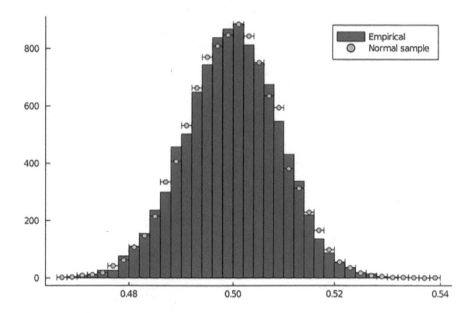

Figure 10-6: Comparing the empirical and theoretical distributions

Note that in order to compare two histograms directly, they must have the same bin width, or both be normalized. In these examples, I allow the routines to compute the bin width automatically, knowing that for similar distributions the widths would be the same.

The Distributions package provides many probability distributions in addition to the normal distribution. It also includes many functions for using these distributions, along with other statistical tools.

Probability Density Functions

One of those tools is pdf(), which stands for *probability density function*. This function describes the distribution in the following sense: if you integrate the probability density function over a certain interval, the result is the probability that an observation lies within that interval. In other words, the probability that an observation lies between *a* and *b* is the area under the distribution curve between *a* and *b*.

Usually, when referring to the graph of a distribution, we mean the graph of its probability density function. The integral over the entire distribution must exist and be equal to 1, because it is certain that any observation must have some value within the range of possible values.

All of the `histogram()` plotting types have an optional `normalize` keyword argument that can be set to `true` to make the histogram plot indicate probabilities rather than raw counts—for example:

```
histogram(averages, label="Empirical", normalize=true)
plot!(rand(nd, 10000), seriestype=:scatterhist, label="Normal sample",
    normalize=true)
❶ plot!(0.46:0.001:0.54, pdf.(nd, 0.46:0.001:0.54), lw=5, label="Normal PDF")
```

Those three lines repeat the plots of the two histograms just plotted in Figure 10-6, but normalized. Now the areas of the histogram rectangles, shown in Figure 10-7, are probabilities rather than raw counts. The new curve is a plot ❶ of the probability density function of the normal distribution with the same mean and standard deviation as the sample. It is a graph of the equation for ϕ, displayed after Figure 10-5. Figure 10-7 shows how accurately it predicts the results of the numerical experiment in Listing 10-4.

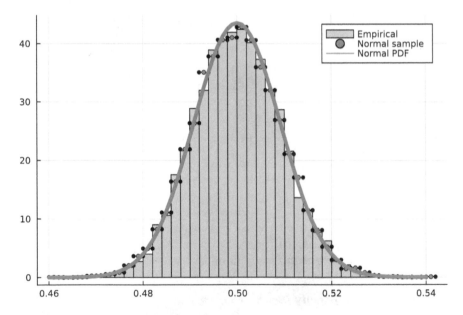

Figure 10-7: Adding the probability density function

Because of the normal distribution's importance, Julia provides another function, similar to `rand()`, that returns normally distributed random numbers rather than uniformly distributed ones. The `randn()` function is part of `Base`, so you don't need an `import`. It returns single numbers or arrays, normally distributed with a mean of 0 and a standard deviation of 1.

Let's repeat the plot from Listing 10-1 using `randn()`:

```
using Plots
ra = randn(100000)
scatter(ra, markersize=1, label=nothing)
```

The only difference is in using `randn()` instead of `rand()`. Figure 10-8 shows the result. As in Figure 10-1, each of the 10^5 numbers is represented by a tiny dot, but now the dots are not uniformly distributed.

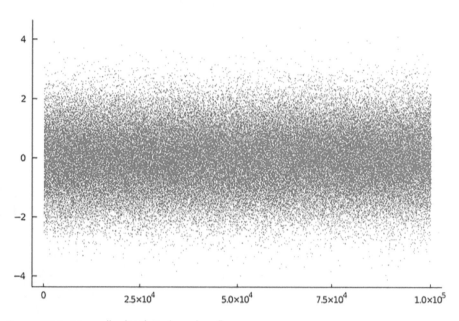

Figure 10-8: Normally distributed random floats

Instead, they are crowded around the value 0 on the vertical axis, with their density getting thinner the farther they are from 0, the mean of their distribution.

Dealing with Data

So far, all the "data" in this chapter has been either made up or the result of collecting results from numerical pseudorandom processes. If you are using Julia for statistical analysis, the odds are good that you have some actual, real-life data to analyze.

In this section, we'll explore the most important methods in Julia for dealing with real data. We'll look at a data type that comes in handy when manipulating data in the real world, how to read data from the most common types of datafiles, how to use dataframes to view and analyze this data, and how to take advantage of Julia's statistical packages to understand and visualize numerical information.

Missing Values

There is an unusual data type I didn't mention in Chapter 8 because I was saving it for this chapter. It's a singleton type called `Missing`, and it is used to represent missing values.

Imagine you have a sensor that is supposed to record the temperature inside a tank of water at regular intervals of time. Unfortunately, every now and then it fails to record a measurement. Those failures are recorded as 0s, but that number is far outside the range of possible measurements, so these failures can't be mistaken for actual temperatures. At the end of the experiment you have two vectors, or perhaps two columns of a matrix, one for the times of the measurements and the other for the temperatures. When analyzing this data, you don't want the false zero temperatures to be included in the analysis because that would distort your calculations. You want a better solution than simply deleting the failed readings because that would create a false record of what actually happened in the experiment, and, to keep the timing and temperature vectors the same length, perhaps for plotting the results, you will have to delete the corresponding entries from the timing vector, leading to a time sequence containing gaps.

The `Missing` type provides one solution to this set of problems and others—for example, in data science, where the concept of missing values arises. It has some properties that may seem peculiar, illustrated in Listing 10-6, which is a REPL session exploring arithmetic on the `Missing` type.

```
julia> m = missing
missing

julia> 3m
missing

julia> 3 + m
missing

julia> missing/3
missing

julia> missing/0
missing

julia> missing + missing
missing

julia> typeof(m)
Missing
```

Listing 10-6: Arithmetic properties of missing values

We see from Listing 10-6 that arithmetic on missing values leads to a missing result, even when dividing by 0.

Usually, missing values are not floating around by themselves, but are found as part of a collection of data. Listing 10-7 is a little function that creates an array, replaces some of its values with missing values, and plots the result.

```
using Plots
function plotmissing()
    a::Vector{Union{Missing, Float64}} = sin.(0:0.03:2π) .+ rand(210)/4
    a[49:54] .= missing
    plot(a, legend=nothing, linewidth=3)
end
```

Listing 10-7: Creating some missing data for plotting

We need to declare the array to be able to accept missing values as well as floating-point numbers. If we omit this declaration, the compiler will complain when we try to assign missing to any location in the array because it will have defined it as Vector{Float64}.

The plot in Figure 10-9 shows that Plots knows how to handle missing data.

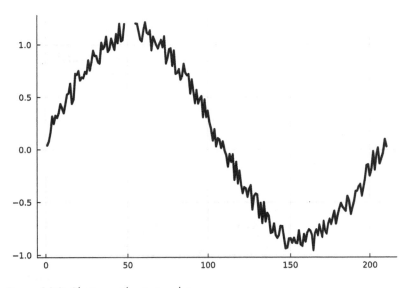

Figure 10-9: Plotting with missing data

By default, it leaves a gap where there are missing values.

Functions for Handling Missing Values

Julia provides several functions to do convenient things with missing values. To illustrate what these do, suppose we have an array, a, with some numbers and some missing elements:

```
a = [1, missing, 2, 3, missing, 4]
```

If you want the sum of the *numbers* in the array, you might try `sum(a)`, but if you refer to Listing 10-6, you will see that, since adding a number to a missing value yields `missing`, the end result of the `sum()` operation will just be `missing`. Here, Julia's `skipmissing()` function, which does as its name suggests, comes to the rescue:

```julia
julia> sum(skipmissing(a))
10
```

The `skipmissing()` function, which is built into `Base`, returns an iterator:

```julia
for i in skipmissing(a)
    println(i)
end
```

If you run that loop, you'll see this:

```
1
2
3
4
```

If you need to make a new array with the `missing` values omitted, use `collect(skipmissing(a))`.

If, instead, you want to make an array with a particular value substituted for the `missing` values in the original array, the function for that is `coalesce()`:

```julia
julia> coalesce.(a, NaN)
6-element Vector{Real}:
   1
 NaN
   2
   3
 NaN
   4
```

Notice how we need to use the dot operator to apply `coalesce()` to all the elements of the vector, and how the type of the returned array is no longer a `Union` with `missing`.

If you have a program that analyzes data, and want to generalize it so it can handle data collections with `missing` elements, the `skipmissing()` function makes that task relatively straightforward. You may only have to replace occurrences of your data arrays with `skipmissing()` acting on those arrays.

You may, however, prefer an approach that does not litter your code with a multitude of calls to `skipmissing()`. You can take advantage of Julia's multiple dispatch to define your own methods for `sum()`, and for any other functions that operate on your data arrays, to handle `missing` elements however you like. If, whenever you `sum()` an array of data (and keeping in mind the warning about type piracy from Chapter 8), you know that you will always want the missing values ignored and the numerical values added together, you can define a method this way:

```
import Base.sum
function sum(a::AbstractArray{Union{Missing, Int64}})
    return sum(skipmissing(a))
end
```

That example works for integers, but it's easily modified for other numerical types.

The function ismissing() returns true if its argument is missing and false otherwise. It's often more expressive than comparing against the Missing type in data expressions.

The Missings package provides a few more convenience functions for dealing with this data type. This package is not in the standard library, so you'll have to add and import it.

Anyone making use of missing values is likely to appreciate two functions from this package. As shown in Listing 10-7, it's a little cumbersome to define a vector that can hold both the needed numerical type and optional values—and, more important, you may have a numerical array that you need to convert to a type that will allow you to add missing values to it. The following little REPL session shows how to use the allowmissing() function from the Missings package, which solves both of these problems:

```
julia> import Missings
julia> a = rand(4)
julia> a = Missings.allowmissing(a)
julia> a[3] = missing;
julia> a
4-element Vector{Union{Missing, Float64}}:
 0.6225362617934931
 0.4473340385496267
  missing
 0.5062746637386624
```

You can convert a Vector{Union{Missing, Float64}} type back into a pure floating-point numerical type using Missings.disallowmissing(), but first you must eliminate any missing values from it.

Logic with Missing Values

Before leaving the topic of Julia's Missing data type, let's look at how it behaves in the context of logic expressions. We typically think of operations on logical values as following a two-valued (Boolean) logic, where the only possible values are true and false, a calculus that is reviewed in "Logic" on page 31. The missing value expands the world of Boolean logic to encompass a third truth state, which is neither true nor false, but indeterminate. In Julia, the missing type, along with bitwise AND (&), bitwise OR (|), bitwise exclusive OR (xor), equality (==), and negation (!), form a system of three-valued logic.

The results of a logical expression thus can be true, false, or missing. The following list shows how the system works, and after some thought, the entries should make intuitive sense. For example, the result of true | missing is true because the result will be true *no matter the truth value of the second operand*. And the result of true & missing must be missing, because it will *depend* on the truth value of the second operand, which is undetermined.

```
true | missing    true
true & missing    true
false | missing   missing
false & missing   false
xor(true, missing)    missing
xor(false, missing)   missing
!missing   missing
missing == missing    missing
missing === missing    true
```

Since the truth value of missing == missing depends on the values of the missing items, it is itself missing. However, since missing is a singleton type, all instances of it are the same object; hence missing === missing must be true.

CSV Files

Data that's of moderate size often comes in the form of a comma-separated value (CSV) file. These are text files with items delimited by commas, and optionally with descriptive headers. They have the considerable advantages of being human readable and amenable to processing with all of the Linux command line tools. But they have the disadvantages of taking up more space than necessary, being less efficient than binary representations, and possibly not faithfully representing the original values after conversion into text. For those reasons, this format is probably not the best choice for storing, say, the output of a physics simulation. However, CSV is perhaps the most common format for distributing what are commonly called "statistics," such as demographic data or the pandemic data that we'll explore later.

You may be tempted to write your own programs for reading CSV files, parsing them, and turning them into some Julia data structure. If you've come this far in the book, you will certainly be able to do so. However, it would be wise to resist the temptation, except as an exercise.

For real work, it's a better idea to use the CSV package, which we'll need to add in the package manager. This package can handle any delimiter, in addition to commas: the popular tab-separated file format as well as any custom format you may come across. It's even able, in many cases, to figure out by itself what delimiter the file is using. This delimiter need not be limited to a single character; it can be a string as well. The CSV package can deal with comments mixed in with the data, column headers, and anything else you're likely to encounter. It can read files from disk or, given a URL, can fetch them over the internet. It can handle dates in any format and transform labels into more code-friendly forms. Perhaps most importantly, it transforms the textual information into a Julia data type that can be further transformed into one of several different table-like data formats designed to be easily manipulated for statistical work.

Dataframes

The most important of these table-like data structures is dataframe, provided by the DataFrames package, which also needs to be added. Indeed, as the data structure returned by CSV after it reads a file is not the most convenient for exploration, the usual strategy is to immediately transform it into a dataframe.

A dataframe is a table of values, like a matrix, but with extra functionality designed for data exploration. Along with the dataframe data type, the DataFrames package exports several functions for manipulating it. In addition, many Julia functions with which you are already familiar have methods that extend their functionality to the dataframe.

It is most useful to think of a dataframe as a set of columns stuck together. Each column has a unique name. A column can be referred to with its integer index, with its name as a string, or with its name as a symbol. When you are examining, plotting, or manipulating data, you are doing these things to dataframe columns.

NOTE *We treat dataframes as sets of columns for data analysis and visualization. However, most Julia functions that operate on collections treat dataframes as collections of rows. See "Further Reading" on page 359 for an illuminating article on this subject.*

Let's consider an example using real-life data that comes in a typically messy form. Our journey through this data will make the earlier discussion of dataframes concrete and introduce the important functions for wrangling data from sources in the wild.

Let's look at some data from the COVID-19 Data Repository maintained by the Center for Systems Science and Engineering (CSSE) at Johns Hopkins University (*https://github.com/CSSEGISandData/COVID-19*). This data comes in the form of CSV files, using an actual comma as a delimiter. The first line contains headings to describe each data column, but the format of those headings will make subsequent manipulation in Julia inconvenient. The first problem is that some of the headers are names of countries or territories that contain spaces. The second is that some of the headers are dates, but these are in a format that we need to take into account so that they are parsed correctly.

NOTE *The datafile used in the examples here is available in the online resource area under the name* time_series_covid19_confirmed_global.csv. *The CSSE data grows in size over time, so some of the plots shown in this section may become unwieldy with future versions of the file from Johns Hopkins.*

Fortunately, the file reading function in the CSV package is equipped to deal with both of those common issues. Listing 10-8 shows the instructions for reading the CSV file and converting it immediately into a dataframe.

```
using CSV, DataFrames
covdat = CSV.File("time_series_covid19_confirmed_global.csv";
    normalizenames=true) |> DataFrame
```

Listing 10-8: Reading a CSV file

The normalizenames option replaces spaces and other troublesome characters in column names with underscores and performs any other transformations needed to turn header text into legal Julia identifiers. The dateformat keyword argument should be self-explanatory.

The first argument to CSV.File() is the name of the file on disk, which I previously downloaded and saved. Another option is to pass the URL of the file here. CSV.File() will recognize this and automatically download the data over the internet. The date format is determined by inspecting the file, whose first line, which contains the column headers, looks like this:

```
Province/State,Country/Region,Lat,Long,1/22/20,1/23/20,1/24/20,...
```

There are 432 columns. The end of the second command in Listing 10-8 converts the CSV.File() object into a DataFrame object, which is stored in the variable covdat. If this is executed in a REPL, Julia will print out a truncated representation of the dataframe. Figure 10-10 shows what that looks like. In this particular case, I've narrowed the REPL window so it fits better on the page.

```
julia> covdat
274×432 DataFrame
 Row │ Province_State              Country_Region        Lat    ⋯
     │ String?                     String                Float ⋯
─────┼──────────────────────────────────────────────────────────
   1 │ missing                     Afghanistan            33.9 ⋯
   2 │ missing                     Albania                41.1
   3 │ missing                     Algeria                28.0
   4 │ missing                     Andorra                42.5
   5 │ missing                     Angola                -11.2 ⋯
   6 │ missing                     Antigua and Barbuda    17.0
   7 │ missing                     Argentina             -38.4
   8 │ missing                     Armenia                40.0
   9 │ Australian Capital Territory Australia            -35.4 ⋯
  10 │ New South Wales             Australia             -33.8
  11 │ Northern Territory          Australia             -12.4

 264 │ Turks and Caicos Islands    United Kingdom         21.6
 265 │ missing                     United Kingdom         55.3 ⋯
 266 │ missing                     Uruguay               -32.5
 267 │ missing                     Uzbekistan             41.3
 268 │ missing                     Vanuatu               -15.3
 269 │ missing                     Venezuela               6.4 ⋯
 270 │ missing                     Vietnam                14.0
 271 │ missing                     West Bank and Gaza     31.9
 272 │ missing                     Yemen                  15.5
 273 │ missing                     Zambia                -13.1 ⋯
 274 │ missing                     Zimbabwe              -19.0
                              430 columns and 252 rows omitted
```

Figure 10-10: Representation of a dataframe in the REPL

The display indicates how much information has been omitted, the names of the visible columns, and the type of data they contain. A question mark after the data type means some values may be missing. Here is a typical use for the missing data type: most of the countries in the files do not have a province listed, but a few do. Missing data is represented in the original CSV file by a number that is . . . missing.

The fancy display of dataframes in the REPL is accomplished by show(), usually implicitly. A print() of a dataframe spits out the whole thing, without the nice formatting or type information, and is usually not what you want. In addition, show() can create HTML and LaTeX versions, and control other aspects of the dataframe display. Consult the REPL help to learn the details.

The @df Macro

For the rest of the chapter, we're going to make extensive use of a macro found in the StatsPlots package called @df. It's part of StatsPlots because it's especially effective at making commands for plotting from dataframes more concise, but its use is not limited to plot() commands. From this point on, the following command is assumed:

```
using StatsPlots, Statistics
```

The @df macro does what macros do best: it rewrites code so that our programs are easier to write and read. This macro has one job: it replaces symbols in an expression with the columns of the dataframe that appears as its first argument. This simple expression rewriting is enough to make this macro popular because it frees the programmer from having to repeat the name of the dataframe multiple times in an expression. Consider the following example:

```
julia> @df covdat print((minimum(:_1_1_21), maximum(:_1_1_21), mean(:_1_1_21)))
(0, 20252310, 306902.8576642336)
```

In this expression, the symbol :_1_1_21 is converted to covdat._1_1_21 each time it appears. The argument of the macro following the name of the dataframe must be a block or a function call, so the above would fail without wrapping the result in the print() function.

Since Symbols are converted into dataframe columns when using the @df macro, we need some syntax to indicate when a Symbol should be left alone— for example, if there is a conflict between a column name and a symbol used for another purpose. The macro provides the "^()" wrapper to handle these conflicts. If, for example, a column called "topleft" happens to be in your dataframe, you'll need to use the syntax legend=^(:topleft) in the plotting command to put the legend in the Northwest.

Indexing and Filtering Dataframes

A dataframe can be indexed and filtered using the same methods that we apply to matrices. However, dataframes come with some extra indexing methods that let us take advantage of their named columns.

I include in this chapter only the indexing and filtering methods that I think are most likely to be useful in the majority of cases. There are, in addition to everything covered here, several packages that supply macros and functions providing yet more ways to select and transform the information in a dataframe. Their intention is to allow a more streamlined syntax for certain common tasks, and these packages can be convenient. However, most of them are in somewhat of a state of flux. As in most sections in this book, I try to confine myself to methods that have solidified—that you can learn once and use forever.

Items in a dataframe can be extracted using the familiar forms of integer indexing. Here are a few examples:

❶
```
julia> covdat[3, 2]
"Algeria"
```

❷
```
julia> covdat[3:6, 2]
4-element Vector{String}:
 "Algeria"
 "Andorra"
 "Angola"
 "Antigua and Barbuda"
```

❸
```
julia> covdat[1, 2:4]
DataFrameRow
 Row │ Country_Region  Lat       Long
     │ String          Float64?  Float64?
─────┼────────────────────────────────────
   1 │ Afghanistan      33.9391    67.71
```

Notice how the data type of the result depends on how we index the dataframe. If we ask for one element ❶, we get back a single value, in this case a string. If we ask for a range of rows in a single column ❷, we get a Vector. Finally, if we extract data horizontally, by indexing a single row and a range of columns ❸, we get a data type that we haven't seen before: a DataFrameRow.

Let's ask Julia for a range of rows and a range of columns:

```
julia> covdat[266:268, 2:4]
3×3 DataFrame
 Row │ Country_Region  Lat        Long
     │ String          Float64?   Float64?
─────┼─────────────────────────────────────
   1 │ Uruguay         -32.5228   -55.7658
   2 │ Uzbekistan       41.3775    64.5853
   3 │ Vanuatu         -15.3767   166.959
```

We get back a smaller dataframe. What else could it be?

We don't have to count indices to refer to columns, but can use their names, as in Listing 10-9.

```
julia> covdat[272:end, [:Country_Region, :Lat, :Long, :_1_22_21]]
3×4 DataFrame
 Row | Country_Region  Lat      Long     _1_22_21
     | String          Float64? Float64? Int64
-----------------------------------------------------
   1 | Yemen            15.5527  48.5164      2118
   2 | Zambia          -13.1339  27.8493     43333
   3 | Zimbabwe        -19.0154  29.1549     30523
```

Listing 10-9: Selecting columns by name

We use Symbols to index the dataframe's columns. For each column title, a Symbol with the same name is created for efficient indexing. We could just as well have used the string versions of the column names in Listing 10-9, but using Symbols is more efficient. This is one reason for using normalizenames when reading the data: headers containing spaces would not be valid Symbol names, and we would be forced to use the string versions. Listing 10-9 shows the last three countries, their latitude and longitude, and the number of COVID cases on January 22, 2021.

The headings of the columns for latitude and longitude have data types printed with question marks. This means somewhere in this table is a country or a province with one or both of these values missing. To see those countries or provinces, we need to find the *row* in the table where :Lat or :Long has the value missing. To select rows from a dataframe where one or more columns satisfy some condition, we can use the filter() function (described in "The filter() Operator" on page 163). The DataFrame package extends the filter() function to operate on dataframes by filtering rows and returning a new dataframe. The following line of code filters our COVID dataframe, looking for the rows with missing latitude or longitude:

```
filter(r -> (r.Lat === missing) || (r.Long === missing), covdat)

1×432 DataFrame
 Row | Province_State         Country_Region  Lat       Long      ...
     | String?                String          Float64?  Float64?  ...
-----------------------------------------------------------------
   1 | Repatriated Travellers Canada          missing   missing   ...
                                                    428 columns omitted
```

The result is a dataframe with a single row, with the curious notation Repatriated Travellers in place of the province.

Rather than use the filter() function, you can get the same result with bitmask indexing or any other technique that works with normal arrays.

Notice in the example just shown how we specified the columns for the filter using the column names as bare words. This is yet another form of indexing, which is convenient in filter expressions. We can also use that syntax to select columns from the dataframe, turning them into Vectors:

```
julia> covdat.Country_Region
274-element Vector{String}:
 "Afghanistan"
 "Albania"
 "Algeria"
 "Andorra"
 ⋮
 "Yemen"
 "Zambia"
 "Zimbabwe"
```

Since selecting columns provides us with Vectors, we can use this form of indexing for plotting:

```
using Plots
plot(covdat.Country_Region, covdat._1_1_21; xrotation=40,
    label="Cases on 1JAN2021", legend=:topleft)
```

Nothing mysterious is going on here. We simply extracted two vectors from the dataframe and plotted them in the usual way, resulting in Figure 10-11.

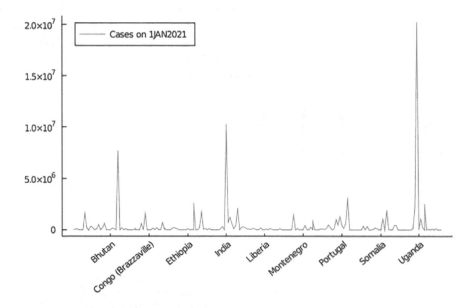

Figure 10-11: Cases vs. country

This plot is not ideal, however. It shows us something about the distribution of the number of cases on the date in question, but the horizontal axis is essentially useless because there is no room for hundreds of country labels. Perhaps, instead of trying to plot all the data at once, it would be more useful to plot some meaningful subset. Let's limit our visualization to the countries with a lot of cases, by using the filtering mechanism we just learned. Also, let's switch to a bar chart, which is the more appropriate visualization for this type of data:

```
covhc = filter(r -> r._1_1_21 > 2*10^6, covdat)
@df covhc bar(:Country_Region, :_1_1_21; xrotation=40,
    label="Cases on 1JAN2021", legend=:topleft)
```

Now we have something useful: a chart of the countries with more than two million cases on New Year's Day 2021, shown in Figure 10-12.

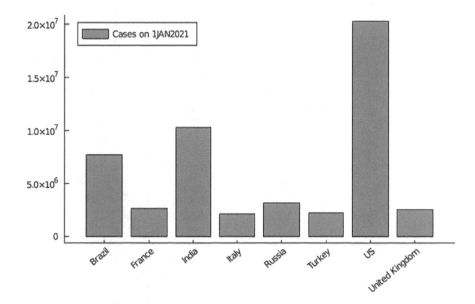

Figure 10-12: Countries with over two million cases

In the previous indexing commands, we used integer indexing to select columns, which worked well, but required us to count to the first column of interest. Also, it was only convenient because we knew that the columns we wanted extended to the end, which simplified the indexing expression.

An alternative that lets us use column names directly is the Between() function. The equivalent expression for selecting the date columns is:

```
covdat[1, Between(:_1_22_20, end)]
```

This can be easily modified to choose any closed interval of columns.

Another option is the Not() function. Here is a selection that returns the same DataFrameRow as the previous one:

```
covdat[1, Not([:Country_Region, :Province_State, :Lat, :Long])]
```

The columns that remain after the listed ones are excluded are just the ones we want: the date columns.

We can also select columns using regular expressions applied to the names of their titles. Here is another way to make the same selection, returning the same DataFrameRow:

```
covdat[1, r"_2"]
```

Sometimes this is the most convenient way to select data. For example, if we want to extract only the columns for February 2021 for Afghanistan, we could just say covdat[1, r"_2_\d*_21"].

But what if we want to make a DataFrameRow with all the date columns *and*, say, the Country_Region column (but none of the other ones)? None of the indexing techniques we've seen so far make this convenient, although you might be able to twist them to get the desired result. There is no need for contortions, however, because we can use the Cols() function. The following lines show four different ways to use this function to get a DataFrameRow similar to the one we created using multiple techniques earlier, but with the addition of the Country_Region column:

```
covdat[1, Cols(:Country_Region, r"_1")]
covdat[1, Cols("Country_Region", r"_1")]
covdat[1, Cols(2, r"_1")]
covdat[1, Cols(2, 5:end)]
```

As we can see, the Cols() function lets you pick out individual columns or ranges of columns using numerical indices, regular expressions, or column names either as symbols or as strings. It can also reorder columns. The following rearranges the covdat dataframe to place the latitude and longitude columns at the end:

```
covdat[:, Cols(1:2, r"_", :Lat, :Long)]
```

With this, we have a large enough toolbox to do most of the indexing, selecting, and rearranging of dataframes that we're likely to encounter in our work.

Mutating Dataframes

The indexing expressions covdat[:, :Country_Region] and covdat.Country_Region both seem to return a Vector with contents identical to the Country_Region column of the dataframe called covdat. However, they are not identical:

```
julia> covdat[:, :Country_Region] == covdat.Country_Region
true

julia> covdat[:, :Country_Region] === covdat.Country_Region
false
```

This tells us that while the two left- and right-hand sides contain the same values, they are not the same object. The syntax `dataframe[:, :col]` makes a *copy* of the column and returns it as a `Vector`. But `covdat.Country_Region` is a *reference* to the column. If you have a choice, avoid making unnecessary copies, as it is slower and consumes memory. Also, if you want to mutate a column by assigning to individual elements, you must use a reference rather than a copy, as shown in Listing 10-10.

```
julia> covdat.Country_Region[1] = "Disneyworld"
"Disneyworld"

julia> covdat
274×432 DataFrame
 Row │ Province_State  Country_Region     Lat       Long    ...
     │ String?         String             Float64?  Float64 ...
─────┼──────────────────────────────────────────────────────────
   1 │ missing         Disneyworld         33.9391   67.71  ...
   2 │ missing         Albania             41.1533   20.168
   : │     :                :                :          :
 274 │ missing         Zimbabwe           -19.0154   29.154
                          429 columns and 271 rows omitted
```

Listing 10-10: Mutating a dataframe

The direct dot syntax used here only works when using a literal column name after the dot, not with a variable holding a column name. If you're using variables to hold the names of columns, you must use square brackets. However, that doesn't mean you are obligated to make copies of columns. Another syntax allows you to use square brackets to reference a column using a variable, and without making a copy: `dataframe[!, var]` means the same thing as `dataframe.columnname` if *var* is set to `"columnname"`.

A command such as `covdat[:, c][1] = "Disneyworld"` will have no effect on the original dataframe. However, the assignment in Listing 10-10 can also be written as

```
covdat[!, :Country_Region][1] = "Disneyworld"
```

which will mutate the dataframe. The meaning of the exclamation point is suggested by its use in mutating functions, introduced in "Functions That Mutate Their Arguments" on page 56.

Transposing Dataframes

Dataframes make it convenient to plot or operate on columns of data. But suppose, using the data in the `covdat` dataframe, that you wanted to plot the time histories of case numbers for various countries. For each country, its time series is the part of the *row* for that country starting in the fifth column. We know, from the indexing section earlier, that we can extract rows from the dataframe, and that doing so gets us not a `Vector`, but a `DataFrameRow`. This means that, for plotting, we need to convert the result into a `Vector`. Here is one way to put all of this together to plot the time histories of COVID cases in the US:

```
using Chain
@chain covdat begin
    filter(r -> r.Country_Region == "US", _)[1, 5:end]
    Vector()
    plot(names(covdat)[5:end], _, xrotation=45, legend=:topleft,
        label="US cases", lw=3)
end
```

I snuck in a function you haven't seen before: `names()` returns the names of the columns in a dataframe in the form of a `Vector` of strings, so it is what we need to make meaningful x-tick labels.

The listing employs the `@chain` macro introduced in "The @chain Macro" on page 174. The pipeline syntax is popular when wrangling data from dataframes, as this activity inherently involves a series of transformations. The code snippet will produce the desired timeline plot, shown in Figure 10-13.

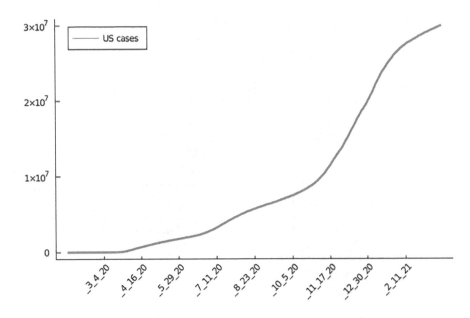

Figure 10-13: US cases vs. date

Now, to compare different countries, I would merely need to repeat the plotting pipeline using `plot!()` to add a new curve, substituting the country name of interest.

You may be thinking that there is a lot to type just to plot a row of data, and that this could be a bit of a drag for interactive work. Again, all this typing is required because the intention behind dataframes is to deal with them as a set of columns, so plotting rows is going against the grain. It would be smoother to go with the dataframe flow and somehow flip the dataframe around first, so the rows become columns. This would make the code easier to write and read. Selecting the data to plot would be more direct, and it would come in the form of a Vector that can be plotted immediately, eliminating the need for conversion.

We want to end up with a series of columns for different countries, with each column containing the series of case numbers for the country. If we have that kind of dataframe, we can plot any country's case number history directly. We would also like a column containing the date labels to use in plots. We can omit the other columns. We don't plan to use the latitude and longitude information in these plots or in our subsequent analysis, but they will remain in the original covdat dataframe if we need them. We are just making a new dataframe as a tool to ease our exploration of the data.

Before proceeding, however, we need to do something about the fact that some of the country names appear more than once, because some of them are listed along with several entries for Province_State. If these country names are to become column titles, they must be unique. A little later on we'll learn how to incorporate this data, but for now, we can simply eliminate the rows with provinces, keeping only the main country entries:

```
covmc = covdat[ismissing.(covdat.Province_State), :]
```

With the troublesome rows deleted, we can now safely exchange rows for columns. It probably sounds like we need some kind of transpose of the dataframe; however, the transpose() function, that we know and love from our work with matrices, will not work here. Fortunately, the DataFrame package comes with a function designed exactly for this purpose. We learned about the permutedims() function in "Adjoints and Transposes" on page 144, as a kind of generalized transpose operation. The DataFrames package extends this function to handle DataFrames; here's how to use it:

```
covmc = covmc[:, Not([:Province_State, :Lat, :Long])]
cdcn = permutedims(covmc, 1, "d")
```

In the first line, we get rid of the columns that we won't need. The transpose happens in the second line, where the first argument to permutedims() is the dataframe to be transposed, the second argument selects the column from the original dataframe whose contents are to be used as column names for the transposed dataframe, and the third argument is the name to give the new column, whose contents will be composed of the column names of the original dataframe. Since we eliminated the Province_State column, the first column of covmc is now Country_Region, so the names in the column of countries are used as the new column titles. We can specify the column to pivot around using any kind of selector, so we could have written the following as well:

```
cdcn = permutedims(covmc, :Country_Region, "d")
```

Our new dataframe, cdcn, appears as shown in Figure 10-14.

```
428×193 DataFrame
 Row │ d              Afghanistan  Albania  Algeria  Andorra ⋯
     │ String         Int64        Int64    Int64    Int64   ⋯
─────┼──────────────────────────────────────────────────────────
   1 │ _1_22_20                 0        0        0        0 ⋯
   2 │ _1_23_20                 0        0        0        0
   3 │ _1_24_20                 0        0        0        0
   4 │ _1_25_20                 0        0        0        0
   5 │ _1_26_20                 0        0        0        0 ⋯
   6 │ _1_27_20                 0        0        0        0
   7 │ _1_28_20                 0        0        0        0
  ⋮  │    ⋮               ⋮         ⋮        ⋮        ⋮      ⋱
 422 │ _3_18_21             56044   119528   115842    11393
 423 │ _3_19_21             56069   120022   115970    11431 ⋯
 424 │ _3_20_21             56093   120541   116066    11481
 425 │ _3_21_21             56103   121200   116157    11517
 426 │ _3_22_21             56153   121544   116255    11545
 427 │ _3_23_21             56177   121847   116349    11591 ⋯
 428 │ _3_24_21             56192   122295   116438    11638
                            188 columns and 414 rows omitted
```

Figure 10-14: The cdcn dataframe in the REPL

There is one problem with our freshly transposed dataframe: some of the column titles now have spaces in their names. You can't see them in the small piece of the dataframe shown in Figure 10-14, but we know that they're there:

```
julia> [c for c in covdat.Country_Region if contains(c, " ")]
46-element Vector{String}:
 "Antigua and Barbuda"
 "Bosnia and Herzegovina"
 "Burkina Faso"
 "Cabo Verde"
 :
 "United Kingdom"
 "United Kingdom"
 "West Bank and Gaza"
```

It's not a serious problem, but, as you now know, legal symbol names are more convenient and lead to neater and more efficient code.

The function rename!() transforms the column names of a dataframe in place (hence the mutation warning sign). It has several methods; the method that we shall use takes a function as its first argument and the dataframe to be altered as its second argument. The supplied function is applied to each column separately. The command in Listing 10-11 replaces spaces with underlines in the column names of cdcn.

```
rename!(x -> replace(x, " " => "_"), cdcn)
```

Listing 10-11: Renaming columns of a dataframe

Did it work? Let's take a peek at a relevant bit of the dataframe:

```julia
julia> cdcn[:, r"^Un"]
428×2 DataFrame
 Row | United_Arab_Emirates  United_Kingdom
     | Int64                 Int64
-----------------------------------------------
   1 |                    0               0
   2 |                    0               0
   : |                    :               :
 428 |               446594         4312908
```

Now we can plot time-dependent case numbers for selected countries with ease:

```julia
@df cdcn plot(:d, [:Zambia :Albania :Afghanistan]; xrotation=35,
          legend=:topleft, lw=3, ls=[:solid :dash :dot])
```

The @df macro from StatsPlots was useful there, as the command refers to several columns using Symbols; without it, we would be obligated to mention the name of the dataframe each time. This plot() command produces the graph in Figure 10-15.

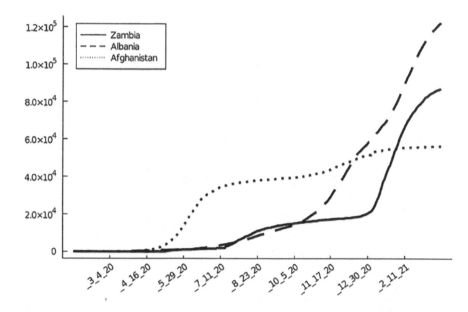

Figure 10-15: Timeline of cases in three countries

In a plot() command inside a @df macro call, the cols() function (note the lowercase) can be used to select a numerical range of columns with cols(a:b), all the columns with cols(), or a column whose Symbol name is stored in a variable, with c = :thecol and cols(c).

Remember that Cols, with an uppercase C, is for column selection within square brackets and is part of DataFrames.jl, whereas cols, using lowercase, is a utility function for use in the @df macro, provided by StatsPlots.jl.

With all the machinery that we now have under our belts, we can do more than plot random selections of countries. One thing that might be interesting is to plot only those countries whose caseloads rise above a certain level on any day included in the dataset. Here is one way to do that, using the @df macro and cols() function from StatsPlots:

```
sc = [Symbol(c) for c in names(cdcn)[2:end] if maximum(cdcn[:, c]) > 3*10^6]
@df cdcn plot(:d, cols(sc); xrotation=35, lw=2, legend=:topleft, ls=:auto)
```

The strategy is to collect the relevant columns as an array of Symbols, so that we can select them in the plot() statements using cols(). Figure 10-16 shows the result.

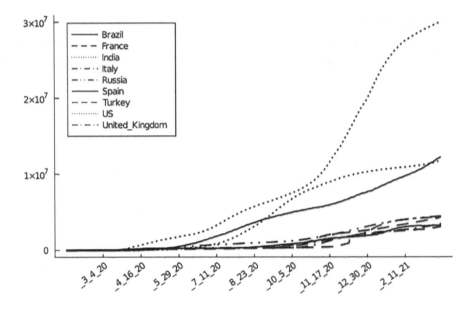

Figure 10-16: Countries with large caseloads

StatsPlots has turned the symbols identifying the columns into strings for the plot, providing a useful legend.

Summarizing Dataframes

Another useful device that DataFrames provides is the combine function. This allows us to map a function onto a set of columns to create a new dataframe that is a summary of an existing dataframe. For example, suppose we want a table that contains the maximum number of cases seen for each country. The combine() function makes this simple:

```
julia> combine(cdcn, 2:190 .=> maximum)
1×189 DataFrame
 Row │ Afghanistan_maximum  Albania_maximum  Algeria_maximum ...
     │ Int64                Int64            Int64            ...
─────────────────────────────────────────────────────────────
   1 │              56192           122295           116438 ...
                                           186 columns omitted
```

For each column in the range of columns defined in the second argument, combine() applies the maximum() function to its contents.

The combine() function creates new column names by appending the name of the function. If you would like to preserve the original name, pass in renamecols = false.

This data is a good candidate for another bar chart, but it would be more convenient to have it transposed, with a column of countries and a column of maximums. We know how to do that now, but something is missing: we need to add a column to hold the new column names. Listing 10-12 combines the methods we've learned to first make a permuted dataframe called cdmp and then, in the last line, copy only the rows with the largest caseloads into another dataframe, cdmpc.

```
cdmax = combine(cdcn, 2:190 .=> maximum, renamecols=false)
cdmax[!, :Country] = ["Maximum"]
cdmp = permutedims(cdmax, :Country)
cdmpc = cdmp[cdmp.Maximum .> 2*10^6, :]
```

Listing 10-12: Plotting maximum caseloads

After executing the code in Listing 10-12, cdmpc looks like this:

```
14×2 DataFrame
 Row │ Country          Maximum
     │ String           Int64
─────────────────────────────────
   1 │ Argentina         2269877
   2 │ Brazil           12220011
   ⋮ │     ⋮                ⋮
  13 │ US               30010928
  14 │ United_Kingdom    4312908
                  10 rows omitted
```

You see that there are only 14 countries that experienced a caseload of more than two million during the time period covered by this dataset. Now we can make a bar chart with this simple command:

```
bar(cdmpc.Country, cdmpc.Maximum, xrotation=45, label=nothing,
    title="Countries with highest maximum caseloads")
```

This creates the graph in Figure 10-17.

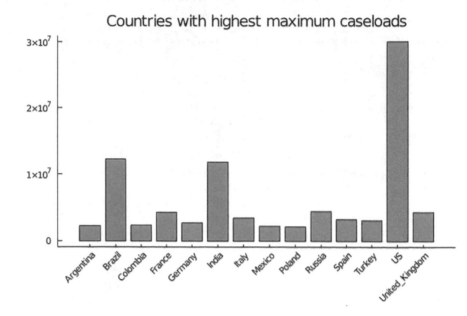

Figure 10-17: The highest maximum caseloads

The need for summary statistics of the data in a dataframe is so common that a function is available that does the foregoing work for us, but it's good to know how to do it "manually," in case you need something it doesn't provide. That function is called describe(), and here's how it works:

```
julia> describe(cdcn, :max; cols=Not(:d))
189×2 DataFrame
 Row │ variable             max
     │ Symbol               Int64
─────────────────────────────────────
   1 │ Afghanistan           56192
   2 │ Albania              122295
   3 │ Algeria              116438
   4 │ Andorra               11638
   5 │ Angola                21836
   6 │ Antigua_and_Barbuda    1080
   ⋮ │          ⋮              ⋮
 184 │ Venezuela            153315
 185 │ Vietnam                2576
 186 │ West_Bank_and_Gaza   230076
 187 │ Yemen                  3703
 188 │ Zambia                86993
 189 │ Zimbabwe              36749
                  177 rows omitted
```

That's certainly easier! By default, describe() returns a DataFrame with the means and medians as well, but those are not meaningful for these timelines, so we limit the statistics calculated by passing a symbol, :max, for the one we want. The function can calculate the other summary statistics as well, such as standard deviation, and automatically skips missing values. It can even report the number of missing values in each column, if you so desire.

Grouping Dataframes

Earlier we threw away some of the data, namely the additional provinces for the several countries for which such entries existed. As promised, we'll now find a way to include that information.

Let's suppose we are not interested in looking at the data for individual provinces, but instead would like to add up the numbers for all the provinces belonging to each country and just look at the total case numbers. This makes a bit more sense than just deleting that data. The most convenient way to do this kind of thing involves the concept of the *grouped dataframe* and an associated new data type, the GroupedDataFrame.

A GroupedDataFrame is something like a vector of dataframes. Each dataframe in the vector is created from a source dataframe by collating the rows that have the same value in a chosen column. In our case, we'll group by Country_Region. Most of the resulting members of the GroupedDataFrame will have a single row because most countries appear only once. But those countries that appear multiple times, because they have Province_State values, will give rise to members of the GroupedDataFrame with more than one row, with one for each Province_State.

One small wrinkle is that the members of a GroupedDataFrame are not actually dataframes, but have a new data type called SubDataFrame; however, the distinction is usually not important.

The following will group the covdat dataframe by country:

```
cvgp = groupby(covdat, :Country_Region)
```

Now cvgp is a GroupedDataFrame. Let's examine it in the REPL:

❶ ```
julia> length(cvgp)
192
```

❷ ```
julia> length(covdat.Country_Region) - length(cvgp)
82
```

❸ ```
julia> cvgp[1]
1×432 SubDataFrame
 Row | Province_State Country_Region Lat   Long   _ ...
     | String?   String   Float64? Float64? I ...
----
   1 | missing   Afghanistan   33.9391   67.71   ...
                                            428 columns omitted
```
```

```
❹ julia> cvgp[183]
12×432 SubDataFrame
 Row | Province_State                Country_Region  La ...
     | String?                       String          Fl ...
--------------------------------------------------------------
   1 | Anguilla                      United Kingdom  1 ...
   2 | Bermuda                       United Kingdom  3
   : |                       :                 :
  12 | missing                       United Kingdom  5
                          430 columns and 9 rows omitted
```

The grouped dataframe has 192 members ❶, which tells us how may distinct countries are included in the data (remembering that one of them is Repatriated Travellers).

Subtracting that from the total number of rows ❷, we learn that 82 countries have provinces listed.

Looking at individual members of cvgp ❸ ❹ confirms that these are dataframes devoted to individual countries. The next step is to add up the case numbers across all provinces for each date, so each country's numbers will include all of its provinces. That's what the combine() function is for. When I introduced combine(), we used it on a dataframe, but when applied to a grouped dataframe, it does exactly what we want, applying the specified function along the selected columns for each group member individually and then returning a normal DataFrame as the result.

First we need an array holding the columns to sum, which are the date columns, and then we can combine() them. We'll store the result in a new variable:

```
dcols = cdcn.d
cvsm = combine(cvgp, dcols .=> sum, renamecols=false)
```

Now cvsm has the same structure as our original covdat, but only 192 rows, one for each country. As before, it will be convenient to have on hand the transpose of this dataframe:

```
cvsp = permutedims(cvsm, :Country_Region, "d")
```

And, as before, it's better to normalize (remove the spaces from) the column names. After repeating the procedure from Listing 10-11 on cvsp, we have a dataframe convenient for plotting.

Now it's easy to compare the timelines for France, both with and without its territories:

```
@df cvsp plot(:d, :France; xrotation=35, label="France with territories", legend=:topleft)
@df cdcn plot!(:d, :France; xrotation=35, label="France minus territories", legend=:topleft,
        ls=:dash)
```

Figure 10-18 shows the results.

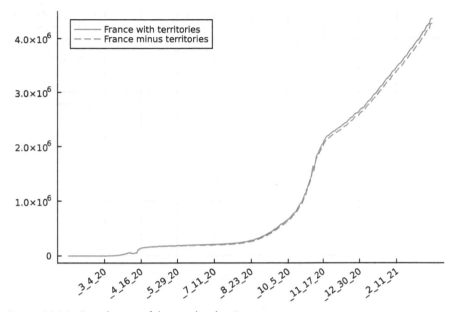

Figure 10-18: Time history of the caseload in France

In most cases, the inclusion of the `Province_State` columns makes a barely visible difference in the plot.

Multivariate Data

The previous examples all dealt with timelines: a single quantity, in this case numbers of infections, as a function of date, for various countries. Another form of data involves the frequencies of a number of events in, say, different places, or compared among different demographic groups. Figure 10-4 showed a simple example of this form of data, where the events are observations of height and the demographic groups are men and women.

When you have data on more than one variable, you can use statistical methods to look for associations among them, always remembering that "correlation does not imply causation." But an association can suggest that it might be worthwhile to look further, and the *lack* of correlation might be useful in ruling out hypotheses.

In the (made up) example of men's and women's heights, if we also had, from the same subjects, data about income level, or age, we could look for associations. Are richer people taller? When does the increase of height with age level off? Julia's `DataFrames`, combined with its convenient statistical functions and the visualizations provided by `StatsPlots`, make this kind of data exploration a relatively easy and pleasant task.

I compiled our second datafile from data maintained by the US Census Bureau (*https://www.census.gov*). It is available in the supplementary website at *https://julia.lee-phillips.org*, in the file named *census.dat*. The file is in tab-separated value format, with one line of column headers and comment lines that each begin with a hash mark (#). The data consists of absolute numbers of reported crimes in several categories in 2011 for each county in the US, plus a column for the total population of the county and one for the percentage of minors who did not complete high school. The comment lines give the totals for each state and for the entire country. Here are the first nine lines of the 3,143-line file:

```
Areaname    Larceny Murder  MVTheft Robbery MinorsNHI   EstimatedPop
##UNITED STATES 6384687 16107    1196608 405471 10.8       295753151
##ALABAMA    97640    308 10796    5636    7.8 4545049
Autauga, AL 1149    0   112 28  8   47870
Baldwin, AL 1973    5   137 37  11.3    162564
Barbour, AL 64  0   7   1   7.8 29452
Bibb, AL    144 0   18  3   8.  21375
Blount, AL  558 0   134 6   11.8    55035
Bullock, AL 54  0   0   3   7.9 10975
```

Clearly, the first thing we need to do is use the CSV package to read this and store it in a dataframe. The CSV.File function will detect that tabs are used as delimiters, and also that the first line is a header, but we should tell it about the comments:

```
cbc = CSV.File("census.dat", comment="#") |> DataFrame
cbc = cbc[cbc.EstimatedPop .!= 0, :]
```

The second line eliminates any rows (there were three) with a zero population. As we plan to divide the absolute numbers by population to convert them into rates, we need to delete those rows. Here is the conversion:

```
for c in 2:5
    cbc[!, c] = cbc[!, c] ./ cbc[!, 7]
end
```

At this point, our dataframe looks like this:

```
julia> cbc
3143×7 DataFrame
  Row | Areaname       Larceny     Murder      MVTheft     Robber ...
      | String         Float64     Float64     Float64     Float6 ...
------------------------------------------------------------------------
    1 | Autauga, AL    0.0240025   0.0         0.00233967  0.0005 ...
    2 | Baldwin, AL    0.0121368   3.07571e-5  0.000842745 0.0002
    3 | Barbour, AL    0.00217303  0.0         0.000237675 3.3953
    4 | Bibb, AL       0.00673684  0.0         0.000842105 0.0001
    5 | Blount, AL     0.010139    0.0         0.00243481  0.0001 ...
    6 | Bullock, AL    0.00492027  0.0         0.0         0.0002
    7 | Butler, AL     0.0227653   9.83381e-5  0.00108172  0.0007
    8 | Calhoun, AL    0.0256511   4.46106e-5  0.00215915  0.0014
    : |    :              :            :           :           :
 3137 | Sheridan, WY   0.0167767   0.0         0.000921795 3.6871 ...
```

```
3138 | Sublette, WY     0.0387191   0.0         0.00262009   0.0
3139 | Sweetwater, WY   0.0296249   2.68341e-5  0.00262974   0.0001
3140 | Teton, WY        0.0197487   0.0         0.00149925   0.0001
3141 | Uinta, WY        0.0283567   0.0         0.00190417   0.0002 ...
3142 | Washakie, WY     0.00425093  0.0         0.000128816  0.0
3143 | Weston, WY       0.0122008   0.0         0.0          0.0001
                            3 columns and 3128 rows omitted
```

How is a particular crime category, say, larceny, distributed among the counties? Are they all the same? How likely is it for a county to have an unusually high larceny rate? We can answer those kinds of questions with a histogram, which we can produce with this command:

```
@df cbc histogram(:Larceny; legend=nothing)
```

In many commands that pull data from the dataframe, the @df macro will save some typing and make the code easier to read. The histogram, shown in Figure 10-19, shows that about 400 counties had no larceny at all during the report year, and most had rates (total number divided by population) below 2 percent. Above that rate, the distribution drops off steadily and fairly rapidly.

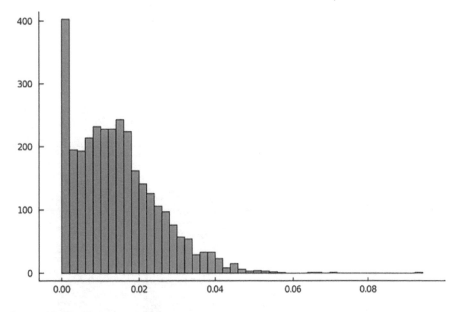

Figure 10-19: Histogram of larcenies

With our dataframe set up, exploring this data in the REPL is simple (the following assumes that Statistics has already been imported):

```
julia> mean(cbc.Larceny)
0.014305068778810368
```

```
julia> @df cbc cor(:Murder, :Larceny)
0.29993876295850447

julia> @df cbc cor(:MVTheft, :Larceny)
0.6528140798664165
```

The average larceny rate is about 1.4 percent. How is this crime correlated with other crimes? The correlation with murder is weak, meaning
that knowledge of a high larceny rate in a particular county tells you nothing
about its murder rate. However, the correlation with vehicle theft is significant: a county with a high larceny rate is a place where you are more likely
to get your car stolen. That may not be surprising, but before we take it se-
riously, we should remember that the correlation coefficients calculated by
the cor() function of the Statistics package are the Pearson coefficients,
which assume a linear relationship between the two variables under consideration. Does such a linear relationship hold between these two crime
categories? The way to answer this kind of question is with a scatterplot:

```
@df cbc scatter(:MVTheft, :Larceny; legend=nothing, markersize=2,
    opacity=0.3, xlabel="Motor vehicle theft", ylabel="Larceny",
    xrange=[0, 0.015])
```

It does look from Figure 10-20 as if there is at least a roughly linear relationship between the two rates, so the correlation coefficient is meaningful.

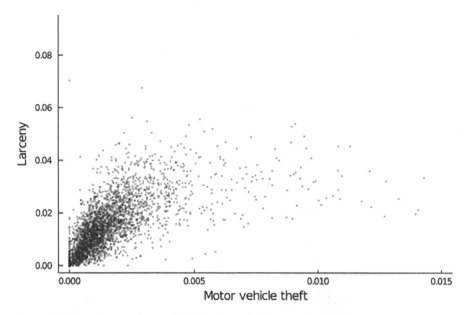

Figure 10-20: Larceny–motor vehicle theft scatterplot

Using a small marker size combined with a low opacity is effective when
making scatterplots with many points. The idea is that there are likely to
be regions with a lot of overlap. Using small, transparent points allows the

point density at any location to appear as a buildup of image density there. Using opaque or larger points would create a plot where we can't distinguish between moderate and high densities once the markers begin to obscure each other.

This idea is made more systematic with a plot recipe from StatsPlots called histogram2d(). As the name suggests, it takes two variables and creates a two-dimensional histogram. The result is similar to a scatterplot, but with the plane divided into cells and the cells colored according to the number of points they contain. Here is how it works:

```
@df cbc histogram2d(:MVTheft, :Larceny; xlabel="Motor vehicle theft",
                    ylabel="Larceny", xrange=[0, 0.015])
```

As with ordinary histograms, we can adjust the number of bins if the automatic calculation is not optimal, but in this case, the algorithm does a good job. The result shown in Figure 10-21 conveys information similar to the scatterplot in Figure 10-20, but now we can read off the number of cases from the color map.

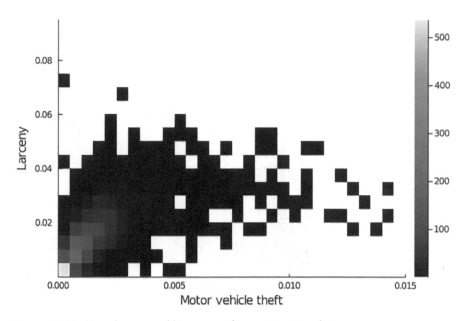

Figure 10-21: Two-dimensional histogram of two categories of crime

The describe() function that we met earlier is useful for getting an overview of this type of data. The result can be made more concise by eliminating the uninteresting bits:

```
julia> describe(cbc, :mean, :max, :nmissing)[2:end,:]
6×4 DataFrame
 Row │ variable     mean      max       nmissing
     │ Symbol       …Union    Any       Int64
─────────────────────────────────────────────────────
```

1	Larceny	0.0143051	0.0925926	0
2	Murder	3.01897e-5	0.000539374	0
3	MVTheft	0.00156298	0.0231045	0
4	Robbery	0.000357696	0.00987096	0
5	MinorsNHI	11.5316	42.9	0
6	EstimatedPop	94099.0	9803912	0

The last column in the description table informs us that there are no missing values. The reason for the composite data types is that the summary dataframe contained a row of county names that we eliminated with the indexing expression, so these columns actually contain a mix of numbers and strings.

You can combine the two-dimensional histogram of Figure 10-21 with normal one-dimensional histograms of each variable using the `marginalhist()` recipe from StatsPlots:

```
@df cbc marginalhist(:MVTheft, :Larceny; xlabel="Motor vehicle theft",
                     ylabel="Larceny")
```

The result, shown in Figure 10-22, is a nice visualization of two distributions simultaneously.

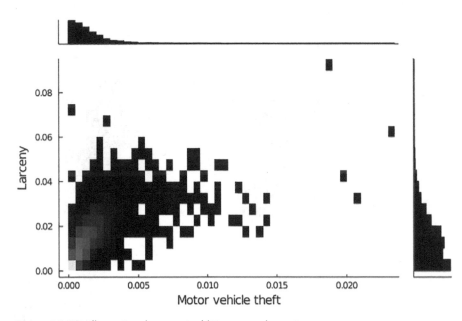

Figure 10-22: Illustrating the marginal histogram plot recipe

The StatsPlots package has another trick up its sleeve. It can combine some of the plots we've already seen into a composite visualization that makes it easy to pick out associations and patterns among a group of variables almost at a glance. This is achieved with the `corrplot()` recipe, as follows:

```
@df cbc corrplot([:MinorsNHI :MVTheft :Robbery]; fillcolor=cgrad(),
                  xrotation=40)
```

We've chosen three variables to look at; it's possible to look at every-thing at once, or any other subset with more than two categories. The need to include the fillcolor argument is a bug that may be fixed by the time you are reading this, so you may want to try omitting it. It controls the palette used in the two-dimensional histograms, and, as you saw earlier, it's not needed in regular histogram2d plots to get the default coloring.

Figure 10-23 shows the result.

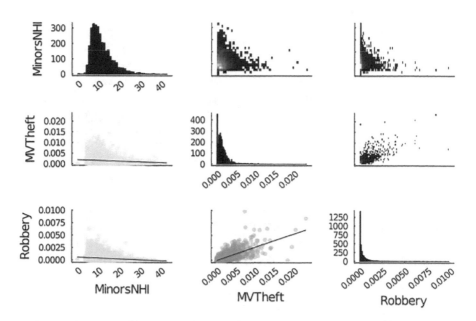

Figure 10-23: A correlation plot

The recipe produces a matrix of plots comparing every possible com-bination of pairs of variables from the vector of arrays provided in the first argument. Along the diagonal of this plot matrix (where the two variables are identical) we have conventional, one-dimensional histograms; above the diagonal, we see all three possible two-dimensional histograms; and below the diagonal, we have all the scatterplots, using transparent points. As a bonus, the scatterplots also feature regression (best fit) lines drawn through the points, and the marker color reflects the type of correlation: positive correlations are blue, lack of correlation is indicated by yellow, and negative correlations are red. This is a powerful visualization that carries a rich pay-load of information. A quick look tells us that failure to complete secondary school is unrelated to rates of vehicle theft or robbery, but those two types of crime are correlated with each other.

Other Packages

This section briefly describes a few more tools that readers interested in statistics will want to be aware of. See "Further Reading" on page 359 for some additional resources you may find useful.

JuliaDB for Out of Core Datasets

Dataframes are powerful data types, but they're intended for data structures that fit in RAM. For data that is too large to fit in memory, a better choice is JuliaDB, which is designed to work efficiently with such "out of core" datasets.

RCall for Interacting with R

The R programming language is a long-established language and system for statistical analysis. Like Julia, R is free software and has a large population of devoted users. However, it is not a good general-purpose programming language, and it can be quite slow for certain types of calculations. If you are starting a new project, and do not happen to have a personal library of R code that you have developed over the years, I recommend using Julia for your statistics needs. It already has a large and capable ecosystem of statistical packages, and more packages are being added every day. Julia won't let you down if your analysis program turns into something that needs to run quickly on big data. Its ability to run on GPUs and other multiprocessor hardware, and the efficiency of its compiled code, means that you won't need to rewrite your programs in order for them to scale.

However, if you have already invested time and effort into writing R routines that you want to keep using, you need not rewrite them. You can use them from, and in combination with, Julia. The RCall package has several macros for interoperating with R routines and data structures, as well as a special REPL mode for interacting directly with R within the Julia session. In fact, as soon as you type using RCall, an R process starts up in the background. It locates your R installation and can even install R for you.

P-hacking

For calculating p-values and performing other analyses to contribute to the replication crisis in science, the HypothesisTests package at *https://github.com/ JuliaStats/HypothesisTests.jl* is invaluable.

Conclusion

The concepts and techniques of statistics cut across all scientific disciplines. Julia, with its statistics packages, puts a lot of exploratory and analytical power at our fingertips. Good integration with the Plots package makes visualization fast and easy as well. While systems such as R, a standard for statistical analysis for decades, offer some functions not yet built into Julia's packages, the latter are developing quickly. Julia has some advantages today over the venerable workhorses: the ease of developing in the language makes it easier to add missing capabilities, and Julia's efficiency frees you from the need to rewrite your code in a faster language when faced with big data or computationally intensive analyses.

We'll revisit some of the concepts introduced in this chapter in the next chapter, with simulated evolution, and in Chapter 13, where we explore the techniques of probabilistic programming to make inferences about models.

FURTHER READING

- For details on the lava lamp entropy project, see *https://blog.cloudflare.com/randomness-101-lavarand-in-production/*.

- The pandemic simulation in this chapter implements a simplified model along the lines of the widely used COVID-19 model developed at *https://github.com/mrc-ide/covid-sim*.

- The formula for the combination of events used in the pandemic simulation is derived in Chapter IV of William Feller's standard work on probability theory, *An Introduction to Probability Theory and Its Applications*, Volume 1 (Wiley 1968).

- An alternative random number generator designed for long-term stability is available at *https://github.com/JuliaRandom/StableRNGs.jl*. You may want to use it if you would like your programs to use the same pseudorandom sequences across future versions of Julia and its packages.

- The RCall package resides at *https://github.com/JuliaInterop/RCall.jl*.

- A frequently updated list of Julia statistics and machine learning packages, with brief descriptions, is available at *https://github.com/JuliaStats*.

- See this 20-minute tutorial video by Juan Klopper for an introduction to statistics in Julia: *https://www.youtube.com/watch?v=xbsr46Dw8hg*.

- A textbook by Yoni Nazarathy and Hayden Klok about doing statistics, data science, and machine learning with Julia is available at *https://statisticswithjulia.org*.

- The headquarters of the JuliaDB package is *https://juliadb.juliadata.org/latest/out_of_core/*.

- More information on dataframes as collections of rows is available at *https://bkamins.github.io/julialang/2023/02/24/dfrows.html*.

11

BIOLOGY

Modern biology is becoming very much a branch of information technology.
–Richard Dawkins

As Professor Dawkins points out, computation has become a central tool in many areas of biology. This was perhaps inevitable, as evolution is the central organizing principle of biology, and evolution occurs through the transmission of information in the form of a digital storage device known as DNA.

The biology ecosystem around Julia is sophisticated, wide-ranging, and growing rapidly. The language and its packages are being used in many areas of biological and medical research, in both industry and academia.

This chapter begins with a brief overview of the Julia biology landscape and proceeds directly to a detailed case study in simulated evolution.

The Julia Biology Ecosystem

Bioinformatics has become a major subfield of biology that is defined by the use of computers. It mainly deals with the analysis and manipulation of protein sequences, so it has a strong computational linguistics flavor. The Bio-Julia GitHub organization provides a starting place for browsing this large collection of packages. It includes, among others, modules for handling the various file types that bioinformaticians have devised over the years.

To discover other Julia packages outside of the bioinformatics organization, we can turn to the general GitHub search methods described in "How to Find Public Packages" on page 80. Many of these packages do not include general tags such as "biology," so you can find them more easily with focused searches using terms such as *phylogenetics* or *ecology*.

The `Pumas` pharmaceutical modeling and simulation toolkit merits particular mention as a major success story for Julia in medicine and biology. `Pumas` is used by major corporations and research groups to develop and test drugs. Its GitHub page contains links to extensive documentation and tutorials.

Many Julia biology packages were created to work with other packages in the areas of statistics, equation solving, or other areas useful in mathematical biology. An example is `EvolutionaryModelingTools`, which works with the `DifferentialEquations` package (see "Combining DifferentialEquations with Measurements" on page 302), providing macros to assist in setting up problems that use Gillespie's algorithm (a method for attacking stochastic differential equations) in the simulation of models of infectious disease propagation and problems with a similar structure.

Simulating Evolution with Agent-Based Modeling

Agent-based modeling (ABM) is a simulation technique using a community of computational entities, the *agents*, interacting with each other and their environment through a set of *rules*. The agents may be representations of life forms, vehicles, or something more abstract, such as information. The rules can depend on time, the distance between agents, their movement, the state of the environment near the agent, or nearly anything else we can imagine. Agents may move, store data, die, and be born. The environment itself can change as well.

Researchers have used ABM to simulate traffic flow, the progress of infectious diseases, the collective behavior of social animals, the spread of opinions, and much more. See "Further Reading" on page 380 for some links to background information about this approach, and to documentation of the main packages used in this section.

Our project will be the simulation of evolution through natural selection in a population of two types of simple creatures representing predators and prey. We will see how the prey creatures, when allowed to inherit their "genes" from their parents, evolve to be better at evading their predators. This evolution results from random mutations in the inherited characteristics combined with the selection pressure from the predators eating the less evasive prey before they have a chance to reproduce.

The `Agents` package provides a framework for a wide variety of ABM calculations. It attends to the lower-level details, such as calculating the motions of agents, enforcing boundary conditions, and searching for neighbors, allowing us to concentrate on programming the rules for agent interaction at a fairly high level.

The space in which the agents live can be a continuous physical space (the one we will use here); a grid space on which agents can only occupy discrete positions; a more abstract tree space, in which agents are not located physically, but within a tree data structure; and even a space defined on an actual road map, using OpenStreetMap data. The space can become an environment containing spatially and temporally varying conditions affecting the agents.

The agents have position and velocity properties and a unique ID. We can endow them, as well, with any data structures convenient for our simulation. We can create or destroy agents, or change any of their properties, based on their proximity to other agents, on time, or on environmental conditions. Agent proximity—nearest neighbors or neighbors within a given radius—is returned by a simple function call.

Any particular project typically will make use of only a small subset of `Agents`'s capabilities, and this section's project is no exception.

Overview of the Simulation Problem

Our universe will contain two types of creatures: predators and prey. Each type has a simple behavior. Predators chase prey. If a predator manages to get very close to its target, it vanishes from the simulation, devoured by its pursuer. The predators choose their targets from among all those within their detection range, but they are polite: they won't chase prey that one of their colleagues is already chasing. Predators have only one speed, which is somewhat faster than the one speed with which the prey are able to run. They turn toward their prey as they chase them, but their superior speed is offset by limited agility: they can turn only through some maximum angle at every simulation step. Like some actual predator species, our simulated predators adjust their reproductive rate to maintain a certain ratio of predator population to prey population.

The prey make turns at regular intervals according to a list of angles; each prey creature has its own list. When it reaches the end of the list, it goes back to the top. Prey don't react to predators, they simply run around making their prescribed turns. One can imagine that their environment is rich with uniformly distributed food, as a property (which is called mojo in the program) gets incremented by a fixed amount at every step. If a prey creature manages to reach a predetermined amount of mojo without getting eaten, it reproduces. Reproduction is fatal; the creature is replaced by two descendants. Each descendant inherits a copy of its parent's table of angles, with some random mutations.

The only property that distinguishes different prey individuals, aside from their locations and velocities, is the list of angles. We initialize the agents with a random list, uniformly distributed from $-\pi$ to π. Some lists of turns will, by chance, be slightly better than others in allowing the agent to survive longer, as they will, on average, make it more difficult for the predators, with their limited agility, to catch it. These agents will be more likely to reproduce, as will their children. Through mutation, some of these children may be even more likely to survive to reproduce. We hope to observe an evolution in the distribution of angles in the prey population, and an average increase in the ability to evade predation, as a result of this selection pressure.

The foregoing is an overview of the structure and aims of the project. In the next few sections, we'll put together all the components of our simulation, in the order in which they appear in the complete program, which is assembled for convenience in the code section of the web supplement for this chapter at *https://julia.lee-phillips.org*. When turning these ideas into a program, we'll have to make everything concrete. For example, we'll decide to make the list of angles contain eight elements. Many of these details are, within limits, arbitrary, and the reader might experiment with altering all or some of them, and perhaps improve upon the experiment described here.

The Predator and Prey Agents

The `Agents` package provides a convenient macro for defining our agents:

```
using Agents, StatsBase, JLD2, Random

@agent Prey ContinuousAgent{2} begin
    mojo::Float64
    moves::Vector{Float64}
end

@agent Predator ContinuousAgent{2} begin
    victim::Int64
end
```

First we import the needed packages. In addition to `Agents`, we need `StatsBase` for creating histograms of the angle distributions, `JLD2` for saving and loading simulation data (see Listing 9-4 on page 289), and `Random` for random numbers (see "Random Numbers in Julia" on page 307).

The `@agent` macro defines the agents as composite types. After executing the macros in the listing, we have an agent type called `Prey` and another called `Predator`. The `ContinuousAgent{2}` notation means that the agents are destined to live in a continuous, two-dimensional space, where their positions are defined by a tuple of two floating-point numbers.

Each instance of `Prey` is endowed with two properties: `mojo`, the float that will determine when it's ready to reproduce; and `moves`, its vector of angles that determines the path it takes as it wanders blindly through the environment.

A predator has only one property: victim will be the ID of the individual prey that it's chasing. If this is 0, it's sitting still and waiting for a potential victim to wander within range.

Constants Defining Model Behavior

Certain parameters determining model behavior are defined in a list of constants, shown in Listing 11-1. We can alter these constants to experiment with evolution under different conditions without making changes to the program. These are declared const, a declaration we should apply to all global quantities in the interests of performance. In general, a program should not use non-const global variables.

```
const NPrey = 16 # Number of Prey agents
const NPred = 8 # Number of Predator agents
const PPR = 0.5 # Predator/prey ratio
const M = 8  # Number of turns
const SBT = 100 # Steps between turns
const TAD = 0.2 # Target acquisition distance
const KD = 0.01 # Kill distance
const LS = 2 # Litter size
const MIPS = 0.1 # Mojo increase per step
const MNFR = 50.0 # Mojo needed for reproduction
const SPEEDR = 1.5 # Ratio (predator speed)/(prey speed)
const LAA = π/128 # Limit of angular agility
const dt = 0.001
const SEED = 43
const rng = Random.MersenneTwister(SEED)
const LF = open("logfile", "a+") # Logfile
const LI = 100 # Log interval
```

Listing 11-1: Constants defining the model

The predator population adjusts itself at every step to maintain the PPR, adding predators if needed and eliminating them if the ratio is more than 5 percent too large.

The parameter M is the length of the vector of angles that amounts to the prey's genome. The prey will proceed in a straight line for SBT steps before turning through the next angle in the angle vector.

A predator can "see" a prey creature if it's closer than the distance TAD. It begins chasing the first such prey that it sees that is not already being chased. If a predator manages to close the distance to its target to within KD, the target is eliminated.

When a prey creature reproduces, it replaces itself with LS descendants.

The prey creatures eat continuously as they run, increasing their mojo by MIPS every step. The mojo is really just a measure of how long a creature has survived. Once a prey creature's mojo has reached MNFR, it reproduces.

The predator's straight-line speed is SPEEDR times the prey's speed. The predator's ability to corner is limited by LAA. It turns in the direction of the prey, adjusting its heading at every step, but can turn no more than LAA radians each time.

The Agents integration routine (a simple Euler step) uses a timestep of dt. This constant serves as an overall scale for agent speeds.

In order to be able to repeat simulations using identical sequences of random numbers, and to create ensembles of simulations when desired, we'll use a random number generator with a seed that we can control (see "Random Numbers in Julia" on page 307). This is the purpose of SEED and the rng. Also, the rand() functions are somewhat more efficient when passed an rng, although this concern is not as acute as it has been in some past versions of Julia and the Random package.

Utility Functions

We'd like to have a few functions to make the code that orients the predators and changes the direction of the prey more concise:

```
function vnorm(v)
    v ./ sqrt(v[1]^2 + v[2]^2)
end

function angle_between(a, b)
    atan(b[2], b[1]) - atan(a[2], a[1])
end

function turn(v, θ)
    M = [cos(θ) -sin(θ); sin(θ) cos(θ)]
    M * [v...]
end
```

We're going to need to normalize velocity vectors, which means adjusting their lengths to unity. This is what vnorm() does. The angle_between() function returns the angle between two vectors. The predators need this to calculate where to turn when chasing their food. And turning, both of predators and prey, relies on turn(), which, when supplied with a starting vector and an angle, returns the vector rotated through the angle.

In addition, we need a function to mutate the moves table. Without this, no evolution takes place:

```
function rmutate!(moves, nms)
    for ms in rand(rng, 1:M, nms) # nms random mutation sites
        θ = moves[ms] + (2rand(rng) - 1) * π/4
        # Keep within ±π:
        if abs(θ) < 1π
            moves[ms] = θ
        else
```

```
            moves[ms] = (θ - sign(θ) * 2.0π) % 2.0π
        end
    end
end
```

This makes a random change to a specified number of the angles in the table by an angle uniformly distributed from $-\pi/4$ to $\pi/4$.

Model Initialization

Every Agents simulation requires, in addition to the agents themselves, three data structures:

```
arena = ContinuousSpace((1, 1); periodic=true)
properties = Dict(:stepno => 0, :total_step => 0)
model = ABM(Union{Prey, Predator}, arena; properties)
```

The arena is the space in which the agents live and interact. Our space will be continuous, have coordinates running from 0 to 1 along each dimension, and have periodic boundary conditions. This makes the space infinite in the sense that an agent running off the right side will reemerge on the left side.

The properties is a dictionary of quantities relating to the simulation as a whole. In our simulation we use it just to keep track of how many steps have passed. For keeping track of when it's time for the prey to make a turn, we use stepno and increment total_step at each step. The former could be derived from the latter, but maintaining the two counters can be convenient when restarting a simulation from a saved state. We initialize both counters to 0.

With these two objects in place we can initialize the model, which maintains the whole simulation state. Checkpointing and restarting the simulation requires merely saving the model to disk. The two positional arguments of its constructor are the agent types and the space. If we had only one type of agent, the call would look like ABM(Prey, arena; properties), for example.

We choose properties for the name of the property dictionary because that name is used for a keyword in the model constructor, which makes the call to ABM simpler (see "Concise Syntax for Keyword Arguments" on page 154).

NOTE   *With the version of Agents used at the time of writing, we get a warning after constructing the model this way. The message warns us about a potential inefficiency when using a Union of agent types. This is an area of ongoing development effort, and the warning will probably disappear in future versions. The inefficiency doesn't actually become a problem unless we use more than three agent types.*

With model defined, we can initialize it by adding the agents:

```
for i in 1:NPrey # Initialize Prey agents
    vel = vnorm(Tuple(rand(model.rng, 2).-0.5))
```

```
❶ moves = π*(2rand(model.rng, M) .- 1)
    add_agent!(Prey, model, vel, 0.0, moves)
end

for i in 1:NPred # Initialize Predator agents
    add_agent!(Predator, model, (0.0, 0.0), 0)
end
```

The add_agent!() function is named using an exclamation point to remind us that it mutates one of its arguments: it alters model by adding agents to it. This function creates an agent at a random position within the arena. It expects an agent type as a first argument, the model in the second position, and a tuple giving the agent's initial *x* and *y* velocities. Positional arguments following the third are passed to the agent constructor. Therefore, in the first loop, each add_agent!() call will create a Prey instance using Prey(0.0, moves). The initial mojo is set to 0, and the starting vector of angles is randomly set ❶.

Functions to Extract Information from the Model

Let's look at some more short utility functions that accept the model as an argument and return information about its current state. We'll use some of them in the calculation and others to extract data that we'll store and use later when we analyze the results.

First we'll need functions to give us a vector of all the prey or predators in the system:

```
function preys(model)
    [a for a in allagents(model) if a isa Prey]
end

function predators(model)
    [a for a in allagents(model) if a isa Predator]
end
```

Inside the list comprehensions we use the allagents() function, which creates an iterator over the agents of a model.

The following suggestively named functions simply call the ones just shown and return the lengths of the agent vectors:

```
function number_of_predators(model)
    length(predators(model))
end

function number_of_preys(model)
    length(preys(model))
end
```

Since the predators do not compete for prey with their colleagues, they need to know if a potential meal is already under pursuit:

```
function being_chased(model)
    [a.victim for a in predators(model)]
end
```

This function returns a vector of all the IDs of prey creatures that are marked as victims by some predator. In order to determine if a potential meal is not already being chased, a predator checks whether its ID is in this list.

As mentioned earlier, we expect the vectors of angles to evolve. One way to get an overview of this process is to observe the evolution of the distribution of angles in the population (see "Distributions" on page 321 for an overview of the concept of a distribution).

The following function gathers all the angles in all the moves vectors from all the prey creatures and returns a Histogram data structure representing a binning of the distribution into 40 equal buckets. We can then normalize and plot the results at various timesteps to analyze one aspect of the simulation:

```
function moves_dist_data(model)
    moves_data = [m.moves for m in preys(model)]
    all_angles = [i for a in moves_data for i in a]
    fit(Histogram, all_angles, -π:2π/40:π)
end
```

This function, and its use of fit() and the Histogram data structure, are the reason we imported the StatsBase package. The pattern in the comprehension in the second line, with its two for loops, is a common way to flatten a collection of collections.

Stepping Through the Simulation

The agent_step!() and model_step!() functions are at the core of any Agents simulation. At every timestep, the agent_step!() function updates each agent as it's selected by the *scheduler*. This update can include moving the agent, changing its velocity, altering the values of its properties, or anything else that makes sense to apply to individual agents. The scheduler is the component of the calculation that selects which agents to update and in what order. In most Agents simulations, we can leave the order unspecified; allowing the scheduler to update the agents in an arbitrary order is the fastest option.

After the agent_step!() function comes (by default) the model_step!() function, which makes updates that apply to the model as a whole. This includes updates that require access to the entire agent population, including those that search for near neighbors.

The agent_step!() function is required, but model_step!() is optional; our calculation uses both. Also, there is an option to perform model_step!() before agent_step!() if the calculation needs that.

Stepping the Agents

The following shows the entire function for updating both predator and Prey agents:

```
function agent_step!(agent, model)
    move_agent!(agent, model, dt)
    if agent isa Predator && agent.victim > 0
        if agent.victim in keys(model.agents)
            if euclidean_distance(agent, model[agent.victim], model) < KD
                kill_agent!(model[agent.victim], model)
                agent.victim = 0
                agent.vel = (0.0, 0.0) # Time to rest a bit ❶
            else
                θp = angle_between(agent.vel,
                        get_direction(agent.pos, model[agent.victim].pos, model))
                θf = min(abs(θp), LAA) * sign(θp) ❷
                agent.vel = Tuple(turn(agent.vel, θf))
            end
        else
            agent.victim = 0 # Already gone
        end
    end
    victims = being_chased(model)
    if agent isa Predator && agent.victim == 0
        food = [a for a in nearby_agents(agent, model, TAD)
                if (a isa Prey && !(a in victims))]
        if !isempty(food)
            agent.victim = food[1].id
            append!(victims, food[1].id)
            agent.vel = SPEEDR .* vnorm(get_direction(agent.pos, food[1].pos, model)) ❸
        end
    end
    if agent isa Prey
        if agent.mojo >= MNFR # Reproduce: add LS new Preys at my position
            for c in 1:LS
                child = add_agent!(agent.pos, Prey, model,
                                    vnorm(Tuple(rand(model.rng, 2).-0.5)), 0, agent.moves)
                rmutate!(child.moves, 2)
            end
            kill_agent!(agent, model) # Reproduction is fatal ❹
        end
        if model.stepno == 0
            vel = turn(agent.vel, agent.moves[1])
            agent.vel = Tuple(vel) ❺
            agent.moves = circshift(agent.moves, -1)
```

```
        end
        agent.mojo += MIPS # I eat as I run
    end
end
```

The agent_step!() function (which can be named anything, but we've used the conventional name) must accept agent and model as arguments. The scheduler passes each agent in turn to the function as it cycles through them.

The first line moves the agent by an amount determined through the timestep, dt.

We then kill off any Prey agents that have been caught by the predators that are chasing them, where "caught" means that the distance between them has become less than KD. We use euclidean_distance(), a function built into the package, to measure this distance.

After the meal, the predator waits, stationary ❶, for another available prey to come within range.

If the prey is too far away to eat, we continue the chase by turning toward it. The first step is finding the current angle between the predator's velocity vector and the vector between the positions of the predator and its prey. Fortunately, Agents comes with a function just for this: get_direction(). In calling this function, we use two additional features of the model: an agent's position tuple is available as agent.pos, and model[i] returns the agent with ID i. Although models aren't arrays, the Agents package defines a getindex() method that enables this. After limiting the turning angle ❷ to the predator's agility, set with the constant LAA, we update its velocity.

We then check for any sufficiently close eligible prey: any Prey agent within a distance TAD that's not already being chased. If we find one, we set the predator's velocity vector to point toward the prey, again using get_direction() ❸.

Turning to the prey creatures, first we check if they have accumulated enough mojo to reproduce. Those who have enough give birth to LS copies, which are then mutated. We kill off the parent using the kill_agent!() function ❹, which is part of the Agents package.

When it's time to make a turn, we rotate the velocity using our turn() function. We need to convert the result to a Tuple ❺ because the package uses those to store agent velocities.

After making the turn, we rotate the agent's private turn table with a function that we're using for the first time: circshift(), which rotates an array. This invocation rotates the moves vector to the left, so its second element becomes its first and its first becomes its last. The outcome is that the prey makes the M turns stored in moves repeatedly (if it survives long enough to do so).

Stepping the Model

After the scheduler updates all the agents, it calls this function, passing the model as an argument:

```
function model_step!(model)
    model.stepno = (model.stepno + 1) % SBT
    model.total_step += 1

    # Maintain predator/prey ratio:
    predators_pop = length(predators(model))
    prey_pop = length(preys(model))
    if predators_pop/prey_pop < PPR
        for i in 1:Int(round(PPR*prey_pop - predators_pop))
            add_agent!(Predator, model, (0.0, 0.0), 0)
        end
    end
    if predators_pop/prey_pop > 1.05PPR
        for i in 1:Int(round(predators_pop - PPR*prey_pop))
            ❶ kill_agent!(random_agent(model, a -> a isa Predator), model)
        end
    end
    # Logging and checkpointing:
    if model.total_step % LI == 0
        write(LF, "$(model.total_step), $prey_pop, $predators_pop \n")
        flush(LF)
    end
end
```

First we increment model_step, using modular arithmetic to maintain a cycle of length SBT; then we increment the total step. Since total_step, as well as its other properties, is stored along with the model, we can checkpoint and seamlessly restart the simulation by using JLD2 to save and reload the model, and total_step will keep track of how long it's been run.

We maintain the predator/prey ratio specified with PPR by adding or removing predators as needed. The add_agent() function from Agents adds an agent at a random position. The tuple in the argument list is its initial velocity, and subsequent arguments are passed to the agent constructor. In this case, there is only one such argument: the initial victim property is set to 0.

We remove agents by passing a random agent to kill_agent() using the function random_agent() ❶. This Agents function takes, in its optional second argument, a function expressing a condition that the potentially doomed agent must satisfy.

Finally, the routine maintains a logfile, writing an entry every LI steps. We flush() the logfile so that we can take a look at it while the simulation is running. Without this call, the file may not be written until the calculation ends.

Running the Simulation

The run!() function is Agents's basic facility for stepping through a model, as shown in Listing 11-2. Its four positional arguments are the model, the function for updating the agents, the optional function for updating the model, and the total number of steps.

```
function evolve!(model, nruns, nsteps_per_run)
    for run in 1:nruns
        adf, mdf = run!(model, agent_step!, model_step!, nsteps_per_run;
                        adata=[:mojo],
                        mdata=[:total_step, number_of_predators,
                                number_of_preys, moves_dist_data])

        jldsave("mdf$run"; mdf)
        jldsave("model$run"; model)
    end
end


evolve!(model, 10, 1000)
```

Listing 11-2: Running the simulation

It returns two dataframes (see "CSV Files" on page 332): one for the agents and one for the model. The adata keyword argument is a Vector of quantities to include in the agent dataframe, and the mdata keyword argument is for the model dataframe. These quantities can be agent or model properties, which become symbols, or functions of the model. In the value for mdata, we're using three functions that we defined with this in mind: we're keeping track of the two population sizes and the angle distribution.

We've wrapped run!() in a function that calls it nruns times, each time asking it to run the model for nsteps_per_run steps, and uses the save function from JLD2 to store the model dataframe and the entire model to disk.

To load the model from its saved version on disk, we can enter

```
mode = load(filepath, "model")
```

where the string argument specifies the variable to be loaded from the file.

Visualizing System Behavior

The most convenient way to get a snapshot of the model at any time, or to create an animation of its progress, is to use two functions provided by the InteractiveDynamics package, which needs a separate import:

```
julia> using InteractiveDynamics, CairoMakie
```

We need to import a Makie library as well because InteractiveDynamics uses it for drawing. Makie is a graphics framework along more or less the same lines as the current standard, Plots.

As we plan to create visualizations of our model with its two agent types, let's create functions that map the agent types to two distinct colors and shapes:

```
function agent_color(agent)
    if agent isa Prey
        return :blue
    end
    if agent isa Predator && agent.victim > 0
        return :red
    end
    return :green
end

function agent_shape(agent)
    if agent isa Prey
        return '●'
    end
    return '⊙'
end
```

These functions, when used together, will render prey creatures as blue dots and predators as circles with dots inside them. Predators on the chase will be red, while idle predators will be green.

After evolving the model to any step using run!(), we can create and save a picture of its state with the following calls:

```
julia> fig, _ = abmplot(model; ac=agent_color, as=20, am=agent_shape)
julia> save("model_snapshot.pdf", fig)
```

The plotting function, abmplot(), returns two values, of which we only need the first. The agent color (ac) and agent shape (am) use our functions defined earlier, and we set the agent marker size (as) to a value that worked well in the visualization. Figure 11-1 shows the result after 10,000 steps.

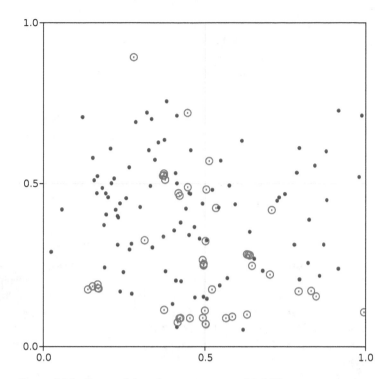

Figure 11-1: The model configuration at step 10,000

At the moment shown in Figure 11-1, there are 139 total agents. None of the predators happen to be idle at this moment, so they are all rendered in the same color.

We can also create an animation of the model using `abmvideo()`, which is supplied by `InteractiveDynamics` as well. It actually runs the model, beginning with the initial state supplied in its second argument, stepping through it using the same step functions that we supply to `run!()`:

```
julia> abmvideo("arena.mp4", model, agent_step!, model_step!;
         ac=agent_color, am=agent_shape,
         frames=500, framerate=30)
```

The run stops after the number of steps given in the `frames` keyword argument, and the video file is saved with the name given in the first argument. We can use constants or, as we did here, functions for agent shapes and colors, as in `abmplot()`. You can view some animations made with this method in the online supplement for this chapter.

Animations are excellent devices for verifying that an ABM simulation is working as intended and for communicating the results when the dynamic behavior is interesting. However, running the model through `abmvideo()` is much slower than running it with `run!()` because, in addition to the model calculations, the function renders an image at each step using `abmplot()` and assembles a video file. A strategy for long-running agent simulations, therefore, may be to run the calculation using `run!()` and then render subsets of steps as animations. This strategy requires periodically saving the model, as we do in our example within `agent_step!()`, so we have various saved states available to start from.

Two additional quirks to note about `abmvideo()` are that it doesn't use the convention of the exclamation point in its name, despite mutating the model, and that it cannot generate dataframes directly as can `run!()`. We can get around this last issue by putting data recording into `model_step!()`, as we did in our example with logging. This is a more flexible approach in any case, as it allows us more control over the recorded data. For example, we might decide to add a row to the dataframes less frequently than every step.

The `CairoMakie` graphics library is appropriate for making high-quality plots and animations saved in files. For more immediate feedback, we can import `GLMakie` instead. If both are imported, the calls `GLMakie.activate!()` and `CairoMakie.activate!()` switch between them. When `GLMakie` is active, `abmplot()` and `abmvideo()` open a dedicated graphics window when using the REPL, or they can insert graphics into a computational notebook.

Analyzing the Results

The call to run the simulation in Listing 11-2 stores the distribution of angles in the prey angle tables in the model dataframe at every timestep. These angles are initially uniformly distributed, so if the distribution changes over time, we know that some form of evolution is occurring. The angle distribution over the population doesn't tell us everything about its character, but if we reach a point where the distribution has stopped evolving, this suggests that the population may have achieved some form of optimum in response to the selection pressure exerted by the predators.

We can plot a histogram of the distribution at any step by extracting `moves_dist_data` from the model dataframe. The dataframe for the 20th run looks like this:

```
julia> mdf20 = load("mdf20", "mdf")
1001×5 DataFrame
  Row | step   total_step  number_of_predators  number_of_preys  moves_dist_data
      | Int64  Int64       Int64                Int64            …Histogram
------------------------------------------------------------------------------------
    1 |    0   19000                      1787             3447  Histogram{Int64, 1, Tuple...
    2 |    1   19001                      1787             3444  Histogram{Int64, 1, Tuple...
    3 |    2   19002                      1787             3438  Histogram{Int64, 1, Tuple...
    4 |    3   19003                      1787             3434  Histogram{Int64, 1, Tuple...
    ⋮ |    ⋮        ⋮                         ⋮                ⋮                      ⋮
```

999	998	19998	2559	5075 Histogram{Int64, 1, Tuple...
1000	999	19999	2559	5072 Histogram{Int64, 1, Tuple...
1001	1000	20000	2559	5069 Histogram{Int64, 1, Tuple...

Here is the call to plot the histogram from the last row in this dataframe:

```julia
julia> using LinearAlgebra, Plots

julia> Plots.plot(normalize(mdf20.moves_dist_data[end], mode=:pdf);
                  xticks=([-π:π/2:π;], ["-π", "-π/2", "0", "π/2", "π"]),
                  legend=false, xlabel="θ", ylabel="PDF(θ)")
```

We need the LinearAlgebra package for the normalize() function, which rescales the histogram of raw counts into one that can be interpreted as a probability density function (see "Probability Density Functions" on page 325). This allows us to compare distributions from populations of different sizes directly. At this stage, there are 5,069 Prey agents, as can be read off from the dataframe, and comparing the distribution at earlier times shows that it seems to have converged to the shape shown in Figure 11-2.

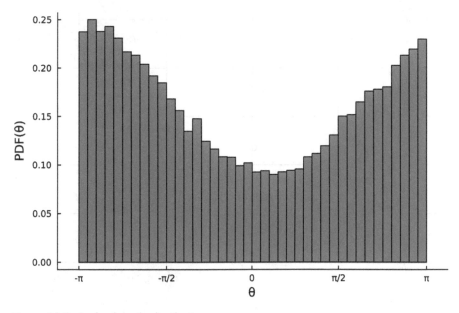

Figure 11-2: Evolved angle distribution

A bit of reflection reveals why the prey creatures may have evolved such a distribution. The predators are significantly faster than their prey (SPEEDR = 1.5) but they have severely limited agility: LAA = π/128, which means that they can turn no more than 1.4° in any step. If the prey try to run in a straight line, the predators are likely to catch them before they have a chance to reproduce. This fact produces the pronounced dip in the distribution near 0°. Making sharp turns of close to 180° buys the most time, and that's where we find the peaks in the distribution.

If this idea, that the prey have "learned" to avoid predators with these particular attributes, is correct, then a different species of predator with different attributes should give rise to a different angle distribution.

To test this idea, we need simply to change the LAA and SPEEDR constants and run the simulation again. After trying this with SPEEDR = 1.05 and LAA = π/16, we observe the distribution shown in Figure 11-3 after 13,000 steps.

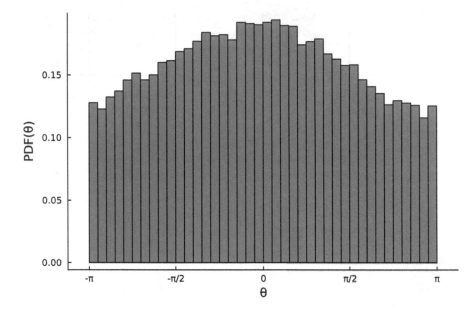

Figure 11-3: Evolved angle distribution with slower but more agile predators

This result is distinctly different and admits a clear intuitive explanation. These predators can only travel 5 percent faster than the prey, so their potential victims can often survive long enough to reproduce by simply continuing in something close to a straight line. Although slow, they are far more agile than the predators in the previous simulation, able to turn through 11.25° at each step, so prey who make many large turns are more likely to be caught. Hence we see a distribution with a broad peak near 0°, falling off at larger angles.

The distribution evolution is suggestive, but let's see if we can confirm the idea that the prey have evolved to be better predator avoiders. We'll do this by comparing the evolved population to unevolved populations with uniform distributions of angles in their moves tables. Since we use a seeded random number generator, we can create ensembles of populations by running the simulation multiple times while varying the SEED.

The ability of a population to survive in an environment with predators of a particular type is its *fitness*. The predators' type in our model is defined by two parameters: SPEEDR and LAA, their speed and agility.

To test the fitness of the initial, unevolved population, we start with 200 Prey agents and 100 Predator agents, and turn off the Prey agents' ability to reproduce. In such a situation, the prey population should decay roughly exponentially, eventually dwindling to zero. We perform this experiment 10 times.

To test the fitness of the evolved population, we load the model after 20,000 steps and extract a random sample of 200 Prey agents from it. We put that sample into the arena with 100 predators and observe the population decay, repeating this experiment 10 times as well. Each experiment uses a different random seed, so we'll get a different random sample each time.

Figure 11-4 shows the results: the evolved population performs distinctly better than the initial population.

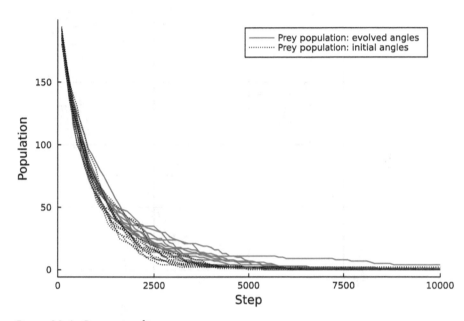

Figure 11-4: Comparing fitness

Of course, the evolved population becomes extinct as well, as it must without the ability to reproduce. But the comparison shows that the sharp-turn strategy suggested by Figure 11-2 is effective, as this population decays more slowly.

Conclusion

In this chapter, I presented a complete, detailed example of a research problem: we began with some curiosity about whether we could simulate natural selection acting on specific attributes of a population. Then we made the question concrete by devising a scenario where behavior was codified by a list of eight numbers. Next, we constructed a simulation capturing the mechanisms we wanted to study and observed that the simulation displayed evolution of the population, apparently converging to some optimum. Lastly, we tested the evolved population and found that it did have increased fitness.

The Agents package, and Julia's expressiveness and efficiency, dramatically streamlined the path from initial speculation to a verifiable, quantitative, and easily visualized result. The ability to try out a variety of scenarios and analyze and view the results, all within a unified interactive environment, and with no compromise in performance, is an unprecedented boon for the researcher.

FURTHER READING

- For more information on BioJulia, the "bioinformatics infrastructure for the Julia language," see *https://biojulia.dev*.

- The article "Julia for Biologists" provides an overview of the use of the language in biology: *https://arxiv.org/abs/2109.09973*.

- More details on `Agents.jl` is available at *https://juliadynamics .github.io/Agents.jl/stable/*.

- Watch a video about `Agents.jl` here: *https://youtu.be/Iaco6v6TVXk*.

- A detailed survey of the field of artificial life is available at *https:// www.ais.uni-bonn.de/SS09/skript_artif_life_pfeifer_unizh.pdf*.

- For interesting anecdotes about artificial life simulations, visit *https:// direct.mit.edu/artl/article/26/2/274/93255/The-Surprising- Creativity-of-Digital-Evolution-A*.

12

MATHEMATICS .

The people of Ulm are mathematicians.
–Motto of Ulm, the birthplace of Albert Einstein

In this chapter, we'll explore several Julia packages for symbolic and numerical mathematics. Symbolic mathematical software can replace tedious pencil-and-paper calculations or long evenings in the company of tables of integrals with automated manipulations of mathematical expressions. Numerical packages include modules for linear algebra, equation solving, and related fields. The two classes of packages have substantial overlap, and both are a boon to the applied mathematician or, potentially, to anyone who uses mathematics in research.

Symbolic Mathematics

This category of software is sometimes called *computer algebra*, but it includes all types of automated symbol manipulation, such as algebraic and trigonometric simplification; generation of Taylor series; calculation of limits, derivatives, and integrals; and more specialized areas such as algebraic number theory.

Symbolic mathematical software is distinguished from the more familiar intersection of computers and math by its ability to handle mathematics as mathematics, rather than by simply performing arithmetic. We feed it expressions incorporating variables, and it returns rewritten expressions, or the solution to a problem, in terms of those variables, rather than numbers.

Numerical-Symbolic Modeling with Symbolics

This section introduces Symbolics, which is described as a symbolic modeling language and as numerical-symbolic software. These descriptions are meant to suggest that Symbolics emphasizes the synergy between symbolic and numerical calculations, and is designed with efficiency in mind. Symbolics does not feature all the abilities of a full-blown computer algebra system—it can't calculate indefinite integrals, for example. But it has other, unique abilities. For example, it can transform a normal Julia function into a symbolic function, and it can create a C program from a Julia Symbolics program. Symbolics is written entirely in Julia, which means that we can reach for any part of the language in working with its symbolic expressions. Symbolics is a key part of the ModelingToolkit package, a framework for automatically parallelized scientific machine learning.

To establish names as symbolic variables, as shown in Listing 12-1, it's most convenient to use a macro supplied by the Symbolics package.

```
@variables a b c φ z;
 5-element Vector{Num}:
 a
 b
 c
 φ
 z
```

Listing 12-1: Declaring Symbolics variables

After calling this macro, we can use the five mentioned variables similarly to how we would use variables in mathematical expressions. They have the type Num and share much of the behavior of the Real type, but they have extra powers, which we'll explore next.

Let's create a rotation matrix as we did in "Matrix Multiplication" on page 146:

```
RM = [cos(φ) -sin(φ); sin(φ) cos(φ)]
```

Since φ is a Symbolics variable, this matrix is a Symbolics expression.

Let's see what happens if we try to rotate a vector with it using matrix multiplication, as we did with the "normal" rotation matrix in Chapter 5:

```
julia> RM * [1, 0]
2-element Vector{Num}:
 cos(φ)
 sin(φ)

julia> RM * [0, 1]
2-element Vector{Num}:
 -sin(φ)
  cos(φ)

julia> RM * [1, 1]
2-element Vector{Num}:
 cos(φ) - sin(φ)
 cos(φ) + sin(φ)

julia> RM * [0.5, 0]
2-element Vector{Num}:
 0.5cos(φ)
 0.5sin(φ)

julia> RM * [0.5, 0.6]
2-element Vector{Num}:
 0.5cos(φ) - 0.6sin(φ)
 0.5sin(φ) + 0.6cos(φ)
```

In each case, the matrix multiplication returns an exact result, correct for any value of φ. The * operator is able to operate on Symbolics expressions, performing matrix multiplication as it does with matrices of numbers. This is another example of the composability of Julia packages. Most array and numerical operators and functions will handle Symbolics expressions the way we would expect.

To compute a numerical result, we can use the substitute() function:

```
julia> substitute(RM * [1, 0], Dict(φ => π/2))
2-element Vector{Num}:
 6.123233995736766e-17
 1.0
```

The result is identical to the one in "Matrix Multiplication" on page 146.

The substitute() function takes a Symbolics expression in its first argument and a dictionary of substitutions to make in its second argument. The resulting expression is not always simplified as we might expect:

```
julia> ex = a^2*z^2 + a^4*z^4;

julia> substitute(ex, Dict(a => sqrt(b)))
```

```
(z^2)*(sqrt(b)^2) + (z^4)*(sqrt(b)^4)

julia> substitute(ex, Dict(a => b^(1//2)))
b*(z^2) + (b^(2//1))*(z^4)
```

Here we have a polynomial that we attempt to write in a slightly simpler form by making a change of variable. Our first attempt is foiled because Symbolics seems not to know that, for example, sqrt(b)^2 = b. We had better luck on our second try.

Symbolics is able to automatically simplify expressions involving multiplication or division of variables raised to integer powers:

```
julia> z^3 * z^5
z^8

julia> a^5/a^3
a^2
```

It also comes with a simplify() function, but it's not able to do much—not even the limited simplification that appears in the documentation. The emphasis of Symbolics, as mentioned previously, is on efficient numeric-symbolic modeling. We can always turn to SymPy, explored in the next section, to perform nontrivial simplifications of an expression, the results of which we can use in a Symbolics program.

An Example: Bessel Functions

As an example of a practical use of Symbolics, let's say we need to compute the Bessel function of the first kind, of various orders, and some of its derivatives. These functions appear throughout physics and engineering. We used a Bessel function in Listing 7-5 on page 206 to represent the shape of a vibrating drumhead, where we gained access to it through the SpecialFunctions package.

To roll our own Bessel function, which we'll denote $J_m(x)$, where m is the order, we can turn to its well-known series representation:

$$J_m(x) = \sum_{k=0}^{\infty} \frac{(-1)^k x^{2k+m}}{2^{2k+m} k!(k+m)!}$$

A Julia function implementing this representation, shown in Listing 12-2, will accept x, m, and a number of terms (because we can't compute an infinite number of terms) that we'll call N.

```
function Jm(x, m::Int, N)
    s = 0
    for k in N:-1:0
        s += (-1)^k * x^(2k + m) / (2^(2k + m)*factorial(k)*factorial(k + m))
    end
    return s
end
```

Listing 12-2: Calculating a Bessel function using its series expansion

This function will return the value of $J_m(x)$ computed using N terms in the series. Because it uses normal integers, rather than big integers, we can only use it with N < 19 (see "'Big' and Irrational Types" on page 216). Keeping nine terms is more than sufficient for an extremely accurate approximation in the interval $0 \leq x \leq 6$.

Our little function Jm() is useful if we need to know the numerical value of $J_m(x)$ at various values of x, especially if we don't know about the Special Functions package. If we happen to need the value of various derivatives of $J_m(x)$, we could calculate them using some finite difference scheme, calling Jm(x, m, N) at two or more closely spaced values of x to compute the derivative at x. However, the numerical error intrinsic to these methods accumulates as the order of the derivative increases, and the repeated evaluations of Jm(x, m, N) are an additional computational cost. Let's see how an approach using Symbolics neatly dispenses with both of those issues.

If we call Jm(x, m, N) with numerical values for x, m, and N, we get a number back, the approximation for the mth Bessel function at x. Listing 12-3 shows what we get if, instead of a number for x, we supply the name of a Symbolics variable.

```
julia> J19 = Jm(z, 1, 9)
(1//1917756584755200)*(z^17) + (1//1474560)*(z^9) +
(1//29727129600)*(z^13) + (1//384)*(z^5) + (1//2)*z -
(1//176947200)*(z^11) - (1//18432)*(z^7) - (1//6658877030400)*(z^15) -
(1//6903923705118720000)*(z^19) - (1//16)*(z^3)
```

Listing 12-3: A Symbolics expression approximating $J_1(z)$

In Listing 12-1, we created the Symbolics variable z, among others. When we pass z to Jm(), it returns the nine terms of the series expansion generated with m = 1 and N = 9, in an unfortunate random order. We assigned this Symbolics expression to the variable J19. We can get the numerical value of this expression through substitution:

```
julia> substitute(J19, Dict(z => 1.2))
0.4982890575672154
```

```
julia> Jm(1.2, 1, 9)
0.4982890575672155
```

The difference in the value in the last place is due to a difference in the order of operations. The strategy shown in Listing 12-2 of adding up the small terms in a series before the larger ones should be somewhat more accurate.

As another example of the power of composing Julia packages, we can use Latexify to render a LaTeX version of a Symbolics expression:

```
julia> using Latexify
```

```
julia> latexify(J19)
L"\begin{equation}
```

```
\frac{1}{1917756584755200} z^{17} + \frac{1}{1474560} z^{9} - [etc.]
\end{equation}
"
```

Copying and pasting the contents (with some line breaks added) of the resulting LaTeX string into the source of this book, which is typeset using LaTeX, shows us the rendered expression:

$$\frac{1}{1917756584755200}z^{17} + \frac{1}{1474560}z^9 - \frac{1}{176947200}z^{11} -$$

$$\frac{1}{18432}z^7 - \frac{1}{6658877030400}z^{15} + \frac{1}{29727129600}z^{13} +$$

$$\frac{1}{384}z^5 - \frac{1}{690392370511872000}z^{19} + \frac{1}{2}z - \frac{1}{16}z^3$$

The process illustrated here, of taking a normal Julia function and re-purposing it to generate a Symbolics expression, is sometimes called *tracing*. Only functions that are in a sense deterministic can be traced. What this means, in the case of our Jm() function, is that we can supply a Symbolics variable for x, but not for the number of terms, N. For that, we must supply an integer. If we try to sneak in a Symbolics variable for the third positional argument, we get a cryptic error message:

```
julia> Jm(z, 1, a)
ERROR: TypeError: non-boolean (Num) used in boolean context
```

The reason we didn't enforce an integer N in the function signature, as we did for m, was to illustrate this behavior.

The problem with attempting to trace Jm() while using a Symbolics variable representing the number of terms is that the loop limits are unknown: what expression is to be returned? We can trace only functions that generate a completely determined expression based on their inputs. The particular error message appearing in this listing is a signal that we've run into this problem.

Differentiating the Bessel Function

Since we're in possession of an *analytic* expression, generated in Listing 12-2, for the approximation to $J_1(z)$, we can derive its analytic derivative at *any order* to get $d^p J_1/dz^p$, the pth derivative. Since J19 is only a polynomial, this is a simple, albeit tedious and error-prone, procedure.

Symbolics can relieve us of the burden of differentiating by hand:

```julia
julia> Differential(z)(J19) |> expand_derivatives
(1//2) + (13//29727129600)*(z^12) + (17//1917756584755200)*(z^16) +
(5//384)*(z^4) + (1//163840)*(z^8) - (19//690392370511872000)*(z^18) -
(11//176947200)*(z^10) - (3//16)*(z^2) - (7//18432)*(z^6) - (1//443925135360)*(z^14)
```

Here we use the `Differential()` function. `Differential(t)` returns another function that calculates the derivative with respect to t of the Symbolics expression that it receives. To actually see the result of this manipulation, we need to pass it to `expand_derivatives()`. The result is the correct differentiation of the polynomial J19, with its terms in yet another random order.

As suggested previously, we can repeatedly apply `Differential()` to generate derivatives at any order without worrying about the accumulation of finite differencing errors. Let's take a look at the first 10 derivatives of the Bessel function:

```julia
julia> using Plots, LaTeXStrings

julia> dnJ19 = [Differential(z)(J19) |> expand_derivatives];
```

❶
```julia
julia> for ord in 2:10
           push!(dnJ19, Differential(z)(dnJ19[ord-1]) |> expand_derivatives)
       end
```

```julia
julia> plot(J19; lw=2, xrange=(0, 6), yrange=(-0.6, 0.6), legend=false,
            xlabel=L"x", ylabel=L"J_1, J_1^\prime, J_1^{\prime\prime}, ...")
```

❷
```julia
julia> for ord in 1:10
           plot!(dnJ19[ord]; linestyle=:auto)
           gui()
       end
```

We intend to plot the derivatives, so first we import `Plots` and, to get typeset math in the axis labels, `LaTeXStrings`. We calculate the derivative of the Bessel function, as we did before, and place the result inside a vector. In a loop ❶ we apply the derivative operator repeatedly to the previous result, generating the first 10 derivatives. We set up the plot by graphing $J_1(x)$, using LaTeX strings for the labels, and then loop through ❷ the elements of the vector of derivatives, adding each one to the visualization. Figure 12-1 shows the result.

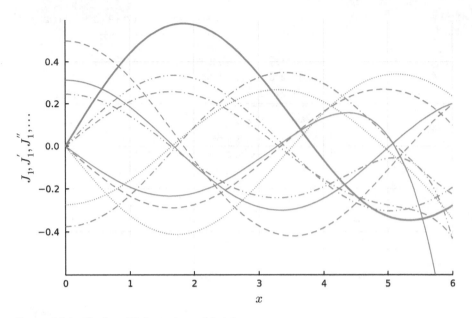

Figure 12-1: The first 10 derivatives of $J_1(z)$

The thick solid line shows $J_1(x)$. The `linestyle=auto` keyword argument to `plot!()` creates a series of lines with different dash patterns, which are plotted using the default line thickness. These are the 10 derivatives.

That we're able to plot these `Symbolics` expressions directly, without setting up vectors of numerical variables or having to make numerical substitutions by hand, is another example of composability. The `Plots` package was written without any knowledge of the (future) `Symbolics` package, yet it's able to deal with `Symbolics` expressions in a natural way.

Math Manipulation with SymPy and Pluto

For more general symbolic mathematics, `SymPy` is probably the best package available at the moment. This package is a Julia wrapper around the highly capable Python library of the same name, so it's limited to Python performance; however, for the kind of work typically done with such packages, raw speed is not usually a crucial consideration.

NOTE *In order to use `SymPy` from Julia, with some systems and configurations it may be sufficient to merely execute add `SymPy` in Julia's package mode, followed by using `SymPy`. On other systems, we need to install the Python `SymPy` library (and perhaps Python itself) outside of Julia. For example, on Linux (where Python is routinely available with most distributions), we can execute `pip3 install sympy` in the shell. However, as there is no official method of installing libraries or resolving dependencies in the Python world, it's impossible to provide a command that will work for everyone. The remainder of this section assumes that you've successfully executed add `SymPy` and using `SymPy` in a Julia environment.*

SymPy works from any such environment, and does a nice job of rendering mathematical notation in the terminal REPL. Its use from Pluto, however, is more delightful, and we'll use examples from that environment. In Pluto, math is automatically rendered in LaTeX, so the results are immediately in the form of beautifully typeset formulas, embedded within the notebook. Pluto uses MathJax for its math rendering. A right-click on any displayed expression brings up a contextual menu providing several options, the most important providing one to copy the LaTeX commands that create the expression to the clipboard.

Another reason Pluto is a natural fit for SymPy is that, when using a computer algebra library, we're usually in discovery or exploration mode, or using Julia with SymPy as a calculator, rather than developing a large program. The reactive nature of Pluto lends itself well to this mode of interaction (see "Pluto: A Better Notebook" on page 17). Because of Pluto's dependency graph, we can know that all the equations displayed in the notebook at any time are consistent with each other, something that is decidedly not true with Jupyter.

The ability to use Pluto is one reason we might prefer to use SymPy from within Julia rather than with Python directly. Another is that the wrapping of functions and data structures provided by SymPy presents a more familiar interface for the Julia programmer and eases interoperation with other Julia programs and libraries. This wrapping is not complete in a sense, however. The user of SymPy will encounter remnants of Python's class-method syntax, as we'll see in such calls as sol.rhs(), for the right-hand side of a solution sol.

Since Pluto is such a powerful (and fun) environment for using SymPy, the examples in this section will take the form of screenshots from a Pluto session (see Chapter 1 for a reminder of how to start up a Pluto notebook session).

Figure 12-2 shows the start of the session.

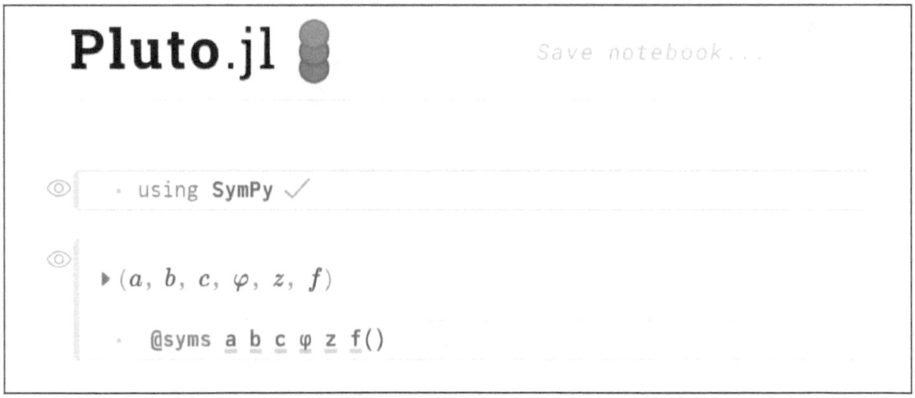

Figure 12-2: Starting a SymPy session within Pluto

After importing the package, we establish some variables as SymPy symbolic names using the @syms macro. This serves the same purpose as the @variables macro used with the Symbolics package. Entering one of the names as f() establishes f as the symbolic name of a function that we can use as an unknown in, for instance, the definition of a differential equation (we'll look at this shortly).

Algebra with SymPy

SymPy can perform algebraic simplification, expansion, and its inverse, factoring, as shown in Figure 12-3.

$$ac - b^2$$

```
simplify((a^2*c^2 - c*a*b^2) / (a*c))
```

$$a^2 + 2ab + b^2$$

```
expand((a + b)^2)
```

$$(a - b)(a + b)$$

```
factor(a^2 - b^2)
```

Figure 12-3: Simplification, expansion, and factoring

The subtle underlines adorning some characters in the input cells in Figure 12-3 indicate which are SymPy symbols—a nice refinement to the interface.

In order to solve systems of algebraic equations, we can place the equations into a vector and call solve() with the vector as an argument, as shown in Figure 12-4.

$$p = \blacktriangleright [2a + 3b - 1, \ a - 2b + 1]$$

```
p = [2a + 3b - 1, a - 2b + 1]
```

$$\blacktriangleright \text{Dict}(\quad a \qquad b \quad)$$

$$\Rightarrow -\frac{1}{7}, \quad \Rightarrow \frac{3}{7}$$

```
solve(p)
```

Figure 12-4: Solving a system of equations

The vector p contains two equations, entered so their right-hand sides equal 0; therefore, p represents the following system:

$$2a + 3b = 1$$

$$a - 2b = -1$$

The result of the call to solve() is the solution $a = -1/7, b = 3/7$.

Numerical Solutions with SymPy

Our example happens to involve linear equations, but SymPy can handle higher-order polynomials, rational equations, and more, and it can find complex and multiple solutions. We can also turn to its built-in numerical solver, useful in cases where no symbolic solution exists.

As an example, let's say we were interested in values of a for which

$$\sin(a) + \log(a) = 1$$

An attempt to throw this at the symbolic solver only gets us an error message lamenting that SymPy knows no algorithms for its analytic solution. This is a job for an approximate, numerical solver.

Intelligent numerical solution behooves us to understand something about the behavior of the equation of interest, at least within and near the neighborhood where we seek solutions. A good first step is to look at a graph of the equation, as shown in Figure 12-5.

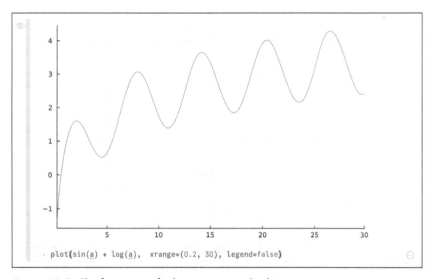

Figure 12-5: The first step in finding a numerical solution

Here we've plotted the left-hand side of the equation; the curve's intersections with the horizontal line at 1 show us where we can expect the solutions. Inspection of the graph shows three solutions near a = 1, 3, and 5.

SymPy's numerical solver is the nsolve() function. It expects a symbolic expression in its first argument and a guess for a root for the expression in its second argument. By calling the function three times with three approximate roots, we can get three precise answers, as shown in Figure 12-6.

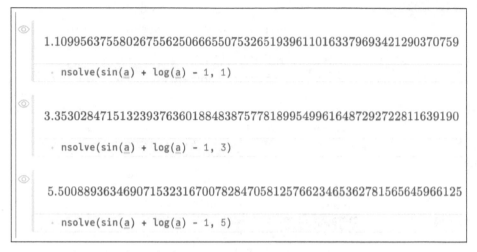

Figure 12-6: Numerical root finding

Integration with SymPy

SymPy knows calculus, and it can largely replace weighty tables of integrals. We'll use the package to evaluate the indefinite and a definite integral of the Gaussian distribution (see "The Normal Distribution" on page 323). We can evaluate these integrals in one step by using the integrate() function, but we can also divide the problem into two stages. The first stage will be to define expressions for the *unevaluated* integrals, shown in Figure 12-7.

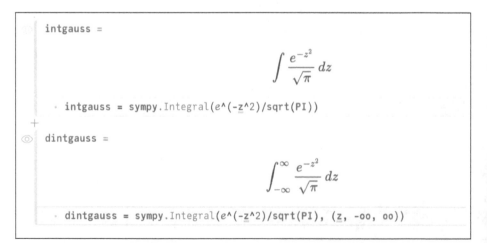

Figure 12-7: Unevaluated integrals

We create an unevaluated integral using the sympy.Integral() function, which requires the namespace prefix because it's not exported by the package. In this case, the expression under the integral has only one independent variable, but if it had more than one, we would supply the variable of integration as a second argument (which we can in any case, with the same result). The second argument appears in the definite integral version, where the tuple contains the variable of integration and the lower and upper limits. Here e is Euler's number, which we can enter by typing **\euler** followed by TAB or by directly entering the Unicode character. We enter symbolic infinity using a double o, and symbolic π using PI—which is not to be confused with the irrational Julia π. The two are not interchangeable: if we use π instead of PI, the former will be converted into an approximation to π, and factors of π will fail to cancel in subsequent manipulations.

There can be several reasons for creating such intermediate expressions, rather than integrating in one step. We may want to use these unevaluated integrals in other calculations, or we may simply want to examine their typeset form to ensure that we've entered them correctly—something that's easier to accomplish with conventional mathematical notation than even the exceptionally legible computerese that Julia makes available to us.

To evaluate the integrals, we pass them to the doit() function, as shown in Figure 12-8.

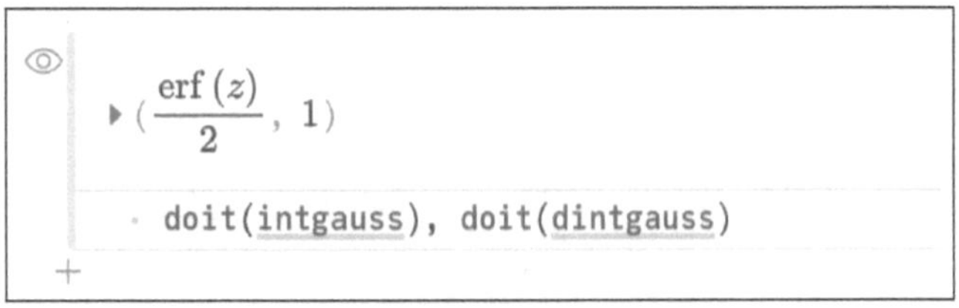

$$\blacktriangleright\ (\ \frac{\mathrm{erf}\,(z)}{2}\ ,\ 1\,)$$

doit(intgauss), doit(dintgauss)

Figure 12-8: Evaluating the integrals

The indefinite integral (antiderivative) of the Gaussian is not expressible in closed form in terms of elementary functions. It's defined as the *error function*, abbreviated erf(z). This is the type of mathematical knowledge built into most capable computer algebra systems, and SymPy is no exception. The $\frac{1}{\sqrt{\pi}}$ factor in the integral normalizes the result so that the definite integral over the whole line yields 1. With this normalization, the integrand is a probability density function, and the definite integral from a to b is the probability of an observation falling within that interval.

Differential Equations with SymPy

SymPy can also solve differential equations. In keeping with our minor theme of the Bessel functions, let's recall that these mainstays of applied mathematics arise as the solutions of differential equations. Figure 12-9 shows a particular example that demonstrates how to define a differential equation in SymPy.

```
beseq =
```

$$z^2 \frac{d^2}{dz^2} f(z) + z \frac{d}{dz} f(z) + (z^2 - 1) f(z) = 0$$

```
beseq = Eq(z^2 * diff(f(z), z, 2) + z * diff(f(z), z, 1) + (z^2 - 1) * f(z), 0)
```
                                                                    114 ms

Figure 12-9: Bessell's equation

Figure 12-9 shows the construction of the differential equation for the Bessel function of the first kind of order 1. We define the equation using the Eq() function, which takes the left-hand and right-hand sides as its two arguments. In the definition, we've used the symbolic differential operator: diff(f(z), z, n) is the nth derivative of f(z) with respect to z. It was with this in mind that we established f() as a symbolic function in Figure 12-2.

To find the solution to a differential equation, we use SymPy's dsolve() function, which takes the equation to solve and the function to solve it for in its first two arguments. But since boundary conditions are essential for nailing down which solutions we're interested in, dsolve() also takes a dictionary of boundary conditions as the value of the keyword argument ics. We can specify values or derivatives at specific points in this dictionary; here we only need a simple condition to exclude another Bessel function that's singular at the origin. Figure 12-10 shows the call that generates the solution of interest.

```
sol =
```

$$f(z) = C_1 J_1(z)$$

```
sol = dsolve(beseq, f(z); ics = Dict(f(0)=>0))
```

$$J_1(z)$$

```
sol.rhs(1)
```

Figure 12-10: Solving a differential equation

Figure 12-10 shows that SymPy uses the conventional notation for the Bessel function (in Pluto; in the REPL it spells out the name). The solution with the supplied boundary condition is undetermined up to a multiplicative constant, which SymPy names C_1. The second cell in Figure 12-10 shows how to extract the rhs (right-hand side) of the solution while specifying a value for the constant, in this case 1. We can use the rhs to plot the solution, as shown in Figure 12-11.

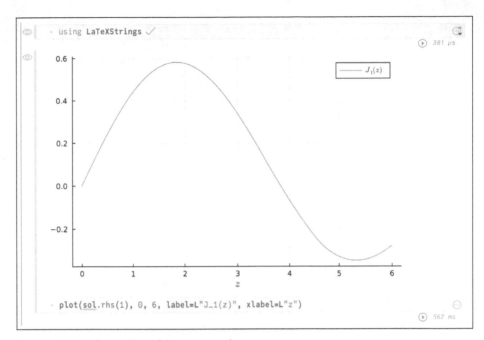

```
· using LaTeXStrings ✓
                                                            381 μs
```

```
· plot(sol.rhs(1), 0, 6, label=L"J_1(z)", xlabel=L"z")
                                                            562 ms
```

Figure 12-11: Plotting the solution to Bessel's equation

The curve shown in Figure 12-11 agrees with the Bessel function calculated by other means in Figure 12-1.

Linear Algebra

As Professor L. Fox says in his 1965 textbook *An Introduction to Numerical Linear Algebra*, about 75 percent of scientific computing involves, wholly or in part, numerical linear algebra. Whatever the current proportion happens to be, linear algebra is, and likely always will be, a central part of any enterprise where we turn to computers to help us solve problems in science, mathematics, or engineering. The fundamental reason for this is because the central problem of numerical linear algebra, the solution of simultaneous systems of linear equations, arises repeatedly in the modeling of an enormous variety of systems—not only those whose behavior is truly linear, but those whose behavior can be linearly modeled within some range of parameters. For example, a system of partial differential equations can often be approximated by a linear algebraic system close to some initial condition or for a small range of a controlling parameter.

Views

In performing calculations using matrices (or arrays of other shapes), we often employ views. A *view* in Julia is a reference to a part of an array that we can create and manipulate without copying any data; modifications to the view modify the original array.

We can create views using the @view or @views macros. The first version immediately precedes the array expression that we want to turn into a view, while the second transforms all the slicing operations within an entire expression or code block into views:

```julia
julia> R = rand(5, 5)
5×5 Matrix{Float64}:
 0.957982  0.206423  0.00489974  0.0881235  0.708827
 0.301785  0.107707  0.524776    0.83413    0.771915
 0.049844  0.031097  0.22972     0.415245   0.735899
 0.438108  0.57943   0.144575    0.131095   0.103629
 0.473649  0.237991  0.148043    0.0351828  0.724837

julia> row1Rview = @view R[1, :]
5-element view(::Matrix{Float64}, 1, :) with eltype Float64:
 0.9579822727773696
 0.20642276219972644
 0.004899741566674942
 0.0881235008776815
 0.7088267041115207
```

❶ ```julia
julia> row1Rview .= 17;
```

❷ ```julia
julia> R
5×5 Matrix{Float64}:
 17.0       17.0      17.0       17.0       17.0
  0.301785   0.107707  0.524776   0.83413    0.771915
  0.049844   0.031097  0.22972    0.415245   0.735899
  0.438108   0.57943   0.144575   0.131095   0.103629
  0.473649   0.237991  0.148043   0.0351828  0.724837

julia> @views row1RviewAgain = R[1, :];

julia> row1RviewAgain === row1Rview
true
```

After creating a view of the first row of the random matrix R, we set all of its elements to 17 ❶. Since modifying a view modifies the original, the first row of R is transformed ❷. We create the same view using the @views macro, and verify that the views are indeed the same with the last expression.

The slice syntax used earlier, without the @view or @views macros, would create a new array with a *copy* of the data from the first row of R. Modifying the copy would do nothing to the original array.

When should we use copies and when should we use views? The answer depends on the pattern of computation to which we intend to subject the data structures. In this example, since arrays are stored in column-major order, manipulating a row uses noncontiguous memory accesses. If, after extracting the row, we use it repeatedly, then the time consumed in creating the copy may be a good investment. However, if the array is large, the copy will consume significant memory that the use of a view would avoid. Copies use more memory, but can lead to faster code. There is no universal answer to the question beginning this paragraph. Whether it's better to use views or copies depends on the size of the arrays involved and how we use the data.

Linear Algebra Examples

Let's look at a simple example problem. Consider the 2×2 system shown in Equation 12.1.

$$a_{11}x_1 + a_{12}x_2 = b_1$$
$$a_{21}x_1 + a_{22}x_2 = b_2$$

(12.1)

In this system of equations, x_1 and x_2 are the unknowns for which we ultimately seek a solution; the a_{xx}s are numerical coefficients, whose indices indicate their positions in the system. The right-hand side of the system consists of the two numbers b_1 and b_2.

In order to apply the machinery of numerical linear algebra, we'll follow the universal convention and write the system more compactly as

$$Ax = b$$

(12.2)

where A is the matrix

$$\begin{bmatrix} a_{11} & a_{12} \\ a_{21} & a_{22} \end{bmatrix}$$

x is the vector $[x_1, x_2]$, and b is the vector $[b_1, b_2]$. The juxtaposition of A and x indicates the usual matrix multiplication.

The form of Equation 12.2 suggests that we can somehow divide by A to solve for x, and that is indeed true. As this is a section on *numerical* linear algebra, in Equation 12.3, let's try some actual numbers in place of the symbols in Equation 12.1:

$$x_1 + 3x_2 = 1$$
$$2x_1 + 4x_2 = 7$$

(12.3)

This equation may, or may not, have a solution for x_1 and x_2. In order to try to solve it numerically, we'll define a Julia matrix and a vector for the right-hand side, corresponding to A and b in Equation 12.2, as shown in Listing 12-4.

```
julia> A = [1 3; 2 4]
2×2 Matrix{Int64}:
 1  3
 2  4

julia> b = [1, 7]
2-element Vector{Int64}:
```

```
1
7
```

Listing 12-4: A small linear system

At this point, if we could make sense of the idea of dividing by a matrix, then we would expect that the solution could be calculated by dividing b by A. This, in fact, will be our first approach to solving the equation system in Listing 12-4.

Of course we're familiar with the / operator for division. Julia comes with a "reverse" version, called the *left division operator*, that we haven't had occasion to use until now:

```
julia> 1 / 3 == 3 \ 1
true
```

Julia's Base extends the left division operator to operate on matrices, calculating the inverse of a matrix and then performing a matrix multiplication. The result should be a column array containing the solution:

```
julia> A \ b
2-element Vector{Float64}:
  8.5
 -2.5
```

This is indeed the solution, as we can immediately verify:

```
julia> A * [8.5, -2.5]
2-element Vector{Float64}:
 1.0
 7.0
```

The result is b, as defined in Listing 12-4.

As mentioned, the meaning of A \ b is the matrix multiplication of the *inverse* of A with b:

```
julia> inv(A) * b
2-element Vector{Float64}:
  8.5
 -2.5

julia> inv(A) == A^-1
true
```

The second input expression shows another way to spell the inverse of a matrix.

Although this is the formal meaning of the \ operator, we should never solve equation systems using inv(), but instead with an expression such as A \ b. This is because the left division operator solves the system using the most efficient algorithm available, which may not involve the calculation of the inverse matrix.

The inverse of a matrix is defined such that $A^{-1} A$ and $A A^{-1}$ are both equal to the *identity matrix*, which has the same shape as A and has 1.0 on the diagonal and 0.0 elsewhere:

```julia
julia> A * inv(A)
2×2 Matrix{Float64}:
 1.0  0.0
 0.0  1.0
```

The identity matrix is conventionally represented as I, and is called thus because it is the identity element under matrix multiplication:

```julia
julia> I22 = A * inv(A);
julia> I22 * A == A * I22 == A
true
```

In general, matrix multiplication is not commutative, but multiplication by the identity matrix, and multiplication of a matrix by its inverse, are.

The LinearAlgebra Package

The examples in this section so far require no package imports, as inv() and the extension of \ to matrices are part of Base. To go further, we need to import the LinearAlgebra package, which is part of the standard library, so it imports quickly and nothing needs to be downloaded. The rest of the code examples in this section assume that you've executed using LinearAlgebra.

The LinearAlgebra package can perform all of the standard operations on matrices. We'll demonstrate using our little matrix A. First, the trace and the determinant:

```julia
julia> tr(A) # Trace of A
5

julia> det(A) # Determinant of A
-2.0
```

Next, the calculations of eigenvalues and eigenvectors ($Ax = \lambda x$ if x is an eigenvector of A and λ is its eigenvalue):

```julia
julia> eigvecs(A) # Eigenvectors
2×2 Matrix{Float64}:
 -0.909377  -0.565767
  0.415974  -0.824565

julia> eigvals(A) # Eigenvalues
2-element Vector{Float64}:
 -0.3722813232690143
  5.372281323269014
```

The nth eigenvector/eigenvalue pair is the nth column of the matrix returned by eigvecs() along with the nth element of the vector returned by eigvals(). We can check to see if the LinearAlgebra functions return the correct values:

```julia
julia> evec1 = eigvecs(A)[:,1];

julia> eval1 = eigvals(A)[1];

julia> A * evec1  - evec1 * eval1
2-element Vector{Float64}:
  0.0
 -5.551115123125783e-17
```

Here we've assigned names to the first eigenvector and its eigenvalue; we should see that A * evec1 is equal to eval1 * evec1. Comparing the two values in the final expression, we see that they are the same within floating-point accuracy.

Specialized Matrix Types

Linear algebra routines, such as eigvals() and others, are written to dispatch an algorithm designed to take advantage of the symmetries or other properties of the matrices involved. The routines check for relevant properties of the matrix arguments passed to them in order to choose the most efficient method of solution. For example, the eigvals() function checks for symmetry of real matrices using the issymmetric() function, and hermiticity of complex matrices using ishermitian().

The matrix properties that are important in choosing an efficient routine include, among others, whether a matrix is symmetric, banded, triangular, hermitian, sparse (see "The Adjacency Matrix" on page 196), or diagonal. Each of these matrix classes has an associated Julia type. We can convert a general matrix to one of these more specific types by creating a view using the appropriate function. For example, Symmetric(M) creates a view of the matrix M that is symmetric. We might want to do this in order to pass the result to a linear algebra function ensuring that it selects the optimal algorithm, in case it doesn't detect the character of the matrix.

To get an idea of how all this works, let's look at the behavior of the eigvals() function. First, we create a moderately large matrix for our timing study, as shown in Listing 12-5.

```julia
julia> N = 3000;

julia> G = rand(N, N);

julia> sG = (G + G') / maximum(G + G');
```

Listing 12-5: Creating a random, symmetric matrix

The final assignment creates a symmetric matrix by adding G, element-wise, to its transpose. Let's compute the eigenvalues of G in several ways, as shown in Listing 12-6. We don't care about the results, but we're interested in the timings.

```
julia> using BenchmarkTools

julia> @btime eigvals(G);
  24.044 s (20 allocations: 69.58 MiB)

julia> @btime eigvals(sG);
  4.612 s (14 allocations: 69.74 MiB)

❶ julia> SsG = Symmetric(sG);

julia> SsG == sG
true

julia> typeof(SsG)
Symmetric{Float64, Matrix{Float64}}

❷ julia> @btime eigvals(SsG);
  4.481 s (14 allocations: 69.74 MiB)
```

Listing 12-6: Timing the calculation of eigenvalues

The first two timings demonstrate that the eigvals() function can exploit the symmetry of the matrix to drastically reduce the calculation time. We also create a Symmetric view of sG ❶, which contains the same values as the original matrix, but is of a different type. In this case, the use of SsG doesn't affect the calculation time ❷, as eigvals() has already detected that sG is symmetric. We could also ask eigvals() to compute eigvals(Symmetric(G)), and it would do so as quickly as it computed the eigenvalues of the actually symmetric matrix just shown. But in this case, the computed eigenvalues would not be the eigenvalues of G, as G is not symmetric.

The eigvals() and eigvecs() functions check for symmetric or hermitian arguments, but not for other properties. We can demonstrate this by calculating the eigenvalues of an upper triangular matrix: a matrix with zero elements below the diagonal. First we need to construct the matrices for use in the test:

```
julia> N = 3000;

julia> G = rand(N, N);

❶ julia> UTt = UpperTriangular(G);

julia> typeof(UTt)
UpperTriangular{Float64, Matrix{Float64}}
```

```
julia> UT = Matrix(UTt);

julia> typeof(UT)
Matrix{Float64} (alias for Array{Float64, 2})
```

❷ ```
julia> UT == UTt
true
```

After making, again, a random matrix G, we create ❶ an UpperTriangular view of this matrix and assign it to UTt. Then we assign it to UT after converting it to a basic Matrix type. This is a convenient way to make a full matrix that happens to be upper triangular. The two objects contain the same elements ❷ but are of different types. The type of UTt tells LinearAlgebra functions that it's upper triangular, so they can take advantage of that in case a specialized algorithm is available. eigvals() is one of these functions:

```
julia> @btime eigvals(UT);
  119.571 ms (18 allocations: 69.53 MiB)

julia> @btime eigvals(UTt);
  35.905 μs (2 allocations: 23.48 KiB)
```

The time to compute the 3,000 eigenvalues is much shorter than for a matrix with no structure (Listing 12-6) due to all the zeros in UT. The time that eigvals() needs to work on the UpperTriangular view of the matrix is drastically reduced (note the units in the timings returned by @btime), as are the memory requirements. The matrices have identical elements, and the computed eigenvalues are the same (but are returned in a different order). However, the information carried by the UpperTriangular type informs eigvals() about the matrix's structure, which is information it can use in dispatching to an algorithm more efficient than the general-purpose one.

The moral of this story is that we should pass the most informative view possible to any LinearAlgebra function.

Equation Solving and factorize()

A *factorization* of a matrix, analogous to the factorization of a number, is a series of matrices that, when (matrix) multiplied together, yield the original matrix. Matrix factoring is often an early step in the solution of a matrix equation (a system of linear equations), and is attempted by the left division operator, the standard function for solving such systems. The factorization can be the most time-consuming part of the calculation of the solution, which often proceeds rapidly after the factorization is complete. As many problems involve the repeated solution of equations in the form of Equation 12.2 using different b vectors, it would save significant time if we could perform the factorization once, separating out that part of the calculation. This is what the LinearAlgebra function factorize() enables:
```

```
julia> N = 8000;

julia> G = rand(N, N);

julia> g = rand(N);

julia> fG = factorize(G);

julia> @btime G \ g;
  10.073 s (6 allocations: 488.40 MiB)

julia> @btime fG \ g;
  37.942 ms (2 allocations: 62.55 KiB)
```

Here we see that solving the equation system using the pre-factored matrix is about 200 times faster, and uses a small fraction of the memory required, than when we use the unfactored matrix. However, the call to factorize() itself takes about as much time as the calculation G \ g. The advantage is that we can use fG in subsequent problems that vary only in their right-hand sides to get solutions cheaply.

Telling \ about the properties of the matrix using views doesn't help, as it did with eigvals():

```
julia> g = rand(3000)

julia> @btime sG \ g;
  504.239 ms (6 allocations: 68.71 MiB)

julia> @btime SsG \ g;
  556.492 ms (8 allocations: 70.18 MiB)

julia> fSsG = factorize(SsG);

julia> @btime fSsG \ g;
  6.161 ms (2 allocations: 23.48 KiB)
```

Here, also, although the Symmetric view doesn't help, we observe a large speedup and decrease in memory consumed when using the factorized matrix.

Conclusion

This chapter covers two large topics that, I believe, are generally useful to scientists, engineers, and other technical users of Julia.

The use of symbolic mathematics packages is potentially valuable for everyone, and my discussions with various students and researchers convinces me that many are unaware that computers can calculate integrals and derivatives, solve equations symbolically, and perform other feats of real mathematical manipulation—not merely arithmetic. Opening this door leads to many possibilities, especially when symbolic and numerical methods are combined, as encouraged by the Symbolics package.

Of course, linear algebra is a vast traditional area for computer application, and we only scratched the surface here. Julia is particularly convenient for calculations in this arena. BLAS (Basic Linear Algebra Subprograms) and LAPACK are the Fortran libraries at the heart of numerical linear algebra, and most languages' linear algebra abilities amount to interfaces to these venerable collections of optimized routines. Julia is unusual in several regards: BLAS and LAPACK are being rewritten in pure Julia, an ongoing project, and, through the libblastrampoline package, Julia offers the unique ability to switch between BLAS implementations on the fly.

FURTHER READING

- See "Symbolic Mathematics on Linux" for more details on symbolic math: *https://lwn.net/Articles/710537/*.

- Documentation for Symbolics.jl is available at *https://symbolics .juliasymbolics.org/stable/*.

- OSCAR is a computer algebra package that covers algebra, geometry, and number theory: *https://oscar.computeralgebra.de*.

- For a list of matrices with special symmetries and structures, visit *https://docs.julialang.org/en/v1/stdlib/LinearAlgebra/#Special -matrices*.

- libblastrampoline is available at *https://github.com/JuliaLinear Algebra/libblastrampoline*.

- The recently developed LinearSolve package provides a unified interface for a selection of linear equation solvers: *https://github .com/SciML/LinearSolve.jl*.

13

SCIENTIFIC MACHINE LEARNING

The bewilderments of the eyes are of two kinds, and arise from two causes, either from coming out of the light or from going into the light.
—Socrates

The topic of this chapter is a rather new approach to solving scientific problems through computation. Much of the recent development in the field of scientific machine learning (SciML) has taken place within the Julia ecosystem and has been led by researchers using Julia in science. Relatively little has been published explaining how to apply the new techniques in a form digestible by those not conversant with machine learning jargon. I hope to fill at least part of that gap here through the selection of simple but concrete examples that clarify the concepts involved so that readers can apply them to a variety of problems.

Scientific machine learning is not machine learning. *Machine learning (ML)* is a branch of artificial intelligence in which computers train themselves (usually guided by human supervision), by practicing on a large corpus of data, to recognize patterns and make classifications. ML techniques are applied to such problems as detecting fraudulent financial transactions or trying to guess what movie you want to watch next. The training replaces the traditional coding of a specific model or algorithm.

SciML extracts several key techniques from ML and applies them to a different class of problem. In SciML, we assume that the system we're studying is described by a particular model, often expressed as a set of differential equations. Certain parameters or other aspects of the model, however, are unknown. If we have data about how the system behaves, SciML techniques allow us to infer the values of these unknown parameters efficiently.

Automatic Differentiation in a Physics Problem

Along with concepts from statistics and probability theory, SciML borrows *automatic differentiation* from ML. This technique is critical to both ML and SciML. Traditionally, differentiation is a mathematical procedure from calculus that finds the slope of a curve (in one dimension) or a surface (in two or more dimensions). We call a derivative of a surface, which involves dealing with several variables, a *gradient*. If your kitchen sink is installed correctly, the negative gradient of its surface points toward the drain at every point, so that when you pull the plug all the water drains out and you're not left with any puddles.

Automatic differentiation is the calculation of a derivative or gradient of a function expressed in a programming language, rather than in mathematical notation. The programmed function can be the direct translation of a mathematical expression. Often, when the expression is complicated, its analytic derivative will involve many terms and be expensive to calculate in the traditional way. Automatic differentiation can be faster. We can even use automatic differentiation to calculate gradients that have no analytic form: the function being differentiated can include nearly any computation, including those not expressible in mathematical notation. Automatic differentiation is not numerical differentiation; it's not a finite-difference calculation. Neither is it symbolic differentiation, as explored in Chapter 12. It applies knowledge of calculus, such as the chain rule for derivatives, with knowledge of the derivatives of specific functions and numerical techniques to differentiate efficiently and accurately.

ML uses automatic differentiation to guide its models in the direction of the correct solutions, and it's used within the SciML machinery in a similar way. We can also use it explicitly for efficient calculations of derivatives in mathematical models, as shown in "Calculating Forces from Potentials" on page 408.

Differentiating with ForwardDiff

We can meet our automatic differentiation needs in this chapter with the derivative() function from the ForwardDiff package, which I'll assume has been imported in the following examples. Its use is simple: we supply a function and a value, and `ForwardDiff.derivative()` returns the derivative of the function evaluated at the supplied value:

```
julia> ForwardDiff.derivative(sin, 0.0)
1.0
```

The result is correct: the derivative of sin(x) is cos(x), and cos(0) = 1.

The `ForwardDiff.derivative()` function can also handle functions defined in Julia that may contain almost any type of computation:

```
julia> function fdst(x)
           (x - floor(x))^2 / ceil(x)
       end
fdst (generic function with 1 method)

julia> plot(fdst, 0, 5; label="fdst(x)", xlabel="x", lw=2);

julia> plot!(x -> ForwardDiff.derivative(fdst, x); label="fdst'(x)", lw=2, ls=:dash)
```

The `floor()` and `ceil()` functions round their arguments to the closest smaller or larger whole number. The `fdst()` function defined in the example is not something that we can look up in a table of derivatives or handle with the familiar techniques of calculus, but Julia's automatic differentiation routine calculates the derivative correctly. Figure 13-1 shows the result.

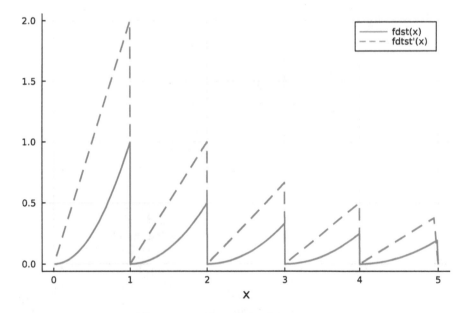

Figure 13-1: Automatic differentiation of a strange function

In Figure 13-1, the legend uses a prime to indicate a derivative. The dashed line shows the result of the automatic differentiation function, which is not troubled by the existence of discontinuities.

Calculating Forces from Potentials

In physics, the force on a body is the negative gradient of its potential energy. If the potential energy depends on only one variable, this is simply the negative of its derivative with respect to that variable. Let's revisit the finite-angle pendulum problem from Chapter 9.

Listing 13-1 recapitulates the problem in one place for convenience.

```
using ForwardDiff
using DifferentialEquations
const L = 1.0
const g = 9.8
const m = 1.0
```

❶
```
function ppot(θ)
    return m*g*L*(1-cos(θ))
end
```

```
function pendulum!(du, u, p, t)
    L, g = p
    θ, ω = u
    du[1] = ω
```
❷`    du[2] = -ForwardDiff.derivative(ppot, u[1])/m`
```
end
```

```
function pendulumF!(du, u, p, t)
    L, g = p
    θ, ω = u
    du[1] = ω
    du[2] = -g/L * sin(θ)
end
p = [L, g] #  <- Parameters
```

```
u0 = [deg2rad(175), 0]
         #  θ    ω  <- Initial conditions
```

```
tspan = (0, 20)
```

```
prob = ODEProblem(pendulum!, u0, tspan, p)
probF = ODEProblem(pendulumF!, u0, tspan, p)
```

❸
```
sol5d = solve(prob)
sol5dF = solve(probF)
```

Listing 13-1: Revisiting the finite-angle pendulum

Listing 13-1 contains something extra, however: the ppot() function, which gives the gravitational potential energy of the pendulum as a function of height ❶. The pendulum!() function now sets up the problem using automatic differentiation to calculate the (negative) derivative of the potential ❷ to derive the force, rather than using the force function directly. A second function, pendulumF!(), sets up the problem as before, using the force function. We proceed just as we did in Chapter 9, but we find two numerical solutions: once using the potential ❸ and again using the force.

Figure 13-2 compares the two methods of solution.

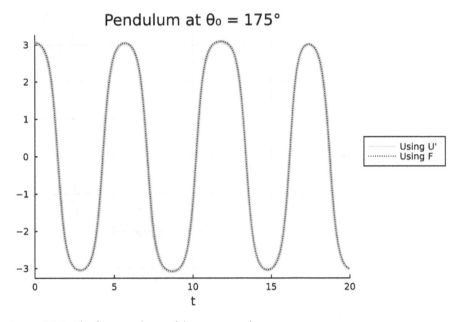

Figure 13-2: The finite-angle pendulum computed two ways

The two solutions agree exactly. Clearly it wasn't necessary to reach for the ForwardDiff package to handle this problem, but we did so to verify that it works as expected. When applying a new technique, it's essential to test it on a relatively simple problem with a known solution first, to gain confidence in our understanding of how to use it, and to confirm that we understand how it works.

Physicists usually think in terms of potentials rather than forces, so when conducting numerical experiments, we're more likely to try different potentials rather than tweak the force function directly. Having a solution program that differentiates the potential for us is more convenient than deriving a new force field at each iteration. Also, the potential functions we work with have a simpler form than the force functions derived from them. This is the case in the next example.

Imagine that we've discovered a new particle with a potential that is strongly repulsive at short range, has a well at a particular distance, and is weakly repulsive at longer ranges. The potential

$$U(r) = \frac{e^{-e^{-0.4\left(r-1\right)^2}}}{\sqrt{r+1}}$$

where r is the distance from the particle, has these properties, as shown in Figure 13-3.

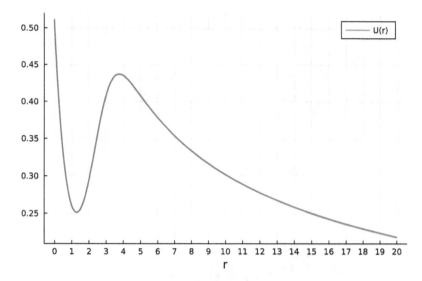

Figure 13-3: The potential of an imaginary particle

Figure 13-3 shows the potential well at $r \approx 1.3$. This is a location at which an interacting particle can be trapped if it lacks the energy to escape.

The system will contain two of these particles, fixed at $r = 0$ and $r = 20$. We'll place a moving particle between them, and use units where its mass is 1. Figure 13-4 shows the combined potential of the two fixed particles.

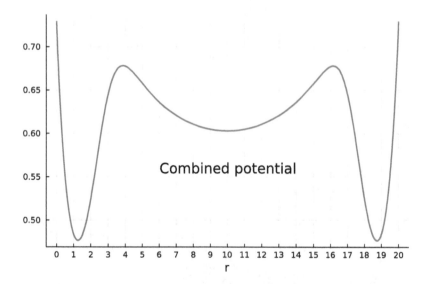

Figure 13-4: The total potential of two imaginary particles

We'll insert the moving particle into the system at $r = 5.0$, with an initial velocity of 0.2035. This positive velocity starts the particle moving to the right at $t = 0$. With a zero initial velocity, it would oscillate within the shallow well centered on $x = 10$, between $x = 5$ and $x = 15$. Its particular initial velocity gives the particle barely enough energy to surmount the potential hill near $x = 16$.

In Listing 13-2, we proceed as in the revisited pendulum problem in Listing 13-1.

```
using DifferentialEquations
using ForwardDiff


U(r) = exp(-(exp((-0.4*(r-1)^2))))/sqrt(r+1)

function particle!(du, u, p, t)
    x1, x2 = p
    r, v = u
    du[1] = v
❶  du[2] = -ForwardDiff.derivative(U, abs(r - x1)) +
            ForwardDiff.derivative(U, abs(r - x2))
end

❷ p = [0.0, 20.0]
❸ u0 = [5.0, 0.2035]

tspan = (0, 650)

prob = ODEProblem(particle!, u0, tspan, p)
sol = solve(prob)
```

Listing 13-2: Solving for the motion between two imaginary particles

We derive the forces by applying automatic differentiation to the potential function, which is the sum of the two contributions from the two fixed particles ❶, evaluating the derivatives at the distance from each particle. The p array holds the positions of these two particles ❷, and the u0 array contains the initial position and initial velocity of the moving particle ❸. After establishing a time span for the solution, we define the ordinary differential equation (ODE) problem and store its solution in sol as before.

A first attempt at a solution is shown in Figure 13-5, which shows the position of the moving particle as a function of time.

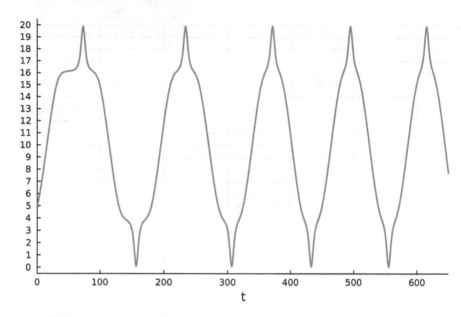

Figure 13-5: An inaccurate solution

We extract the position variable from the solution as explained in Chapter 9.

Scientists should always cast a critical eye over purported numerical solutions to differential equations. Our first instinct should be to examine the output of the solver in light of everything we know about how the solution should behave. In this case, we know that the solution should be periodic, as nothing in the definition of the problem can add or remove energy. The result in Figure 13-5 is clearly not accurately periodic.

The DifferentialEquations package provides many options for solution methods and exposes several parameters for tweaking the behavior of the solvers. See "Further Reading" on page 427 for a link to the relevant part of the documentation. As the differential equation set up in Listing 13-2 is not of a difficult type, we can probably stick with the default solver. The accuracy issue is most likely caused by the nature of the potential and the initial velocity, which, as mentioned, is near a critical value that determines whether the particle will surmount a local potential maximum. This suggests that simply applying an error bound may be sufficient. The reltol parameter, supplied as a keyword argument to solve(), adjusts the adaptive timestepping as needed to limit the local error to the value that we supply, as described in "Parametric Instability" on page 300. Its default is 0.001, which is probably not stringent enough for this problem. Smaller changes in the initial velocity have a large effect on the particle's motion. If we try again using sol = solve(prob; reltol=1e-6), we get the solution shown in Figure 13-6.

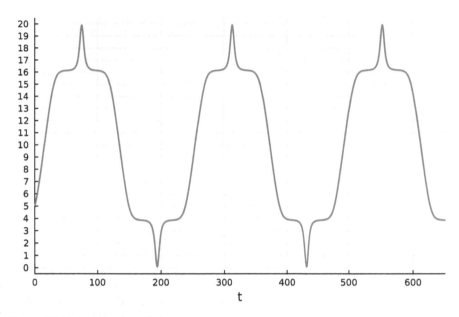

Figure 13-6: An accurate solution

The new solution appears to be accurately periodic. Furthermore, reducing `reltol` further doesn't change the solution, which supplies some reassurance that it's converged to the right answer.

The derivative of U happens to be

$$-\frac{(0.8 - 0.8r)\, e^{-0.4\left(r-1\right)^2} e^{-e^{-0.4\left(r-1\right)^2}}}{\sqrt{r+1}} - \frac{e^{-e^{-0.4\left(r-1\right)^2}}}{2\left(r+1\right)^{\frac{3}{2}}}$$

which would be somewhat more annoying to work with directly.

Probabilistic Programming

This section introduces the `Turing` package through several examples. This package allows us to infer likely causes given observed effects. We'll assume some comfort with several of the ideas discussed in Chapter 10—in particular, probability and probability distributions. We'll need to be familiar with these ideas to understand the output from `Turing` and to interpret its results.

Testing for Fairness of a Coin

This simple example introduces the basic concepts and procedures for using `Turing` in probabilistic programming.

Suppose we flip a coin L number of times and observe that we get a total of *Nheads* heads. We want to assess whether what we observed shows that the coin is *fair* or not, where *fair* means that the probability of coming up heads is $1/2$, or very close to it. This is the type of question that probabilistic programming claims to be able to answer: given an effect, or a set of observations, what was the cause? Here the effect is the proportion of heads, and the cause is the probability of heads.

NOTE   *I'm cognizant that the foregoing brief analysis may not please everyone, but wish to avoid becoming mired in metaphysics. The actual causes of our observations will be the physical details of the coin's construction and the method of tossing. The probability of heads represents a summary of the cumulative effect of this myriad of unknown details; the description of cause as a probability reflects our incomplete knowledge.*

The first step in using Turing is to construct a probabilistic model describing the probability distributions of each of the random variables in the problem. For some variables, these distributions are unknown, in which case we need to assume something reasonable, such as a uniform or normal distribution that includes all possible values, perhaps centered on the value that we think is most likely. For others, the description of the problem implies a particular distribution, one that is usually parameterized by observations or the values of some of the other variables.

In this example we have one unknown random variable, *Pheads*. We'll assume that it can have any value from 0 to 1, uniformly distributed. This assumption means that we don't have any a priori belief about the nature of the coin. If we had reason to think that it was almost certainly fair, we could instead assert that it was normally distributed with a mean of 1/2 and a small variance.

In Turing models, we represent assertions about the distributions of random variables using the ~ operator. Our assumption about the distribution of the probability of heads takes the form Pheads ~ Uniform(0, 1). The Uniform() function comes from Distributions.jl, which Turing automatically imports (see "Distributions" on page 321).

Listing 13-3 shows the complete Turing model.

```
julia> using Turing, StatsPlots

julia> @model function coin(Nheads, L)
           Pheads ~ Uniform(0, 1)
        ❶ Nheads ~ Binomial(L, Pheads)
       end;
```

Listing 13-3: A simple probabilistic program

After importing Turing and StatsPlots, which will be useful for visualizing the output, we use the @model macro from Turing to define the model. We can call the function that @model acts on anything we want; the macro understands the ~ operator and transforms the function into a Turing model.

The inputs are the observed number of heads and L, the total number of flips. As mentioned, we assume a uniform distribution for Pheads, the quantity that we're trying to infer. The number of heads observed when we flip a coin L times is a random variable that we know has a binomial distribution parametrized by L and Pheads ❶ (see "Further Reading" on page 427 for a link to a brief introduction).

To understand, in outline, how Turing carries out its inductive process to infer the unknowns in the model (Pheads in this case) from the observations, we'll imagine how we might do it manually. For the simple problem here, we might choose a series of Pheads values from 0 to 1, either deterministically or randomly, perhaps using rand(). For each of these values for Pheads, we can calculate the expectation value, or mean, of Nheads from its binomial distribution. The expectation value closest to the observed value of Nheads is our inferred value for Pheads.

This inference procedure would be fairly efficient because we have a simple formula for the mean of the binomial distribution. If we were dealing with less tractable distributions, including ones depending on many parameters, each with its own distribution, the only way to extract the expectation value would be through the numerical experiment of sampling from the distribution. As pointed out in "Random Numbers in Julia" on page 307, the rand() function allows us to sample directly from a distribution. However, as we'll see soon, a more realistic problem may include thousands of random variables and thousands of distributions. Naive sampling from each of them would take a prohibitively long time.

This is the problem that Turing solves. It allows us to do no more than tell it what the probability distributions are, then it samples from them efficiently, calculates expectation values as needed, and reports the results and their uncertainties and error estimates. We won't go into the details of how Turing accomplishes this feat, except to say that it implements the technology of Markov chain Monte Carlo (MCMC) sampling, a starting point for readers who are interested in investigating the theoretical background.

To tell Turing to generate a report about its inferences, we issue one command using its sample() function:

```
julia> flips = sample(coin(60, 100), SMC(), 1000)
```

Here coin() is the model function from Listing 13-3. Its arguments are the number of heads and the total number of flips—in this case 60 heads out of 100 coin tosses. The next argument selects a sampling strategy from among the handful supplied by the Turing package. The initials SMC stand for sequential Monte Carlo, which performs well on simple problems. The choice of sampler can be a matter of trial and error; different samplers are best suited to different problems. (See "Further Reading" on page 427 for links to some documentation for Turing's samplers.) The final argument, 1000, is the number of sampling experiments to conduct. Each one produces an estimate for Pheads, and Turing reports the mean of these estimates, which is its most likely value, as shown in Listing 13-4.

```
Chains MCMC chain (1000×3×1 Array{Float64, 3}):

Log evidence      = -4.5014682572661195
Iterations        = 1:1:1000
```

```
Number of chains  = 1
Samples per chain = 1000
Wall duration     = 12.73 seconds
Compute duration  = 12.73 seconds
parameters        = Pheads
internals         = lp, weight
```

Summary Statistics

parameters	mean	std	naive_se	mcse	ess	rhat	ess_per_sec
Symbol	Float64	Float64	Float64	Float64	Float64	Float64	Float64
Pheads	0.6024	0.0460	0.0015	0.0023	410.5088	1.0002	32.2499

Quantiles

parameters	2.5%	25.0%	50.0%	75.0%	97.5%
Symbol	Float64	Float64	Float64	Float64	Float64
Pheads	0.5058	0.5719	0.6092	0.6319	0.6862

Listing 13-4: The report from Turing

The report, which appears after 12.73 seconds on my laptop, contains a lot of information, but only a few numbers are essential for us. Under Summary Statistics, the Symbols are the random variables whose inferred values we want: in this case, only Pheads. The best guess that Turing has for Pheads is 0.6024. Another number to keep an eye on is rhat, which is 1.0002 in this example. If this number is far from 1.0, the sampling process did not converge properly, and we need to try a different sampler or alter the controls passed to the sampler, if it's one that accepts parameters.

Now we can think about addressing the question implied in the title of this section: is the coin fair? We can gain some insight by looking at the distribution of the 1,000 inferences for Pheads resulting from the sampling procedure. The histogram() function (see "Distributions" on page 321) gains the power to plot this with a simple call to histogram(flips; normalize=true) courtesy of the Turing and StatsPlots packages. We'll plot the histogram with a normal distribution curve on the same graph with the following:

```julia
julia> histogram(flips; normalize=true)
julia> plot!(Normal(0.6024, 0.0460); lw=2)
```

The parameters in the normal distribution, plotted in the second line, are the mean and standard deviation taken from the report in Listing 13-4. Figure 13-7 shows the result, where we can see that the sampling distribution from Turing is quite a good approximation to the normal distribution with the parameters that it reports.

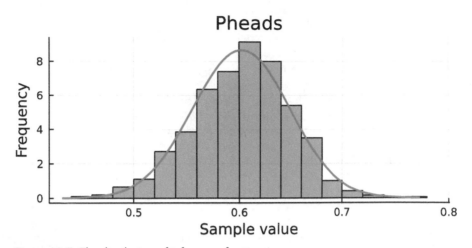

Figure 13-7: The distribution of inferences for Pheads

Why should the distribution of the mean values of Pheads be normal? After all, we set Pheads up with a uniform distribution in the model. The answer is that the distribution in Figure 13-7 is the distribution of *mean values* of the random variable Pheads. As demonstrated in "The Normal Distribution" on page 323 (using the same uniform distribution), the distribution of the means will be normal (Gaussian). This will be true regardless of the underlying distribution of the variable itself, which is an important theorem in probability theory and the fundamental reason for the ubiquity of the normal distribution.

We can apply any criterion we choose to decide whether this coin is fair after examining the sampling results. Although the most likely value for the probability of heads is very close to 0.6, strongly suggesting that we have a biased coin, it's *possible* that the coin is fair. We can estimate the probability that Pheads is $1/2$ directly from the normalized histogram. The two bars surrounding 0.5 on the horizontal axis have an area of about (0.52 - 0.48) × 0.8 = 0.32, yielding a probability of 3.2 percent that the coin is fair. The value of 0.8 comes from visually estimating the average height of the two relevant bins. We can also calculate this from the normal distribution:

```
julia> cdf(Normal(0.6024, 0.0460), 0.52) - cdf(Normal(0.6024, 0.0460), 0.48)
0.032725277247186525
```

The cdf() function, which stands for *cumulative density function*, returns the integral of the distribution supplied in the first argument from negative infinity to the value supplied in the second argument. Therefore, to extract the probability that a random variable governed by the distribution lies between two values, we need merely to subtract the results from two calls to cdf(). The value of 3.3 percent agrees pretty well with our estimate for the same interval from the histogram.

This coin has only a 3.3 percent chance of being fair. Is that strong enough evidence to convict it of bias? That's up to us.

Flipping the coin 100 times provides pretty strong evidence of its shady character. Intuitively, we understand that if we had flipped it only 10 times, and happened to observe six heads, that wouldn't be strong evidence of any non-fairness in the coin. Similarly, an observation of 600 heads after tossing the coin 1,000 times would be pretty conclusive.

We can see the results of these two scenarios by calling sample() twice and passing the result directly to histogram():

```julia
julia> histogram(sample(coin(6, 10), SMC(), 1000); normalize=:probability, fc=:lightgray)
julia> histogram!(sample(coin(600, 1000), SMC(), 1000); normalize=:probability, fc=:gray)
```

This is a quick way to compare the distributions when we're not interested in the detailed report.

NOTE   *Because the results returned by sample() are generated partly through random sampling, the details will be different every time. Everyone running the code samples in this section will observe slightly different distributions and means, although the overall conclusions should be invariant. In an important problem, a good practice would be to run more than one sampling experiment, try different samplers, and perhaps vary some of the details in the model concerning assumed distributions.*

Figure 13-8 shows the result.

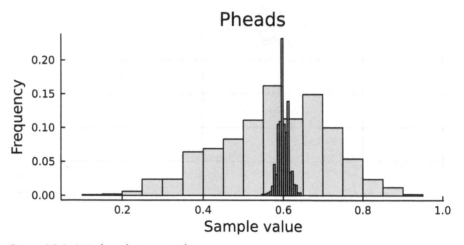

Figure 13-8: Weak and strong evidence

The lighter histogram, showing the inferences from 10 flips, clearly indicates that we have no evidence for bias in the coin. It's about as likely that Pheads is 1/2 as it is 6/10. However, the observation using 1,000 flips is unambiguous: 600 heads in that experiment makes it nearly impossible for the coin to be fair. The darker gray overlay of the second histogram shows a narrow distribution around Pheads = 0.6.

Inferring Model Parameters from Series Observations

In most applications of probabilistic programming, scientists are interested in inferring the causes of a series of observations taken over time, rather than merely a single number. We can extend the approach in the previous section to handle time series by considering the data gathered at each point in time to be a separate measurement with a distribution around some predicted value. The values can be predictions from nearly any type of model, as long as we can express it as a Julia function.

A Simple Mathematical Model

To demonstrate the approach, we'll first consider the problem of fitting a pair of parameters in a simple expression that we assume to be the cause of a series of observations. The model is a sine function and the two unknown parameters are its amplitude A and its frequency f, as shown in Listing 13-5.

```
const t = 0:π/50:4π;
A0 = 3.4; f0 = 2.7;
data = A0*sin.(f0*t) + 0.5 .* randn(length(t));

@model function wave(data)
    f ~ Uniform(0, 3)
    A ~ Uniform(0, 4)
❶ prediction = A*sin.(f*t)
    for i in eachindex(t)
      ❷ data[i] ~ Normal(prediction[i], 0.5)
    end
end;
```

Listing 13-5: The sine function with unknown frequency and amplitude as a model

After defining a series of times, we pick values for the A (amplitude) and f (frequency) parameters. We use these to generate some simulated observations, containing normally distributed errors, that we store in data. Our plan is to pretend we don't know the values of A and f and to use the data, along with the assumed sinewave dependence, to infer their values.

In the model, we assert a priori uniform distributions for the frequency and amplitude that establish limits for their possible values. For each possible set of values, we have a prediction ❶ for the time series that would result. We consider the data passed to the model to be a set of physical measurements, so we assume that the observation at each time is normally distributed around the "true" (predicted) value at that time, with a standard deviation of 0.5 ❷.

The inference through sampling proceeds as in the previous section. However, the SMC sampler seems to work poorly for this class of problems. The MH sampler (for Metropolis-Hastings) works far more reliably, and it's quite fast as well, but is a poor performer in other problems. (As mentioned earlier, we may need to experiment with a variety of sampling algorithms and their input parameters.) Listing 13-6 shows the sampling command and its truncated output.

```
julia> wavesample = sample(wave(data), MH(), 1000)
Chains MCMC chain (1000×3×1 Array{Float64, 3}):

Iterations        = 1:1:1000
Number of chains  = 1
Samples per chain = 1000
Wall duration     = 0.92 seconds
Compute duration  = 0.92 seconds
parameters        = f, A
internals         = lp

Summary Statistics
```

parameters	mean	std	naive_se	mcse	ess	rhat	ess_per_sec
Symbol	Float64	Float64	Float64	Float64	Float64	Float64	Float64
f	2.6876	0.0247	0.0008	0.0039	8.9062	1.1077	9.7230
A	3.4323	0.3867	0.0122	0.0681	2.5378	2.1700	2.7706

Listing 13-6: Inferring the values of parameters

The sampler returns reasonable results in less than one second. This is impressive, considering that the algorithm is sampling two parameters 1,000 times and using 200 data points, each with its own distribution, to infer the final distributions of A and f and their expectation values.

Let's visualize the inferred solution using the returned means of A and f superimposed on the simulated data and what we know is the true solution:

```
julia> plot(t, A0*sin.(f0*t); lw=2, legend=false, ylabel="A(t)", xlabel="t")
julia> plot!(t, data)
julia> A1 = 3.4323; f1 = 2.6876;
julia> plot!(t, A1*sin.(f1*t); ls=:dot)
```

In the first two lines, we plot the model with a thick line and the noisy data with a thinner line. The final plot command plots a sinewave using the inferences for A and f as a dotted line. Figure 13-9 shows the combined plot.

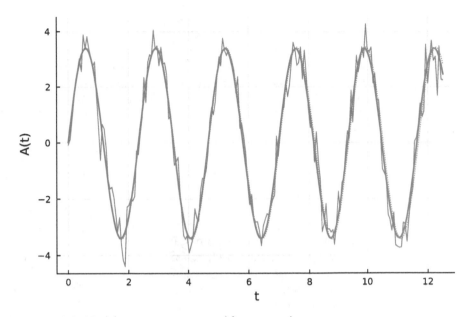

Figure 13-9: Model parameters recovered from noisy data

Figure 13-9 shows how the correct signal was recovered from the noisy observations. The periodic nature of the model means that the slight error in the inferred frequency will cause the curves to diverge further at later times.

An ODE Model

The model used for generating the prediction need not be a known function; it can be a set of differential equations. This is possible because Turing and DifferentialEquations are composable, another benefit of Julia's type system. The combination is immensely powerful, and opens up new arenas for research. In science our models often take the form of differential equations that encode, in general terms, our hypotheses about how the system works. Some of the details of the system may remain as parameters with unknown, or partially known, values. Probabilistic programming, using the general procedure outlined in "Inferring Model Parameters from Series Observations" on page 419, allows us to infer the most likely values of these parameters and then check, quantitatively, how well our purported model performs.

For example, we may measure the trajectory of a cannonball and think we know that its path is governed by Newton's laws of motion and the forces of gravity and air resistance. But we might not know the correct value of the gravitational acceleration on our planet or the coefficient of drag for the cannonball in its atmosphere. Assuming our differential equations are correct, we can use Turing and DifferentialEquations to infer the values of those two numbers from the observed trajectory, and then plug them back into the model to see whether we can reproduce the data. This approach eliminates a huge amount of trial and error, and it lets us iterate fluidly over variations in our models.

Returning to the parametric instability problem from Chapter 9, let's go backward: assume that we know we have a pendulum in a gravitational field, with a varying string length, and that we know the values for gravity, the pendulum mass, and the mean length of the string, but that the frequency and amplitude of the oscillation in the string's length are unknown. We will, however, assume that the function defining that oscillation is a sin(t), where, as before, t is time.

This example will show how we can work backward from data about the pendulum's behavior to an estimate of the driving frequency and amplitude, using the assumption of the underlying physical model behind the data. Naively, we might approach this problem by solving the differential equation, using the techniques from Chapter 9, multiple times, with various values of the unknown parameters, until we hit upon a solution that is close enough to the data. But this process will be computationally expensive and may not provide systematic knowledge of the uncertainty in the final result.

Listing 13-7 shows the problem set up for solution by the Differential Equations package, assembled here for convenience from Listings 9-8 and 9-9.

```
using DifferentialEquations

function pendulum!(du, u, p, t)
    L, g = p
    θ, ω = u
    du[1] = ω
    du[2] = -g/L(t) * sin(θ)
end

❶ g = 9.8; A = 0.2; f = 0.97
L(t) = 1.0 + A * cos(f*2*sqrt(g)*t)
p = [L, g]

u0 = [deg2rad(5), 0]
#    θ   ω   <- Initial conditions

tspan = (0, 80)

sol = solve(ODEProblem(pendulum!, u0, tspan, p); saveat=0.1)
```

Listing 13-7: The parametrically driven pendulum

In this example, the driving frequency is set to 3 percent smaller than the parametric resonance frequency ❶.

Before we proceed to apply Turing to this problem, let's take a look at how varying the f and A values affects the results. First, we'll plot the solution at resonance and slightly "detuned," at 0.95 resonance:

```
g = 9.8; A = 0.2; f = 1.0
L(t) = 1.0 + A * cos(f*2*sqrt(g)*t)
p = [L, g]
plot(solve(ODEProblem(pendulum!, u0, tspan, p)); idxs=1,
    legend=false, ylabel="A(t)")

f = 0.95
L(t) = 1.0 + A * cos(f*2*sqrt(g)*t)
p = [L, g]
plot!(solve(ODEProblem(pendulum!, u0, tspan, p)); idxs=1, lw=2)

annotate!(40, 1, ("Thin line:\nparametric forcing at resonance", 8))
annotate!(40, -0.5, ("Thick line:\n5% detuning", 8))
```

Figure 13-10 shows the two solutions.

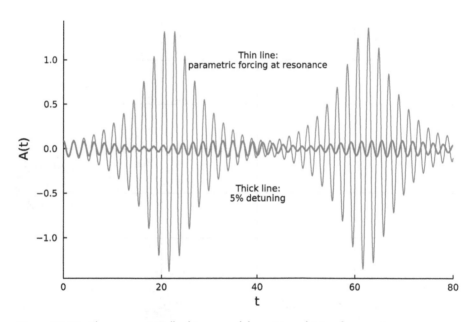

Figure 13-10: The parametrically driven pendulum at two driving frequencies

As Figure 13-10 makes clear, the solution is quite sensitive to the driving frequency.

Changing the driving amplitude also has a strong effect on the solution. Figure 13-11 shows the effect of two different forcing amplitudes at the same frequency.

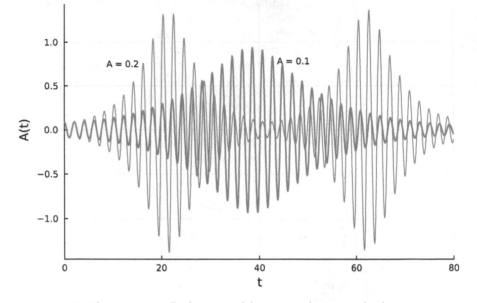

Figure 13-11: The parametrically driven pendulum at two driving amplitudes

Changing the forcing amplitude alone changes the envelope amplitude, the envelope timescale, and the frequency of the response.

When we compare these solutions, we can see that amplitude and frequency are interdependent. It's not a simple matter to infer either driving parameter from the response. Let's see how well probabilistic programming with Turing does with this problem. First we'll define a model with A and f uniformly distributed within reasonable intervals:

```
using Turing

@model function pdpen(observation)
    A ~ Uniform(0.0, 0.3)
    f ~ Uniform(0.9, 1.1)
    g = 9.8
    L(t) = 1.0 + A * cos(2*f*sqrt(g)*t)
    p = [L, g]
    prediction = Array(solve(ODEProblem(pendulum!, u0, tspan, p); saveat=0.1))[1, :]
    mstd = 0.1 * maximum(abs.(prediction))
    for i in eachindex(prediction)
        observation[i] ~ Normal(prediction[i], mstd)
    end
end
```

As in the simple sinewave model, we'll generate some noisy simulated data from the solution returned by DifferentialEquations for given values of A and f, and then use the Turing model to try to infer those numbers from the data. The program in the following listing goes through this procedure for a small set of values for A and f and plots the inferred numbers with the known values:

```
plot(; xrange=(0, 0.3), yrange=(0.9, 1.1), legend=false,
    xlabel="A", ylabel="f")
for A in range(0.02, 0.25; length=3)
    for f in range(0.95, 1.05; length=3)
    ❶  L(t) = 1.0 + A * cos(2*f*sqrt(g)*t)
        p = [L, g]
    ❷  sol = solve(ODEProblem(pendulum!, u0, tspan, p); saveat=0.1)
        mstd = 0.1 * maximum(abs.(Array(sol)[1, :]))
        observation = Array(sol)[1, :] + mstd * randn(length(sol))
    ❸  psamples = sample(pdpen(observation), MH(), 3000)
        scatter!([A], [f]; mc=:lightgray, ms=9)
        scatter!([mean(psamples[:A])], [mean(psamples[:f])];
                xerror=std(psamples[:A]), yerror=std(psamples[:f]),
                mc=:black, shape=:hexagon, ms=9)
    end
end
plot!()
```

For each A,f pair, the program defines a forcing function ❶ and generates a solution ❷ from the differential equation. We tell the solver to save solution points at regular intervals using the saveat keyword argument and scale the simulated noise to the amplitude of the solution. The purpose of the solution is to generate the simulated noisy observations, which we then feed to the sampler ❸. The next command places a mark on the A-f plane of the plot corresponding to the true values of A and f. Then we place a mark for the inferred values, with error bars taken from the standard deviations of the distributions returned by sample().

We can access the sampling results for individual parameters using indexing on the name of the parameter as a symbol, so psamples[:A] is an array of all 3,000 values for A in the distribution generated by the sampler. The mean of this array is its expectation value (and the value printed in the report printed in the REPL). The std() function calculates the standard deviation of an array, returning the same number as in the report under std.

Figure 13-12 shows the result.

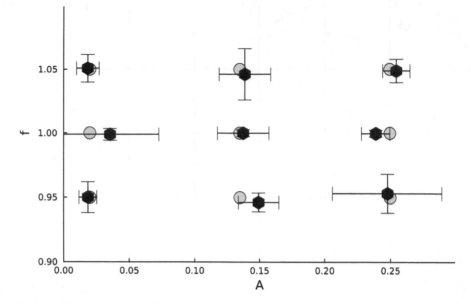

Figure 13-12: Inference of forcing parameters in the parametric pendulum

The experiment works well using 3,000 samples; however, the same program run with 1,000 samples performs distinctly worse. Figure 13-12 shows that each inferred value is correct within its reported standard deviation, and most of those spreads are small. Despite the complexity and sensitivity of this problem, Turing and DifferentialEquations were able to work together to confirm the faithfulness of the model and accurately induce the correct model parameters. Doubtless with further tuning of the sampling method, we could improve the results even further.

Conclusion

The field of scientific machine learning is making impressive strides and expanding rapidly as I write this. Julia users are perfectly positioned to take advantage of recent research in this field, as it finds application in the packages of the SciML ecosystem. Scientific machine learning selects some of the technologies developed in ML that can be fruitfully applied to science and engineering concerns. A survey of the entire field would be a book in itself. In this chapter we've explored a few central ideas and applied them to problems that, while interesting in themselves, are simple enough not to obscure the working of the SciML machinery with too much incidental detail. These ideas and techniques can be applied to all areas of quantitative science. This is an exciting field to follow. Wherever it goes, it will inevitably become a pillar of computational science.

FURTHER READING

- See "The Essential Tools of Scientific Machine Learning (Scientific ML)" by Christopher Rackauckas for an introduction to existing open source tools: *http://www.stochasticlifestyle.com/the-essential-tools-of-scientific-machine-learning-scientific-ml/*.

- A solid mathematical introduction to automatic differentiation is available at *http://www.ams.org/publicoutreach/feature-column/fc-2017-12*.

- Here is a hub for Julia's SciML documentation: *https://docs.sciml.ai/*.

- For a description of the various solver options for the `Differential Equations.jl` package, visit *https://docs.sciml.ai/DiffEqDocs/stable/basics/common_solver_opts/*.

- Details on the binomial distribution can be found at *https://www.itl.nist.gov/div898/handbook/eda/section3/eda366i.htm*.

- Documentation for the Turing package resides at *https://turinglang.org/dev/docs/using-turing/get-started*.

- For a tutorial on the use of Turing, visit *https://turinglang.org/dev/docs/using-turing/guide*.

14

SIGNAL AND IMAGE PROCESSING

I studied Latin in high school, and I was reading stuff from Cicero. And that signal took a few thousand years to get to me. But I was still interested in what he had to say.
–Seth Shostak

This chapter contains examples from problems in both signal and image processing. The two subjects are usually considered germane to unrelated areas of research: signal processing interests the audio or electrical engineer, while image processing is relevant to biologists and astronomers. However, they belong together because they use many of the same techniques, and the relevant tools have the same mathematical foundations. For many purposes, we can think of an image as just a two-dimensional signal, and apply similar algorithms to transform, smooth, filter, and more, extending the single time dimension to two (or three) space dimensions.

We'll first look at one-dimensional signals, considering the common case of an independent coordinate representing time. After that, we'll explore Julia's packages for image processing.

Signals in Time

Sound comes to us as a time-varying air pressure, and we store it as a record of amplitude versus time, where the amplitude may represent direct measurements of pressure or its conversion to electrical voltages or some other quantity by our measuring apparatus. We'll explore signal processing in Julia by working with a sound from nature.

Exploring a Sound Sample

Our real-life sound is the call of the endangered cactus ferruginous pygmy owl (*Glaucidium brasilianum cactorum*), a native of Arizona. I found the sound sample at *http://www.naturesongs.com/falcstri.html#cobo* and saved it on disk with the filename *cfpo1.wav*. The sample is a WAV file: a common file format for audio that nearly any music playback or sound editing software, on any operating system, can play. Listening to the sample reveals a call consisting of a short, medium-high-pitched vocalization repeated about three times per second for about 12 total seconds.

NOTE   *WAV files are often described erroneously as "uncompressed" audio. The audio data they contain is almost always compressed using one of a handful of available lossless compression algorithms (similar to the compression used in the ZIP family of file compression utilities). They take up far more space than the same sound compressed using a perceptual encoder such as that used for MP3 files, but such files are not useful for scientific signal processing and analysis.*

In a Linux terminal, we can get some information about the file using the file command:

```
$ file cfpo1.wav
cfpo1.wav: RIFF (little-endian) data, WAVE audio, Microsoft PCM, 8 bit, mono 8000 Hz
```

The output reflects the most common file format; the data is little-endian because the WAV format was invented at Microsoft. The third clause names the compression algorithm; Microsoft PCM is the most common. The rest of the output means that the samples were saved with 8 bits of precision, providing 2^8 = 256 available amplitude levels per point, and that we have one channel sampled at 8,000 samples per second.

Back in the Julia REPL, let's read in the sample, assign it to cfpo, and plot the waveform:

```
julia> using SignalAnalysis, SignalAnalysis.Units, Plots

julia> cfpo = signal("cfpo1.wav");

julia> plot(cfpo)
```

First we import two convenient packages for signal analysis. All the other examples in this section assume this `using` statement. The `SignalAnalysis` `.Units` package provides time and frequency unit abbreviations, and a handy form of time-based indexing that we'll use later.

The `signal()` function has many methods. When supplied with a string, it loads the named file and packages the data into a type defined in the package. The `SignalAnalysis` package also extends `Plots` to be able to plot signals directly. Figure 14-1 shows the waveform of the owl call.

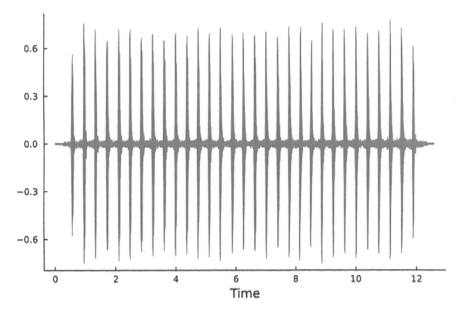

Figure 14-1: The call of the cactus ferruginous pygmy owl

As the sound sample contains 100,558 elements, plotting is not instantaneous. The plot recipe uses information about the sample rate to create a correct time axis, and labels the axis as well. The `signal()` function rescales the 8-bit samples to `Float64` numbers ranging from −1.0 to 1.0.

The `SignalAnalysis` package supplies several functions for extracting information about the signal. The following are the most important of these:

```
julia> framerate(cfpo)
8000.0f0

julia> nframes(cfpo)
100558

julia> duration(cfpo)
12.56975f0
```

The term `nframes` refers to samples and `duration()` reports the length of the signal in seconds.

Figure 14-1 shows the three-chirps-per-second structure of the owl call clearly, but we can't tell what note the owl is singing. Let's zoom in:

```
julia> one_chirp = plot(cfpo[2.05:2.25s]);

julia> chirp_zoomed = plot(cfpo[2.1:2.11s]);

julia> plot(one_chirp, chirp_zoomed; layout=(2, 1))
```

The first two plot statements take advantage of the convenient time-based indexing that the `SignalAnalysis` package enables. It frees us from having to convert between time and index number of the signal data. The indexing works only with seconds and only with a range of floats. To access the single frame at two seconds, we can write `cfpo[2.0:2.0s]`.

Figure 14-2 shows the combined plot: two segments of the signal at two different scales. The plot recipe always labels the plots beginning at t = 0, but we can always define `xticks` to reference the original time interval if desired.

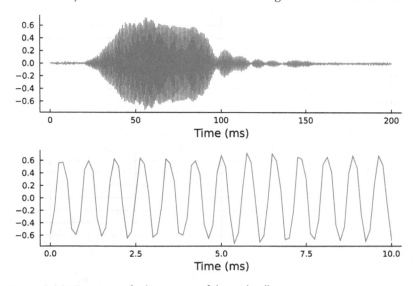

Figure 14-2: Two magnified segments of the owl call

The bottom plot in Figure 14-2 is in the middle of one of the chirps, and is sufficiently magnified to allow us to count cycles easily. There appear to be about 3.25 cycles in 2.5 ms (most easily counted from $t = 5.0$ ms, where a peak of the wave happens to align exactly with a grid line, to $t = 7.5$ ms), which is a frequency of $3.25/2.5\text{e}{-}3 = 1{,}300.0$ Hz, which is very close to the musical note E_6.

Analyzing Frequencies

One of the senses of the word *analysis* is the separating of something into component parts. We'll perform two types of frequency analysis of signals. The first type converts the signal, a function of amplitude versus time, into a function of amplitude versus frequency. This is the purpose of the Fourier transform, which assumes that the signal is periodic, and analyzes it into a sum of periodic functions (sines and cosines of various amplitudes, sines or cosines of various phases and amplitudes, or complex exponentials—all equivalent representations). The representation as a sum of frequencies is the signal's *spectrum*. The second type combines temporal and frequency information into a *spectrogram*. Here we no longer assume that the signal is periodic. The spectrogram shows us the spectrum as it varies in time.

The SignalAnalysis package provides several plotting routines we can use to visualize both types of frequency analysis. The psd() function plots the *power spectral density* of a signal based on its Fourier transform. Its interpretation is straightforward when applied to a periodic signal, which describes the owl call pretty well:

```
julia> psd(cfpo; xticks=0:100:4000, xrot=90, lw=2)
```

Since psd() uses the Plots package, we can supply the familiar keyword arguments. Figure 14-3 shows the spectrum.

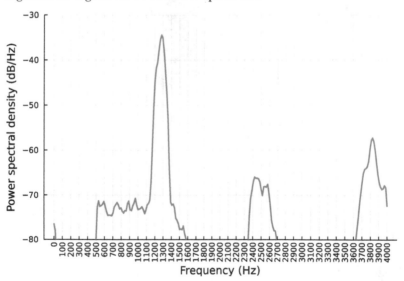

Figure 14-3: Fourier spectrum of the call of an owl

The spectrum has a peak just barely below 1,300 Hz, which agrees with our estimate from counting cycles of the waveform. We can also see peaks close to the second and third harmonics (twice and thrice 1,300 Hz).

Displays such as Figure 14-3 are useful analytic and diagnostic tools, but they don't convey a full idea of the nature of the signal under investigation. We can see that the signal is dominated by a 1,300 Hz frequency, with two strong overtones, but there's no hint of the rapid staccato performance.

For a fuller analysis, we turn to the spectrogram. The `SignalAnalysis` package also provides a function to create these visualizations easily:

```julia
julia> specgram(cfpo; c=:grayC)
```

Figure 14-4 contains the spectrogram, and clearly shows the frequency distribution of energy in the signal: the strong component near 1,300 Hz and the two higher harmonics at lower amplitudes. We can also see the temporal structure; the chirps repeating at about three times per second are obvious.

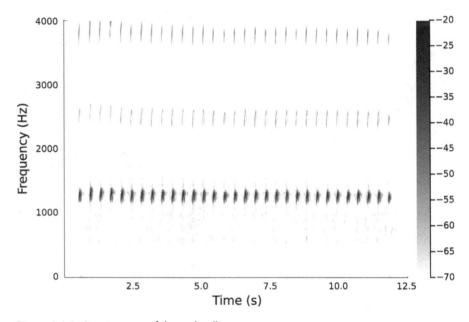

Figure 14-4: Spectrogram of the owl call

Spectrograms use Fourier transforms and a *window* sliding over the signal to calculate the spectrum as it evolves, resulting in a visualization combining frequency and time information. They're more informative than a `psd()`-type plot for any except periodic signals. Practical Fourier transform routines, such as the ones used by `psd()`, also use windowing, but for the purpose of eliminating the inevitable discontinuities at the edges of the signal and the resulting "leakage" of spurious high-frequency components.

NOTE   *This section presents the quickest and most convenient methods for signal analysis, with an emphasis on getting to the visualizations that interest most scientists. For* *more control, or to obtain direct access to spectra, import the* `DSP.jl` *package. The* `SignalAnalysis` *package wraps many of its routines, but importing* `DSP` *grants access to its definitions for various Fourier transform windows and other details that we can invoke with keyword arguments to the higher-level* `SignalAnalysis` *routines such as* `psd()`.

Now that we've dealt with two ways to examine the frequency spectra of signals, in the next section we'll explore methods for transforming the signal by altering the spectrum.

Filtering

A *filter* in the context of signal processing is a circuit, device, or, in our case, a computation, that attenuates some of the frequencies present in a signal. Perhaps the most familiar examples are the crossover circuits in speakers that route the high frequencies to the tweeters and the low frequencies to the woofers.

Filters are also important in empirical science—for example, in reducing noise in measurements. Imagine a sensor that records the variations in depth of a waterway. We might be interested in measuring the effect of tides, and detecting any long-term change in the average depth. These changes occur on the timescales of hours and longer. However, the measurements will be polluted by the more rapid changes caused by wind, weather, and passing boats. Using filtering, we can seek to erase the irrelevant data from the signal by eliminating frequencies faster than, say, one cycle per hour.

This strategy suggested in the previous paragraph is called a *low-pass* filter, because it attenuates frequencies *above* a specified cutoff, allowing those below the cutoff to pass. An example of a *high-pass* filter would be the crossover circuit leading to a speaker's tweeter.

Another type of filtering common in scientific instrumentation is a *notch* filter: one that attenuates frequencies near a target frequency. Notch filters are useful for eliminating 60 or 50 Hz power line noise from instruments through which the signal passes (but are only useful if the signal doesn't contain information near the power line frequency).

A *band-pass* filter attenuates anything outside a narrow band around a target frequency.

Making Filters with fir()

The `SignalAnalysis` package makes it easy to construct any of these types of filters and apply them to signals. In each case we begin with the `fir()` function to construct the filter. Its basic use involves three positional arguments and an optional keyword argument named `fs`, giving the sampling frequency of the signal.

The first argument is an integer number of *taps*, which is related to the number of terms retained in the polynomial that describes the filter. Essentially, a greater number of taps causes the filter to be more selective and its response to be smoother. The second and third arguments are the lower and upper bounds of the unfiltered frequency range. If we provide the fs keyword, we supply these arguments in Hz, kHz, or another unit from SignalAnalysis.Units. For example, Listing 14-1 shows how to make a low-pass filter that filters out everything above 2,000 Hz.

```
lpf = fir(127, 0, 2kHz; fs=8kHz);
```

Listing 14-1: Constructing a low-pass filter

The example makes a 127-tap filter, which is a typical value.

The lower bound for a low-pass filter is 0, as in the example. To make a high-pass filter, we pass nothing as the upper bound.

The SignalAnalysis package provides a plotting function to visualize the filters created with fir(). To see a plot of the frequency response of the lpf filter defined previously, we need simply enter:

```
julia> plotfreqresp(lpf; fs=8000)
```

This creates the plot shown in Figure 14-5.

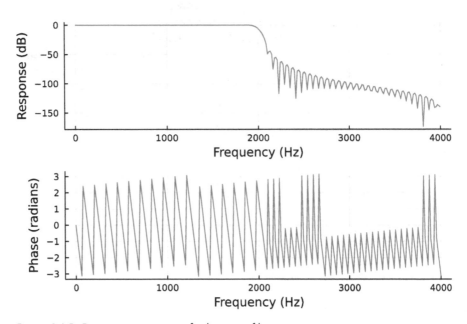

Figure 14-5: Frequency response of a low-pass filter

The top graph in Figure 14-5 indicates the amount by which the frequency component, given on the horizontal axis, will be reduced when the filter is applied to a signal. The units are in dB (decibels), which is conventional in signal processing. Figure 14-5 shows 0 dB, or no change, to the frequencies until we approach 2,000 Hz, when the signal is rapidly attenuated. For normal sounds, a reduction of 20 dB effectively silences the component it's applied to; therefore, the oscillations in the filter response below −50 dB have no audible effect.

The bottom graph shows the phase shifts created by the filter. These are usually inaudible, but may or may not be relevant, depending on one's plans for the filtered signal.

NOTE *For more detailed control over the filter characteristics, we can import DSP.jl and pass a method keyword to fir() using one of the filter construction methods described at* https://docs.juliadsp.org/stable/filters/.

The dB numbers in the frequency response plot are directly added to the values of frequency component peaks displayed in the psd() plot of a signal, which are also displayed in dB. To calculate the change in amplitude of the signal itself, we use the formula

$$\Delta dB = 20 \log_{10} \left(\frac{V_f}{V} \right)$$

where V is the amplitude of the component in the input signal and V_f is the filtered amplitude. Therefore, a 6 dB reduction halves the amplitude:

$$20 \log_{10}(1/2) \approx -6.021$$

To see the effect of larger tap values, we can make two additional low-pass filters with the same frequency ranges but with more taps:

```
lpf_255 = fir(255, 0, 2kHz; fs=8kHz);
lpf_1027 = fir(1027, 0, 2kHz; fs=8kHz);
```

A higher tap number will produce a filter with a response closer to ideal, as Figure 14-6 shows.

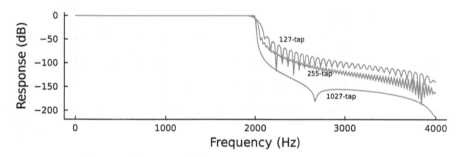

Figure 14-6: A low-pass filter using different tap numbers

Although using a higher tap number creates a cleaner filter with a sharper cutoff, it leads to a more expensive filtering calculation. The added calculation time makes no difference for our example, using a stored signal of moderate length, but it can be a consideration with real-time filtering, for example.

Applying Filters

To filter the signal, we can use the function sfilt():

```
julia> cfpo_lp = sfilt(lpf, cfpo);
```

This applies the low-pass filter defined in Listing 14-1 to the owl sample and assigns the result, a new signal, to cfpo_lp. Plotting the power spectrum of the filtered signal using psd() shows the effect of the filtering (see Figure 14-7).

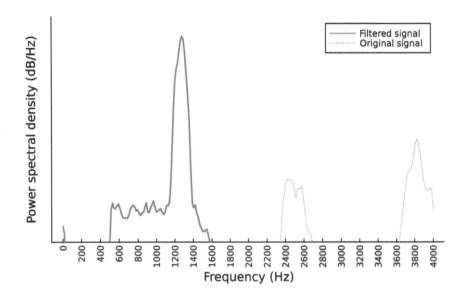

Figure 14-7: The filtered owl call

This plot displays the original, unfiltered spectrum using a dotted line and the filtered spectrum with a thicker, solid line. The spectrum below the low-pass cutoff at 2 kHz is untouched, while all frequencies above have been eliminated.

We create Figure 14-7 with the following commands:

```
julia> using Plots.PlotMeasures

julia> psd(cfpo_lp; lw=2, label="Filtered signal", legend=true)

julia> psd!(cfpo; ls=:dot, ticks=0:200:4000, xrot=90, label="Original signal",
            legend=true, margin=5mm)
```

It's necessary to repeat some of the keyword arguments when adding to psd() plots because the plotting recipe resets them.

The spectrogram of the filtered signal in Figure 14-8 also shows the elimination of the second and third harmonics with the preservation of the signal otherwise.

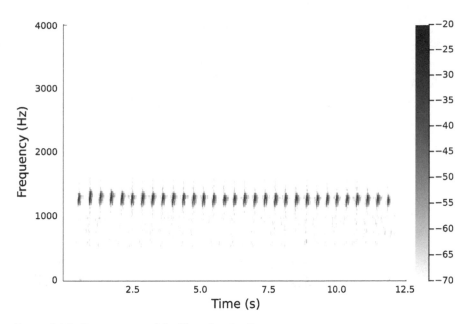

Figure 14-8: Spectrogram of the filtered owl call

Synthetic Signals

In order to ensure that we understand, quantitatively, signal analysis and filtering, let's start with a signal synthesized from known frequency components. Another method of signal() creates a signal with embedded sampling rate information from a normal vector. In Listing 14-2, we create a vector consisting of the addition of two sine waves, representing data with two components at 1,000 and 2,050 Hz sampled at 8 kHz. We then package the data into a signal.

```
julia> sin1000_2050 = signal(sin.((0.0:1.0/8000:1.0)*2π*1000) .+
                        0.5 .* sin.((0.0:1.0/8000:1.0)*2π*2050), 8000);
```

Listing 14-2: Creating a synthetic signal

We assigned the result to sin1000_2050. The second argument to signal() gives the sampling rate. The component at 2,050 Hz has half the amplitude of the component at 1,000 Hz. The power spectrum should show two peaks, with the higher-frequency peak 6 dB lower than the lower-frequency peak. Figure 14-9 shows the result of Listing 14-3.

```
julia> psd(sin1000_2050; xrange=(500, 2500), xticks=600:100:2500,
            xminorticks=2, yticks=-61:3:-02, xrot=45, margin=5mm)
```

Listing 14-3: Spectrum of a synthetic signal

Because the signal contains embedded sampling rate information, psd() is able to scale the plot correctly.

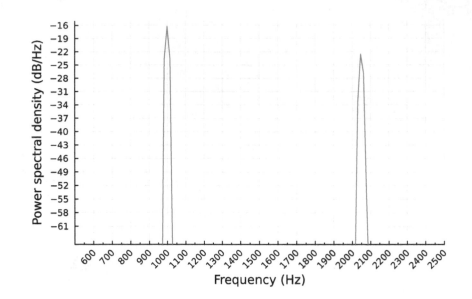

Figure 14-9: Spectrum of a synthetic signal with two frequency components

Figure 14-9 shows the power spectrum with two narrow peaks where we put them, and the correct 6 dB difference in their amplitudes.

Now let's measure the effect of filtering. We'll use the lpf filter defined in Listing 14-1, but first we need to take a closer look at it near its cutoff frequency:

```julia
julia> plotfreqresp(lpf; fs=8000, xrange=(1800, 2100), yrange=(-50, 1),
                     yticks=0:-4:-50, xticks=1800:50:2100, right_margin=5mm)
```

The expanded plot of the filter response in Figure 14-10 (with the phase response omitted) shows that the filter should reduce the 2,050 Hz component by 16 dB.

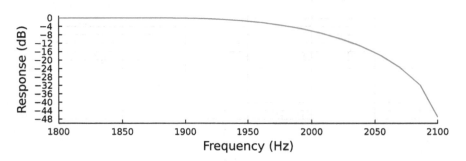

Figure 14-10: The cutoff region of the low-pass filter

We can check whether the filter is working as expected by overlaying the power spectrum of the filtered signal onto the plot created in Listing 14-3:

```
julia> psd!(sfilt(lpf, sin1000_2050), xrange=(500, 2500), xticks=600:100:2500,
            xminorticks=2, yticks=-61:3:-02, xrot=45, margin=5mm)
```

Figure 14-11 shows that the higher-frequency peak is reduced by 16 dB while the lower-frequency peak is unchanged.

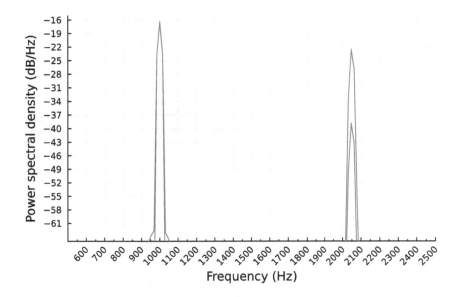

Figure 14-11: Power spectrum of the filtered synthetic signal

This little exercise shows that the filters have predictable effects, altering the spectra without introducing artifacts.

Saving Signals

We can read a WAV file from disk into a signal using the signal() function, but saving a signal as a WAV file requires importing the WAV.jl package:

```
julia> using WAV
julia> wavwrite(cfpo_lp, "cfpo_lp.wav"; compression=WAVE_FORMAT_PCM, nbits=8)
```

The keyword arguments select a compression format and word size that's compatible with a wide variety of software. After making the wavwrite() call, a WAV file called *cfpo_lp.wav* will exist on the disk drive.

If we want to save our sin1000_2050 signal as a WAV file, we first have to scale it to have unit amplitude:

```
julia> scaled = sin1000_2050 ./ maximum(sin1000_2050)
```

Then we save it using wavwrite() as before and play it using any audio software.

Image Processing

Let's consider an image interpretation task common in medicine and laboratory biology: how many blood cells are in a photograph of a blood sample taken through a microscope? The traditional method of acquiring this "blood count" was to enumerate the cells manually, a tiresome and error-prone process. We'll see how to use various image processing techniques with Julia to automate the procedure. The result will be a faster and more accurate count that doesn't require tedious labor. However, the techniques we'll investigate here aren't limited to blood counts. We could apply them to everything from counting bacteria to analyzing satellite reconnaissance.

Loading and Converting Images

The command using Images imports the file and image input-output functions, including optimized routines for most image types:

```
julia> using Images
```

```
julia> frog_blood = load("frogBloodoriginal.jpg");
```

After the import, a simple load() command reads the file into an image, which in Julia is an array of pixels.

When working in a notebook, such as Pluto, the results of image operations are displayed as images; in the terminal REPL, they're displayed similarly to other arrays. For graphical image display from the REPL, the ImageView package supplies the imshow() function. The window opened by imshow() features a few GUI powers, the most useful of which is a display of pixel address and color value in response to moving the mouse pointer over the image.

Images can be matrices of numbers or pixel types. There are several types of pixels, but the ones we'll be using are RGB and Gray pixels. Since we loaded the frog_blood image from a color picture, it's an array of RGB (red-green-blue) pixels:

```
julia> eltype(frog_blood)
RGB{N0f8}
```

This is clearly a parametric type (see "Parametric Types" on page 248). The parameter N0f8 is another (parametric) type that maps unsigned 8-bit integers to floats in the range [0.0, 1.0]. An element of frog_blood looks like the following:

```
julia> frog_blood[1, 1]
RGB{N0f8}(0.361,0.008,0.384)
```

This would be purple: nearly equal amounts of red and blue and almost no green.

If we want to replace the extreme upper-left pixel with pure green, we could execute:

```
frog_blood[1, 1] = RGB{N0f8}(0.0, 1.0, 0.0)
```

However, we won't.

We can convert the color image to a grayscale version by broadcasting Gray() as a conversion function to the image array:

```
frog_blood_gs = Gray.(frog_blood);
save("frog_blood_gs.jpg", frog_blood_gs)
save("frog_blood_gs.png", frog_blood_gs)
```

The listing also shows how to save images in files. The save() function converts image data to the file format indicated by the filename extension. Here we've saved two versions of the same image, one as a *.jpg* file and one as a *.png* file.

Figure 14-12 shows the grayscaled image.

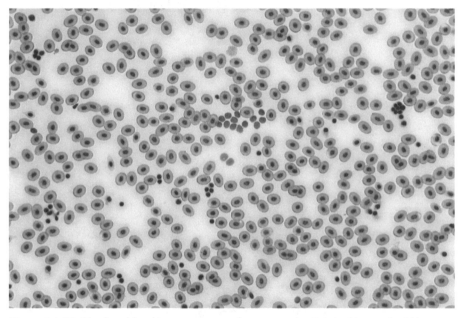

Figure 14-12: The frog blood image converted to grayscale. Original image by Wayne Large (CC BY-ND 2.0). Available from https://flic.kr/p/cBDUEG.

Other useful color conversion functions are red(), green(), and blue(), which extract the named color channels from an RGB pixel and can also, of course, be broadcast to entire images to separate them into their color channels.

In order to compare two, or several, versions of an image, perhaps to eyeball the effect of a transformation or processing step, the mosaicview() function is handy:

```
julia> imshow(mosaicview(red.(frog_blood), green.(frog_blood),
        blue.(frog_blood), frog_blood_gs; ncol=2, npad=6))
```

This command creates four images showing the three color channels of the original frog_blood image and the composite grayscale version, sticks them together in a grid, then displays them. If working in a notebook, we don't need the imshow() call. The ncol argument specifies the numbers of columns in the image grid (an nrows is also available), and the npad argument puts a border of the specified number of pixels between the images.

Figure 14-13 shows what mosaicview() produces.

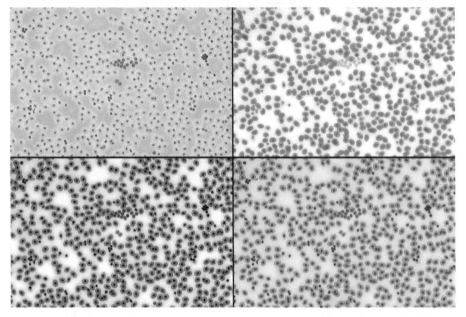

Figure 14-13: The red, green, blue, and all channels (top to bottom, left to right) of the frog blood image

The original image, containing all of the color channels, is in the lower-right quadrant.

Counting Cells Using an Area Fraction

Our first attempt at automating the counting of blood cells will use the ImageBinarization package. This package contains a handful of algorithms for separating an image into a "foreground" and a "background," coloring the foreground pure black and the background pure white. In other words, each pixel in the original image is assigned either 0.0 or 1.0, depending on the results of the algorithm invoked. The package documentation displays examples of the results of all the available algorithms on a variety of image types.

The goal is to generate an image that separates the blood cells from everything else, as much as possible. This binary image will then be a good starting point for further analysis. We've already made some progress in this direction through the color separations shown in Figure 14-13. The blue channel, at the bottom, seems to have increased the contrast between the (larger) red blood cells and the other particles. Instead of binarizing the original color image, we'll start with the blue channel:

```julia
julia> using ImageBinarization

julia> frog_blood_blue = blue.(frog_blood);

julia> frog_blood_b1 = binarize(frog_blood_blue, Intermodes())
```

The binarize() function takes the image as the first argument and the name of the binarization algorithm as the second argument, and returns the binarized image. The documentation describes the details of the Intermodes algorithm. For our purposes, it does a good job at detecting discrete structures, such as cells, against a plain background.

Figure 14-14 shows the binarized image.

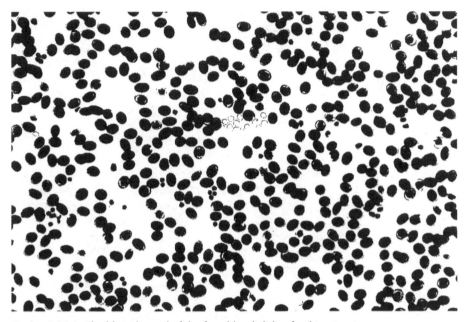

Figure 14-14: The blue channel of the frog blood slide after binarization

We'll use this image as the basis for the blood count.

If we knew the average area of the blood cells in the image, we could divide that into the total area occupied by all blood cells to arrive at an estimate of the number of cells. The cells appear to be approximately elliptical (in this two-dimensional image).

Using the GUI in the imshow() window, I used the pixel readout to measure the major and minor axis lengths of four typical cells at 26.8 pixels and a typical minor axis at 24.5 pixels. Using $A = \pi r_1 r_2$ for the area of an ellipse with radii r_1 and r_2, the average of the four areas was 511.3 square pixels.

Finding the total blood fraction is simple using the binarized image. In frog_blood_b1, the cells are black, with a pixel value of 0, and the background is white, with a value of 1. The total cell count is therefore sum(1 .- frog_blood_b1), which evaluates to 255,029.0. Dividing this result by the average cell area yields 499 cells.

Counting Cells by Recognizing Features

We can improve on the estimate in the previous section by exploiting algorithms that search for features with particular shapes in the image. The Hough transform (see "Further Reading" on page 465 for background) is one such class of algorithms that can be specialized to various shapes. The `ImageFeatures` package, which we'll assume is imported in the following examples, offers implementations for detecting lines and circles. As the features we need to detect resemble circles, we'll use the `hough_circle_gradient()` function, an implementation of the Hough transform for circles.

Before applying the algorithm, we'll process the image to make its task easier and produce a more accurate result. One problem with the image is that the cells we want to count are not circles, but elongated. Hough transforms for ellipses do exist, but are not yet available in the `ImageFeatures` package. Another problem is that many cells are touching, and a few are overlapping. The Hough transform can deal with touching and overlapping circles, but it has a better time with cleanly separated shapes.

Nature has provided some assistance with the second problem: each cell has a nucleus, clearly delineated in the picture. Even when blood cells are in contact or overlapping, their nuclei are separated. If we could eliminate most of everything except the nuclei from the image, we could simply count those to get the blood count.

Here we are fortunate: the color of the nuclei makes them easy to distinguish from everything else in the image. This may not be apparent to the eye, but by placing the mouse cursor on the nuclei in the `imshow()` window, and comparing with other locations, we can see that the nuclei are unique in having a green value close to 0 while having a red value > 0.2. We can confirm this in other ways—for example, by plotting the three color components along lines through the image.

The following array comprehension creates a new image from the original pixel by pixel, by leaving the pixels within the nucleus color range unchanged, while turning the others white:

```
julia> nuclei = Gray.([(green(e) < 0.1) & (red(e) > 0.2) ? e :
            RGB{N0f8}(1.0, 1.0, 1.0) for e in frog_blood]);
```

We also transform the result into a grayscale image for further processing and printing. Figure 14-15 shows the result.

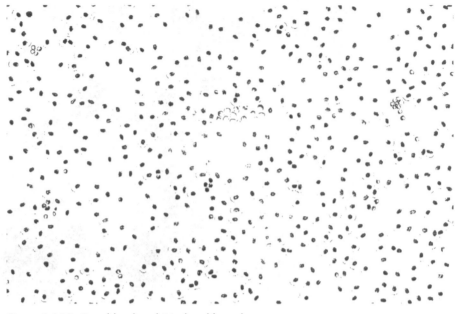

Figure 14-15: Frog blood nuclei isolated by color

We've managed to isolate the nuclei pretty well and eliminate some of the particles that are something other than blood cells.

Figure 14-15 is a good candidate for the circle-finding algorithm, but we must complete two preliminary steps first. The hough_circle_gradient() function doesn't operate on actual images, but on maps of *edges* and *phases*. The edge map is the output of an edge-detection algorithm, transforming the image into, essentially, a line drawing tracing its shapes. The map of phases is a matrix of angles calculated from the edge map, giving the direction at every point of its gradient, as an angle from $-\pi$ to π.

The canny() function is an excellent edge detector:

```julia
julia> edges = canny(nuclei, (0.15, 0.0))
```

Its second argument is a tuple of thresholds used for defining an edge from the input image (which must be grayscale). I arrived at the values it contains through trial and error, aiming for a set of edges that captured the nuclei while ignoring most of the scattering of white blood cells and other particles. Figure 14-16 shows the output of the canny() function.

Figure 14-16: Edge detection of the nuclei image

This is a pretty clean result, and is what we were aiming for.

The phase calculation itself requires two steps—first the gradient map itself and then the phases derived from it:

```julia
julia> dx, dy = imgradients(edges, KernelFactors.ando5);

julia> phases = phase(dx, dy);
```

With the edges and phases computed, we can run the Hough transform:

```julia
julia> centers, radii = hough_circle_gradient(edges, phases, 1:5; min_dist=20);
```

After this call, centers contains a vector of indices giving the locations of each circle and radii a vector of their corresponding radii. The length of either vector gives the number of circles found. In this case, the length is 534, which is in reasonable agreement with the estimate of 499 we arrived at earlier.

The third argument to hough_circle_gradient() gives the allowed range for the circle radii, in pixels. The min_dist keyword argument is the minimum allowed distance between circle centers.

To see how well the circle fitting did, and how much confidence we should lend to the estimate of 534 blood cells, we can use the centers array to draw circles directly on the original image where the hough_circle_gradient() function says they should be:

```
julia> using ImageDraw

julia> for p in centers
           draw!(frog_blood, CirclePointRadius(p, 15; thickness=8, fill=false))
       end
```

The draw!() function, provided by ImageDraw, mutates its first argument by drawing shapes on it, in white by default. The CirclePointRadius() in the second argument creates a circle at point p with radius 15; the fill=false creates an open circle with perimeter thickness controlled by the thickness keyword.

Figure 14-17 shows the result of drawing the circles on top of the (grayscale version of) the original image.

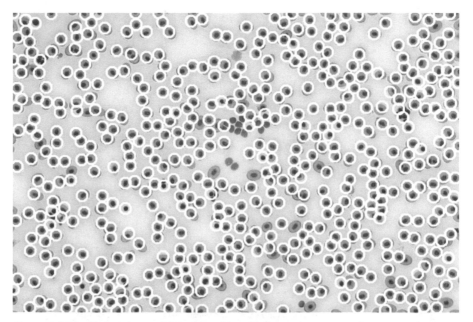

Figure 14-17: Circles detected by a Hough transform

Figure 14-17 shows that the Hough transform did an excellent job. Nearly every blood cell is marked with a circle, and most of the other objects are ignored. There are a few misses and a few false detections, but, on the whole, the count of 534 is quite accurate.

The image processing pipeline described in this section would be practical for automating blood counts, although the specific parameters would need to be adjusted for different types of samples, different stains, and so on. The approach is far faster and probably more accurate than manual counting.

Applying Advanced Array Concepts

As an image is an array, various advanced array concepts available in Julia can make their manipulation more convenient and concise. This section explores techniques for dealing with arrays that we haven't used directly up to now, although we've seen how they're used in several packages. Placed within an image processing context, their use becomes easier to visualize.

Views

A *view* is a reference to another array or to a section of another array. The other array is called the *parent*. A view is a kind of virtual array, which occupies almost no memory: it shares memory with the parent, so modifying one modifies the other.

NOTE   *It is dangerous to alter the shape of the parent array after creating a view. Subsequent operation on the view may create out-of-bounds memory accesses or segmentation faults.*

To see how views work, we'll create a small grid of middle-gray values and a view pointing to every other element in the grid:

```
julia> rgi = rand(Float64, (10, 10)) .* 0.2 .+ 0.4;

julia> checkers = @view rgi[1:2:end, 1:2:end];

julia> size(checkers)
(5, 5)

julia> checkers .= 0.0;

julia> black_squares = heatmap(rgi; c=:grays, clim=(0.0, 1.0), colorbar=false);

julia> checkers .= 1.0;

julia> white_squares = heatmap(rgi; c=:grays, clim=(0.0, 1.0), colorbar=false);

julia> plot(black_squares, white_squares)
```

❶

The second line shows how to create a view with the @view macro. The checkers view, defined by selecting alternate squares of the parent array, forms a checkerboard pattern. Its size is half that of the parent. After setting all its elements to 0.0 ❶, the corresponding elements in the parent are likewise modified. We can change the values of elements in the view repeatedly, and these updates are reflected in the parent. Figure 14-18 shows the outcome.

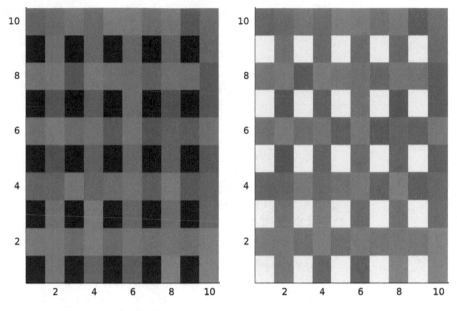

Figure 14-18: Patterns created using a view

This example shows how views can simplify certain expressions. They're also useful as an aid to memory parsimony. If a computation uses parts of arrays as intermediate containers, which we don't need in the final result, we can avoid allocating memory to hold these temporary structures by using views instead.

As an illustration, here are two versions of a little function that returns the difference between the sums of alternate elements in an array:

```
function odd_even_difference(a::AbstractArray)
    return sum(a[begin:2:end]) - sum(a[begin+1:2:end])
end

function odd_even_difference2(a::AbstractArray)
❶ return @views sum(a[begin:2:end]) - sum(a[begin+1:2:end])
end

julia> using BenchmarkTools

julia> @btime odd_even_difference(rand(Int(1e7)));
  96.716 ms (6 allocations: 152.59 MiB)

julia> @btime odd_even_difference2(rand(Int(1e7)));
  62.116 ms (2 allocations: 76.29 MiB)
```

The @views macro ❶ transforms all slice operations in the expression to its right into view operations. The first version of the program creates two arrays and computes the sum of odd and even indexed elements. The second performs the same computation, but by creating views instead of new arrays. The timing runs show that using views cut the memory consumption in half while also decreasing runtime by a third. Avoiding unnecessary array copying by using views where possible is an easy optimization.

AxisArrays

With the AxisArrays package, we can give names to array dimensions and axes, give units to arrays, and enjoy more flexible indexing. Dataframes (see "Dataframes" on page 333) also allow us to name rows and columns, but are limited to two dimensions.

The following example shows how to name the rows and columns of a matrix:

```
julia> using AxisArrays

julia> ae = AxisArray(reshape(1:100, 10, 10); row='a':'j', col='A':'J')
2-dimensional AxisArray{Int64,2,...} with axes:
    :row, 'a':1:'j'
    :col, 'A':1:'J'
And data, a 10x10 reshape(::UnitRange{Int64}, 10, 10) with eltype Int64:
    1   11  21  31  41  51  61  71  81   91
    2   12  22  32  42  52  62  72  82   92
    3   13  23  33  43  53  63  73  83   93
    4   14  24  34  44  54  64  74  84   94
    5   15  25  35  45  55  65  75  85   95
    6   16  26  36  46  56  66  76  86   96
    7   17  27  37  47  57  67  77  87   97
    8   18  28  38  48  58  68  78  88   98
    9   19  29  39  49  59  69  79  89   99
   10   20  30  40  50  60  70  80  90  100
```

With this definition, we can index using the numbers that we're used to or the names that we've assigned to the axes, or mix them up:

```
julia> ae['a', 'B']
11

julia> ae[1, 2] == ae['a', 2] == ae[1, 'B']
true
```

❶
```
julia> ae['a':'c', 'B':'D']
2-dimensional AxisArray{Int64,2,...} with axes:
    :row, ['a', 'b', 'c']
    :col, ['B', 'C', 'D']
And data, a 3x3 Matrix{Int64}:
```

```
11  21  31
12  22  32
13  23  33
```

❷ `julia> ae[col=2, row=1]`
`11`

The example shows that we can slice with our custom names ❶ as we do with numerical indices, and that, if we use the names of the dimensions, we can supply indices in any order ❷. We can use any names where we use row and col here. They're defined only within index expressions; they don't exist as variables outside the brackets.

The next example shows how to incorporate units into the definition of an array:

```julia
julia> using Unitful

julia> mm = u"mm";

julia> cm = u"cm";

julia> rgin = AxisArray(rand(Float64, (10, 10)) .* 0.2 .+ 0.4,
            Axis{:y}(0mm:1mm:9mm), Axis{:x}(0cm:1cm:9cm));

julia> rgin[x=3, y=2] == rgin[1mm, 2cm] == rgin[2, 3] == rgin[x=2cm, y=1mm] ==
       rgin[2, 2cm]
true
```

This shows the use of the `Axis{}()` constructor, and, in the final line, various ways we can index into the array, including mixing numerical and unit indices.

We can use an ellipsis, from the automatically imported `EllipsisNotation` package, to represent ranges of units:

```julia
julia> rgin[1mm .. 2mm, 1cm .. 3cm] == rgin[1mm .. 2.3mm, 10mm .. 30mm]
true
```

This illustrates two properties of dimension ranges. We can use equivalent units, here using 10 mm = 1 cm, and the endpoints of the intervals need not lie exactly on an element of the array. Beware that the indexing rounds *down* and not to the nearest element.

Let's define a rectangle using ranges of lengths, paint it white, and plot the resulting array:

```julia
julia> rgin[2mm .. 7.2mm, 3cm .. 4.9cm] .= 1.0;

julia> heatmap(rgin; c=:grays, clim=(0.0, 1.0), colorbar=false, ratio=1,
           xticks=(1:10, ["$(i)mm" for i in 0:9]),
           yticks=(1:10, ["$(i)cm" for i in 0:9]),
           xrange=(0, 11))
```

The plotting command is an example of custom labeled ticks. Figure 14-19 shows the new state of rgin.

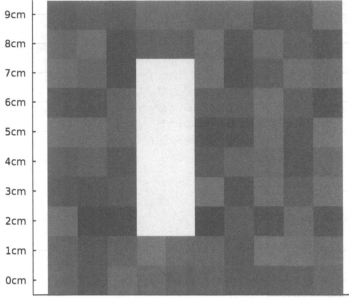

Figure 14-19: We paint this white rectangle by specifying physical lengths.

The direct use of physical dimensions to index arrays frees us from the mental or programmatic labor of constantly translating between integer indices and the quantities that they represent in our models.

OffsetArrays

Those with experience in Python or C, when encountering Julia for the first time, sometimes complain about its 1-based indexing, whereas old Fortran hands know that it's a better choice. The former group may be pleased to know that in Julia, as in Fortran, we can make arrays that start anywhere.

DON'T ASSUME 1-BASED INDEXING

Assuming that an array passed to a function will be 1-based is a source of occasional bugs in public packages. The existence of OffsetArrays is the reason for our earlier warning not to iterate over arrays with:

```
for i = 1:length(A) # Do not do this.
    # ...expressions with A[i]...
```

Instead, use eachindex(A) or another construction that generates legal indices. But there is another reason: using eachindex() generates more efficient memory accesses for certain types of arrays.

The OffsetArrays package provides several ways to create an OffsetArray. We can call the OffsetArray() function with the source array and each dimension's *offset* as positional arguments. A dimension's offset is how far its indices are shifted from their normal position. An offset of 0 means no shift, and an offset of −2 means that the dimension's index runs from −1 to two less than its length. To illustrate how an OffsetArray works, we'll start with our random gray matrix again:

```julia
julia> using OffsetArrays, Random

julia> rgen = MersenneTwister(7654);

julia> rgi = rand(rgen, Float64, (10, 10)) .* 0.2 .+ 0.4;

julia> rgi_offset = OffsetArray(rgi, -3, 2);

julia> rgi[1, 1]
0.5447560977385423

julia> rgi_offset[-2, 3]
0.5447560977385423
```

In this example, we use a seeded random number generator (see "Random Numbers in Julia" on page 307) so that the results will be identical for readers trying these commands. The (-2, 3) position of rgi_offset corresponds to the (1, 1) position of rgi.

This use of OffsetArray() creates a view, rather than a copy of the original, as shown in Listing 14-4.

```julia
julia> rgi_offset[-2, 3] = 0.0
0.0

julia> rgi[1, 1]
0.0
```

Listing 14-4: OffsetArrays are views.

Since the two arrays share memory, modifying rgi_offset modifies rgi. Of course, we can make a new array using copy() if needed:

```julia
julia> rgi_offset_copy = copy(OffsetArray(rgi, -3, 2));

julia> rgi_offset_copy[-2, 3] = 1.0
1.0

julia> rgi[1, 1]
0.0
```

Painting part of the array white illustrates that ranges work as before, taking into account the offsets:

```julia
julia> rgi_offset[0:5, 8:11] .= 1.0;
```

Figure 14-20 shows the image of the array, with the black element set in Listing 14-4 and the white rectangle set in this example. The plotting grid for heatmaps is centered on the elements, so we can examine which elements were changed to verify that we understand the indexing ranges.

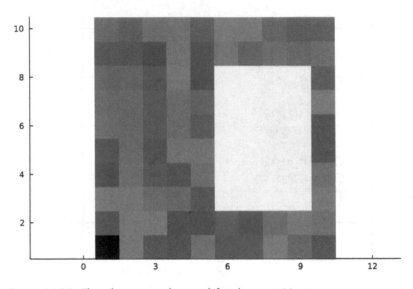

Figure 14-20: The white rectangle was defined as an OffsetArray.

Plotting with heatmap() doesn't work with OffsetArrays unless we explicitly supply coordinate vectors. In other words, we can call heatmap(rgi), but must use heatmap(1:10, 1:10, rgi_offset) to prevent the plotting routine from getting confused. The two calls produce the same image in this case, as the two arrays share memory.

OffsetArray() provides another syntax, using ranges of indices rather than single offsets. This method is convenient when extracting a subset of an existing array:

```julia
julia> passage = Float64.(Gray.(load("titanPassage.jpg")));

julia> passage = reverse(passage; dims=1);

julia> middle_passage = OffsetArray(passage[300:600, 400:700], 300:600, 400:700); ❶

julia> passage[300:600, 400:700] .= 0.0;

julia> passage[350:550, 450:650] = middle_passage[350:550, 450:650]; ❷
```

First we load a color photograph, convert it to grayscale, and then to a floating-point array, assigning the result to the passage. Since we plan to inspect the images in this example using heatmap(), we flip the image vertically for convenience to undo the effect of the orientation of the vertical axis.

Using OffsetArray(), we extract a square portion of the image and assign it to middle_passage ❶. This line shows another way to establish the offset indices: instead of a single integer offset, we supply the range of indices indexing the array. We choose these to be identical to the indices used to extract the sub-image, so that a pixel addressed in the extracted part will correspond to the pixel in the original image with the same indices. This technique greatly simplifies programs where we want to maintain a correspondence between an array and a sub-array, eliminating the need to constantly translate indices. The middle_passage matrix is a new array, not a view, because the index ranges create a copy.

The next line paints the square region, from which we took the extract, black.

In the final line, we replace a portion of the black square with a portion of the extracted part of the image ❷. Since the index ranges in both arrays are identical, the replaced part of the image will exactly correspond to what was there originally. The result is a black frame around a part of the image, with nothing else altered, as Figure 14-21 shows.

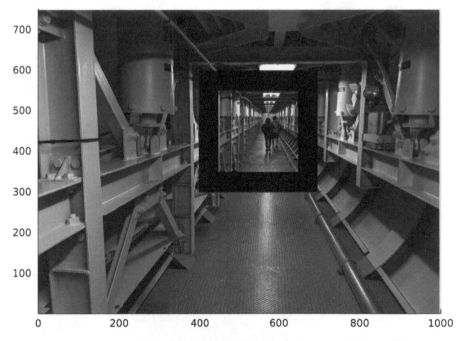

Figure 14-21: OffsetArrays make many image manipulations easier. Original photograph taken inside a Titan missile facility by Lee Phillips (CC BY-ND 2.0).

The use of offset indices makes this code easier to write and read, and less prone to errors. With conventional arrays we would have been forced to add lines performing array arithmetic to translate between pixel ranges in the large and extracted images, or construct the frame from pieces.

The OffsetArrays package proves two additional ways to construct array offsets automatically, both of which can be convenient in image processing. We can order up an OffsetArray centered on an array:

```
julia> passage = Float64.(Gray.(load("titanPassage.jpg")));
```

❶ julia> OffsetArrays.center(passage)
```
(375, 500)
```

```
julia> passage[375, 500]
0.25098039215686274
```

❷ julia> passage_centered = OffsetArrays.centered(passage);

```
julia> passage_centered[0, 0]
0.25098039215686274
```

The center() function ❶ from OffsetArrays returns the index of the center of an array (if the array has an odd number of elements along some dimension, it rounds down). The package's centered() function ❷ creates an OffsetArray with the index [0, 0] at its center. We usually need to qualify these function names with the package name because of collisions.

Having the center of index space at the center of an array is helpful in the common situation where the array represents a quantity in physical space, or in space and time, where we often use a coordinate system with the origin at the center. Here's another visual example, where having the [0, 0] point at the center of an image simplifies calculations:

```
julia> dmax = minimum(size(passage_centered))/2

julia> for j in eachindex(passage_centered[1, :]),
           i in eachindex(passage_centered[:, 1])
           passage_centered[i, j] *= max(0.0, 1.0 - sqrt(i^2 + j^2)/dmax)
       end
```

We've set dmax to the distance from the center to end along the shorter dimension. Then we multiply each pixel by a decreasing function of distance from the center. Figure 14-22 shows the result, a centered circular frame darkening toward the edges.

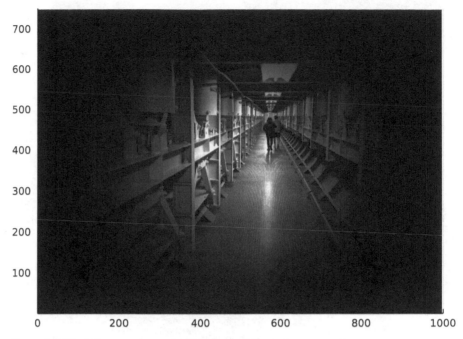

Figure 14-22: OffsetArrays make it easy to reference the center of an array.

Using a centered OffsetArray simplifies the code, allowing us to dispense with the index arithmetic usually needed to reference the center of an array.

Cartesian Indices

Julia's *cartesian indices* are a powerful tool that can greatly simplify all kinds of computations with arrays. The two relevant types built into Julia are the CartesianIndex and CartesianIndices. A CartesianIndex represents an address of an element in an array of any size. CartesianIndices are iterators that span a rectangular region, of any dimensionality, within an array.

For concreteness, and so that we can look at pictures, we'll concentrate on two-dimensional arrays, as shown in Listing 14-5.

```
julia> ci = CartesianIndex(1, 1)
CartesianIndex(1, 1)

julia> collect(5ci:8ci)
4×4 Matrix{CartesianIndex{2}}:
 CartesianIndex(5, 5)  CartesianIndex(5, 6)  CartesianIndex(5, 7)  CartesianIndex(5, 8)
 CartesianIndex(6, 5)  CartesianIndex(6, 6)  CartesianIndex(6, 7)  CartesianIndex(6, 8)
 CartesianIndex(7, 5)  CartesianIndex(7, 6)  CartesianIndex(7, 7)  CartesianIndex(7, 8)
 CartesianIndex(8, 5)  CartesianIndex(8, 6)  CartesianIndex(8, 7)  CartesianIndex(8, 8)
```

Listing 14-5: Iterating over CartesianIndices

This example shows how using CartesianIndices simplifies iterating over a rectangular region. First we assign the CartesianIndex corresponding to the index [1, 1] to ci. Then we iterate from CartesianIndex(5, 5), represented as 5ci, to 8ci, using collect() to instantiate the iteration so we can inspect it. The power is in how a linear iteration is expanded into a nested iteration over both dimensions, spanning the rectangle between the two corners [5, 5] and [8, 8]. We can use this type of iteration in any number of dimensions:

```
julia> collect(CartesianIndex(1, 1, 1):CartesianIndex(3, 3, 3))
3×3×3 Array{CartesianIndex{3}, 3}:
[:, :, 1] =
 CartesianIndex(1, 1, 1)  CartesianIndex(1, 2, 1)  CartesianIndex(1, 3, 1)
 CartesianIndex(2, 1, 1)  CartesianIndex(2, 2, 1)  CartesianIndex(2, 3, 1)
 CartesianIndex(3, 1, 1)  CartesianIndex(3, 2, 1)  CartesianIndex(3, 3, 1)

[:, :, 2] =
 CartesianIndex(1, 1, 2)  CartesianIndex(1, 2, 2)  CartesianIndex(1, 3, 2)
 CartesianIndex(2, 1, 2)  CartesianIndex(2, 2, 2)  CartesianIndex(2, 3, 2)
 CartesianIndex(3, 1, 2)  CartesianIndex(3, 2, 2)  CartesianIndex(3, 3, 2)

[:, :, 3] =
 CartesianIndex(1, 1, 3)  CartesianIndex(1, 2, 3)  CartesianIndex(1, 3, 3)
 CartesianIndex(2, 1, 3)  CartesianIndex(2, 2, 3)  CartesianIndex(2, 3, 3)
 CartesianIndex(3, 1, 3)  CartesianIndex(3, 2, 3)  CartesianIndex(3, 3, 3)
```

Here the iteration represents a cube. Without CartesianIndices, we would have to write it as three nested loops, but here it's a simple range expression.

In fact, CartesianIndices are more general than what's shown in these examples. They need not represent contiguous rectangular regions:

```
julia> collect(CartesianIndex(1, 1):CartesianIndex(2, 2):CartesianIndex(5, 5))
3×3 Matrix{CartesianIndex{2}}:
 CartesianIndex(1, 1)  CartesianIndex(1, 3)  CartesianIndex(1, 5)
 CartesianIndex(3, 1)  CartesianIndex(3, 3)  CartesianIndex(3, 5)
 CartesianIndex(5, 1)  CartesianIndex(5, 3)  CartesianIndex(5, 5)
```

Their utility is in compactly representing nested iterations, and in constructing "portable" ranges of indices we can use in different arrays. Listing 14-6 illustrates this idea.

```
julia> by2 = CartesianIndex(1, 1):CartesianIndex(2, 2):CartesianIndex(5, 5)
CartesianIndices((1:2:5, 1:2:5))

julia> reshape(1:100, 10, 10)[by2]
3×3 Matrix{Int64}:
 1  21  41
 3  23  43
 5  25  45
```

Listing 14-6: Using CartesianIndices to construct "portable" ranges of indices

Here we've assigned a `CartesianIndices` iterator to `by2`, which we then used to extract nine noncontiguous elements from a 10×10 matrix. This example also shows a more compact way to define the iterators, suggested to us by the form of the result returned on the first line:

```julia
julia> CartesianIndices((1:3, 1:3, 1:3)) ==
       CartesianIndex(1, 1, 1):CartesianIndex(3, 3, 3)
true
```

To help visualize `CartesianIndices`, we'll start with a 100×100 version of our random gray matrix and select a rectangle within it by iterating over multiples of `ci`, defined in Listing 14-6:

```julia
julia> rgi = rand(rgen, Float64, (100, 100)) .* 0.2 .+ 0.4;

julia> rgi[5ci:20ci] .= 0.0;
```

Figure 14-23 shows what this does to `rgi`.

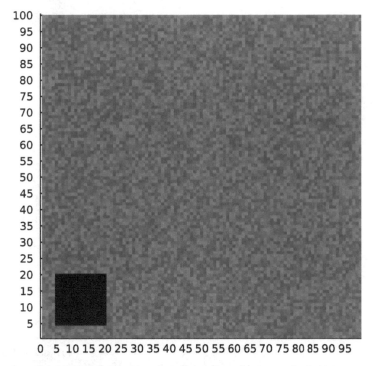

Figure 14-23: Defining a rectangular region with CartesianIndices

Julia's `CartesianIndices` equip us with a way to define a rectangular region that we can perform direct arithmetic on, to, for example, shift it to various locations around an array. This kind of "moving window" operates behind the scenes in the fast Fourier transform and spectrogram functions that we used earlier in this chapter. It's also a big part of solving partial differential equations on a grid, a major enterprise in computational science. Those with experience programming such stencil operations in a traditional language such as Fortran know how tricky the process can be. Here we'll apply the idea to a photograph, by sliding a square window around the image to create a blurred, pixel-averaged version:

```
julia> monk = Float64.(load("monk-mintons-1947.jpg"));

❶ julia> average_monk = similar(monk);

julia> cim = CartesianIndices(monk);

julia> ws = 1; # Window size

❷ julia> c1 = CartesianIndex(ws, ws);

julia> for i in cim
           n = s = 0.0
           for j in max(first(cim), i - c1):min(last(cim), i + c1)
               n += 1
               s += monk[j]
           end
           average_monk[i] = s/n
       end
```

After loading the image, we initialize an array to hold the averaged version using similar() ❶, which makes a copy of an array with the same size and types. We'll use the cim variable to iterate over the entire original image. The size of the moving square window is assigned to ws, which is used to define its extent ❷. The for loop visits each point in the original, replacing it with the average of all the pixels in the square window centered on that point.

The purpose of the max() and min() calls is to handle the border regions, where the moving window would extend beyond the edge of the matrix. This works because of how max() and min() treat CartesianIndex types:

```
julia> max(CartesianIndex(3, 4), CartesianIndex(-2, 9))
CartesianIndex(3, 9)

julia> min(CartesianIndex(3, 4), CartesianIndex(-2, 9))
CartesianIndex(-2, 4)
```

The functions return a new CartesianIndex where each dimensional index is individually maximized or minimized; therefore, we need only refer to the corners of the original array to ensure that no index component is too large or too small.

The functions act differently on tuples:

```
julia> max((3, 4), (-2, 9))
(3, 4)
```

Here the tuples (or vectors) are ordered by their first elements, and the return value is always one of the arguments.

Figure 14-24 shows the original image and the results of averaging over 1, 4, and 8 pixels.

Figure 14-24: Thelonious Monk, 1947. Original and with averaging over 1, 4, and 8 pixels, left to right and top to bottom. Photo by William Gottlieb (public domain, http://hdl.loc.gov/loc.music/gottlieb.06191).

The result is an increasing softening of the original image, the result of a simple form of low-pass filtering.

We can use a similar technique to create a reduced image—for example, by a factor of two in each dimension:

```
julia> smaller_monk = zeros(size(monk) .÷ 2);
julia> cism = CartesianIndices(smaller_monk);
julia> c1 = CartesianIndex(1, 1)
julia> for i in cism
           n = s = 0.0
         ❶ for j in max(first(cim), 2i - c1):min(last(cim), 2i + c1)
```

```
                    n += 1
                    s += monk[j]
            end
        smaller_monk[i] = s/n
        end
```

After initializing an array half the size of the original to hold the reduced image, we create a `CartesianIndices` iterator spanning it, assigned to `cism`. The outer loop iterates over the smaller array and sets each of its elements to the average of the pixels surrounding the corresponding pixel in the original. The indexing ❶ is due to the fact that for location [i, j] in the reduced image, the corresponding location in the original is [2i, 2j].

Figure 14-25 shows the original alongside the reduced version.

Figure 14-25: Piano four hands: reducing an image with pixel averaging

Of course, we could also create a quick reduced image with `original[1:2:dy, 1:2:dx]`, but averaging pixels leads to a better outcome, especially in the appearance of diagonal lines. Professional image reduction algorithms usually employ a larger window with a sampling method more elaborate than the simple arithmetic mean in this example.

Conclusion

In this chapter, we've analyzed and manipulated artifacts from the physical world of sounds and images. We've explored a variety of tools from packages for signal and image processing, but also found that the power of Julia's facilities for array manipulation make difficult jobs easy, allowing us to write short and simple programs that perform complex tasks.

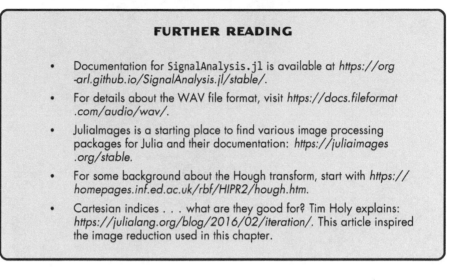

FURTHER READING

- Documentation for SignalAnalysis.jl is available at *https://org-arl.github.io/SignalAnalysis.jl/stable/*.

- For details about the WAV file format, visit *https://docs.fileformat.com/audio/wav/*.

- JuliaImages is a starting place to find various image processing packages for Julia and their documentation: *https://juliaimages.org/stable*.

- For some background about the Hough transform, start with *https://homepages.inf.ed.ac.uk/rbf/HIPR2/hough.htm*.

- Cartesian indices . . . what are they good for? Tim Holy explains: *https://julialang.org/blog/2016/02/iteration/*. This article inspired the image reduction used in this chapter.

15

PARALLEL PROCESSING

If one ox could not do the job they did not try to grow a bigger ox, but used two oxen.
—Grace Hopper

 Parallel processing is a class of strategies for computation where we divide a problem into pieces and tackle each piece with a different computer or different processing units on a single computer—or a combination of both approaches. This chapter treats *true parallel processing*, where different computations occur simultaneously, and *concurrent processing*, where we ask the computer to do several things at once, but it may have to alternate among them.

While writing effective parallel programs can be tricky, Julia goes a long way toward making parallel and concurrent processing as easy as possible. The same program may run in parallel or merely concurrently, depending on machine resources, but Julia's abstractions free us to write one version of the program that can take advantage of varying runtime environments.

This chapter will provide an overview of how to implement the major concurrency paradigms using facilities built into Julia and several convenient packages.

Concurrency Paradigms

A natural distinction from the programmer's point of view is between *multithreading* and *multiprocessing*, and that's the major divide that organizes this chapter. This area suffers from some terminological inconsistency. We use multithreading to mean programming *aimed* at parallel execution on multiple CPU cores on a single machine. A *core* is a processing unit within a CPU chip. Each one is equipped with its own resources, such as caches and arithmetic logic units, and can execute instructions independently, although it may share some resources with other cores. If someone happens to run a multithreaded program on a computer with only one core, there won't be any parallelism happening, but that need not concern us when we're writing the program. The same code will run faster on a multicore machine if we've written it correctly.

We use multiprocessing to refer to a style of programming where we launch tasks that can be executed by different processes on a single machine or by multiple machines (or both).

The most important distinction between the two styles of programming has to do with access to memory: all of the threads in a multithreaded program have access to the same pool of memory, while the processes in a multiprocessing program have separate memory areas.

Multithreading

This section deals with speeding up the work within a single process by dividing it among a number of *tasks*. Since all these tasks exist within the same process, they all have access to the same memory space. The task is the basic concept upon which Julia's parallel and concurrent processing is built. It's a discrete unit of work, usually a function call, that's assigned to a particular thread by the *scheduler*. Tasks are inherently asynchronous; once launched, they continue on their assigned thread until they're done or suspend themselves by yielding to the scheduler. However, we can synchronize and orchestrate the tasks' life cycles in various ways.

NOTE *You may have done parallel computing with Julia without knowing it. Many linear algebra routines, including the matrix multiplication dispatched by *, run multithreaded BLAS (Basic Linear Algebra Subprograms) routines that automatically take advantage of all CPU cores, transparently to the user. You can verify this by executing a matrix multiply in the REPL and keeping an eye on your CPU meters.*

When we enter the Julia REPL or use the julia command to run a program stored on the disk, we have several available command line options.

Unless we use the -t option, Julia uses exactly one thread (and, consequently, one CPU core), no matter the hardware configuration on which it's running.

To allow Julia to use all the available threads, use the -t auto argument. In that case, all of the "available" threads will be all of the *logical* threads on the machine. This is often not optimal. A better choice can be -t *n*, where *n* is the number of *physical* cores. For example, the popular Intel Core processors provide two logical cores for each physical core using a technique called *hyperthreading*. Hyperthreading can yield anything from a modest speedup to an actual slowdown, depending on the type of calculation.

On Linux we can use the lscpu command at the system shell to get information about the CPU. For example, if the output contains the lines

```
Thread(s) per core:        2
Core(s) per socket:        2
Socket(s):                 1
```

then the machine has a total of two physical compute cores and four logical threads provided by hyperthreading. We usually need to experiment to discover whether -t *n* (in this case, -t 2) or -t auto leads to a better outcome.

Within a program, or in the REPL, we can check for the number of available threads with

```
Threads.nthreads()
```

which reports the total number in use and is blind to how many of them represent real cores.

With multiple threads, we can speed up our programs by assigning tasks to run on more than one CPU core simultaneously, either automatically or by applying various levels of control.

Easy Multithreading with Folds

One automatic way of launching tasks is with the Folds package, which provides multithreaded versions of map(), sum(), maximum(), minimum(), reduce(), collect(), and a handful of other functions over collections. Its use is as easy as replacing, for example, sum() with Folds.sum(). The parallelized function takes care of dividing the work among all the available threads.

As an example, Listing 15-1 shows the parallelized map of an expensive function over an array.

```
julia> using BenchmarkTools, Folds

julia> f(x) = sum([exp(1/i^2) for i in 1:x]);

julia> time_serial = @belapsed map(f, 100_000:105_000)
13.989536582

julia> time_parallel = @belapsed Folds.map(f, 100_000:105_000)
7.606663313
```

```
julia> time_parallel / time_serial
0.5437394776026614

julia> Threads.nthreads()
2
```

Listing 15-1: Easy parallelism with `Folds.jl`

The `@belapsed` macro is part of `BenchmarkTools`. Like the `@btime` macro that we've used before, it runs the job repeatedly and reports an average of resource utilizations. This version is convenient when we just want the CPU time consumed.

The parallelized version of `map()` gives each thread an approximately equal portion of the loop over 5,001 numbers. Ideally, the total compute time should be $1/N$, where N is the number of threads. Behind the scenes, it's creating tasks, each with some portion of the loop, and assigning them to available threads; it may use two tasks, or more. It also synchronizes the computation, waiting for all the tasks to complete before returning.

This REPL session was started using the `-t 2` flag. The results show that the parallel version used just slightly more than half the time of the serial computation. Since we are running on two (physical) threads, the result indicates an almost ideal parallel speedup.

However, we're not always so lucky. Whether parallelizing a computation helps, hinders, or has no effect is the result of the trade-off between the overhead of setting up and managing a set of tasks and the benefits of dividing up the work. It's sensitive to the cost of the calculation per array element, the size of the array, and the patterns of memory access. The same calculation on a smaller array has a better outcome using the serial `map()`:

```
julia> time_serial = @belapsed map(f, 1:41)
2.4464e-5

julia> time_parallel = @belapsed Folds.map(f, 1:41)
2.5466e-5
```

Here, working on a single processor is actually faster than trying to parallelize the short computation. Successful parallel computing requires a good deal of testing. We need to ensure that we're taking good advantage of the hardware and that the results running on multiple cores are identical to the results run serially, aside from small numerical differences that reordering of floating-point calculations can cause in some programs.

Manual Multithreading with @threads

The `Folds` package is a higher-level interface to the manual multithreading that's the subject of this section. Going manual requires more care, but it can provide an extra degree of control that we sometimes need.

Threads.@threads

The main facility for multithreading in Julia is the `Threads.@threads` macro, which is part of `Base`, so it's always available. To run a loop in parallel, we preface it with the macro. As an introduction, Listing 15-2 tackles the same problem as in the previous section.

```
julia> f(x) = sum([exp(1/i^2) for i in 1:x]);

julia> time_serial = @belapsed for x in 100_000:105_000
           r = f(x)
       end
13.933373843

julia> time_parallel = @belapsed Threads.@threads for x in 100_000:105_000
           r = f(x)
       end
7.507556971
```

Listing 15-2: Timing a threaded loop

Apparently, the `@threads` version performs similarly to the wrapper from the `Folds` package.

The `@threads` macro works by dividing the loop into N segments and assigning each segment to a separate task. The scheduler apportions these tasks among the available threads. Normally N is a small multiple of the number of threads, so if we have two cores and have used the `-t 2` flag, `@threads` will probably divide the loop over 5,001 elements into two or four loops of approximately equal length.

The `@threads` loop is synchronized in the sense that computation does not continue past the end of the loop until all tasks are complete. Different parts of the loop, hence different tasks, may take different amounts of time. If this difference is large, some threads will be idle waiting for the others to catch up. This is why, as mentioned previously, this style of multithreading works best when all iterations take roughly the same computing time.

Instead of throwing out the result, let's try adding together all the f(x)s:

```
function sumf_serial(n)
    s = 0.0
    for x in 1:n
        s += f(x)
    end
    s
end

function sumf_parallel(n)
    s = 0.0
    Threads.@threads for x in 1:n
        s += f(x)
    end
```

```
        s
end
```

```
julia> sumf_serial(1000)
502900.5422006599
```

```
julia> sumf_parallel(1000)
376606.37463883933
```

```
julia> sumf_parallel(1000)
376453.03112871706
```

The parallel results not only differ from the serial result, but it seems that we can get different answers for different runs of the parallel program. What did we do wrong?

Atomic Theory

The problem arises when we update s within the parallel loop. Multiple independent threads trying to access and write to the same scalar variable creates a *race condition*, a conflict where the result depends on an order of operations which the program does not control. We can get different results from different runs because the timings will differ, based on unknown influences such as the other tasks that the operating system happens to be performing during the run. There's no problem when updating array locations because in the threaded loop, arrays will be divided among the threads and no thread will step on another thread's data.

Julia provides several strategies for protecting a scalar during multi-threaded execution. One way is to use *atomic variables*, as Listing 15-3 shows.

```
function sumf_parallel_locked(n)
    s = Threads.Atomic{Float64}(0);
    Threads.@threads for x in 1:n
        Threads.atomic_add!(s, f(x))
    end
    s[]
end
```

```
julia> sumf_parallel_locked(1000)
502900.5422006605
```

Listing 15-3: Using an atomic variable

We've initialized s as an atomic variable using the built-in Threads.Atomic declaration. It allows only simple types: the various floats, integers, and the Bool type. We update atomic variables using a small collection of functions for the purpose, all namespaced with Threads. In addition to Threads.atomic_add!(), we have atomic_sub!() for subtraction, several logical operators, atomic_xchg!() for setting the variable to a new value, and a few more. We access the value of an atomic variable with the odd-looking syntax in the last line of the program.

The result is close to the serial result, so the atomic variable fixed the problem. The results are close, but not equal: they vary in the last few decimal places. The result of a series of floating-point operations can depend on their order, and the order varies between serial and parallel runs and among parallel runs with different numbers of threads. We'll also get a minutely different result if we run the serial code counting backward in the loop:

```
function sumf_serial_reversed(n)
    s = 0.0
    for x in n:-1:1
        s += f(x)
    end
    s
end
```

```
julia> sumf_serial_reversed(1000)
502900.5422006606
```

These small variations in the least significant parts of the answers are normal and expected, and are something that the numericist must be alert to when comparing the results from a parallelized program when run on different computers with possibly different numbers of cores.

We can also get a correct summation using a different strategy:

```
function sumf_parallel2(n)
    s = zeros(Threads.nthreads())
    Threads.@threads for x in 1:n
    ❶ s[Threads.threadid()] += f(x)
    end
    sum(s)
end
```

```
julia> sumf_parallel2(1000)
502900.5422006605
```

We've essentially given each thread its private copy of the summation variable and added all the copies together at the end. We use Threads.nthreads() to create a vector the same length as the number of threads. Within each thread, Threads.threadid() returns that thread's unique integer identifier. We use this identifier to index into the array of summations ❶, ensuring that each thread updates only the element that belongs to it. The sum of sums in the last line should be the same as the scalar s in the other versions of the program.

The technique of using an array instead of an atomic variable can be faster, because before a thread is allowed to read or update an atomic variable, it must wait until it's released by any other thread that's using it. The use of arrays eliminates this *locking* and the consequent waiting time. However, it uses a bit more memory for the new arrays.

Spawning and Synchronizing Tasks

The techniques we've described in the previous two sections implement parallelism by dividing the work among tasks and launching them behind the scenes. Here we'll learn how to take control of spawning and synchronizing tasks.

Launching Tasks with Threads.@spawn

We can also launch tasks manually with the `Threads.@spawn` macro, as shown in Listing 15-4.

```
function sumf_atomic(f)
    s = Threads.Atomic{Float64}(0.0);
❶ @sync for x in 100_000:105_000
        Threads.@spawn Threads.atomic_add!(s, f(x))
    end
return s
end

julia> @belapsed s = sumf_atomic(f)
8.101242794

julia> s = sumf_atomic(f);

julia> s[]
5.126145395914207e8
```

Listing 15-4: Introducing task spawning

Since `@belapsed` and the other benchmarking tools in `BenchmarkTools` run code multiple times, we place the timed code within a function to force the atomic variable to be initialized in each trial run.

The `@sync` macro ❶ works for any block, not just for loops. It synchronizes all tasks launched within the lexical scope of the block, which means that the statement following its end statement will wait until they're all done. In Listing 15-4, `@sync` ensures that when we access `s[]`, it will have its final value, and that the timings include the time for completion of all tasks.

The block in Listing 15-4 is a version of the function in Listing 15-3, with manually spawned tasks. In general, the loop

```
Threads.@threads for i in 1:N
    something
end
```

is semantically equivalent to

```
@sync for i in 1:N
    Threads.@spawn something
end
```

but their implementations are different, in that, as mentioned earlier, `Threads` `.@threads` is *coarse-grained*, dividing the loop into a small number of tasks. The manually spawned version creates a new task for every loop iteration.

The fact that the timings in these two examples are almost the same demonstrates that spawning a task in Julia has almost no overhead; we can spawn thousands of tasks with little performance penalty. If we move a program using tasks to a different machine with more cores, it should run faster with no changes required on our part.

NOTE *In this chapter we perform many timings on bare loops at the top level in order to compare the effects of different approaches to concurrency and parallelism in as few lines of code as possible. In developing a real program, all timing studies should be on functions, preferably in modules. Many compiler optimizations are available only for code in functions.*

Synchronizing

Using `Folds.map()` or `@threads` synchronizes tasks for us. However, if we launch tasks with `Threads.@spawn` manually, we can't know which have completed their work at any particular point in the program. That's why the program in Listing 15-4 needs a `@sync` macro.

The following example illustrates what can happen if we neglect synchronization:

```
W = zeros(5);

for i in 1:5
    Threads.@spawn (sleep(1); W[i] = i)
end
println(W)
```

If we run this program, we'll see the following output:

```
[0.0, 0.0, 0.0, 0.0, 0.0]
```

Each loop iteration launches a task that mutates the global array, writing to one of its locations. However, at the end of the loop, the array W doesn't seem to have changed.

Each `@spawn` sends off a task to do its work, and the loop continues to the next iteration immediately. Although each spawned job has a built-in delay created by the `sleep()` call, the loop itself is complete almost instantaneously.

We then execute the statement following the loop, printing the value of W, which hasn't yet been written to.

If we want to wait at the end of the loop for all tasks spawned within it to complete, so that W is up to date, we use the @sync macro:

```
W = zeros(5);

@sync for i in 1:5
    Threads.@spawn (sleep(1); W[i] = i)
end
println(W)
```

When we run this program, we see:

```
[1.0, 2.0, 3.0, 4.0, 5.0]
```

Instead of synchronizing all the tasks within a block, we can wait for some of them to complete, letting the others run their courses:

```
W = zeros(5);

jobs = Vector{Any}(undef, 5);

for i in 1:5
    jobs[i] = Threads.@spawn (sleep(i); W[i] = i)
end
wait(jobs[2])
println(W)
```

We initialize a jobs vector to hold the return values of each call to @spawn. These are Tasks, a data type that holds information about an asynchronous task. The wait() function pauses execution until its argument is ready. We change the loop a bit to wait on each iteration for i seconds, so each task will take longer than the preceding one. As soon as the second job is complete, the next instruction, printing W, is run.

The program produces this output:

```
[1.0, 2.0, 0.0, 0.0, 0.0]
```

We can see that when the println() statement is reached, the first two elements of W are modified, but the remaining tasks are still running (sleeping).

Another useful synchronization function is fetch(). Like wait(), it receives a Task as an argument and waits for the task to finish:

```
W = zeros(5);

jobs = Vector{Any}(undef, 5);

for i in 1:5
    jobs[i] = Threads.@spawn (sleep(i); W[i] = i)
```

```
end
job2 = fetch(jobs[2])
println(W)
println(job2)
```

That function prints this output:

```
[1.0, 2.0, 0.0, 0.0, 0.0]
2
```

Since the result returned by an assignment is the value assigned, the task that executes W[2] = 2 returns 2, and this gets assigned to job2 by the call to fetch(). The condition of W at this point is its state immediately after the second task is complete.

Yielding

After the scheduler places tasks on all available threads, any remaining spawned tasks are on the *queue*, waiting for their turn to run. They will have to wait until one of the running tasks finishes or *yields* its place. This system is called *cooperative multitasking*, and it's the model Julia usually applies to task scheduling. Some operations cause a task to yield automatically. The more important ones are waiting for I/O and sleeping. But if a program involves multiple tasks that perform long calculations, it's our job to break up the calculations manually and insert yield()s in order to provide opportunities for other tasks to run, *unless* we don't mind each thread waiting for each expensive task on it to finish (which may indeed be acceptable).

Listing 15-5 contains two functions that each do the identical piece of busywork, applying f(x), which was defined in Listing 15-1, to a range of numbers. The difference between the two functions is that the first does the job in one lump, while the second divides the range into two halves, calling yield() between them. The yield() function tells the scheduler that it may suspend the task and run the next task from the queue, if there is one waiting. After that task is complete, the suspended task will resume.

```
function task_timer(n)
    push!(times, (n, time()))
    map(f, 100_000:102_000)
    push!(times, (n, time()))
end

function task_yield_timer(n)
    push!(times, (n, time()))
    map(f, 100_000:101_000)
    yield()
    map(f, 101_000:102_000)
    push!(times, (n, time()))
end
```

Listing 15-5: Inserting an opportunity to yield

The functions assume the existence of a global array named times. They place the result of calling time(), within a tuple with the integer n identifying the task, onto the end of this array as soon as they begin and just before they return. The time() function returns the system time in seconds to approximately microsecond precision. Its value is uninteresting, but we can use the difference between two calls to time() to find out how much time passed between two code locations, which is a pretty accurate measure of how long the intervening calculation took.

Listing 15-6 spawns three tasks using the first function, recording the saved times, and then does the same using the modified function with the yield() call.

```
times = []
@sync for n in 1:3
    Threads.@spawn task_timer(n)
end
times_noyield = times[:]

times = []
@sync for n in 1:3
    Threads.@spawn task_yield_timer(n)
end
times_yield = times[:]
```

Listing 15-6: Testing the effects of yielding

Figure 15-1 plots the task numbers versus the *elapsed* times from the start of each thread-spawning loop, for experiments on a single thread.

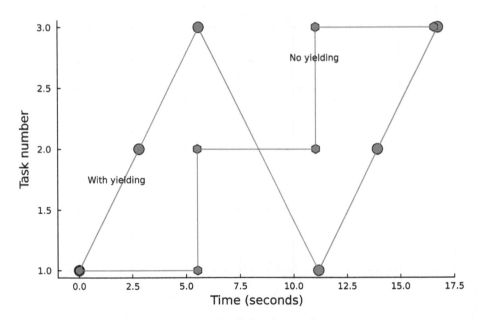

Figure 15-1: Timings for cooperative and selfish tasks

We can see from Figure 15-1 that each complete loop takes about 5.5 seconds. The experiment with yielding (circles) shows that each task does its half loop and then allows the next task in the queue to run. It doesn't resume until all subsequent tasks have completed their first halves and yielded. In the experiment without yielding (hexagons), each task monopolizes the thread until it's finished.

With only one thread active, the order of task operations is predictable. Also, when using one thread it's impossible for yielding or any rearrangement of tasks to decrease the time to completion of all the calculations; we can't get something for nothing. However, in cases where lighter tasks are mixed with more time-consuming ones, allowing the latter to yield will get us access to the results of the lighter tasks sooner, which can be desirable in some programs. When multiple threads are available, yielding gives the scheduler a chance to migrate tasks among threads, keeping them all occupied and potentially increasing the total throughput. This rearrangement of tasks is called *load balancing*.

Multiprocessing

If we decide to run with Grace Hopper's metaphor that starts this chapter, we might say that the multithreading explored in the previous section amounts to yoking together a team of oxen to pull a big load, while we can compare the multiprocessing explored in this section to dividing the load into separate carts and letting each ox pull its cart at its own pace.

Multiprocessing and distributed computing are closely related concepts, and the two terms are often used interchangeably. This style of computation divides the work into multiple *processes* that have their own memory spaces. The processes may share resources on a single computer or on multiple networked computers. Julia's abstractions make it possible to write the multiprocessed program once and run it in a variety of environments.

Because the various processes don't have access to the same memory, any data that they need must be copied and sent to them, possibly over a network. Because of this, distributed computing is most suited to handling time-consuming tasks on small data, especially if computing resources are communicating over a slow network such as the internet.

Running on a cluster uses multiprocessing to distribute the work to an array of processors usually communicating over a higher-bandwidth network, combined with the multithreading of the previous section to make the best use of each node.

Multiprocessing is based on the same concept of an asynchronous task that forms the basis of the multithreading described previously. It adds the concept of the process and the possibility of spawning tasks on more than one process. It allows us to do this automatically or with control of individual tasks, with program interfaces similar to the ones we explored with multithreading.

Easy Multiprocessing with pmap

To start the Julia REPL or runtime in multiprocessor mode, use the -p flag. As with the -t flag, it usually makes the most sense to ask for a number of processes equal to the number of hardware threads available. On a machine with two cores, start Julia using `julia -p2`. This creates two *worker processes* that can accept tasks. We'll have (in this case) a total of three processes: the two workers and the executive process, in which the REPL runs if we're working interactively. We can assign tasks to workers automatically or by specifying the process number.

With the -p2 flag, each process will be single-threaded, and each will run on its own thread on the two-core machine. We can also use the flags -p2 -t2, which creates two worker processes, each with access to two threads. Then we have the option of spawning tasks on either process, and, within each task, running multithreaded or multiprocessing loops. At this point it may seem as if we have too many options, and that it would be difficult to decide on a strategy. One rational approach that takes good advantage of all available computing resources is to launch one worker process on each remote machine, using the mechanism described in the next section, and use the -t auto flag. This strategy allows each networked machine to use all its available threads for shared-memory parallel computing and helps to avoid unnecessary data movement.

Starting Julia with the -p flag automatically performs the equivalent of using `Distributed`, loading the standard library package that provides utilities for multiprocessing. We can retrieve the number of available processes with `nworkers()`, provided by `Distributed`. One of the useful utilities from `Distributed` is `pmap()`, a distributed version of `map()`, as shown in Listing 15-7.

```
❶ julia> @everywhere f(x) = sum([exp(1/i^2) for i in 1:x]);

julia> time_serial = @belapsed map(f, 100_000:105_000)
13.934491874

julia> time_mp = @belapsed pmap(f, 100_000:105_000)
7.944081133
```

Listing 15-7: The distributed map

Since each process has its own memory, we have to give copies of all function definitions to the workers. That's what the @everywhere macro does ❶. We also need to decorate module imports, constant definitions, and everything else that the workers need to use with @everywhere.

Once all the workers have copies of the f() function, we can repeat our timing tests from Listing 15-1 using pmap(). This works similarly to Folds.map(), but instead of orchestrating a synchronized computation by spawning tasks to multiple threads in the current process, it spawns tasks in multiple processes. If we've launched Julia with the worker process number equal to the number of physical cores, as suggested earlier, normally each of the processes launched by pmap() will occupy its own hardware thread, and pmap()

will assign tasks to processes, and hence to threads, in a way that attempts to balance the load.

Networking with Machine Files

Julia makes multiprocessing on a collection of networked computers almost as easy as on a single computer. The first step is to create a text file that contains the network addresses of the machines that we want to enlist in helping with the calculation, along with some other details. The machines in question must have Julia installed, and should contain a directory path identical to the path from which we're running the controlling program. We need to have passwordless ssh access to each machine. Leaving out some optional details, the *machine file* contains one line per machine, in the following form:

```
n*host:port
```

Here *n* is the number of workers to start on the machine at *host*, which can be an IP address or a hostname that the controlling computer can resolve. The *:port* part is optional and only needed for nonstandard ssh ports (ports other than 22).

For this example, I put two computers into a machine file named *machines*. Here's the entire file:

```
2*tc
2*pluton:86
```

Both hostnames are resolved into their IP addresses by entries in my */etc/hosts* file. I could have used the IP numbers directly as well. The computer called tc is in my house, and pluton, a server I maintain mostly for serving Pluto notebooks that I drafted for this exercise, is about 1,200 miles away. It listens on port 86 for ssh connections, whereas tc uses the standard port. The machine file specifies that each machine will use two worker processes.

To start a REPL that will use these remote resources as well as two worker processes on the machine where the REPL is running, we execute

```
julia -p2 --machine-file=machines
```

omitting other options, such as specifying a project directory.

After a modest delay, we get a REPL prompt. At this point the Julia workers on both remote computers are running and waiting to receive tasks. Let's check that everyone's listening:

```
julia> pmap(_ -> run(`hostname`), 1:6)
    From worker 4:    tc
    From worker 3:    sp3
    From worker 2:    sp3
    From worker 5:    pluton
    From worker 6:    pluton
    From worker 7:    tc
```

```
6-element Vector{Base.Process}:
 Process(`hostname`, ProcessExited(0))
 Process(`hostname`, ProcessExited(0))
 Process(`hostname`, ProcessExited(0))
 Process(`hostname`, ProcessExited(0))
 Process(`hostname`, ProcessExited(0))
 Process(`hostname`, ProcessExited(0))
```

The host sp3 is the laptop where the REPL is running. We use pmap() to launch six processes, asking each one to run the system command hostname. There's no guarantee that they'll be equally divided, as it turns out in this example, or that every machine receives a job—but in this case it turns out that six tasks was enough. Using run() provides a report identifying which worker ID is assigned to which machine. If we need merely the output from the shell command, we can use readchomp() instead of run().

The worker numbers range from 2 to 7 because process 1 is the REPL process. We can get a list of workers anytime with:

```
julia> workers()
6-element Vector{Int64}:
 2
 3
 4
 5
 6
 7
```

Let's repeat the timing in Listing 15-7 on our three-machine network, as shown in Listing 15-8.

```
julia> @belapsed pmap(f, 100_000:105_000)
5.255985404
```

Listing 15-8: A distributed map over a network of computers

The machines pluton and tc each have two CPU cores, so we have tripled the number of cores available for the calculation. We did observe a speedup, but only by about 50 percent over performing the calculation confined to the local machine. Computing over the internet incurs significant overhead. Monitoring the remote machine's CPU usage shows that both of tc's CPU cores were active during the calculation, at about 70 percent utilization, while pluton's two cores were nearly quiescent. The ping time to pluton during the experiment was about 50 times longer than to tc, as we might expect from their relative distances. Clearly Julia's scheduler sent more units of work to the closer computer while waiting to receive responses from the distant machine.

Going Manual with @spawnat

The @spawnat macro spawns an asynchronous task, just as @spawn does, but on a worker process. We can leave the decision about which process is to receive the task by using @spawnat :any, or pick one with @spawnat *n*. The macro is part of Distributed, so it is always available if we've started Julia with the -p flag.

Let's check that the macro does what we expect by using it to ask each machine to report its hostname:

```
for p in 2:7
    @spawnat p @info "Process $(myid()) is running on $(readchomp(`hostname`))"
end
```

The myid() function returns the process number of the process where it is called. The program prints this message when run:

```
From worker 3:      [ Info: Process 3 is running on sp3
From worker 2:      [ Info: Process 2 is running on sp3
From worker 4:      [ Info: Process 4 is running on tc
From worker 7:      [ Info: Process 7 is running on tc
From worker 5:      [ Info: Process 5 is running on pluton
From worker 6:      [ Info: Process 6 is running on pluton
```

We observed a modest speedup when running a pmap() over a network of three computers in Listing 15-8. Listing 15-9 shows what happens if we try a version of the loop with manual spawning.

```
@sync for x in 100_000:105_000
    @spawnat :any r = f(x)
end
```

Listing 15-9: Spawning too many distributed processes

We would observe terrible performance, worse than performing the calculation on a single thread. This is because, unlike the coarse-grained concurrency that pmap() transforms the loop into, the manual multiprocessing in this loop launches thousands of tasks on a handful of processes. Each one requires interprocess communication to manage, which far outweighs any gains from concurrency. The situation is different from the version in Listing 15-4, where the fine-grained loop performs as well as the coarse-grained loop, because in that case, all computation takes place on one process. Creating tasks within a process is very cheap, but interprocess communication is not; therefore, @spawnat is best used for small numbers of expensive tasks that don't require massive copying of data.

Multiprocessing Threads with @distributed

The multiprocessed analogy to the `Threads.@threads` macro is the `@distributed` macro. While the former divides a loop into a coarse-grained set of tasks on the available threads of the local machine or process, the latter divides a loop into a coarse-grained set of tasks spawned across processes, which may be across machines on a network.

Listing 15-10 shows the `@distributed` version of the threaded loop in Listing 15-2.

```
julia> @belapsed @sync @distributed for x in 100_000:105_000
           r = f(x)
       end
3.668112229
```

Listing 15-10: Using @distributed

I performed this timing test on my little network of three machines, each with two CPU cores. It's the best time we've achieved for this loop so far. We need to use the `@sync` macro with this use of `@distributed`, unlike with `Threads.@threads`, which always synchronizes. (Even though we're not using the results of the calculations, leaving off the `@sync` renders the timing meaningless, as in that case the loop will return immediately after spawning its tasks.)

A common pattern is to combine the results from each iteration of a loop, as we did in Listing 15-4, using an atomic variable. If we insert a function between the `@distributed` macro and the `for` keyword, the macro will gather the results from each iteration, reduce them using the function, and return the result of combining the reductions from each process. Since returning this final result implies synchronization, we can leave off the `@sync` when supplying a reduction function:

```
julia> @distributed (+) for x in 100_000:105_000
           r = f(x)
       end
5.126145395914206e8
```

The loop is equivalent to

```
sum(pmap(f, 100_000:105_000))
```

which also automatically performs a reduction across multiple processes.

Why is the loop in Listing 15-10 faster than the `pmap()` version shown in Listing 15-8? Both approaches perform the same calculation distributed over the same machines. As always, when setting out to increase performance through concurrency, we're obligated to analyze the workloads in our programs. The loop in this case is over 5,001 function evaluations that are nontrivial, but also not very expensive (on the local machine `f(105_000)` takes 2.77 ms to evaluate). The pmap() function, by default, spawns a new task for each iteration of the loop. The scheduler will attempt load balancing by apportioning these tasks to various processes as they're spawned. The speedup through concurrency is partially offset by the overhead of scheduling and interprocess communication. Due to these considerations, pmap(), with no additional tuning parameters, works best with a small number of expensive tasks, which doesn't describe the situation in this example.

In contrast, the coarse-grained concurrency of the @distributed loop works well in this case, with a large number of relatively light tasks. Far fewer tasks are spawned, and more computer time is devoted to calculation, with less interprocess communication and scheduling overhead.

In the multithreaded examples, there's little difference in performance between the coarse-grained Threads.@threads version and the fine-grained Folds.map() version. This is because there's no interprocess communication in that case and spawning tasks is very fast.

We can tell pmap() to break up the loop into larger chunks using the batch_size keyword argument:

```
julia> @belapsed pmap(f, 100_000:105_000; batch_size=1000)
4.370967232

julia> @belapsed pmap(f, 100_000:105_000; batch_size=2501)
3.746921853
```

The default for batch_size is 1, meaning one task spawned for each iteration. A batch_size of *n* divides the loop into segments of length *up to n*, sending each loop segment off to a worker process as a separate task. The example shows that we can get performance similar to the @distributed loop from pmap() by dividing the work into halves.

Summary of Concurrency in Julia

It's likely that any program intended for large-scale, high-performance computing will take advantage of a combination of multiprocessing and multithreading. The former allows the program to distribute its work over the nodes of a supercomputing cluster, while the latter exploits multiple cores on each node. Therefore, Julia programs are often run using combinations of startup flags such as -p, -t, and a reference to a --machine-file.

Julia's abstractions go far in allowing us to write one version of our program that will run fast on a single thread, faster on multicore hardware, and even faster on a network of computers. Nevertheless, for the best performance, we can't escape the need to carefully consider the patterns of computation in our programs and make it possible for Julia's scheduler and the operating system to take the best advantage of the hardware.

Table 15-1 is a highly simplified summary of the main utilities for parallel and distributed processing that we've explored throughout this chapter.

Table 15-1: Multithreaded and Distributed Processing

Model	Threaded (shared memory)	Distributed (private memory)
Startup	`julia -t n`	`julia -p n`
Loops	`Threads.@threads for`	`@distributed for`
Maps	`Folds.map()`	`pmap()`
Launch task	`Threads.@spawn`	`@spawnat (p or :any)`

Before tuning the parallelization of a program, we should strive to achieve the best single-thread performance possible, by applying the optimization principles discussed in previous chapters. The most important of these are type stability, correct order of memory accesses, and caution around globals. However, even more important than these common pitfalls is the choice of an appropriate algorithm, a subject largely beyond the scope of this book.

Conclusion

The subject of concurrency in Julia is large and complicated, and could consume a book of this size on its own. The next topics of interest after mastering the material in this chapter might be using *shared arrays*, which allow multiprocessing-style programming using shared memory; *GPU programming*, which uses a graphical processing unit as an array processor; and using the *message passing interface (MPI)* library, which is popular in Fortran programs for high-performance scientific computing, from within Julia. "Further Reading" contains links to starting points for all of these topics.

FURTHER READING

- The Folds package resides at *https://github.com/JuliaFolds/Folds.jl*.
- "A quick introduction to data parallelism in Julia" by Takafumi Arakaki, the author of Folds.jl, is especially welcome, as Folds has little documentation: *https://juliafolds.github.io/data-parallelism/tutorials/quick-introduction/*.
- General Julia performance tips are available at *https://docs.julialang.org/en/v1/manual/performance-tips/*.
- For documentation on shared arrays, visit *https://docs.julialang.org/en/v1/stdlib/SharedArrays/*.
- The GitHub organization JuliaGPU (*https://juliagpu.org*) serves as an umbrella for Julia packages that implement or can exploit graphics processing units for parallelization.
- Examples of GPU programming with Julia are available at *https://enccs.se/news/2022/07/julia-for-hpc*.
- The JuliaParallel GitHub organization is home to a number of packages for parallel computing in Julia, including the MPI package (*https://github.com/JuliaParallel/MPI.jl* and the ClusterManagers package (*https://github.com/JuliaParallel/ClusterManagers.jl*) for managing job schedulers like Slurm on high-performance computing clusters.

INDEX

distribution assertion (~), 414
Distributions package, 324–326
DivideError, 179
division, 27
division operator (÷), 28
DNA, 361
do blocks, 166–167
docstrings, 67
documentation
    with docstrings, 67–68
    and Markdown, 68–69
doit() function, 393
double semicolon (;;), 191
drugs, 362
drum, modes of vibration, 206–207
dsolve() SymPy function, 394
DSP package, 435–437
duration() function, 432

E

e (Euler's number), 219
eccentricity in the Ptolemaic
        system, 201
editors, 5, 14–15
eigenvalues, 399
eigenvectors, 399
eigvals() function, 399–400
    of symmetric matrix, 401
    of triangular matrix, 402
eigvecs() function, 399
Einstein, Albert, 381
Elixir, 169
ellipsis operator (..) , 453
eltype() function, 221
Emacs, 15
    REPL interaction, 15
end multiline comment (=#), 59
entropy sources, 307
enumerate() function, 147–148
epicycles, 201–205
Eq() SymPy function, 394
erf() (error function), 393
error operator (±), 281
error propagation, 280–284
errors, 178–186
    combining with units, 283
Euler's number, 219
@everywhere macro, 480
evolution, simulated, 362–379

EvolutionaryModelingTools package, 362
exceptions, 178–186
    types of, 178–179
executive process, 480
expand_derivatives() function, 387
expint() function, 264
exponential integral, 264
expression, 26
    from string, 168
expression objects, 168–170
    interpolation of values, 169–170
expression quotation (:), 168
Expr type, 168
:extra_kwargs entry, 257

F

f0 numerical suffix, 281
factorial, 216
factorial() function, 217, 313
factorization, matrix, 402–403
factorize() function, 402–403
factor trees, 197–198
@fastmath performance macro, 176–177
FedEx, 61
fetch() function, 476
fill() function, 139
fillrange plotting attribute, 257
filter() function, 163–164
finally keyword, 186
findfirst() function, 131–132
findlast() function, 131–132
findnext() function, 132
fir() function, 435–437
fish, 193
flattening a collection, 369
Float16 type, 215
Float32 type, 215, 281
Float64 type, 27, 214
floatmax() function, 216
floatmin() function, 216
fluid dynamics, 284–294
foldl() function, 164
foldr() function, 164
Folds package, 469–470
football fields, 270
force from potential energy, 408–413
Fortran, xxi–xxii, 404, 454
ForwardDiff package, 406–413
Fourier transform, 433

lowered form, 243
lscpu command, 469
LuaLaTeX, 274, 279
Luxor package, 190–192, 239, 251, 285, 294
   coordinate system, 192
   defaults, 191
   fonts, 192
   scale factor, 191

M

machine file, 481
macOS, 4–5
@macroexpand macro, 177
macros, 170–177
   adding syntax to Julia, 171–173
   for broadcasting, 173–174
   for chaining functions, 174–175
   collision avoidance, 171
   creating, 171
   difference from functions, 171
   for information, 177
   invocation syntax, 171
   for performance, 175–177
   for string formatting, 177
   for timing, 175
map() operator, 161–163
   and broadcasting, 162–163
mapreduce() operator, 166
marginalhist() plotting function, 356
Marx, Groucho, 123
MathJax, 274–275, 389
math symbols, 13
MATLAB, xxii
matrix, 37
   identity, 399
   special types, 400–402
   triangular, 401
matrix factorization, 402–403
matrix inverse, 147
matrix multiplication, 146–147
maximum() function, 166
mean() function, 319–321
measurement() function, 282
Measurements package, 280–284
   combining with
      DifferentialEquations, 302–303
median() function, 319
membership, 43

membership operator (∈), 43
Meta.parse() function, 168
metaprogramming, 167–177
MethodError, 179
methods, 229–233
methods() function, 231
minimum() function, 166
missing() function, 330
Missings package, 331
missing type, 328–330
   and logic, 331
   and Plots, 329
MIT, xxi
mode() function, 320
modular arithmetic operator (%), 29
module paths, 66
modules
   creating, 65–67
   current, 66
   exported names, 63
   naming, 63
   paths and dots, 66–67
   renaming imported, 65
Monk, Thelonious, 462
Monty Hall problem, 310–311
mosaicview() function, 443
MP3, 430
multiple dispatch, xxii, 229–233, 241
multiplication by juxtaposition, 29–30
multiprocessing, 468, 479–485
multithreading, 468–479
mutable keyword, 236
mutation, 55–59
   arrays, 55–56
   by functions, 56–57
   strings, 58
mutually assured destruction, 457
myid() function, 483

N

Nof8 type, 442
named tuples, 138–139
names() function, 342
namespaces, 62, 66
NASA, 191, 270
native types, 216
Netflix, 406
networked computing, 481–482, 484
nframes() function, 432

RESOURCES

Visit *https://nostarch.com/practical-julia* for errata and more information.